Frommer's®

5th
Edition

Puerto Rico

by Darwin Porter
& Danforth Prince

D0348415

IDG Books Worldwide, Inc.
An International Data Group Company
Foster City, CA • Chicago, IL • Indianapolis, IN • New York, NY

ABOUT THE AUTHOR

Ever since the age of 17, when **Darwin Porter** sold his first article on Puerto Rico to a travel magazine, he has been visiting and writing about the island. A bureau chief of the *Miami Herald* at the age of 21, Porter has traveled frequently and extensively throughout Puerto Rico and the rest of the Caribbean. His coauthor is **Danforth Prince,** formerly of the Paris bureau of the *New York Times.* Together, they share their secrets and discoveries of travel to Puerto Rico with you.

IDG BOOKS WORLDWIDE, INC.

An International Data Group Company
919 E. Hillsdale Blvd.
Suite 400
Foster City, CA 94404

Find us online at **www.frommers.com**

Copyright © 2000 by IDG Books Worldwide, Inc.
Maps copyright © 2000 by IDG Books Worldwide, Inc.

All rights reserved. No part of this book may be reproduced or transmitted in any form or by any means, electronic or mechanical, including photocopying, recording, or by any information storage and retrieval system, without permission in writing from the Publisher.

FROMMER'S is a registered trademark of Arthur Frommer. Used under license.

ISBN 0-7645-6088-3
ISSN 1062-4775

Editor: Lisa Torrance
Production Editor: Tammy Ahrens
Photo Editor: Richard Fox
Design by Michele Laseau
Staff Cartographers: John Decamillis, Roberta Stockwell, Elizabeth Puhl
Additional Cartography: Nicholas Trotter
Page Creation: IDG Books Indianapolis Production Department

SPECIAL SALES

For general information on IDG Books Worldwide's books in the U.S., please call our Consumer Customer Service department at 1-800-762-2974. For reseller information, including discounts, bulk sales, customized editions, and premium sales, please call our Reseller Customer Service department at 1-800-434-3422.

Manufactured in the United States of America

5 4 3 2 1

Contents

List of Maps

AN INVITATION TO THE READER

In researching this book, we discovered many wonderful places—hotels, restaurants, shops, and more. We're sure you'll find others. Please tell us about them, so we can share the information with your fellow travelers in upcoming editions. If you were disappointed with a recommendation, we'd love to know that, too. Please write to:

Frommer's Puerto Rico, 5th Edition
IDG Books Worldwide, Inc.
909 Third Avenue
New York, NY 10022

AN ADDITIONAL NOTE

Please be advised that travel information is subject to change at any time—and this is especially true of prices. We therefore suggest that you write or call ahead for confirmation when making your travel plans. The authors, editors, and publisher cannot be held responsible for the experiences of readers while traveling. Your safety is important to us, however, so we encourage you to stay alert and be aware of your surroundings. Keep a close eye on cameras, purses, and wallets, all favorite targets of thieves and pickpockets.

WHAT THE SYMBOLS MEAN

✪ Frommer's Favorites

Our favorite places and experiences—outstanding for quality, value, or both.

The following abbreviations are used for credit cards:

AE	American Express	EC	Eurocard
CB	Carte Blanche	JCB	Japan Credit Bank
DC	Diners Club	MC	MasterCard
DISC	Discover	V	Visa
ER	enRoute		

FIND FROMMER'S ONLINE

www.frommers.com offers up-to-the-minute listings on almost 200 cities around the globe—including the latest bargains and candid, personal articles updated daily by Arthur Frommer himself. No other Web site offers such comprehensive and timely coverage of the world of travel.

The Best of Puerto Rico

Whatever you want to do on a tropical vacation or business trip—play on the beach with the kids (or gamble away their college fund), enjoy a romantic honeymoon, or have a little fun after a grueling negotiating session—you'll find it in Puerto Rico. But you don't want to waste precious hours once you get here searching for the best deals and the best experiences. We've done that work for you. During our years of traveling through the islands that form the Commonwealth of Puerto Rico, we've tested the beaches, toured the sights, reviewed countless restaurants, inspected hotels, and sampled the best scuba, hikes, and other outdoor adventures. We've even learned where to get away from it all when you want to escape the crowds.

Here's what we consider to be the best that Puerto Rico has to offer.

1 The Best Beaches

White sandy beaches put Puerto Rico and its offshore islands on tourist maps in the first place. Many other Caribbean destinations have only jagged coral outcroppings or black volcanic-sand beaches that get very hot in the noonday sun.

- **Condado Beach:** Although not the best in the Caribbean, San Juan's Condado Beach is the most famous—which helps explain the wintertime crowds. It is also the most popular in Puerto Rico because of its proximity to San Juan. Once the stamping ground of the rich, including the Vanderbilts and the Rockefellers, this 2-mile band of white sand winds between a blue lagoon and some of the Caribbean's finest resort hotels. High society began coming here after Cornelius Vanderbilt constructed the Vanderbilt Condado Beach Hotel in 1919. In the 1970s, the beach's popularity mushroomed as fast-food restaurants, water-sports concessions, restaurants, and condos emerged from a massive construction boom. See chapter 6.
- **Luquillo Beach:** About 30 miles east of San Juan, Luquillo Beach sits in a crescent-shaped bay edged by a vast coconut grove, which makes it not only the best beach in Puerto Rico, but one of the finest in the entire Caribbean. Coral reefs protect the crystal-clear lagoon from Atlantic waters that can batter the coast. Much photographed because of its white sands, it also has tent sites and other facilities, including picnic areas with changing rooms, lockers,

and showers. Regrettably, Luquillo Beach isn't as well maintained as it used to be, although it remains the favorite of beach buffs from San Juan. In winter, it's also inhabited by "snowbirds" (condo owners from up north who live nearby). See chapter 7.

• **Playa Dorado:** West of San Juan, Playa Dorado consists of six white-sand beaches along the northern coast, reached by a series of winding roads. This whole area is dominated by the Hyatt resorts, Cerromar and Dorado. Because the hotels offer numerous children's programs, the Dorado beaches have become a family favorite. Originally, the beaches opened onto a grapefruit and coconut plantation owned by Clara Livingston, Puerto Rico's first female pilot. As fruit prices declined in the 1950s, she sold off her 1,600 acres to Laurence Rockefeller, who began hotel construction. See chapter 7.

• **Playa de Ponce:** The beaches on the southeast coast west of Ponce, the "second city" of Puerto Rico, are far less crowded than those of the Condado, Luquillo, and Dorado. This long strip of white sand opens onto the tranquil waters of the Caribbean. Several very good seafood restaurants are in the vicinity. See chapter 8.

• **Boquerón Beach:** South of Mayagüez, Boquerón Beach is the Cape Cod of Puerto Rico. This beach town stands at the heart of a 3-mile bay, with palm-fringed white sand curving away on both sides. Fishermen, sailors, scuba divers, and windsurfers, as well as beach devotees, are attracted to this beach, where fresh oysters shucked on the spot and doused with Tabasco are sold from shacks. Here the ice cream is made with sweet corn and dusted with paprika (it sounds awful, but tastes good). See chapter 9.

• **The Secret Beaches:** The main island is filled with isolated sandy coves that only the locals seem to know about. The best, all guaranteed to delight the escapist in you, stretch between Cabo Rojo (the southwesterly tip of Puerto Rico) all the way east to Ponce. Beginning in the west, directly east of Cabo Rojo, you'll discover Bahia Sucia Beach, Rosada Beach, Santa Beach, Manglillos Beach (with a recreation area), Caña Gorda Beach, Tamarindo Beach, and Ballena Beach. Access to many of these is limited because of poor roads, but the effort is worth it. Bring along the supplies you'll need. See chapter 9.

• **Doral Palmas del Mar Resort** (Humacao; ☎ 800/725-6273 in the U.S. or 787/852-6000): The huge Palmas del Mar resort near Humacao on the eastern coast of Puerto Rico has been called "the new American Riviera." Although the architectural dream of this 2,750-acre playground resort built on a former coconut plantation hasn't been realized yet, the site is fully functional and sports 3 miles of white-sand beaches. Unlike some of the rough-water beaches near Rincón in the west, the sea here is tranquil and calm year-round. There's also a water-sports center and marina. See chapter 10.

• **The Beaches of Vieques & Culebra:** To escape the crowds, head for the isolated beaches of the offshore islands of Vieques and Culebra. In Vieques alone there are some 40 beaches, most of them unnamed even though U.S. sailors have nick-named their favorites—everything from Green Beach to Orchid. Sun Bay (Sombe), a public beach on Vieques, is one of our favorites—a splendid crescent of sand with picnic tables and a bathhouse. The beaches of the less-visited island of Culebra are known to savvy aficionados. Here you will find white-sand strips studding the island and opening onto coral reefs and clear waters. Playa Flamenco Beach is the best, lying on the north shore of the island. This 3-mile-long crescent has shade trees and facilities including picnic tables. It's popular with day-trippers from Fajardo, especially on weekends. See chapter 11.

2 The Best Scuba Diving

With the continental shelf surrounding it on three sides, Puerto Rico has an abundance of coral reefs, caves, seawalls, and trenches for divers of all experience levels to explore. See "The Active Vacation Planner" in chapter 2 for detailed information.

- **Metropolitan San Juan:** This easy beach dive off the Condado district in San Juan is not as spectacular as other dives mentioned here, but certainly more convenient. Lava reefs sculptured with caverns, tunnels, and overhangs provide hiding areas for schools of snapper, grunts, and copper sweepers. In the active breeding grounds of the inner and outer reefs, divers of all levels can mingle with an impressive array of small tropical fish—French angels, jacks, bluehead wrasse, butterfly fish, and sergeant majors, among them—along with sea horses, arrow crabs, coral shrimp, octopuses, batfish, and flying gunards. Visibility is about 10 to 20 feet. The Condado reef is also ideal for resort courses, certification courses, and night dives. See chapters 2 and 6.
- **Mona Island:** Mona Island, 40 miles west of the city of Mayagüez in western Puerto Rico, is considered to be the Caribbean version of the Galápagos Islands. Renowned for its pirate tales, cave-pocked cliffs, 3-foot-long iguanas, and other natural wonders, its waters are among the cleanest in Puerto Rico, with horizontal visibility at times exceeding 200 feet. More than 270 species of fish have been found in Mona waters, including more than 60 reef-dwelling species. Larger marine animals, such as sea turtles, whales, dolphins, and marlins, visit the region during migrations. Various types of coral reefs, underwater caverns, drop-offs, and deep vertical walls ring the island. The most accessible reef dives are along the southern and western shores. Getting there is a pain, however. You must brave a 5-hour boat ride across the often rough Mona Passage. See chapters 2 and 8.
- **Southern Puerto Rico:** The continental shelf drops off precipitously several miles off the southern coast, producing a dramatic wall 20 miles long and teeming with marine life. Compared favorably to the Cayman Islands' wall, the Puerto Rican version has become the Caribbean's newest world-class dive destination. Paralleling the coast from the seaside village of La Parguera to the city of Ponce, the wall descends in slopes and sheer drops from 60 to 120 feet before disappearing into 1,500 feet of sea. Scored with valleys and deep trenches, it is cloaked in immense gardens of staghorn and elkhorn coral, deep-water gorgonians, and other exquisite coral formations. Visibility can exceed 100 feet. There are more than 50 dive sites around Parguera alone. See chapters 2 and 9.
- **Fajardo:** This coastal town in eastern Puerto Rico offers divers the opportunity to explore reefs, caverns, miniwalls, and channels near a string of palm-tufted islets. The reefs are decked in an array of corals ranging from delicate gorgonians to immense coral heads. Visibility usually exceeds 50 feet. You can hand-feed many of the reef fish that inhabit the corals. Sand channels and a unique double-barrier reef surround Palomino Island, where bandtailed puffers and parrot-fish harems are frequently sighted. Cayo Diablo farther to the east provides a treasure box of corals and marine animals, from green moray eels and barracudas to octopuses and occasional manatees. See chapters 2 and 10.
- **Humacao Region:** South of Fajardo are some 24 dive sites in a 5-mile radius off the shore. Overhangs, caves, and tunnels perch in 60 feet of water along mile-long Basslet Reef, where dolphins visit in spring. The Cracks, a jigsaw of caves, alleyways, and boulders, hosts an abundance of goby-cleaning stations and a

number of lobsters. With visibility often exceeding 100 feet, the Reserve offers a clear look at corals. At the Drift, divers float along with nurse sharks and angelfish into a valley of swim-throughs and ledges. For the experienced diver, Red Hog is the newest site in the area, with a panoramic wall that drops from 80 to 1,160 feet. See chapters 2 and 10.

3 The Best Golf & Tennis

- **Rio Mar Golf Course** (Palmer; ☎ **787/888-8811**): A 45-minute drive from San Juan on the northeast coast, the 6,145-yard Rio Mar Golf Course is shorter than those at both Palmas del Mar and Dorado East. One avid golfer recommended it to "those whose games and egos have been bruised by the other two courses." Wind here can seriously influence the outcome of your game. The greens fees are a lot less expensive than those of its two major competitors. See chapter 7.
- **Hyatt Resorts at Dorado** (Dorado; ☎ **800/233-1234** in the U.S. or 787/ 796-1234): With 72 holes, Dorado has the highest concentration of golf on the island. Two courses—east and west—belong to the Hyatt Regency Cerromar and the Hyatt Dorado Beach resorts. Dorado East is our favorite. Designed by Robert Trent Jones, Sr., it has been the site of the Senior PGA Tournament of Champions throughout the 1990s.

  And true tennis buffs head here, too. The Dorado courts are the best on the island, and both hotels sponsor tennis weeks and offer special tennis packages. The Hyatt Regency Cerromar has 14 Laykold courts alone, two of them lit for night play. The Hyatt Regency Dorado weighs in with five Laykold courts, two of them lighted. See chapter 7.
- **Wyndham El Conquistador Resort & Country Club** (Las Croabas; ☎ **800/ 468-5228** in the U.S. or 787/863-1000): This sprawling resort east of San Juan is one of the island's finest tennis retreats, with seven Har-Tru courts and a pro on hand to offer guidance and advice. If you don't have a partner, the hotel will find one for you. Only guests of the hotel are allowed to play here. See chapter 10.
- **Club de Golf at Doral Palmas del Mar Resort** (Humacao; ☎ **800/725-6273** in the U.S. or 787/852-6000): Lying on the southeast coast on the grounds of a former coconut plantation, the Palmas del Mar resort boasts the second-leading course in Puerto Rico—a par-72, 6,803-yard layout designed by Gary Player. Crack golfers consider holes 11 through 15 the toughest five successive holes in the Caribbean. See chapter 10.
- **Doral Palmas del Mar Resort** (Humacao; ☎ **800/725-6273** or 787/ 852-6000): On the eastern coastline, this resort complex on the grounds of a former coconut plantation has 20 courts, of which 5 are Har-Tru and 15 are Tenneflex (a harder surface). Seven of the courts are lighted. The resort offers tennis packages, and an on-site pro conducts private lessons. See chapter 10.

4 The Best Hikes

Bring your boots. Puerto Rico's mountainous interior offers ample opportunity for hiking and climbing, with many trails presenting spectacular panoramas at the least-expected moments. See "The Active Vacation Planner" in chapter 2 for detailed information.

- **El Yunque** (☎ **787/888-5670** for information): Containing the only rain forest on U.S. soil, this Caribbean National Forest east of San Juan offers a number of walking and hiking trails. The rugged El Toro trail passes through four different forest systems en route to the 3,523-foot Pico El Toro, the highest peak in the forest. The El Yunque trail leads to three of the recreation area's most panoramic lookouts, and the Big Tree Trail is an easy walk to La Mina Falls. Just off the main road is La Coca Falls, a sheet of water cascading down mossy cliffs. See chapters 2 and 7.

- **Guánica State Forest** (☎ 787/721-5495 for information): At the opposite extreme of El Yunque's lush and wet rain forest, Guánica State Forest's climate is dry and arid, the Arizona-like landscape riddled with cacti. The area, cut off from the Cordillera Central mountain range, gets little rainfall. Yet it's home to some 50% of all the island's terrestrial bird species, including the rare Puerto Rican nightjar, once thought to be extinct. The forest has 36 miles of trails through four forest types. We prefer the mile-long Cueva Trail, where hikers look for the endangered bufo lemur toad, another species thought to be extinct but still jumping in this area. Within the forest, El Portal Tropical Forest Center offers 10,000 square feet of exhibition space and provides information. See chapter 9.
- **Mona Island:** Off the western coast of Puerto Rico, this fascinating island noted for its scuba-diving sites provides hiking opportunities found nowhere else in the Caribbean. Called the Galápagos of Puerto Rico because of its unique wildlife, Mona is home to giant iguanas and three species of endangered sea turtles. Some 20 endangered animals also have been spotted here. Ecotourists like to hike among Mona's mangrove forests, coral reefs, cliffs, and complex honeycomb of caves, ever on the alert for the diversity of both plant and animal life, including 417 plant and tree species, some of which are unique and 78 of which are rare or endangered. More than 100 bird species (2 unique) have been documented. Hikers can camp at Mona for $1 a night. Contact the **Puerto Rico Department of Natural Resources** (☎ 787/721-5495) for more information. See chapter 8.

5 The Best Natural Wonders

- **El Yunque** (☎ 787/888-5670 for information): Forty-five minutes by road east of San Juan in the Luquillo Mountains, and protected by the U.S. Forest Service, El Yunque is Puerto Rico's greatest natural attraction. Some 100 billion gallons of rain fall annually on this home to four forest types containing 240 species of tropical trees. Families can walk one of the dozens of trails that wind past waterfalls, dwarf vegetation, and miniature flowers, while the island's colorful parrots fly overhead. You can hear the sound of Puerto Rico's mascot, the *coquí,* a small frog. See chapters 2 and 7.
- **Río Camuy Cave Park** (☎ 787/898-3100): Some 2¹/₂ hours west of San Juan, visitors board a tram to descend into this forest-filled sinkhole at the mouth of the Clara Cave. They walk the footpaths of a 170-foot-high cave to a deeper sinkhole. Once they're inside, a 45-minute tour helps everyone, including kids, learn to differentiate stalactites from stalagmites. At the Pueblos sinkhole a platform overlooks the Camuy River, passing through a network of cave tunnels. See chapter 7.
- **Las Cabezas de San Juan Nature Reserve** (☎ 787/722-5882): This 316-acre nature reserve about 45 minutes from San Juan encompasses seven different ecological systems, including forestland, mangroves, lagoons, beaches, cliffs, and offshore coral reefs. Five days a week (Wednesday to Sunday), the park staff conducts tours in Spanish and English, the latter at 2pm only. Each tour lasts 2¹/₂ hours and is conducted with electric trolleys that traverse most of the park.

Tours end with a climb to the top of the still-working 19th-century lighthouse for views over Puerto Rico's eastern coast and nearby Caribbean Islands. Call to reserve space before going, as bookings are based on stringent restrictions as to the number of persons who can tour the park without damage to its landscape or ecology. The cost is a relative bargain at $5 for adults and $2 for persons under 13. See chapter 10.

6 The Best Family Resorts

Puerto Rico has a bounty of attractions, natural wonders, and resorts welcoming families who choose to play together.

- **Condado Plaza Hotel & Casino** (San Juan; ☎ **800/468-8588** in the U.S. or 787/721-1000): This resort offers Camp Taíno, a regular program of activities and special events for children ages 4 to 12. The cost of $25 per child includes lunch. The main pool has a kids' water slide starting in a Spanish castle turret, plus a toddler pool. For teenagers, the hotel has a video game room, tennis courts, and various organized activities. For the whole family, the resort offers two pools and opens onto a public beach. It also has the best collection of restaurants of any hotel on the Condado. See chapter 4.

- **El San Juan Hotel & Casino** (San Juan; ☎ **800/468-2818** in the U.S. or 787/791-1000): The grandest hotel in Puerto Rico lies on Isla Verde, the less-famous strip of beach connected to the Condado. Its Kids Klub features trained counselors and group activities for the 5-to-13-year-old set. A daily fee of $28 buys lunch and an array of activities. The hotel opens onto a good beachfront and has some of the best restaurants in San Juan. See chapter 4.

- **Hyatt Resorts at Dorado** (Dorado; ☎ **800/233-1234** in the U.S. or 787/ 796-1234): Sitting 18 miles west of San Juan, the Hyatt Regency Cerromar Beach Resort & Casino and the Hyatt Dorado Beach Resort & Casino share a Camp Hyatt program available for guests ages 3 to 12. Certified counselors direct programs of educational, environmental, and cultural activities. In the evening, movies, talent shows, and video games occupy the agenda. All this costs $40 a day per kid. Parents find one of the largest beaches and resort complexes in the Caribbean, including the world's longest freshwater river pool. See chapter 7.

- **Wyndham El Conquistador Resort & Country Club** (Las Croabas; ☎ **800/ 468-5228** in the U.S. or 787/863-1000): Located 31 miles east of San Juan, this resort offers Camp Coquí on Palomino Island for children 3 to 12 years of age. The hotel's water taxi takes kids to the island for a half or full day of water sports, nature hikes, and island crafts, costing $19 for a half day or $38 for a full day. This resort has some of the best facilities and restaurants in eastern Puerto Rico. See chapter 10.

- **Doral Palmas del Mar Resort** (Humacao; ☎ **800/725-6273** in the U.S. or 787/852-6000): The major rival in the east to El Conquistador, this sprawling resort has an Adventure Club for children ages 3 to 13. Supervised activities include arts, crafts, and sports, plus horseback riding for those old enough. For nonguests, the cost is $22 per half day or $28 per day, including lunch; guests are free. Family packages are sold for as low as $100 per person per night, based on four-person occupancy of a room. The resort is one of the most extensive in the Caribbean, with beaches, restaurants, and lots of water sports. See chapter 10.

7 The Best Honeymoon Resorts

- **El San Juan Hotel & Casino** (San Juan; ☎ 800/468-2818 in the U.S. or 787/791-1000): If you want Vegas-style shows, gambling, nightlife, great restaurants, and the most famous beach in Puerto Rico, El San Juan is at your disposal. It has the most glamorous lobby in the Caribbean and is set on 12 acres of Isla Verde, a strip of beach connected to the Condado. Options include a suite in the main tower with a whirlpool or your own private casita with a sunken Roman bath. The best deal is a package, costing from $459 per night for 5 nights. A lot of freebies are thrown in, including champagne and tropical fruit, daily tennis, one dinner, continental breakfast, and two massages. See chapter 4.

- **Hyatt Dorado Beach Resort** (Dorado; ☎ 800/233-1234 in the U.S. or 787/796-1234): This resort offers a more tranquil atmosphere than the nearby Hyatt Regency Cerromar, yet guests can use all the facilities and attractions of the neighboring hotel. You can book one of the elegantly furnished upper-level rooms in the Oceanview Houses and enjoy romantic vistas of two crescent-shaped beaches. There's casino and disco action, plus a spa, a health club, jogging trails, and 14 tennis courts. Packages in low season begin at $2,135 for two for the week, including one breakfast, champagne, T-shirts, $25 in casino chips, two massages, one dinner with wine, and transfers to and from the airport. In high season the tab rises by $1,000 a week per honeymooning couple, but breakfast and dinner are included. See chapter 7.

- **Ponce Hilton and Casino** (Ponce; ☎ 800/HILTONS in the U.S. or 787/259-7676): A first-class act at Puerto Rico's "second city" on the south coast, this sprawling resort is set in an 80-acre garden. On-site amenities include a casino and disco, plus a whirlpool, tennis courts, and a fitness room. The two restaurants serve the best food on the south coast. Five suites are ideal for honeymoons. The first night costs $219, including a bottle of champagne, truffles, chocolates, and fresh strawberries as a gift. The package includes breakfast daily, plus $25 in casino chips. You also receive a coupon granting 50% off on your next visit. Each additional night is only $170. See chapter 8.

- **Horned Dorset Primavera** (Rincón; ☎ 800/633-1857 in the U.S. or 787/823-4030): The most romantic place for a honeymoon on the island, unless you stay in a private villa somewhere, this small, tranquil estate lies on the Mona Passage in western Puerto Rico, a pocket of posh where privacy is almost guaranteed. Accommodations are luxurious in the Spanish neocolonial style. The property opens onto a long secluded beach of white sand. There are no phones, TVs, or radios in the rooms to interfere with the soft sounds of pillow talk. This is a retreat for adults only, with no facilities for children. Seven-night packages, including a bottle of champagne, breakfast, dinner, and airport transfers, range from $3,000 to $3,850 per couple, depending on the season. See chapter 9.

- **Wyndham El Conquistador Resort & Country Club** (Las Croabas; ☎ 800/468-5228 in the U.S. or 787/863-1000): If you're looking for good food and diversions rather than a tranquil retreat, El Conquistador is the best big-time resort on the island. Atop a 300-foot bluff in eastern Puerto Rico, it has virtually everything for outdoor play, including golf and tennis, but when you want seclusion you can post the PRIVADO sign and the world is yours. It offers a $475 per night honeymoon package (based on 3 nights and 4 days), with many specials such as champagne, a golf clinic, a half-day snorkeling trip, nonmotorized water sports, and even transfers to and from the airport. If you stay a full week, the cost of this package is reduced to $405 per night. See chapter 10.

- **Doral Palmas del Mar Resort** (Humacao; ☎ 800/725-6273 in the U.S. or 787/852-6000): This luxury resort complex sits on 2,750 acres of a former coconut plantation on Puerto Rico's southeast coast. Only an hour's drive from San Juan, this sheltered spot is like another world, with its Mediterranean villas, cobblestone plazas, condos, and Spanish-style fountains. You get some of the best golf on the island here, along with 20 tennis courts, a spa and health club, and miles of hiking and jogging trails. The Palmas Inn suites are best for honeymooners, unless you want to rent a private villa. Honeymoon packages, many of them configured for 7 nights and 8 days, cost for two people from $1,148 to $1,237 for a double room, to $1,590 for a suite. Included in the package are such frills as daily breakfasts, one lunch, one dinner, and baskets of fruit and bottles of champagne. Whereas this particular arrangement is offered only between April and December, other cost-conscious packages are available during high season (December to April) as well, on slightly different terms.

8 The Best Big Resort Hotels

- **El San Juan Hotel & Casino** (San Juan; ☎ 800/468-2818 in the U.S. or 787/791-1000): An opulent circular lobby sets the haute style at the Caribbean's most elegant resort. From its location along Isla Verde Beach, it houses some of the capital's finest restaurants and is the city's major entertainment venue. Guest rooms are tropically designed and maintained in state-of-the-art condition. See chapter 4.
- **Ritz-Carlton** (San Juan; ☎ 800/241-3333 or 787/253-1700): At last Puerto Rico has a Ritz-Carlton, and this truly deluxe, oceanfront property is one of the island's most spectacular resorts. Guests are pampered in a setting of elegance and beautifully furnished guest rooms. Hotel dining is second only to that at El San Juan, and a European-style spa features 11 treatments "for body and beauty." See chapter 4.
- **Hyatt Dorado Beach Resort** (Dorado; ☎ 800/233-1234 in the U.S. or 787/796-1234): Lying on the former stamping grounds of the Rockefellers, these low-rise buildings blend into the lush surroundings of a grapefruit and coconut plantation. Spacious rooms open onto a long stretch of secluded beach, and grounds include an 18-hole Robert Trent Jones–designed championship golf course. Tennis, windsurfing, pool swimming, and dozens of water sports are available, as well as the most elegant dining in Dorado. See chapter 7.
- **Westin Rio Mar Beach Resort, Country Club & Ocean Villas** (Rio Grande; ☎ 800/4-Riomar or 787/888-6000): This $180 million 481-acre resort, 19 miles east of the San Juan airport, is one of the three largest hotels in Puerto Rico. In spite of its size, personal service and style are hallmarks of the property. Twelve restaurants and lounges boast an array of cuisines. Along with its proximity to two golf courses, entertainment, such as an extensive program of live music, is a key ingredient in the hotel's success. See chapter 7.
- **Wyndham El Conquistador Resort & Country Club** (Las Croabas; ☎ 800/468-5228 in the U.S. or 787/863-1000): The finest resort in Puerto Rico, this is a world-class destination—a sybaritic haven for golfers, honeymooners, families, and anyone else. Three intimate "villages" combine with one grand hotel, draped along 300-foot bluffs overlooking both the Atlantic and the Caribbean at Puerto Rico's northeastern tip. The 500 landscaped acres include tennis courts, an 18-hole

Arthur Hills–designed championship golf course, and a marina filled with yachts and charter boats. See chapter 10.

- **Doral Palmas del Mar Resort** (Humacao; ☎ 800/725-6273 in the U.S. or 787/852-6000): Although not as impressive as El Conquistador, this sprawling complex evokes a Mediterranean village, opening onto over 3 miles of beach on the east coast of Puerto Rico. Palm trees grow everywhere. The complex boasts the largest tennis center in the Caribbean and an 18-hole Gary Player championship golf course. Additional amenities include a horseback riding center for beach rides, water sports galore, an outstanding scuba-diving program, and deep-sea fishing charters. There's even a casino and nine restaurants. See chapter 10.

9 The Best Moderately Priced Hotels

- **Gallery Inn at Galería San Juan** (San Juan; ☎ 787/722-1808): The most whimsically bohemian hotel in the Caribbean sits in the heart of the historic city. Once the home of an aristocratic Spanish family, it is today filled with verdant courtyards and adorned with sculpture, silk screens, and original paintings. Staying in one of these comfortable rooms is like living in an art gallery. See chapter 4.
- **At Wind Chimes Inn** (San Juan; ☎ 800/946-3244 in the U.S. or 787/727-4153): This renovated and restored Spanish manor house is one of the best guesthouses in the Condado district. It lies only a short block from Puerto Rico's most famous beach. A favorite with families, the inn offers spacious rooms with kitchens and has recently added a swimming pool. See chapter 4.
- **Copamarina Beach Resort** (Caña Gorda; ☎ 800/468-4553 in the U.S. or 787/821-0505): Near Ponce, this resort was once the private vacation retreat of local cement barons, the de Castro family. Today it's been converted into one of the best beach hotels along Puerto Rico's southern shore. In fact, its beach is one of the island's best. Set in a palm grove, the resort is handsomely decorated and comfortably furnished, with a swimming pool and two tennis courts. See chapter 9.
- **Hotel Paradores Joyuda Beach** (Cabo Rojo; ☎ 787/851-5650): South of Mayagüez in scenic Cabo Rojo, this idyllic little beachfront hotel is far removed from the tourist-trodden districts. It's on one of the island's finest beaches, and it offers well-furnished and air-conditioned bedrooms. It's a favorite with Puerto Rican honeymooners. See chapter 8.
- **Hacienda Tamarindo** (Vieques; ☎ 787/741-8525): On the site of a 1990s nightclub, this expanded inn has style, flair, and charm, and a desirable location—just inland from a great white sandy beach. Built around a massive 2-century-old tamarind tree and operated by a couple from Vermont, the inn has comfortable and appealing accommodations, which are often furnished with antiques. The welcome is warm. See chapter 11.

10 The Best Attractions

- **The Historic District of Old San Juan:** There's nothing like it in the Caribbean. Partially enclosed by old walls dating from the 17th century, Old San Juan was designated a U.S. National Historic Zone in 1950. Some 400 beautifully restored buildings fill this district, which is chockablock with tree-shaded squares, monuments, and open-air cafes, as well as shops, restaurants, and bars. If you're interested in history, there is no better stroll in the West Indies. See chapter 6.

- **Castillo San Felipe del Morro:** In Old San Juan and nicknamed El Morro, this fort was originally built in 1540. It guards the bay from a rocky promontory on the northwestern tip of the old city. Rich in history and legend, the site covers enough territory to accommodate a nine-hole golf course. See chapter 6.
- **The Historic District of Ponce:** Second only to Old San Juan in terms of historic significance, the central district of Ponce is a blend of Ponce Créole and art deco building styles, dating mainly from the 1890s to the 1930s. One street, Calle Isabel, offers an array of Ponceño architectural styles, which often incorporate neoclassic details. The city underwent a massive restoration preceding the celebration of its 300th anniversary in 1996. See chapter 8.
- **Museo de Arte de Ponce:** Also in Ponce, this museum has the finest collection of European and Latin American art in the Caribbean. The building itself was designed by Edward Durell Stone, who also designed the Museum of Modern Art in New York. Contemporary work by Puerto Ricans is displayed, as well as an array of old masters, including Renaissance and baroque works from Italy. See chapter 8.
- **Tropical Agriculture Research Station** (Mayagüez): These tropical gardens contain one of the largest collections of tropical species intended for practical use. These include cacao, fruit trees, spices, timbers, and ornamentals. Adjacent to the Mayagüez campus of the University of Puerto Rico, the site attracts botanists from around the world. See chapter 8.
- **The City of San Germán:** In the southwestern corner of Puerto Rico, and founded in 1512, this small town is Puerto Rico's second-oldest city. Thanks to a breadth of architectural styles, San Germán is also the second Puerto Rican city (after San Juan) to be included in the National Register of Historic Places. Buildings, monuments, and plazas fill a 36-acre historic zone. Today's residents descend from the smugglers, poets, priests, and politicians who once lived here in "the city of hills," so-called because of the mountainous location. See chapter 8.
- **Iglesia Porta Coeli** (San Germán): The main attraction of this ancient town is the oldest church in the New World. It was originally built by Dominican friars in 1606. The church resembles a working chapel, although mass is held here only three times a year. Along the sides of the church are treasures gathered from all over the world. See chapter 8.

11 The Best Restaurants

- **Chef Marisoll** (San Juan; ☎ 787/725-7454): One of Puerto Rico's best chefs, Marisoll Hernández, prepares Old Town's finest cuisine in this Spanish colonial building in the heart of the historic district. With a strong background in classic cooking, she has expanded her repertoire to include innovative and memorable dishes, including curried chicken with fried sweet bananas, homemade mango chutney, and saffron risotto. Or try her grilled swordfish with calamata olives. See chapter 5.
- **Parrot Club** (San Juan; ☎ 787/725-7370): This recent addition to the San Juan scene has already been claimed as one of the finest and most innovative restaurants on the island. Its chef serves a Nuevo Latino cuisine that is a happy medley of Puerto Rican delights, drawing upon the Spanish, African, and even Taíno influences of the island. Menu items are based on updated interpretations of old-fashioned regional dishes—everything from *criola*-styled flank steak to a pan-seared tuna served with a sauce of dark rum and essence of oranges. See chapter 5.

- **Ramiro's** (San Juan; ☎ 787/721-9049): Chef Jesús Ramiro has some of the most innovative cookery along the Condado beachfront strip, along with the city's best wine list. Ramiro has made his culinary reputation with such dishes as quail stuffed with lamb in a port sauce and lamb loin in a tamarind coriander sauce, both equally delectable. His dessert menu is two pages long, including the town's best soufflés. His death-by-chocolate mousse on a green grape leaf is equaled only by his caramelized fresh mango napoleon. See chapter 5.
- **Ajili Mójili** (San Juan; ☎ 787/725-9195): Also on the Condado beachfront, Ajili Mójili provides the most refined interpretation of classic Puerto Rican cookery on the island. Locals find it evocative of the food they enjoyed at their mother's table. Examples include *mofongos,* green plantains stuffed with veal, chicken, shrimp, or pork. The chefs take that cliche dish, *arroz con pollo* (stewed chicken with saffron rice), and raise it to celestial levels. The restaurant takes its name from the lemon-garlic sweet chili salsa that's traditionally served here with fish or meat. See chapter 5.
- **Augusto's Cuisine** (San Juan; ☎ 787/725-7700): Originally from Austria, much-awarded chef August Schreiner is a five-time winner of *El Nuevo Día's* Five Fork Award, honoring the island's great chefs. Try any of his lobster or game dishes, such as venison. His chocolate soufflé Grand Marnier is the island's finest. His mother may not have taught him how to make one of the city's best seafood paellas, but somebody did—or else he invented it himself. See chapter 5.
- **The Landing** (Barrios Puntas/Playa Antonio; ☎ 787/823-3112): One of the best dining spots along the western coast of Puerto Rico, this restaurant has a setting like a stylish private home. Its international cuisine draws hundreds of patrons nightly who enjoy jerk chicken and lobster kebabs, among other dishes, while taking in a view of Ricón legendary surf. See chapter 9.
- **El Ancla** (Ponce; ☎ 787/840-2450): One of the best restaurants along the southern coast, this is the best place to go for regional specialties and fresh seafood. The cuisine is prepared with zest and flavor, as exemplified by its red snapper stuffed with shrimp and lobster. The chef specializes in paella for two persons and makes a wicked sautéed conch, which one frequent habitué calls "sexy conch." See chapter 8.
- **La Cava** in the Ponce Hilton (Ponce; ☎ 787/259-7676): The stellar restaurant of this first-class hotel, La Cava was designed to resemble a 19th-century coffee plantation. It's the most elegant restaurant along the southern tier, and it serves a delectable international cuisine. From the ever-changing menu you are likely to be served everything from grilled lamb sausage on a bed of couscous to tuna loin seared with sesame oil. See chapter 8.

12 The Best Offbeat Travel Experiences

- **Attending a Cockfight:** Although a brutal sport that many find distasteful, cockfighting is legal in Puerto Rico and has its devotees. The most authentic cockfights are in the town of Salinas in the southeast. But it's not necessary to go that far to witness one of these bouts. Three fights a week are held at the **Coliseo Gallistico,** Route 37 (☎ 787/791-6005), in San Juan. Betting is heavy when these roosters take to the ring. See chapter 6.
- **Doing the "Wet and Dry Tour" in Guánica** (near Ponce): Southern Puerto Rico is the site of the world's largest remaining tract of dry coastal forest, and this part of the island allows you to explore miles of mangrove channel systems.

Tropix Wellness Tours (☎ 787/268-2173) takes you into a part of the island rarely explored by visitors. Two expeditions combine a dry forest hike with mangrove kayaking at sunset. After traversing waterways by kayak, you're led to secluded island beaches. It's a 4-day, 3-night adventure that is fully escorted. See chapter 2.

- **Diving off Mona Island** (Mayagüez): Surrounded by some of the most beautiful coral reefs in the Caribbean, Mona Island has the most pristine, extensive, and well-developed reefs in Puerto Rican waters. In fact, they have been nominated as a U.S. National Marine Sanctuary. The tropical marine ecosystem around Mona includes patch reefs, black coral, spore and groove systems, underwater caverns, deep-water sponges, fringing reefs, and algal reefs. The lush environment attracts octopuses, lobster, queen conch, rays, barracuda, snapper, jack, grunt, angelfish, trunkfish, filefish, butterfly fish, dolphin, parrot fish, tuna, flying fish, and more. The crystal waters afford exceptional horizontal vision from 150 to 200 feet, as well as good views down to the shipwrecks that mark the site—including some Hispanic galleons. Five species of whales visit the island's offshore waters. See chapter 8.

- **Visiting Vieques & Culebra:** Puerto Rico's offshore islands—still relatively undiscovered by the modern world—remain an offbeat adventure, and they've got great beaches too. The most developed is Vieques, off the east coast (as is Culebra). Vieques attracts with its gorgeous stretches of sand with picnic facilities and shade trees. It is an ideal retreat for snorkelers and tranquillity seekers. The beaches are nearly always deserted, even though they are among the Caribbean's loveliest. Although nearly three-quarters of the island is owned by the U.S. Navy, you'll never know you're visiting a military complex. The even less-developed Culebra has a wildlife refuge, coral reefs, and Playa Flamenco, another of the Caribbean's finest beaches. And is it ever sleepy here! See chapter 11.

- **Spending the Evening at Mosquito (Phosphorescent) Bay** (Vieques Island): At any time except when there's a full moon, you can swim in glowing waters lit by dinoflagellates called *pyrodiniums* (whirling fire). These creatures light up the waters like fireflies, and swimming among them is one of the most unusual things to do anywhere—truly a magical, almost psychedelic experience. It's estimated that a gallon of bay water might contain about three-quarters of a million of these little glowing creatures. See chapter 11.

- **Sampling the Island's Nosh Pits:** Think of Puerto Rico as one gigantic fast-food joint, for no other island in the Caribbean offers such a delectable array of roadside eats. Snack food lies around virtually every turn in the road. As you drive throughout the island, stop and take your pick of the roadside dives. They may look junky, even trashy, but the food is often a delight—and cheap too.

  You'll find succulent barbecued pig, *pastelillos* (pastry turnovers filled with meat, cheese, or seafood), *surullitos* (deep-fried cornmeal sticks), *alcapurrias* (a filling of fish or meat in a deep-fried casing of finely grated green plantains and taro root), *bacalaitos* (deep-fried codfish fritters), *papas rellenas* (stuffed potatoes), and *arañitas* ("little spiders"—actually, deep-fried clusters of shredded green plantains).

  You don't have to go far for barbecued pig—just head to the roadside food stands in Luquillo Beach, to the east of San Juan. It makes for a great picnic at the beach.

  A truck stop, **Café Restaurant La Nueva Union,** 35 miles west of San Juan at the junction of Carretera 2 and Highway 22 between Arecibo and Hatillo

(☎ 787/878-2353), serves the most succulent traditional fare. Sample its fresh octopus salad, its meaty goat stew, and definitely its *guisados,* or beef stew. Don't leave without an order of coconut flan.

If you make it all the way around the island to La Parguera, stop at **El Quenepo,** a lunch wagon parked under a towering *quenepa* (a tropical fruit tree) on Route 116 between routes 304 and 324. Usually you can spot it by a line of cars letting passengers out to sample the delights from its crowded peanut-size kitchen. El Quenepo offers a vast array of Puerto Rican specialties, many of which you may never have sampled before: cold codfish soup, even a green bean omelet, and *piononos* (a "mountain" composed of fried eggs, plantain strips, and seasoned meat filling).

2 Planning a Trip to Puerto Rico

This chapter discusses the where, the when, and the how of your trip to Puerto Rico—everything required to plan your trip and get it on the road. Here we've concentrated on what you need to do *before* you go.

In addition to helping you decide when to take your vacation, we've put a wealth of insider information at your fingertips. This chapter also explores different possibilities for getting to Puerto Rico, including not only the most obvious ones but also some that may not have crossed your mind. We also discuss various ways to travel around the island and suggest an itinerary to help you get the most out of a week's vacation. You'll find tips on deciding where to stay, where to dine, and what to buy. Capping off the chapter is a quick-reference list of helpful "Fast Facts" about Puerto Rico.

1 The Regions in Brief

Although the many geological divisions of Puerto Rico might not be immediately apparent to the ordinary visitor, its people take great pride in the island's diversity. The most important geological and political divisions are detailed below.

SAN JUAN

The largest and best-preserved complex of Spanish colonial architecture in the Caribbean, Old San Juan (founded in 1521) is the oldest capital city under the U.S. flag. Once a linchpin of Spanish dominance in the Caribbean, it has three major fortresses, miles of solidly built stone ramparts, a charming collection of antique buildings, and a modern business center. The city's economy is the most stable and solid in all of Latin America.

San Juan is the site of the official home and office of the governor of Puerto .Rico (La Fortaleza), the 16th-century residence of Ponce de León's family, and several of the oldest places of Christian worship in the western hemisphere. Its bars, restaurants, shops, and nightclubs attract an animated group of fans. In recent years, the old city has become surrounded by acres of densely populated modern buildings, including an ultramodern airport, which makes San Juan one of the most dynamic cities in the West Indies.

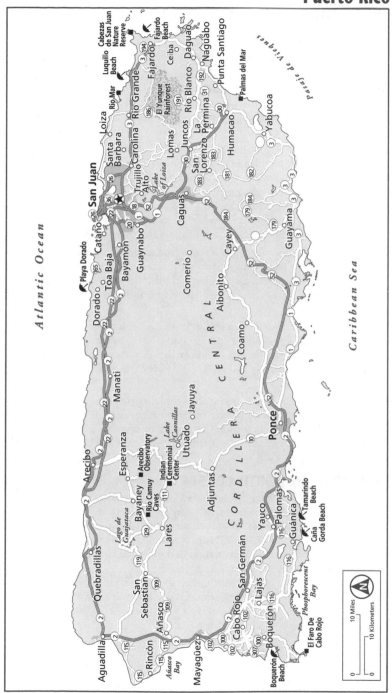

THE NORTHWEST: ARECIBO, RÍO CAMUY, RINCÓN & MORE

A fertile area with many rivers bringing valuable water for irrigation from the high mountains of the Cordillera, the northwest also offers abundant opportunities for sightseeing. The region's principal districts include the following:

AGUADILLA   Christopher Columbus landed near Aguadilla during his second voyage to the New World in 1493. Today the town has a busy airport, fine beaches, and a growing tourism-based infrastructure. It is also the center of Puerto Rico's tiny lace-making industry, a craft imported here many centuries ago by immigrants from Spain, Holland, and Belgium.

ARECIBO   Located on the northern coastline a 2-hour drive west of San Juan, Arecibo was originally founded in 1556. Although little remains of its original architecture, the town is well known to physicists and astronomers around the world because of the radar/radio-telescope that fills a concave depression between six of the region's hills. Equal in size to 13 football fields and operated jointly by the National Science Foundation and Cornell University, it studies the shape and formation of the galaxies by accumulating and deciphering radio waves from space.

RINCÓN   Named after the 16th-century landowner Don Gonzalo Rincón, who donated its site to the poor of his district, the tiny town of Rincón is famous throughout Puerto Rico for its world-class surfing and beautiful beaches. The lighthouse that warns ships and boats away from dangerous offshore reefs is one of the most powerful on Puerto Rico.

RÍO CAMUY CAVE PARK   Located near Arecibo, this park's greatest attraction is underground, where a network of underground rivers and caves provides some of the most enjoyable spelunking in the world. At its heart lies one of the largest known underground rivers. Covering 300 acres aboveground, the park is sought out by cave explorers the world over.

UTUADO   Small, sunny, and nestled amid the hills of the interior, Utuado is famous as the center of the (hillbilly) culture of Puerto Rico. Some of Puerto Rico's finest mountain musicians have come from Utuado and mention the town in many of their ballads. The surrounding landscape is sculpted with caves and lushly covered with a variety of tropical plants and trees.

DORADO & THE NORTH COAST

Playa Dorado, directly east of San Juan at Dorado, is actually a term for a total of six white-sand beaches along the northern coast, reached by a series of winding roads. Dorado is the island's oldest resort town, the center of golf, casinos, and two major Hyatt resorts (see chapter 7). At the Hyatt Resorts Puerto Rico at Dorado, you'll find 72 holes of golf, the greatest concentration in the Caribbean—all designed by Robert Trent Jones.

The complex is quite family-friendly, with its Camp Hyatt, which offers programs for children ages 3 to 15. There is also a water playground at the Hyatt Regency Cerromar Beach Hotel, with a 1,776-foot-long fantasy pool—the world's longest freshwater swimming pool.

Another resort of increasing importance is also found along the north coast: El Conquistador at Palomino Island, a private island paradise with sandy beaches and recreational facilities. This resort lies near Las Croabas, a fishing village on the northeasternmost tip of Puerto Rico's north coast.

Challenging both the Hyatt Resorts and El Conquistador is the Westin Rio Mar Beach Resort, Country Club & Ocean Villas, lying 19 miles to the east of the San Juan international airport.

THE NORTHEAST: EL YUNQUE, A NATURE RESERVE & FAJARDO

The capital city of San Juan (see above) dominates Puerto Rico's northeast. Despite the region's congestion, there are still many remote areas, including some of the island's most important nature reserves. Among the region's most popular towns, parks, and attractions are the following:

EL YUNQUE　In the Luquillo Mountains, 35 miles east of San Juan, El Yunque is a favorite escape from the capital. Teeming with plant and animal life, it is a sprawling tropical forest (actually a national forest) whose ecosystems are strictly protected. Some 100 billion gallons of rainwater fall here each year, allowing about 250 species of trees and flowers to flourish.

FAJARDO　Small and sleepy, this town was originally established as a supply depot for the many pirates who plied the nearby waters. Today, a host of private yachts bob at anchor in its harbor, and the many offshore cays provide visitors with secluded beaches. From Fajardo, ferryboats make choppy but frequent runs to the offshore islands of Vieques and Culebra.

LAS CABEZAS DE SAN JUAN NATURE RESERVE　About an hour's drive from San Juan, this is one of the island's newest ecological refuges. It was established in 1991 on 316 acres of forest, mangrove swamp, offshore cays, coral reefs, and freshwater lagoons—a representative sampling of virtually every ecosystem on Puerto Rico. There is a visitor center, a 19th-century lighthouse (El Faro) that still works, and ample opportunity to forget the pressures of urban life.

THE SOUTHWEST: PONCE, MAYAGÜEZ, SAN GERMÁN & MORE

One of Puerto Rico's most beautiful regions, the southwest is rich in local lore, civic pride, and natural wonders.

BOQUERÓN　Famous for the beauty of its beach and the abundant birds and wildlife in the nearby Boquerón Forest Reserve, this small and sleepy village is now ripe for large-scale tourism-related development. During the early 19th century, the island's most-feared pirate, Roberto Cofresi, terrorized the Puerto Rican coastline from a secret lair in a cave nearby.

CABO ROJO　Established in 1772, Cabo Rojo reached the peak of its prosperity during the 19th century, when immigrants from around the Mediterranean, fleeing revolutions in their own countries, arrived to establish sugarcane plantations. Today, cattle graze peacefully on land originally devoted almost exclusively to sugarcane, while the area's many varieties of exotic birds draw bird-watchers from throughout North America. Even the offshore waters are fertile; it's estimated that nearly half of all the fish consumed on Puerto Rico are caught in waters near Cabo Rojo.

LA PARGUERA　Named after a breed of snapper (*pargos*) that abounds in the waters nearby, La Parguera is a quiet coastal town best known for the phosphorescent waters of La Bahía Fosforescente (Phosphorescent Bay). Here, sheltered from the waves of the sea, billions of plankton (luminescent dinoflagellates) glow dimly when they are disturbed by movements of the water. The town comes alive on weekends, when crowds of young people from San Juan arrive to party the nights away. Filling modest rooming houses, they temporarily change the texture of the town as bands produce long and loud sessions of salsa music.

MAYAGÜEZ　The third-largest city on Puerto Rico, Mayagüez is named after the *majagua*, the Amerindian word for a tree that grows abundantly in the area. Because of an earthquake that destroyed almost everything in town in 1917, few old buildings remain. The town is known as the commercial and industrial capital of Puerto Rico's western sector. Its botanical garden is among the finest on the island.

PONCE   Puerto Rico's second-largest city, Ponce has always prided itself on its independence from the Spanish-derived laws and taxes that governed San Juan and the rest of the island. Long-ago home of some of the island's shrewdest traders, merchants, and smugglers, it is enjoying a renaissance as citizens and visitors rediscover its unique cultural and architectural charms. Located about 90 minutes by car from the capital on Puerto Rico's southern coast, Ponce contains a handful of superb museums, one of the most charming main squares in the Caribbean, an ancient cathedral, dozens of authentically restored colonial-era buildings, and a number of outlying mansions and villas that, at the time of their construction, were among the most opulent on the island.

SAN GERMÁN   Located on the island's southwestern corner, small, sleepy, and historic San Germán was named after Ferdinand of Spain's second wife, Germaine de Foix, whom he married in 1503. San Germán's central church, Porta Coeli, was built in 1606. At one time, much of the populace was engaged in piracy, pillaging the ships that sailed off the nearby coastline. The central area of this village is still sought out for its many reminders of the island's Spanish heritage and colonial charm.

THE SOUTHEAST: PALMAS DEL MAR & MORE

The southeastern quadrant has some of the most heavily developed, as well as some of the least developed, sections of the island.

COAMO   Although today Coamo is a bedroom community for San Juan, originally it was the site of two different Taíno communities. Founded in 1579, it now has a main square draped with bougainvillea and one of the best-known Catholic churches on Puerto Rico. Even more famous, however, are the mineral springs whose therapeutic warm waters helped President Franklin D. Roosevelt during his recovery from polio. (Some historians claim that these springs inspired the legend of the Fountain of Youth, which in turn set Ponce de León off on his vain search of Florida.)

HUMACAO   Because of its easy access to San Juan, this small, verdant inland town has increasingly become one of the capital's residential suburbs.

PALMAS DEL MAR   This sprawling vacation and residential resort community is located near Humacao. A splendid golf course covers some of the grounds. Palmas del Mar is at the center of what has been called the "New American Riviera"—3 miles of white-sand beaches on the eastern coast of the island. Palmas del Mar is the largest resort in Puerto Rico, lying to the south of Humacao on 2,800 acres of a former coconut plantation—now devoted to luxury living and the sporting life.

The Equestrian Center at Palmas is the finest riding headquarters in Puerto Rico, with trails cutting through an old plantation and jungle along the beach. The resort is ideal for families and has a supervised summer activities program for children ages 5 to 12.

THE OFFSHORE ISLANDS: CULEBRA, VIEQUES & MORE

Few *norteamericanos* realize that Puerto Rico has at least four well-known islands and a multitude of tiny cays lying offshore. The most famous of these include:

CAYO SANTIAGO   Lying off the southeastern coast is the small island of Cayo Santiago. Home to a group of about two dozen scientists and a community of rhesus monkeys originally imported from India, the island is a medical experimentation center run by the U.S. Public Health Service. Monkeys are studied in a "wild" but controlled environment both for insights into the behavioral sciences and for possible cures for such maladies as diabetes and arthritis. Casual visitors are not permitted on Cayo Santiago, but they can cruise along the shore and watch the monkeys.

CULEBRA & VIEQUES   Located off the eastern coast, these two islands are among the most unsullied and untrammeled areas in the West Indies, even though Vieques is being belatedly discovered. Come here for sun, almost no scheduled activities, fresh seafood, clear waters, sandy beaches, and teeming coral reefs. Vieques is especially proud of its phosphorescent bay.

MONA   Remote, uninhabited, and teeming with bird life, this barren island off the western coast is ringed by soaring cliffs and finely textured white beaches. The island has almost no facilities, so visitors seldom stay for more than a day of swimming and picnicking. The currents that surround Mona on all sides are legendary for their dangerous eddies, undertows, and sharks.

2 Visitor Information

For information before you leave home, contact one of the following **Puerto Rico Tourism Company** offices: 575 Fifth Ave., New York, NY 10017 (☎ **800/223-6530** or 212/586-6262); 3575 W. Cahuenga Blvd., Suite 405, Los Angeles, CA 90068 (☎ **800/874-1230** or 213/874-5991); or 901 Ponce de León Blvd., Suite 604, Coral Gables, FL 33134 (☎ **800/815-7391** or 305/445-9112).

In Canada contact the company at 41-43 Colbourne St., Suite 301, Toronto, ON M5E 1E3 (☎ **416/368-2680**).

If you have Internet access, visit **City.Net** (www.city.net), which has links, organized by location and then by subject, to sites with information about many destinations. To find Puerto Rico, click on the "Caribbean" heading; when a map of the region appears, click on the island. Here you will find a number of links regarding Puerto Rico.

One of the best Caribbean Web sites is **Caribbean-On-Line** (www.webcom.com/ earleltd/), a series of virtual guidebooks full of information on hotels, restaurants, and shopping, along with sights and detailed maps of the islands. The site is still a work in progress, and at press time Puerto Rico information was not yet accessible. However, the site also includes links to travel agents and cruise lines that are up on the Web.

You may also want to contact the U.S. State Department for background bulletins, which supply up-to-date information on crime, health concerns, import restrictions, and other travel matters. Write the Superintendent of Documents, **U.S. Government Printing Office,** Washington, DC 20402 (☎ **202/512-1800**).

A good travel agent can be a source of information. Make sure your agent is a member of the American Society of Travel Agents (ASTA). If you get poor service from an ASTA agent, you can write to the **ASTA Consumer Affairs Department,** 1101 King St., Alexandria, VA 22314 (☎ **703/739-8739;** www.astanet.com).

3 Entry Requirements & Customs

ENTRY REQUIREMENTS
DOCUMENTS   U.S. citizens who fly from the mainland to Puerto Rico and return to the mainland don't need passports because Puerto Rico is a territory of the United States.

Canadians, however, should carry a passport or some form of identification. Acceptable documents include an ongoing or a return ticket, plus a current voter registration card or a birth certificate. In addition, you will need some photo ID, which

Tip for Travel Documents

Before leaving home, make two copies of your most valuable documents, including your passport, your driver's license, or any other identity document; your airline ticket; and any hotel vouchers. (If you're on medication, you should also make copies of prescriptions.)

---

could be a driver's license or an expired passport. Driver's licenses alone are not acceptable as ID.

Visitors from the United Kingdom, New Zealand, Ireland, and most western European nations need only a valid passport as long as they plan to stay in Puerto Rico 90 days or less. Citizens of Australia need just a passport to enter Puerto Rico.

VACCINATIONS   Vaccinations are not required for entry to Puerto Rico if you're coming from the United States or Canada.

Infectious hepatitis has been reported on other Caribbean islands but less frequently on Puerto Rico. Consult your doctor about the advisability of getting a gamma-globulin shot before you leave home.

Typhoid, poliomyelitis, and tetanus are not common diseases on the island, and inoculations against them are recommended mainly to visitors who plan to rough it in the wilds. If you're staying in a regular Puerto Rican hotel, such preventive measures are generally not needed, but your doctor can advise you, based on your destination and travel plans.

CUSTOMS

U.S. citizens do not need to clear Puerto Rican Customs upon arrival by plane or ship from the mainland. All non-U.S. citizens must clear Customs and are permitted to bring in items intended for their personal use, including tobacco, cameras, film, and a limited supply of liquor (usually 40 oz.).

U.S. CUSTOMS   On departure, U.S.-bound travelers must have their luggage inspected by the U.S. Agriculture Department because laws prohibit bringing fruits and plants to the U.S. mainland. Fruits and vegetables are not allowed, but otherwise, you can bring back as many purchased goods as you want without paying duty.

For more specifics, write to the **U.S. Customs Service,** 1301 Constitution Ave., P.O. Box 7407, Washington, DC 20044 (☎ **202/927-6724;** www.customs.ustreas.gov), and request the free pamphlet *Know Before You Go.*

CANADIAN CUSTOMS   Canadians who have spent 24 hours or less outside the country are allowed a C$50 exemption from taxation goods they've bought, but any tobacco or liquor products purchased abroad are subject to Canadian duty. For Canadians who have spent more than 48 hours outside the Canadian border, a C$300 exemption is granted on goods they've purchased, and they're allowed to bring back duty-free 200 cigarettes, 200 grams of tobacco, 40 imperial ounces of liquor, and 50 cigars. For Canadians who have spent 7 days or more outside the country, the exemption is raised to C$750, and the same quantities of tobacco and liquor mentioned above can be brought in duty-free.

In addition to the exemptions noted above, and regardless of the amount of time they spend away from Canada, Canadians are allowed to mail gifts from abroad to friends, clients, and relatives in Canada (but not to themselves), at the rate of C$60 per day, provided that the gifts are unsolicited and aren't alcohol or tobacco products. Be sure to write "Unsolicited gift, under C$60 value" on the outside of the package.

All valuables such as expensive cameras and jewelry should be declared on Form Y-38 before your departure from Canada, and, whenever it's possible, with the notation of the article's serial number. When serial numbers aren't available, as in the case of jewelry, it's wise to carry a photocopy of either the original bill of sale or a bona fide appraisal.

For more information, contact Revenue Canada, 2265 St. Laurent Blvd., Ottawa, ON K1G 4K3 (☎ 613/993-0534), and ask for the free booklet *I Declare.*

BRITISH CUSTOMS   On returning from the Caribbean, British subjects who either arrive directly in the United Kingdom or arrive via a port in another European Community (EC) country and who did not pass through Customs controls with all their baggage must go through U.K. Customs and declare any goods in excess of 200 cigarettes or 50 cigars or 250 grams of tobacco; 2 liters of still table wine and 1 liter of spirits or strong liqueurs over 22% volume, or 2 liters of fortified or sparkling wine or other liqueurs; 60cc (ml) of perfume; 250cc (ml) of toilet water; and £145 worth of all other goods, including gifts and souvenirs. (No one under 17 years of age is entitled to a tobacco or alcohol allowance.) Only go through the green "nothing to declare" line if you're sure that you have no more than the Customs allowances and no prohibited or restricted goods. For further details on U.K. Customs, contact H.M. Customs and Excise Office, Dorset House, Stamford Street, London SE1 9PY, England (☎ 020/8910-3744; fax 0171/202-4216; www.hmce.gov.uk).

AUSTRALIAN CUSTOMS   The duty-free allowance in Australia is A$400 or, for those under 18, A$200. Personal property mailed back from Puerto Rico should be marked "Australian goods returned" to avoid payment of duty. Upon returning to Australia, citizens can bring in 250 cigarettes or 250 grams of loose tobacco, and 1125ml of alcohol. If you're returning with valuable goods you already own, including foreign-made cameras, you should file Form B263. A helpful brochure, available from Australian consulates or Customs offices, is *Know Before You Go.* For more information, contact Australian Customs Services, GPO Box 8, Sydney, NSW 2001 (☎ 02/9213-2000).

NEW ZEALAND CUSTOMS   The duty-free allowance for New Zealand is NZ$700. Citizens over 17 years of age can bring in 200 cigarettes, or 50 cigars, or 250 grams of tobacco (or a mixture of all three if their combined weight doesn't exceed 250g); plus 4.5 liters of wine and beer, or 1.125 liters of liquor. There is no limit on how much currency you can carry in or out of New Zealand. Fill out a certificate of export, listing the valuables you are taking out of the country; that way, you can bring them back without paying duty. Most questions are answered in a free pamphlet available at New Zealand consulates and Customs offices: *New Zealand Customs Guide for Travellers,* Notice no. 4. For more information, contact New Zealand Customs, 50 Anzac Ave., P.O. Box 29, Auckland, New Zealand (☎ 09/359-66-55).

4 Money

CURRENCY   The U.S. dollar is the coin of the realm. Keep in mind that once you leave Ponce or San Juan, you might have difficulty finding a place to exchange foreign money (unless you're staying at a large resort), so it's wise to handle your exchange needs before you head off into rural parts of Puerto Rico.

CURRENCY EXCHANGE   The currency exchange facilities at any large international bank within Puerto Rico's larger cities can exchange non-U.S. currencies for dollars. You can also exchange money at the Luis Muñoz Marín International Airport.

Also, you'll find foreign-exchange facilities in large hotels and at the many banks in Old San Juan or along Ashford Avenue in Condado. In Ponce, look for foreign-exchange facilities at large resorts and at banks such as Banco Popular, Plaza Las Delicias (☎ 787/843-8000).

TRAVELER'S CHECKS   Although it's now perfectly easy to find ATM machines in Puerto Rico and get cash from them as you would at home (see "ATM Networks," below), some travelers still like the security of carrying traveler's checks so that they can get a refund in the event of theft.

Most large banks sell traveler's checks, charging fees that average between 1 and 2% of the value of the checks you buy, although some out-of-the-way banks, in rare instances, have charged as much as 7%. If your bank wants more than a 2% commission, it may pay to call the traveler's check issuers directly for the address of outlets where this commission will be less.

American Express (☎ 800/221-7282; www.americanexpress.com) in the United States and Canada, with many regional representatives around the world, is one of the largest issuers of traveler's checks. American Express platinum cardholders get traveler's checks issued commission-free at American Express offices or through the American Express service number (☎ 800/553-6782). Gold cardholders can get commission-free checks only through the American Express service number; other cardholders pay a commission. The **American Automobile Association (AAA)** does not charge its members a fee for American Express traveler's checks purchased at AAA offices.

Citicorp (☎ 800/645-6556 in the U.S. and Canada, or 813/623-1709 collect from other parts of the world) is another major issuer. **Thomas Cook** (☎ 800/223-7373 in the U.S. and Canada, or 609/987-7300 collect from other parts of the world; www.thomascook.com) issues MasterCard traveler's checks, and **Interpayment Services** (☎ 800/221-2426 in the U.S. and Canada, or 212/858-8500 collect from other parts of the world) sells Visa traveler's checks.

CREDIT CARDS   Credit cards are widely used in Puerto Rico. Visa and Master-Card are the major cards, although American Express and, to a lesser extent, Diners Club are also popular. We've noted which cards are accepted at every hotel and restaurant reviewed in this book.

ATM NETWORKS   Plus, Cirrus, and other automated-teller machine (ATM) networks operate in Puerto Rico. Before departing, check to see if your PIN number must be reprogrammed for use at Caribbean ATMs to withdraw money on either your ATM or your credit card.

Always determine what the frequency limits for withdrawals and cash advances are on your bank or credit card. For locations of Cirrus (www.mastercard.com/atm/) abroad, call ☎ 800/424-7787 in the United States. For Plus (www.visa.com/atms) usage abroad, dial ☎ 800/843-7587. ATMs give a better exchange rate than banks, but some ATMs exact a service charge on every transaction.

MONEYGRAMS   Sponsored by American Express, **Moneygram** (☎ 800/926-9400) is the fastest-growing money-wiring service in the world. Funds can be transferred from one individual to another in less than 10 minutes between thousands of locations throughout the world. An American Express phone representative will give you the names of four or five offices near you. (You don't have to go to an American Express office; some locations are pharmacies or convenience stores in small communities.) Acceptable forms of payment include cash, Visa, MasterCard, or Discover, and occasionally, a personal check. Service charges collected by American Express are $40 for the first $500 sent, with a sliding scale of commissions for larger sums. Included in

What Things Cost in Puerto Rico	U.S. $
Taxi from the airport to Condado	12.00
Average taxi fare within San Juan	12.00
Typical bus fare	.25–.50
Local telephone call	.10
Double room at the Caribe Hilton (very expensive)	320.00
Double room at El Canario by the Lagoon (moderate)	100.00
Double room at Wind chimes Inn (inexpensive)	65.00
Lunch for one at Amadeus (moderate)	15.00
Lunch for one at La Bombonera (inexpensive)	13.00
Dinner for one at Ramiro's (very expensive)	46.00
Dinner for one at El Patio de Sam (moderate)	28.00
Dinner for one at Tony Roma's (inexpensive)	16.00
Draft beer in a bar	3.75
Coca-Cola in a cafe	1.50
Glass of wine in a restaurant	3.75
Roll of ASA 100 color film, 36 exposures	8.50
Admission to Castillo San Felipe del Morro	Free
Movie ticket	6.00
Theater ticket	13.00–65.00

the transfer is a 10-word telex-style message. The deal also includes a free 3-minute phone call to the recipient. Funds are transferred within 10 minutes, and they can then be retrieved by the beneficiary at the most convenient location when proper photo ID, and in some cases, a security code established by whomever provides the funds, is presented.

5 When to Go

CLIMATE
Puerto Rico has one of the most unvarying climates in the world. Temperatures year-round range from 75 to 85°F (24 to 29°C). The island is wettest and hottest in August, averaging 81°F (27°C) and 7 inches of rain. San Juan and the northern coast seem to be cooler and wetter than Ponce and the southern coast. The coldest weather is in the high altitudes of the Cordillera, the site of Puerto Rico's lowest recorded temperature—39°F (4°C).

THE HURRICANE SEASON
The curse of Puerto Rican weather, the hurricane season lasts—officially, at least—from June 1 to November 30. But there's no cause for panic. In general, satellite forecasts give adequate warnings so that precautions can be taken.

If you're heading to Puerto Rico during the hurricane season, you can call your local branch of the **National Weather Service** (listed in your phone directory under the U.S. Department of Commerce) for a weather forecast.

It'll cost 95¢ per query, but you can get information about the climate conditions in any city you plan to visit by calling ☎ **800/WEATHER.** When you're prompted, enter your Visa or MasterCard account number and then punch in the name of any of 1,000 cities worldwide whose weather is monitored by the **Weather Channel** (www.weather.com).

Average Temperatures on Puerto Rico

	Jan	Feb	Mar	Apr	May	June	July	Aug	Sept	Oct	Nov	Dec
Temp. (°F)	75	75	76	78	79	81	81	81	81	81	79	77
Temp. (°C)	25	24	24	24.4	25.6	26	27	27	27	27	27	26

THE "SEASON"

In Puerto Rico, hotels charge their highest prices during the peak winter period from mid-December to mid-April, when visitors fleeing from cold north winds flock to the islands. Winter is the driest season along the coasts but can be wet in mountainous areas.

If you plan to travel in the winter, make reservations 2 to 3 months in advance. At certain hotels it's almost impossible to book accommodations for Christmas and the month of February.

SAVING MONEY IN THE OFF-SEASON

Puerto Rico is a year-round destination. The island's "off-season" runs from late spring to late fall, when temperatures in the mid-80s (about 29°C) prevail throughout most of the region. Trade winds ensure comfortable days and nights, even in accommodations without air-conditioning. Although the noonday sun may raise the temperature to around 90°F (32°C), cool breezes usually make the morning, late afternoon, and evening more comfortable here than in many parts of the U.S. mainland.

Dollar for dollar, you'll spend less money by renting a summer house or fully equipped unit in Puerto Rico than you would on Cape Cod, Fire Island, Laguna Beach, or the coast of Maine.

The off-season in Puerto Rico—roughly from mid-April to mid-December (rate schedules vary from hotel to hotel)—amounts to a summer sale. In most cases, hotel rates are slashed from 20% to a startling 60%. It's a bonanza for cost-conscious travelers, especially families who like to go on vacations together. In the chapters ahead, we'll spell out in dollars the specific amounts hotels charge during the off-season.

OTHER OFF-SEASON ADVANTAGES

Although Puerto Rico may appear inviting in the winter to those who live in northern climates, there are many reasons why your trip may be much more enjoyable if you go in the off-season:

- After the winter hordes have left, a less-hurried way of life prevails. You'll have a better chance to appreciate the food, culture, and local customs.
- Swimming pools and beaches are less crowded—perhaps not crowded at all.
- Year-round resort facilities are offered, often at reduced rates, which may include snorkeling, boating, and scuba diving.
- To survive, resort boutiques often feature summer sales, hoping to clear the merchandise they didn't sell in February to accommodate stock they've ordered for the coming winter.
- You can often appear without a reservation at a top restaurant and get a table for dinner, a table that in winter would have required a reservation far in advance. Also, when waiters are less hurried, you get better service.

- The endless waiting game is over: no waiting for a rented car (only to be told none is available), no long wait for a golf course tee time, and quicker access to tennis courts and water sports.
- The atmosphere is more cosmopolitan in the off-season than it is in winter, mainly because of the influx of Europeans. You'll no longer feel as if you're at a Canadian or American outpost. Also, since the Puerto Ricans themselves travel in the off-season, your holiday will become more of a multicultural experience.
- Some package-tour fares are as much as 20% lower, and individual excursion fares are also reduced between 5 and 10%.
- All accommodations and flights are much easier to book.
- Summer is an excellent time for family travel, not usually possible during the winter season.
- Finally, the very best of Puerto Rican attractions remain undiminished in the off-season—sea, sand, and surf, with lots of sunshine.

OFF-SEASON DISADVANTAGES

Let's not paint too rosy a picture. Although the advantages of off-season travel far out-weigh the disadvantages, there are nevertheless drawbacks to traveling in summer:

- You might be staying at a construction site. Hoteliers save their serious repairs and their major renovations until the off-season when they have fewer clients. That means you might wake up early in the morning to the sound of the hammer.
- Single tourists find the cruising better in winter when there are more clients, especially the unattached. Families predominate in summer and there are fewer chances to meet fellow singles than in the winter months.
- Services are often reduced. In the peak of winter, everything is fully operational. But in summer, many of the programs such as water sports might be curtailed. Also, not all restaurants and bars are fully operational at all resorts. For example, for lack of business, certain gourmet or specialty dining rooms might be shut down until house count merits reopening them. In all, the general atmosphere is more laid-back when a hotel or resort might also be operating with a reduced staff. The summer staff will still be adequate to provide service for what's up and running.

HOLIDAYS

Puerto Rico has many public holidays when stores, offices, and schools are closed: New Year's Day, January 6 (Three Kings Day), Washington's Birthday, Good Friday, Memorial Day, July 4, Labor Day, Thanksgiving, Veterans Day, and Christmas, plus such local holidays as Constitution Day (July 25) and Discovery Day (November 19). Remember, U.S. federal holidays are holidays in Puerto Rico too.

Puerto Rico Calendar of Events

January

- **Three Kings Day,** island-wide. On this traditional gift-giving day in Puerto Rico, there are festivals with lively music, dancing, parades, puppet shows, caroling troubadours, and traditional feasts. January 6.
- **San Sebastián Street Festival,** Calle San Sebastián in Old San Juan. Nightly celebrations with music, processions, crafts, and typical foods, as well as graphic arts and handicraft exhibitions. January 20 to 23. For more information, call ☎ 787/721-1476.

February

- **San Blas de Illescas Half Marathon,** Coamo. International and local runners compete in a challenging 13.1-mile half-marathon in the hilly south-central town of Coamo. February 6. Call Delta Phi Delta Fraternity (☎ 787/825-4077).
- **Coffee Harvest Festival,** Maricao. Folk music, a parade of floats, typical foods, crafts, and demonstrations of coffee preparation in Maricao, a 1-hour drive east of Mayagüez in the center of one of the island's coffee-growing districts. February 18 to 20. For more information, call ☎ 787/838-2290 or 787/856-1345.

March

- **Carnival Ponceño,** Ponce. The island's Carnival celebrations feature float parades, dancing, and street parties. One of the most vibrant festivities is held in Ponce, known for its masqueraders wearing brightly painted horned masks. Live music includes the folk rhythms of the plena, which originated in Africa. Festivities include the crowning of a carnival queen and the closing "burial of the sardine." March 1 to 7. For more information, call ☎ 787/284-4141.
- **Emancipation Day,** island-wide. Commemoration of the emancipation of Puerto Rico's slaves in 1873, held at various venues. March 22.
- **Good Friday and Easter,** island-wide. Celebrated with colorful ceremonies and processions. Date varies.

April

- **José de Diego Day,** island-wide. Commemoration of the birthday of José de Diego, a patriot, lawyer, writer, orator, and political leader who was the first president of the Puerto Rico House of Representatives under U.S. rule. April 17.
- **Sugar Harvest Festival,** in the western town of San Germán. Festival marks the end of the island's sugar harvest, with live music, crafts, and typical foods, as well as exhibitions of sugarcane plants and past and present harvesting techniques. Late April.

June

- ● **Casals Festival,** San Juan. *Sanjuaneros* and visitors alike eagerly look forward to the annual Casals Festival, the Caribbean's most celebrated cultural event. The bill at San Juan's Performing Arts Center includes a glittering array of international guest conductors, orchestras, and soloists. They come to honor the memory of Pablo Casals, the renowned cellist who was born in Spain to a Puerto Rican mother. When Casals died in Puerto Rico in 1973 at the age of 97, the Casals Festival was 16 years old and attracting the same class of performers who appeared at the Pablo Casals Festival in France, founded by Casals after World War II. When he moved to Puerto Rico in 1957 with his wife, Marta Casals Istomin (past artistic director of the John F. Kennedy Center for the Performing Arts), he founded not only this festival but also the Puerto Rico Symphony Orchestra to foster musical development on the island.

    Where: Performing Arts Center in San Juan. **When:** June 3 to 20. **How:** Ticket prices for the Casals Festival range from $20 to $40. A 50% discount is offered to students, senior citizens over 60, and persons with disabilities. Tickets are available through the Performing Arts Center in San Juan (☎ 787/721-7727). Information is also available from the Puerto Rico Tourism Company, 575 Fifth Ave., New York, NY 10017 (☎ 800/223-6530 in the U.S. or 212/586-6262).
- **Heineken JazzFest,** San Juan. The 10th annual jazz celebration will be staged at Parque Sixto Escobar. Each year a different jazz theme is featured. The open-air

pavilion is in a scenic oceanfront location in the Puerta de Tierra section of San Juan near the Hilton. June 10 to 13. For more information, call ☎ 787/277-9200.

* **San Juan Bautista Day,** island-wide. Puerto Rico's capital and other cities celebrate the island's patron saint with week-long festivities. At midnight, *sanjuaneros* walk backward into the sea (or nearest body of water) three times to renew good luck for the coming year. June 24.

* **Aibonito Flower Festival,** at Road 722 next to the City Hall Coliseum, in the central mountain town of Aibonito. This annual flower-competition festival features acres of lilies, anthuriums, carnations, roses, gardenias, and begonias. June 25 to July 4. For more information, call ☎ 787/735-3871.

July

* **Luis Muñoz Rivera's Birthday,** island-wide. A birthday celebration commemorating Luis Muñoz Rivera (1829 to 1916), statesman, journalist, poet, and resident commissioner in Washington, D.C. July 15.

* **Loíza Carnival.** An annual folk and religious ceremony honoring Loíza's patron saint, John (Santiago) the Apostle. Colorful processions take place, with costumes, masks, and bomba dancers (the bomba is a lively Afro-Caribbean dance rhythm). This jubilant celebration reflects the African and Spanish heritage of the region. July 24 to August 3 for 2001. For more information, call ☎ 787/876-3570.

August

* **El Gigante Marathon,** Adjuntas. This is a 15-kilometer race. Early August.

* **Cuadragésimo Cuarto Torneo de Pesca Interclub del Caribe, Cangrejos Yacht Club.** International blue marlin fishing tournament. Crafts, music, local delicacies, among other activities. August 10 to 13. For more information, call ☎ 787/791-1015.

September

* **International Billfish Tournament,** at Club Náutico. This is one of the premier game-fishing tournaments and the longest consecutively held billfish tournament in the world. Fishers from many countries angle for blue marlin that can weigh up to 900 pounds. September 3 to 10. For further information, call ☎ 787/722-6624.

* **Inter-American Festival of the Arts,** at the Luis A. Ferré Performing Arts Center in San Juan. A 3-week series of musical art performances that includes classical, popular, and folk music; ballet and modern dance productions; and musical theater. Approximately September 20 to October 10. Call ☎ 787/721-7727 for more information.

October

* **La Raza Day (Columbus Day),** island-wide. Commemoration of Columbus's landing in the New World. October 12.

* ✪ **National Plantain Festival,** in the northern town of Corozal. Annual festivity with crafts, paintings, agricultural products, exhibition, and sale of plantain dishes; *neuva trova* music and folk ballet are performed. October 30 to November 2. For more information, call ☎ 787/859-1259.

November

* **Puerto Rican Day of Bomba and Plena,** Ponce. Festivities celebrate two local rhythms and dances, the bomba and the plena, which are still popular today. Groups from all over the island present their repertoires. A colorful parade, handicraft exhibits, and typical food—a selection that ranges from grilled island specialties to hot dogs. Dates vary. For more information, call ☎ 787/842-2540.

- **Start of Baseball Season,** in Hiram Bithorn Park in San Juan and throughout the island. Six Puerto Rican professional clubs compete. Professionals from North America also play here from around November 2 until February. For more information, contact Professional Baseball of Puerto Rico (☎ 787/765-6285).
- **Puerto Rico Discovery Day,** island-wide. This commemorates the "discovery" by Columbus in 1493 of the already inhabited island of Puerto Rico. He is thought to have come ashore at the northwestern municipality of Aguadilla, although the exact location is unknown. November 19.
- **Festival of Puerto Rican Music,** San Juan. Annual classical and folk music festival. One of its highlights is a *cuatro*-playing contest. Mid-November. For more information, call ☎ 787/721-5274.
- **Jayuya Indian Festival,** at Jayuya. This fiesta features the culture and tradition of the island's original inhabitants, the Taíno Indians, and their music, food, and games. More than 100 artisans exhibit and sell their works. There is also a Miss Taíno Indian Pageant, in which contestants are judged by their features and garments that are designed to evoke—both in style and materials—the typical dress of a Taíno woman. November 18 to 21. For more information, call ☎ 787/828-0900.

December

- **Old San Juan's White Christmas Festival,** Old San Juan. Special musical and artistic presentations take place in stores, with window displays. December 1 to January 12.
- **Bacardi Artisans' Fair,** San Juan. The best and largest artisans' fair on the island is held the first two Sundays in December, when more than 100 artisans turn out to exhibit and sell their wares. The fair includes shows for adults and children, a Puerto Rican troubadour contest, rides, typical food and drink—all sold by nonprofit organizations. Held on the grounds of the world's largest rum-manufacturing plant in Cataño, an industrial suburb set on a peninsula jutting into San Juan Bay. December 2 and 10. For more information, call ☎ 787/788-1500.
- **Las Mañanitas,** Ponce. A religious procession starts out from Lolita Tizol Street toward the city's Catholic church, led by mariachis singing songs to honor Our Lady of Guadeloupe, the city's patron saint. The lead song is the traditional Mexican birthday song, *Las Mañanitas.* There's a 6am mass. December 12. For more information, contact the Ponce City Hall (☎ 787/284-4141).
- **Puerto Rico International Offshore Cup,** in San Juan Bay. First of its kind on the island, this competition matches local speedboat racing teams with some of the best offshore teams from the United States and the Caribbean. December 14. For more information, call Pepe Llama at the Puerto Rico Offshore Association (☎ 787/753-7715).
- **Hatillo Masks Festival,** at the northwestern coastal town of Hatillo. A tradition celebrated since 1823 represents the biblical story of King Herod's ordering the death of all infant boys in an attempt to kill the baby Jesus. Men with colorful masks and costumes represent the soldiers, who run or ride through the town from early morning looking for the children. Food, music, and crafts exhibits in the town square. December 28. For more information, call ☎ 787/898-3835.
- **Lighting of the Town of Bethlehem,** between San Cristóbal Fort and Plaza San Juan Bautista in Old San Juan. During the Christmas season.

YEAR-ROUND FESTIVALS

In addition to the individual events described above, Puerto Rico has two year-long series of special events.

Many of Puerto Rico's most popular events are during the **Patron Saint Festivals** *(fiestas patronales)* in honor of the patron saint of each municipality. The festivities, held in each town's central plaza, include religious and costumed processions, games, local food, music, and dance.

At **Festival La Casita,** prominent Puerto Rican musicians, dance troupes, and orchestras perform; puppet shows are staged; and painters and sculptors display their works. It's on every Saturday at Puerto Rico Tourism's "La Casita" Tourism Information Center, Plaza Darsenas, across from Pier 1, Old San Juan.

For more information about all these events, contact the **Puerto Rico Tourism Company,** 575 Fifth Ave., New York, NY 10017 (☎ **800/223-6530** or 212/586-6262).

6 Health & Insurance

STAYING HEALTHY

Finding a good doctor in Puerto Rico is easy, and most speak English. See "Fast Facts: Puerto Rico," later in this chapter, for the locations of hospitals.

POTENTIAL PROBLEMS   It's best to stick to bottled mineral water here. Although tap water is said to be safe to drink, many visitors experience diarrhea, even if they follow the usual precautions. The illness usually passes quickly without medication if you eat simply prepared food and drink only mineral water until you recover. If symptoms persist, consult a doctor.

The sun can be brutal, especially if you haven't been exposed to it in some time. Experts advise that you limit your time on the beach the first day. If you do over-expose yourself, stay out of the sun until you recover. If your exposure is followed by fever or chills, a headache, or a feeling of nausea or dizziness, see a doctor.

Sandflies (or "no-see-ums") are one of the biggest insect menaces in Puerto Rico. They appear mainly in the early evening, and even if you can't see these tiny bugs, you sure can "feel-um," as any native Puerto Rican will attest. Screens can't keep them out, so you'll need to use your favorite insect repellent.

Although mosquitoes are a nuisance, they do not carry malaria in Puerto Rico.

Hookworm and other intestinal parasites are relatively common in the Caribbean, though you are less likely to be affected on Puerto Rico. Hookworm can be contracted by just walking barefoot on an infected beach. Schistosomiasis (also called bilharzia), caused by a parasitic fluke, can be contracted by submerging your feet in rivers and lakes infested with a certain species of snail.

And don't forget that Puerto Rico has been especially hard hit by AIDS. Exercise *at least* the same caution in choosing your sexual partners, and in practicing safe sex, as you would at home.

For conditions such as epilepsy, a heart condition, diabetes, or allergies, consider wearing a **Medic Alert Identification Tag.** For a lifetime membership, the cost is $35 for a steel tag, $45 if silver plated, and $60 if gold plated. In addition, there is a $15 annual fee. Contact the Medic Alert Foundation, P.O. Box 1009, Turlock, CA 95381-1009 (☎ **800/825-3785;** fax 209/669-2495; www.medicalert.org). Medic Alert's 24-hour hotline enables a foreign doctor to obtain your medical records.

Take along an adequate supply of any **prescription medications** you need and a written prescription specifying the generic name of the drug—not the brand name.

However, U.S. brand names are commonly available at most pharmacies. You may also want to take such over-the-counter items as first-aid cream, insect repellent, aspirin, and Band-Aids.

INSURANCE

Before purchasing insurance, check your current homeowner's, automobile, and medical insurance policies, as well as the membership contracts of automobile and travel clubs and credit/charge cards, for any coverage extended to you while you travel.

Many credit- and charge-card companies insure their users in case of a travel accident when the travel cost was paid with their card. Sometimes fraternal organizations have policies that protect members in case of sickness or accidents abroad.

Many homeowner's insurance policies cover theft of luggage during foreign travel and loss of such documents as your passport and your airline ticket. Coverage is usually limited to about $500. Remember that to submit a claim on your insurance, you'll need police reports or a statement from a local medical authority that you did suffer the loss or experience an illness. Some policies provide advances in cash or arrange for immediate transferals of funds.

Companies offering special travel insurance policies include the following:

Travel Guard International, 1145 Clark St., Stevens Point, WI 54481-9970 (☎ **800/826-1300** outside Wisconsin or 715/345-0505; www.travel-guard.com), offers a comprehensive travel protection policy that covers lost luggage, emergency assistance, accidental death, trip cancellation, and medical coverage abroad. Package costs start at $45 and are based on your total trip cost. Children under 16 are automatically covered if accompanying adults have purchased a policy.

Travelers Insurance PAK, Travel Insured International, P.O. Box 280568, East Hartford, CT 06128-0568 (☎ **800/243-3174;** www.travelinsured.com), offers illness and accident coverage costing from $10 for 6 to 10 days. For lost or damaged luggage, $500 worth of coverage costs $20 for 6 to 10 days. Trip cancellation insurance is $5.50 per $100 of coverage to a limit of $10,000 per person.

Wallach and Co., 107 W. Federal St., P.O. Box 480, Middleburg, VA 20118-0480 (☎ **800/237-6615**), offers coverage for between 10 and 120 days at $4 per day; this policy includes accident and sickness coverage up to $250,000. Medical evacuation is also included, along with $25,000 accidental death and dismemberment compensation. Provisions for trip cancellation can also be written into this policy at a nominal cost.

Travelex, P.O. Box 9408, Garden City, NJ 11530 (☎ **800/228-9792**), offers insurance packages priced from $10 to $59 per person for a trip lasting between 1 and 31 days. Included in these packages are travel assistance services and financial protection against trip cancellation, trip interruption, bankruptcy, flight and baggage delays, accident and sickness, and medical evacuation. Major credit-card holders can file their application for insurance over the phone at the number listed above.

7 Tips for Travelers with Special Needs

FOR TRAVELERS WITH DISABILITIES

The Americans with Disabilities Act is enforced as strictly in Puerto Rico as it is on the U.S. mainland—in fact, a telling example of the act's enforcement can be found in Ponce, where the sightseeing trolleys come equipped with ramps and extra balustrades to accommodate travelers with disabilities. Unfortunately, hotels rarely give much publicity to the facilities they offer persons with disabilities, so it's always wise to contact the hotel directly, in advance. Tourist offices usually have little data about such matters.

You can obtain a free copy of *Air Transportation of Handicapped Persons,* published by the U.S. Department of Transportation. Write for Free Advisory Circular No. AC12032, Distribution Unit, U.S. Department of Transportation, Publications Division, 3341Q 75 Ave., Landover, MD 20785 (☎ **301/322-4961;** fax 301/386-5394). Only written requests are accepted.

For names and addresses of operators of tours specifically for visitors with disabilities, and other relevant information, contact the **Society for the Advancement of Travel for the Handicapped (SATH),** 347 Fifth Ave., Suite 610, New York, NY 10016 (☎ **212/447-7284;** fax 212/725-8253; www.sath.org). Yearly membership dues in the society are $45, $30 for senior citizens and students. Send a self-addressed, stamped envelope. SATH will also provide you with hotel/resort accessibility for Caribbean destinations.

For blind or visually impaired persons, the best source of information is the **American Foundation for the Blind,** 11 Penn Plaza, Suite 300, New York, NY 10001 (☎ **800/232-5463** or 212/502-7600). It acts as a referral source for travelers and can offer advice on the transport and border formalities for Seeing Eye dogs.

One of the best organizations serving the needs of persons with disabilities is **Flying Wheels Travel,** 143 West Bridge (P.O. Box 382), Owatonna, MN 55060 (☎ **800/535-6790** or 507/451-5005), offering various customized, all-inclusive vacation packages in the Caribbean.

For a $25 annual fee, you can join **Mobility International USA,** P.O. Box 10767, Eugene, OR 97440 (☎ **541/343-1284** voice and TDD; fax 541/343-6812; www.miusa.org). It answers questions on various destinations and also offers discounts on its programs, videos, and publications. Its quarterly newsletter, *Over the Rainbow,* provides information on Caribbean hotel chains, accessibility, and transportation.

TIPS FOR BRITISH TRAVELERS WITH DISABILITIES   The **Royal Association for Disability and Rehabilitation (RADAR),** Unit 12, City Forum, 250 City Rd., London, EC1V 8AF (☎ **020/7250-3222;** fax 020/7250-0212), publishes holiday "fact packs," three in all, which sell for £2 each or all three for £5. The first one provides general information, including planning and booking a holiday, insurance, finances, and useful organization and holiday providers. The second outlines transportation available abroad and equipment for rent. The third deals with specialized accommodations.

FOR GAY & LESBIAN TRAVELERS

Puerto Rico is the most gay-friendly destination in the Caribbean, with lots of accommodations, restaurants, clubs, and bars that actively cater to a gay clientele. A free monthly newsletter, *Puerto Rico Breeze,* lists items of interest to the island's gay community; it's distributed at the Atlantic Beach Hotel (see chapter 4) and many of the gay-friendly clubs mentioned in this book (see chapter 6).

Men can order *Spartacus,* the international gay guide ($32.95), or *Odysseus, The International Gay Travel Planner,* a guide to international gay accommodations ($27). Both lesbians and gay men might want to pick up a copy of *Ferrari Travel Planner* ($16), which specializes in general information, as well as listings of bars, hotels, restaurants, and places of interest for gay travelers throughout the world. These books and others are available from **Giovanni's Room,** 1145 Pine St., Philadelphia, PA 19107 (☎ **215/923-2960**).

Our World, 1104 N. Nova Rd., Suite 251, Daytona Beach, FL 32117 (☎ **904/441-5367**), is a magazine devoted to options and bargains for gay and lesbian travel worldwide. It costs $35 for 10 issues. *Out and About,* 8 W. 19th St., Suite 401,

New York, NY 10011 (☎ **800/929-2268** or 212/989-4850), has been hailed for its "straight" reporting about gay travel. It profiles the best gay or gay-friendly hotels, restaurants, gyms, clubs, and other places, with coverage of destinations throughout the world. The cost is $49 a year for 10 information-packed issues, plus four events calendars. It aims for the more upscale gay male and lesbian traveler, and it has been praised by everybody from *Travel and Leisure* to the *New York Times*. Both of these publications are also available at most gay and lesbian bookstores.

The **International Gay and Lesbian Travel Association (IGLTA),** 4331 N. Federal Hwy., #304, Ft. Lauderdale, FL 33308 (☎ **800/448-8550** or 954/776-2626; fax 954/776-3303; www.iglta.org), encourages gay and lesbian travel worldwide. With more than 1,300 member agencies, it specializes in networking, providing the information travelers would need to link up with the appropriate gay-friendly service organization or tour specialist. It offers quarterly newsletters, marketing mailings, and a membership directory that's updated four times a year. Travel agents who are IGLTA members will be tied into this organization's vast information resources.

FOR SENIORS

Though much of the island's sporting and nightlife activity is geared toward more youthful travelers, Puerto Rico also has much to offer the senior citizen. The best source of information for seniors is the Puerto Rico Tourism Company (see "Visitor Information," above), or, if you're staying in a large resort hotel, the activities director or the concierge.

For information before you go, obtain a free copy of *101 Tips for the Mature Traveler,* available from Grand Circle Travel, 347 Congress St., Suite 3A, Boston, MA 02210 (☎ **800/221-2610** or 617/350-7500; fax 617/346-6700). This tour operator offers extended vacations, escorted programs, and cruises that feature unique learning experiences for seniors at competitive prices.

SAGA International Holidays, 222 Berkeley St., Boston, MA 02115 (☎ **800/343-0273**), is known for its all-inclusive tours and cruises for seniors, preferably those 50 years of age or older. Both medical insurance and trip-cancellation insurance are included in the net price of any of its tours, except cruises.

AARP (American Association of Retired Persons) is the best organization in the United States for seniors. It offers discounts on car rentals and hotels. For more information, contact AARP at 601 E St., NW, Washington, DC 20049 (☎ **800/424-3410** or 202/434-AARP).

Information is also available from the **National Council of Senior Citizens,** 8403 Colesville Rd., Suite 1200, Silver Spring, MD 20910 (☎ **301/578-8800;** fax 301/578-8999). For a fee of $13 per person or couple, you receive a monthly newsletter, part of which is devoted to travel tips. Reduced discounts on hotel and auto rentals are available.

Mature Outlook, P.O. Box 9390, Des Moines, IA 50306-9519 (☎ **800/336-6330;** fax 515/252-7855), is a travel organization for people over 50. Members receive a bimonthly magazine and are offered discounts at ITC-member hotels. ITC is an international hotel club offering discounts to members. Annual membership is $14.95 to $19.95.

FOR SINGLES

Puerto Rico's thriving nightlife makes it a stellar destination for singles looking for romance. Two of the best clubs for meeting people are Babylon (if you're straight) and Eros (if you're gay). See the write-up of each club in "San Juan After Dark" in chapter 6.

Unfortunately for the 85 million or so single Americans, the travel industry is far more geared toward couples, so singles often wind up paying the penalty. It pays to travel with someone. One company that resolves this problem is Travel Companion, which matches single travelers with like-minded companions. It's headed by Jens Jurgen, who charges $99 for a 6-month listing in his well-publicized records. People seeking travel companions fill out forms stating their preferences and needs and receive a listing of potential travel partners. Companions of the same or opposite sex can be requested. A lengthy, bimonthly newsletter also gives numerous money-saving travel tips of special interest to solo travelers. A sample copy is available for $5. For an application and more information, contact Jens Jurgen at **Travel Companion,** P.O. Box P-833, Amityville, NY 11701 (☎ **516/454-0880;** fax 516/454-0170).

Since single supplements on tours carry a hefty price tag, some tour companies will arrange for you to share a room with another single traveler of the same gender. One such company that offers a "guaranteed-share plan" is Cosmos. Book through your travel agent or call ☎ **800/221-0090.**

FOR FAMILIES

Puerto Rico is a terrific family destination. The smallest toddlers can spend blissful hours on sandy beaches and in the shallow seawater or pools specifically constructed for them. There's no end to the fascinating pursuits available for older children, ranging from boat rides to shell collecting to horseback riding and hiking. Perhaps your children are old enough to learn to snorkel and explore the wonderland of underwater Puerto Rico. Skills such as swimming and windsurfing are taught here, and there are a variety of activities unique to the islands. Most resort hotels will advise you on what there is in the way of fun for the young, and many have play directors and supervised activities for various age groups. Look for the "Family-Friendly Hotels" and "Family-Friendly Restaurants" boxes we've included throughout the book, pointing you to places that cater to kids.

Family Travel Times, which is published 10 times a year by Travel With Your Children (TWYCH), includes a weekly call-in service for subscribers. Subscriptions cost $40 a year and can be ordered by contacting TWYCH, 40 5th Ave., New York, NY 10011 (☎ **212/477-5524;** www.familytraveltimes.com).

8 Getting There: Flying to Puerto Rico

Puerto Rico is by far the most accessible of the Caribbean islands, with frequent airline service. It's also the major airline hub of the Caribbean Basin.

THE AIRLINES

With San Juan as its hub for the entire Caribbean, **American Airlines** (☎ **800/ 433-7300;** www.aa.com) offers nonstop daily flights to San Juan from Baltimore, Boston, Chicago, Dallas–Fort Worth, Hartford, Miami, Newark, New York (JFK), Orlando, Philadelphia, Tampa, Fort Lauderdale, and Washington (Dulles), plus flights to San Juan from both Montréal and Toronto with changes in Chicago or Miami. There are also at least two daily flights from Los Angeles to San Juan that touch down in Dallas or Miami.

American, because of its wholly owned subsidiary, **American Eagle,** also is the undisputed leader among the short-haul local commuter flights of the Caribbean. It usually flies in propeller planes carrying between 34 and 64 passengers. Collectively, American Eagle, along with its larger associate, American Airlines, offers service to 37 destinations on 31 islands of the Caribbean and the Bahamas, more than any other carrier.

Delta (☎ 800/221-1212; www.delta-air.com) has four daily nonstop flights from Atlanta on Monday to Friday, nine nonstop on Saturday, and seven nonstop on Sunday. Flights into Atlanta from around the world are frequent, with excellent connections from points throughout Delta's network in the South and Southwest.

United Airlines (☎ 800/241-6522; www.ual.com) offers daily nonstop flights from Chicago to San Juan. **Northwest** (☎ 800/225-2525; www.nwa.com) has one daily nonstop flight to San Juan from Detroit, as well as at least one (and sometimes more) connecting flights to San Juan from Detroit. United also offers flights to San Juan, some of them nonstop, from both Memphis and Minneapolis, with a schedule that varies according to the season and the day of the week.

TWA (☎ 800/892-4141; www.twa.com) offers three daily nonstop flights throughout the year between New York's JFK and San Juan. There are also daily nonstop flights to San Juan from St. Louis in winter, but none in summer.

US Airways (☎ 800/428-4322; www.usairways.com) also competes, with daily direct flights between Baltimore and San Juan, in which flights make an intermediate stop in Charlotte, North Carolina, before continuing nonstop to San Juan. The airline also offers three daily nonstop flights to San Juan from Philadelphia, and one daily nonstop flight to San Juan from Pittsburgh.

British travelers can take a **British Airways** (☎ 0345/222111 in the U.K., 800/217-9297 in the U.S.) weekly flight direct from London to San Juan on Sunday. **Lufthansa** (☎ 01/803-803-803 in Germany, 800/645-3880 in the U.S.) passengers can fly on Saturday (one weekly flight) from Frankfurt to San Juan via Condor (a subsidiary operating the flight). And **Iberia** (☎ 1/587-8156 in Spain, 800/772-4642 in the U.S.) has two weekly flights from Madrid to San Juan, leaving on Thursday and Saturday.

SAVING ON AIRFARES

In recent years, the traditional expectation that winter fares to the Caribbean were higher than those in summer has changed. On their island routes, most airlines now divide their year into peak season and basic season, eliminating what used to be known as shoulder season. **Peak season** for fares between North America and Puerto Rico now generally means midwinter and midsummer, whereas the less expensive **basic season** covers spring and fall.

Also noteworthy is the fact that most airlines are eliminating business class on their routes from North America to Puerto Rico. Instead, they are offering only economy class and first class. (On most American Eagle flights, first class has been eliminated entirely in favor of single-service flights; since most intra-Caribbean American Eagle flights rarely exceed 90 minutes, no one seems to mind.)

OTHER WAYS TO SAVE

Proceed with caution through the next suggestions. What constitutes good value changes almost daily in the airline industry. It's hard to keep up, even if you are a travel agent or regularly surf the net (see the "Cyber Deals for Net Surfers" box, below). Fares, especially to Puerto Rico, change all the time — what was the lowest possible fare one day can change the very next day when a new promotional fare is offered.

CHARTER FLIGHTS　These flights allow you to travel at rates lower than those of regularly scheduled flights. Many of the major carriers offer charter flights at rates that can cost 30% less than the regular airfare.

There are some drawbacks to charter flights that you need to consider. Advance booking, for example, of up to 45 days or more may be required, and there are hefty cancellation penalties, although you can take out insurance against emergency cancellation. Also, you must depart and return on your scheduled dates or else you'll lose your money. If you don't have proper insurance, it will do you no good to call the airline and tell them you've had a ski accident in Aspen. If you're not on the plane, you can kiss your money good-bye.

Since charter flights are so complicated, it's best to go to a good travel agent and ask him or her to explain the problems and advantages. Sometimes charters require ground arrangements, such as prebooking hotel rooms.

One company that arranges charters is **Council Travel,** 205 E. 42nd St., New York, NY 10017 (☎ **800/226-8624** in the U.S. or 212/661-1414; www.counciltravel.com).

Another is **Travac,** 989 Sixth Ave., New York, NY 10018 (☎ **800/TRAV-800** or 212/563-3303; www.travac.com). Other Travac offices include 2601 E. Jefferson St., Orlando, FL 32803 (☎ **407/896-0014**).

BUCKET SHOPS (CONSOLIDATORS)   In its purest sense, a bucket shop acts as a clearinghouse for blocks of tickets that airlines discount and consign during normally slow periods of air travel (for Puerto Rico, that usually means from mid-April to mid-December). Charter operators and bucket shops used to perform separate functions, but their offerings have often become blurred in recent years. Many outfits perform both functions.

Tickets are sometimes—but not always—discounted as much as 20 to 35%. Terms of payment can vary, from perhaps 45 days prior to departure to the last minute. Some consolidators require you to buy their discounted tickets through a regular travel agent, who usually marks up the ticket 8 to 10%, maybe more, thereby greatly reducing your discount. If you go through an agent, ask him or her to comparison-shop for you, since prices can vary from consolidator to consolidator.

A survey conducted of flyers who use consolidator tickets found only one major complaint: such a ticket doesn't qualify you for an advance seat assignment, so you are likely to be assigned a poor seat on the plane at the last minute.

Another possible hitch: many people who booked consolidator tickets reported no savings at all, since the airlines will sometimes match the price of the consolidator ticket by announcing a promotional fare. Because the situation is a bit tricky, you need to investigate carefully just how much you can expect to save.

To be doubly cautious, since some bucket shops have proved dishonest in the past, you should confirm your flight with the airline to make sure that the bucket shop actually made the reservation for you. Do not rely solely on the word of the bucket shop. Bucket shops can ticket you on both charters and scheduled flights. Even though a scheduled flight may cost more, you have a greater assurance that it will leave on time.

One more bit of advice: inquire as to any and all restrictions, and always pay by credit card.

Although bucket shops abound from coast to coast (look for their usually small ads in your local newspaper's Sunday travel section), few specialize in the highly competitive Caribbean market. One of these is **TFI Tours International,** 34 W. 32nd St., 12th Floor, New York, NY 10001 (☎ **800/745-8000** in the U.S. or 212/736-1140 in New York State).

REBATERS   To make matters even more confusing, rebaters also compete in the low-airfare market. Rebaters are organizations that pass along to the passenger part of their commission, although many of them assess a fee for their services. And although rebaters are not the same as travel agents, they sometimes offer roughly similar services. Sometimes a rebater will sell you a discounted travel ticket and also offer discounted land arrangements, including hotels and car rentals. Most rebaters offer discounts

Cyber Deals for Net Surfers

It's possible to get some great deals on airfare, hotels, and car rentals via the Internet. So go grab your mouse and start surfing before you hit the real waves—you could save a bundle on your trip. The Web sites highlighted below are worth checking out, especially since all services are free.

Microsoft Expedia (www.expedia.com)   The best part of this multipurpose travel site is the "Fare Tracker": you fill out a form on the screen indicating that you're interested in cheap flights from your hometown, and, once a week, they'll e-mail you the best airfare deals. The site's "Travel Agent" will steer you to bargains on hotels and car rentals, and you can book everything, including flights, right online. This site is useful even once you're booked: Before you go, log on to Expedia for oodles of up-to-date travel information, including weather reports and foreign exchange rates.

Preview Travel (www.reservations.com and www.vacations.com)   Another useful travel site, Reservations.com has a "Best Fare Finder," which will search the Apollo computer reservations system (a huge database used by travel agents world-wide) for the three lowest fares for any route on any days of the year. Say you want to go from Chicago to Orlando and back between December 6 and 13: Just fill out the form on the screen with times, dates, and destinations, and within minutes, Preview will show you the best deals. If you find an airfare you like, you can book your ticket right online—you can even reserve hotels and car rentals on this site. If you're in the preplanning stage, head to Preview's Vacations.com site, where you can check out the latest package deals around the world by clicking on "Hot Deals."

Travelocity (www.travelocity.com)   This is one of the best travel sites out there. In addition to its "Personal Fare Watcher," which notifies you via e-mail of the lowest airfares for up to five destinations, Travelocity will track the three lowest fares for any routes on any dates in minutes. You can book a flight right then and there, and if you need a rental car or hotel, Travelocity will find you the best deal via the SABRE computer reservations system (another huge travel agent database). Click on "Last Minute Deals" for the latest travel bargains, including a link to **H.O.T. Coupons (www.hotcoupons.com),** where you can print electronic coupons for travel in the United States and Canada.

Trip.Com (www.thetrip.com)   This site is really geared toward the business traveler, but vacationers-to-be can also use Trip.Com's valuable fare-finding engine, which will e-mail you every week with the best city-to-city airfare deals on your selected route or routes.

Discount Tickets (www.discount-tickets.com)   Operated by the European Travel Network (ETN), this site offers discounts on airfares, accommodations, car

averaging anywhere from 10 to 25% (but this varies from place to place), plus a $25 handling charge.

Travel Avenue, 10 S. Riverside Plaza, Suite 1404, Chicago, IL 60606 (☎ **800/ 333-3335** in the U.S. or 312/876-1116), is one of the oldest agencies of its kind. It offers up-front cash rebates on every airline ticket over $350 it sells. It sells airline tickets to independent travelers who have already worked out their travel plans. Also available are tour and cruise fares, plus hotel bookings.

TRAVEL CLUBS   Travel clubs supply an unsold inventory of tickets that are discounted from 20 to 60%. After you pay an annual fee, you're given a hotline number to call to find out what discounts are available. Some discounts become available a few rentals, and tours. It deals in flights between the United States and other countries, not domestic U.S. flights, so it's most useful for foreign travelers.

E-Savers Programs   Several major airlines offer a free e-mail service, via which they'll send you their best bargain airfares on a weekly basis. Here's how it works: Once a week (usually Wednesday), subscribers receive a list of discounted flights to and from various destinations, both international and domestic. Now here's the catch: These fares are available only if you leave the very next Saturday (or sometimes Friday night) and return on the following Monday or Tuesday. It's really a service for the spontaneously inclined and travelers looking for a quick getaway. But the fares are cheap, so it's worth taking a look. If you have a preference for certain airlines (in other words, the ones you fly most frequently), sign up with them first. Another caveat: You'll get frequent-flier miles if you purchase one of these fares, but you can't use miles to buy the ticket.

Here's a list of airlines and their Web sites, where you can not only get on the e-mailing lists but also book flights directly:

- **American Airlines:** www.aa.com
- **Continental Airlines:** www.flycontinental.com
- **TWA:** www.twa.com
- **Northwest Airlines:** www.nwa.com
- **US Airways:** www.usairways.com

Other airlines also maintain Web sites worth browsing, including **British Airways** (www.british-airways.com), **Lufthansa** (www.lufthansa-usa.com), and **Iberia** (www.iberia.com).

Travel and Booking Agencies   **Preview Travel** (www.previewtravel.com) is the most user-friendly of several travel agency sites, offering some incredible vacation, airline, and hotel deals and updating its offerings every day. It even lets you book your vacation online. **Moments Notice** (www.moments-notice.com) promotes itself as a travel service, not an agency, providing a vacation bargain hunter's dream. The Web site, updated each morning, advertises many deals that are snapped up by the end of the day. A drawback is that many of these vacations require you to drop everything and go almost immediately. **180096hotel.com** offers budget reservations at prestigious hotels all over the world, many accommodations up to 65% off. Booking can be done online. **America Online** (www.aol.com) is the most comprehensive online site offering direct links to many of these sites and others.

days in advance of actual departure, some a week in advance, and some as much as a month. Of course, you're limited to what's available, so you have to be flexible. Some of the best of these clubs are listed below.

Moment's Notice, 7301 New Utrecht Ave., Brooklyn, NY 11204 (☎ 718/234-6295; fax 718/234-6450), charges $25 per year for membership, which allows spur-of-the-moment participation in dozens of tours. Its discounted air and land packages to all Caribbean islands sometimes represent substantial savings over what you'd have paid through more conventional channels. Members can call the hotline (☎ 212/873-0908) to learn what options are available. Most of the company's best-valued tours depart from the northeast.

Travelers Advantage, 3033 South Parker Rd., Suite 900, Aurora, CO 80014 (☎ **800/ 548-1116**), offers a 3-month trial participation for $1 and an annual membership fee starting at $49. You'll get offers for members-only vacation packages at reductions of 5 to 30%. For specific information about prices, call ☎ **800/TEL-TRIP.**

Another club, **Encore Travel Club,** 4501 Forbes Blvd., Lanham, MD 20706 (☎ **800/ 638-8976** in the U.S.), charges $69.95 a year for membership, which offers up to 50% discounts at more than 4,000 hotels. It also offers discounts on airfare, cruises, and car rentals through its volume purchase plans. Membership includes a travel package outlining the company's many services and use of a toll-free phone number.

9 Package Tours

If you want everything done for you and want to save money as well, consider taking a package tour. Besides general tours, many have specific themes—tennis, golf, scuba and snorkeling, and honeymoons. Puerto Rico is prominently featured by most package tour companies.

Economy and convenience are the chief advantages of a package tour—the costs of transportation (usually by plane), a hotel room, food (sometimes), and sightseeing (sometimes) are combined and neatly tied up with a single price tag. There are extras, of course, but in general you'll know in advance roughly what the cost of your vacation will be, and you can budget accordingly. The disadvantage is that you may find yourself, for example, in a hotel you dislike but cannot leave because you've already paid for it.

If you're a serious foodie who likes to dine around, beware of packages that include all meals. Eating all your meals at one hotel on a package plan is almost always cheaper than if you dine around à la carte. However, if you're seeking variety in your dining experiences, you won't find it unless your hotel is particularly adept at creating new taste sensations nightly. To still save money and to savor different dining experiences, ask if you can opt for a Modified American Plan (MAP) that will allow you to eat breakfast at your hotel and either lunch or dinner, at your choice. That way, you're free to have either lunch or dinner outside your hotel. On the MAP we'd opt for a "free" lunch at the hotel, then go out for dinner at one of the many restaurants recommended in this guide.

Choosing the right package can be a bit of a problem. It's best to go to a travel agent, tell him or her what island (or islands) you'd like to visit, and see what's currently offered.

Packages are available because tour operators can mass-book hotels and make volume purchases. You generally have to pay the cost of the total package in advance. Transfers between your hotel and the airport are often included (this may be more of a break than it sounds at first since some airports are situated a $40-or-more taxi ride from a resort). Many packages carry several options, including the possibility of low-cost car rentals. Nearly all tour packages are based on double occupancy.

To save time comparing the price and value of all the package tours out there, consider calling **TourScan Inc.,** P.O. Box 2367, Darien, CT 06820 (☎ **800/962-2080** in the U.S. or 203/655-8091; fax 203/655-6689). Every season, the company gathers and computerizes the contents of about 200 brochures containing 10,000 different vacations in the Caribbean, the Bahamas, and Bermuda. TourScan selects the best value at each hotel and condo. Two catalogs are printed each year. Each lists a broad-based choice of hotels on most of the islands of the Caribbean, in all price ranges. Write to TourScan for their catalogs, costing $4 each, the price of which is credited to any TourScan vacation.

Some of the leading tour operators to the Caribbean include the following:

Caribbean Concepts Corp., 1428 Brickell Ave., Suite 402, Miami, FL 33131 (☎ **888/741-7711** in the U.S. or 305/373-8687; fax 305/373-8310), offers all-inclusive low-cost air and land packages to the islands, including apartments, hotels, villas, or condo rentals.

Another good deal might be a combined land and air package offered by one of the major U.S. carriers. Call their toll-free numbers for more information: **American Airlines Fly-Away Vacations** (☎ **800/321-2121**), **Delta's Dream Vacations** (☎ **800/872-7786**), **TWA Getaway Vacations** (☎ **800/GETAWAY**), and **United Airlines Vacations** (☎ **800/328-6877**).

Other options for general independent packages include:

Horizon Tours, 1634 Eye St., NW, Suite 301, Washington, DC 20006 (☎ **888/SUN-N-SAND** in the U.S. or 202/393-8390; fax 202/393-1547; www.horizontours.com), specializes in all-inclusive upscale resorts in Puerto Rico. Finally, **Liberty Travel,** 69 Spring St., Ramsey, NJ 07446 (☎ **888/271-1584;** fax 201/934-3888; www.libertytravel.com), advertises more packages to the Caribbean than any other agency.

For a dive, adventure, and leisure outfitter for travelers, consider **Experience the Adventure Tours Inc.,** 1350 SW 57th Ave., Suite 315, Miami, FL 33144 (☎ **800/815-5019** or 305/267-6644). This outlet offers both packages of 4 days/3 nights or 8 days/7 nights, centered at the historic city of Ponce. Round-trip airfares are offered from Miami, Orlando, or Newark. Visits are possible to the most historic sights on the southern coast, including Guanica Dry Forest. Scuba diving, sea kayaking, and horseback riding can also be arranged.

Experience the Adventure Tours (see above) also features a number of golf packages at the top resorts of Puerto Rico, ranging from Palmas del Mar in the east to two Hyatt resorts at Dorado, directly west of Puerto Rico. Round-trip air packages are possible from Miami, Orlando, and Newark. The company also offers a series of scuba-diving packages off the southwest coast, featuring two-tank boat dives per day.

If you'd like to explore Puerto Rico as part of a horseback riding tour package, consult **PRwest Vacation Services** (☎ **888/779-3788** or 787/727-4752). A dozen well-trained Paso Fino horses are available to accommodate both the advanced and novice rider. In northwest Puerto Rico, you can explore cavernous cliffs and tropical forests—all on horseback. Tours last 7 days and 6 nights.

Elena's Ecotour Safaris (reached only by e-mail at **elena@elyunque.com**) offers all-inclusive trips that take in sailing, hiking, kayaking, snorkeling, rain-forest jaunts, trips to hot springs, volcanic sights, and boat trips to offshore cays. Trips last 7 nights and 8 days. Safari trekkers spend the nights in *paradores* or island B&Bs. Sometimes camping safaris are organized with tent accommodations provided.

Puerto Rico Tours, Condo Inter-Suite, Suite 5M on Isla Verde in San Juan (☎ **787/306-1540;** fax 787/791-5479), offers specially conducted private sightseeing tours of Puerto Rico, including trips to the rain forest, Luquillo Beach, the caves of Camuy and other attractions such as a restored Taíno Indian village.

Backstage Partners (☎ **787/748-9123;** fax 787/763-0701) offers customized tours that take in a wide range of the island attractions, including ecotours, deep-sea fishing, scuba diving and snorkeling, safaris, and golf packages.

PACKAGES FOR BRITISH TRAVELERS

British travelers can contact **Caribbean Connection,** Concorde House, Forest Street, Chester, England CH1 1QR (☎ **01244/355300**), which offers all-inclusive packages (airfare and hotel) to the Caribbean and customizes tours for independent travel. It publishes two catalogs of Caribbean offerings, one featuring more than 160 properties on all the major islands, and a 50-page catalog of luxury all-inclusive properties.

Other Caribbean specialists operating out of England include **Kuoni Travel,** Kuoni House, Dorking, Surrey RH5 4AZ (☎ **01306/742-222**). **Caribtours,** 161 Fulham Rd., London SW3 6SN (☎ **020/7581-3517**), a small, very knowledgeable organization, also specializes in Caribbean travel and will tailor itineraries.

Although Australians are welcome to visit Puerto Rico, as are New Zealanders and other nationals, there are no special packages or deals for them.

10 For the Cruise-Ship Traveler

If you'd like to sail the Caribbean in a hotel with an ocean view, a cruise ship might be for you. Cruises are slow and easy and are no longer enjoyed only by the idle rich who have months to spend away from home. In fact, most cruises today appeal to the middle-income traveler who probably has no more than 1 or 2 weeks of vacation.

Miami is the cruise capital of the world, but San Juan is second. Unless you have never visited Miami and would like to include it as part of your extended Caribbean itinerary, there is justification in flying directly to San Juan by plane and beginning your cruise here. It puts you immediately in the Caribbean, which means you save a 2-day ocean voyage just to get here. Instead of sailing from Florida, you can spend the time getting to know Puerto Rico.

Most cruise-ship operators emphasize the concept of a total vacation. Some are mostly activity centered; others offer the chance to do nothing but relax. Cruise ships are self-contained resorts, offering a large variety of services and activities on board and sightseeing once you arrive in a port of call.

For those who don't want to spend all their time at sea, some lines offer a fly-and-cruise vacation. You spend a week cruising the Caribbean and another week staying at an interesting hotel at reduced prices. These total packages should cost less than the cruise and air portions purchased separately.

Another version of fly-and-cruise is to fly to and from the cruise. Most plans offer a package deal from the principal airport closest to your residence to the major airport nearest to the cruise departure point. It's possible to purchase your air ticket on your own and book your cruise ticket separately, but you'll save money by combining the fares in a package deal.

Most cruise ships travel at night, arriving the next morning at the day's port of call. In port, passengers can go ashore for sightseeing, shopping, and a local meal. Cruise prices vary widely. Sometimes the same route with the same ports of call can carry different fares, depending on the ship's luxury (as well as your accommodations on board). Consult a good travel agent for the latest offerings.

Some of the most likely contenders include the following: **Ambassador Tours,** 120 Montgomery St., Suite 400, San Francisco, CA 94104 (☎ **800/989-9000** or 415/357-9876); **Cruises Inc.,** 5000 Campuswood Dr. E., Syracuse, NY 13057 (☎ **800/854-0500** or 315/463-9695); **Cruises of Distinction,** 2750 S. Woodward Ave., Bloomfield Hills, MI 48304 (☎ **800/634-3445**); **Cruise Masters,** Century Plaza Towers, 2029 Century Park E., Suite 950, Los Angeles, CA 90067 (☎ **800/ 456-4FUN** or 310/556-2925); **Kelly Cruises,** 1315 W. 22nd St., Suite 105, Oak Brook, IL 60521 (☎ **800/837-7447** or 630/990-1111); and **Hartford Holidays Travel,** 626 Willis Ave., Williston Park, NY 11596 (☎ **800/828-4813**). Any of these stay tuned to last-minute price wars brewing among such megacarriers as Carnival, Princess, Royal Caribbean, and Holland America, as well as such low-budget contenders as Premier.

Vacations to Go, 1502 Augusta Dr., Suite 415, Houston, TX 77057 (☎ **800/ 338-4962**), provides catalogs and information on discount cruises through the Caribbean, as well as the Atlantic and Mediterranean.

WHILE WAITING FOR YOUR SHIP TO SAIL

While waiting for the departure of your cruise vessel, you might spend the day enjoying the historic district of Old San Juan with its endless sightseeing possibilities and merchandise-crammed shops. Another day can be devoted to the Condado with its beaches, gambling casinos, and sporting possibilities in the Greater San Juan area, including almost unlimited golf, tennis, and water sports. Even if you have only hours to spend before your ship's departure, you can explore the historic old city, either taking a tour or going on your own. You'll find beaches galore on upcoming islands, but nothing to equal this historic sector.

WHEN YOUR SHIP COMES IN

The Port of San Juan is the busiest ocean terminal in the West Indies, with an estimated half of the Caribbean's trade passing through here. There are about 710 cruise-ship arrivals every year, bringing nearly 860,000 passengers.

A spacious walkway connects the piers to the cobblestone streets of Old San Juan, so you can walk there to shop. You can also take a waiting taxi to the beaches of Condado. For advice and maps, contact the **Tourist Information Center** at La Casita, near Pier 1 in Old San Juan (☎ **787/721-2400**). The dock area, now restored, is an attractive place for strolling, with its plazas, fountains, promenades, and beaches.

THE CRUISE LINES

Here's a brief rundown of some of the cruise lines serving San Juan and the Caribbean. For detailed information, pick up a copy of our companion guide in this series, *Frommer's Caribbean Cruises and Ports of Call.*

- **Carnival Cruise Lines** (☎ **800/327-9501**), a specialist in the maintenance of some of the biggest and most brightly decorated ships afloat, is the richest, boldest, brashest, and most successful mass-market cruise line in the world. Nine of its vessels depart from Florida or Caribbean ports that include, among others, San Juan, Miami, Tampa, and New Orleans. Two of the ships *(Carnival Inspiration* and *Carnival Fascination)* define San Juan as their home port, from which 7-day excursions are made to such southern Caribbean ports as St. Thomas, Sint Maarten, Dominica, Barbados, Guadeloupe, Martinique, Grenada, St. Lucia, and Santo Domingo. If you prefer to depart from one of the ports of Florida (especially Miami), know in advance that many of the company's cruises make San Juan a focal point of their stopovers. Most of the company's Caribbean cruises offer good value, last between 4 and 11 days (in most cases, 7 days), and feature nonstop activities, lots of glitter, and the hustle and bustle of armies of clients and crew members embarking and disembarking at every port. Cuisine and party-colored drinks are plentiful, although with vessels of this size, they are, by necessity, mass-produced. The overall atmosphere is comparable to that of a floating theme park with hordes of visitors, loaded with whimsy, and with lots of emphasis on partying in a style you might have expected in Atlantic City. Lots of single passengers, some of them with gleams in their eye, opt for this line, and some actually get lucky. Despite the presence of lots of unattached or loosely attached adults, the line makes special efforts to amuse and entertain children between 2 and 17. The average onboard age ranges from 38 to 42, although individual passengers range from 3 to 95.

- **Celebrity Cruises** (☎ 800/327-6700) maintains five newly built, medium-to-large ships offering cruises of between 7 and 15 nights to such ports as Key West, Grand Cayman, St. Thomas, Ocho Rios, Antigua, and Cozumel, Mexico, among others. Passengers interested in maximum exposure to Puerto Rico usually opt to cruise aboard *Galaxy,* a 77,713-ton megaship that's based (late October to late April only) in San Juan, and which embarks every week throughout the year for tours to such southern Caribbean islands as Barbados, Martinique, and Antigua. Alternatively, passengers might opt for a 14-night Panama Canal cruise that involves either eastbound or westbound treks between San Juan and Acapulco. Pre- or postcruise vacation extenders allow additional days in Puerto Rico as an add-on bonus to your trip.

  Despite a recent merger of Celebrity with the larger and better-financed Royal Caribbean International, Celebrity will maintain its own identity and corporate structure within the larger framework. The niche this line has created is unpretentious but classy, several notches above mass market, but with pricing that's nonetheless relatively competitive. Accommodations are roomy and well equipped, and the cuisine is among the most intensely cultivated of any of its competitors afloat.

- **Costa Cruise Lines** (☎ 800/462-6782), the U.S.-based branch of an Italian cruise line that has thrived for about a century, maintains hefty to megasize vessels that are newer than those of many other lines afloat. Two of these offer virtually identical jaunts through the western and eastern Caribbean on alternate weeks, each of them departing from Fort Lauderdale. Ports of call during the eastern Caribbean itineraries of both vessels include a stopover in San Juan, followed by visits to St. Thomas, Serena Cay (a private island off the coast of the Dominican Republic known for its beaches), and Nassau. There is an Italian flavor and lots of Italian design on board here, and an atmosphere of relaxed indulgence. The ships—*CostaRomantica* and *CostaVictoria*—feature tame versions of ancient Roman Bacchanalia, as well as such celebrations as *Festa Italiana,* and focaccia and pizza parties by the pool.

- **Princess Cruises** (☎ 800/421-0522) has a large and far-flung fleet that totals 7 megavessels. Four of these cruise at various times of the year through Caribbean and Bahamian waters sometimes with stops at San Juan as part of the itinerary. The one most closely associated with Puerto Rico, however, is *Dawn Princess,* a state-of-the-art megaship that defines San Juan as its home port. Departing weekly, every Saturday, it pays calls at ports that include St. Thomas, Sint Maarten, Barbados, Martinique, and St. Lucia. On alternate weeks, it stops at Aruba, Caracas, Grenada, St. Thomas, and Dominica. The *Dawn Princess*'s sibling ship, *Sun Princess,* pinpoints San Juan and Acapulco as the beginning or end point of transcanal cruises that last between 10 and 11 days each. Princess is one of the very few in the world offering luxury accommodations and upscale service as a standard feature aboard its megaships. These usually carry a smaller number of passengers than similarly sized vessels on less elegant lines. The company's clientele is upscale, with an average passenger age of 55 or over. A respectable percentage of the staff is British.

- **Radisson Seven Seas Cruises** (☎ 800/285-1835) is noted for the level of glamour and prestige that permeates its cruises. It sends only one of its ships, the *Radisson Diamond,* into the Caribbean on a regular basis. Designed along lines distinctly different from those of every other cruise line afloat, it's a relatively slow but stable ship floating atop submerged pontoons similar to those used by catamarans or oil-drilling platforms in the North Sea. Despite the fact that its design is not likely to be duplicated anytime soon within the cruise industry, passengers appreciate it for its fine cuisine, upscale service, and suitability for corporate conventions at sea. Cruises are relatively expensive compared to those offered by less prestigious lines, and roam freely, with less allegiance to a fixed home port than many other vessels. During a brief period of every year, the *Diamond* defines San Juan as its home port, but only between November and February, when it embarks on short-term cruises of no more than 6 days in duration. Stopovers include Tortola, St. Barts, and Sint Maarten. The rest of the time, the ship's Caribbean ports include cities along the coast of Costa Rica, as well as Curaçao, Aruba, Grand Cayman, Cayman Brac, Cartagena, St. Barts, Sint Maarten, St. Thomas, and Cozumel.

- **Royal Caribbean International** (☎ 800/327-6700) leads the industry in the development of megaships. Most of this company's dozen or so vessels weigh in at around 73,000 tons, are among the largest of any line afloat, and represent a roster of floating hardware that's more impressive than that of many national navies. Marketed as a mainstream mass-market cruise line whose components have been fine-tuned through endless repetition, the line encourages a restrained house-party theme that's somehow a bit less frenetic than that found aboard the more raucous megaships of other cruise lines. The company is well run, and there are enough onboard activities to suit virtually any taste and age level. Though accommodations and accoutrements are more than adequate, they are not upscale, and cabins aboard some of the line's older vessels tend to be a bit more cramped than the industry norm. Using either Miami or San Juan as their home port, RCI ships call regularly at such oft-visited ports as St. Thomas, Ocho Rios, Sint Maarten, Grand Cayman, St. Croix, and Curaçao. Most of the company's cruises last for 7 days, although some weekend jaunts from San Juan to St. Thomas are available for 3 nights, and some Panama Canal crossings last for 11 or 12 nights. Royal Caribbean is the only cruise line in the business that owns, outright, two tropical beaches (one in the Bahamas, the other along an isolated peninsula in northern Haiti) whose sands and water-sports facilities are the focus of many of the company's Caribbean cruises.

- **Royal Olympic Cruises** (☎ 800/872-6400), formed in 1995 from a merger between Sun Lines and Epirotiki Cruises, is a well-respected Greek shipping line that operates the only Greek-registered ship in the Caribbean, the aging but comfortable and well-maintained *Stella Solaris*. Many of this ship's stopovers at Caribbean ports (San Juan, Sint Maarten, St. Lucia, Antigua, and St. Thomas) are configured either as annual Christmas cruises or as visits en route to either the Amazon or the Panama Canal. Despite the age of the ship, its many restorations and the cheerfulness of one of the best staffs of any vessel afloat make it consistently popular.

11 Getting Around

BY PLANE

American Eagle (☎ 800/433-7300 or 787/749-1747; www.aa.com) flies from Luis Muñoz Marín International Airport to Mayagüez, which can be your gateway to western Puerto Rico. Most round-trip fares are $124 to $176. It also offers two daily flights between San Juan and Ponce for $85 to $176 round-trip, depending on the ticket. However, prices are known to fluctuate, so call for last-minute details. For information about air connections to the offshore islands of Vieques and Culebra, see chapter 11.

BY RENTAL CAR

Rental cars are readily available, but many of your fellow readers have offered this advice: *Drive on Puerto Rico only if necessary.* They point out that local drivers are often dangerous, as evidenced by the number of fenders with bashed-in sides. The older coastal highways provide the most scenic routes but are often congested. Some of the roads, especially in the mountainous interior, are just too narrow for automobiles. Proceed with caution along these poorly paved and maintained roads, which most often follow circuitous routes. Cliffslides or landslides are not uncommon.

If you do rent a vehicle, some local agencies may tempt you with special reduced prices. But if you're planning to tour the island by car, you won't find any local branches to help you if you experience trouble. And some of the agencies widely advertising low-cost deals won't take credit cards and want cash in advance. Also, watch out for "hidden" extra costs, which sometimes proliferate among the smaller and not very well-known firms, and difficulties connected with resolving insurance claims.

If you do rent a vehicle, it's best to stick with the old reliables: **Avis** (☎ 800/ 331-1212 or 787/253-5926; www.avis.com), **Budget** (☎ 800/527-0700 or 787/ 791-3685), or **Hertz** (☎ 800/654-3131 or 787/791-0840). Each of the "big three" companies offers minivan transport to its office and car depot. Be alert to the minimum age requirements for car rentals in Puerto Rico. Both Avis and Hertz require that renters be 25 or older, while at Budget, renters between the ages of 21 and 24 pay a $5 daily surcharge to the agreed-upon rental fee.

None of these companies rents Jeeps, four-wheel-drive vehicles, or convertibles.

Added security comes from an antitheft double-locking mechanism that has been installed in most of the rental cars available in Puerto Rico. Car theft is high on Puerto Rico, so extra precaution is always needed.

Distances are often posted in kilometers rather than miles (1km = 0.62 mile), but speed limits are reckoned in miles per hour.

INSURANCE   Each company offers an optional collision damage waiver priced at around $12 to $14 a day. Purchasing the waiver eliminates most or all of the financial responsibility you would face in case of an accident. With it, you can simply go home, leaving the rental company to sort it all out. Without it, you would be liable for up to the full value of the car in case it was damaged. Paying for the rental with certain credit or charge cards sometimes eliminates the need to buy this extra insurance. Also, your own automobile insurance policy may cover some or all of the damages. You should check with both your own insurer and your credit-card issuers before leaving home.

GASOLINE   There is usually an abundant supply of gasoline in Puerto Rico, especially on the outskirts of San Juan, where you'll see all the familiar signs, such as Mobil. Gasoline stations are also plentiful along the main arteries traversing the island. However, if you're going to remote areas of the island, especially on Sunday, it's advisable to start out with a full tank. *Note:* In Puerto Rico, gasoline is sold by the liter, not by the gallon.

DRIVING RULES   Driving rules can be a source of some confusion. Speed limits are often not posted on the island, but when they are, they're given in miles per hour. For example, the limit on the San Juan–Ponce *autopista* (superhighway) is 70 mph. Speed limits elsewhere, notably in heavily populated residential areas, are much lower. Since you're not likely to know what the actual speed limit is in some of these areas, it's better to confine your speed to no more than 30 mph. The highway department places *lomas* (speed bumps) at strategic points to deter speeders. Sometimes these are called "sleeping policemen."

Highway Signs

Road signs using international symbols are commonplace in the San Juan metropolitan area and other urban centers, but they are written in Spanish. The following translations will help you figure out what they mean:

Spanish	English
Autopista	Expressway
Balneario	Public beach
Calle sin salida	Dead end
Carretera cerrada	Road closed to traffic
Carretera dividida	Divided highway
Carretera estrecha	Narrow road
Cruce	Crossroad
Cruce de peatones	Pedestrian crossing
Cuesta	Hill
Desprendimiento	Landslide
Desvío	Detour
Estación de peaje	Toll station
Manténgase a la derecha	Keep right
No entre	Do not enter
No estacione	Do not park
Parada de guaguas	Bus stop
Peligro	Danger
Puente estrecho	Narrow bridge
Velocidad máxima	Speed limit
Zona escolar	School zone

Puerto Ricans drive, as do U.S. and Canadian motorists, on the right-hand side of the road.

ROAD MAPS   One of the best and most detailed road maps of Puerto Rico is published by **International Travel Maps,** 345 W. Broadway, Vancouver, BC, Canada V5Y 1P8 (☎ 604/879-3621), and distributed in the United States by Rand McNally. It's available in some bookstores and is a good investment at $8.95. The **Gousha Puerto Rico Road Map,** which sells for $8.95 in the United States and Canada, has a good street map of San Juan but lacks detailed information about minor highways on the island and is very similar to the map of Puerto Rico distributed free at tourist offices.

BREAKDOWNS AND ASSISTANCE   All the major towns and cities have garages that will come to your assistance and tow your vehicle in for repairs if necessary. There's no national emergency number to call in the event of a mechanical breakdown. If you have a rental car, call the rental company first. Usually, someone there will bring motor assistance to you. If your car requires extensive repairs because of a mechanical failure, a new one will be sent to replace it.

BY PUBLIC TRANSPORTATION

Cars and minibuses known as *públicos* provide low-cost transportation around the island. Their license plates have the letters "P" or "PD" following the numbers. They serve all the main towns of Puerto Rico; passengers are let off and picked up along the way. Rates are set by the Public Service Commission. Públicos usually operate during daylight hours, departing from the main plaza (central square) of a town.

Information about público routes between San Juan and Mayagüez is available at **Lineas Sultana,** Calle Esteban González 898, Urbanización Santa Rita, Río Piedras (☎ 787/765-9377). Information about público routes between San Juan and Ponce is available from **Choferes Unidos de Ponce,** Terminal de Carros Públicos, Calle Vive in Ponce (☎ 787/764-0540).

Fares vary according to whether the público will make a detour to pick up or drop off a passenger at a specific locale. (If you want to deviate from the predetermined routes, you'll pay more than if you wait for a público beside the main highway.) Fares from San Juan to Mayagüez range from $16 to $30; from San Juan to Ponce, from $15 to $25. Be warned that although prices of públicos are admittedly low, the routes are slow, with frequent stops, often erratic routing, and lots of inconvenience.

12 The Active Vacation Planner

Puerto Rico offers a wide variety of participant and spectator sports, including golf, tennis, horseback riding, and all kinds of water sports—from scuba diving to deep-sea fishing.

Many resorts offer a large choice of sports activities, and various all-inclusive sports-vacation packages are available from hotels and airlines serving Puerto Rico.

Dorado Beach, Cerromar Beach, and Palmas del Mar are the chief centers for golf, tennis, and beach life. San Juan's hotels on the Condado–Isla Verde coast also generally offer a complete array of water sports.

BEACHES

With 272 miles of Atlantic and Caribbean coastline, Puerto Rico obviously has plenty of beaches. The **Condado** and **Isla Verde** beaches in San Juan are the most frequented. Good snorkeling is possible, and rental equipment is available for water sports at both. These and other beaches, such as the excellent **Luquillo,** 30 miles east of San Juan (see chapter 7), are overcrowded, especially on Saturday and Sunday. On the other hand, others are practically deserted. The public beaches on the north shore of San Juan at **Ocean Park** and **Park Barbosa** are good and can be reached by bus.

Some of the best deserted beaches stretch between Cabo Rojo, on the southwesterly tip of Puerto Rico, eastward all the way to Ponce. Beginning in the west, directly east of Cabo Rojo, you'll discover **Bahia Sucia Beach, Rosada Beach, Santa Beach, Manglillos Beach** (with a recreation area), **Caña Gorda Beach, Tamarindo Beach,** and **Ballena Beach.** Access to many of these beaches is limited because of poor roads, but the effort to reach them is worth it. Bring along what supplies you'll need.

The best surfing beaches in the Caribbean are on the west coast north of Mayagüez, including the beach at **Punta Higüero,** on Route 413 near the town of Rincón, which is said to be one of the finest surfing spots in the world (see chapter 10).

Some of Puerto Rico's public beaches are practically deserted. You will be charged for parking and for use of *balneario* facilities, such as lockers and showers, at public beaches. They are closed on Monday (if Monday is a holiday, they are open then but closed on Tuesday). In winter, public beach hours are from 9am to 5pm; in summer, from 9am to 6pm. For more information about the island's many beaches, call the **Department of Sports and Recreation** (☎ 787/722-1551).

The following public beaches have balnearios:

        Punta Salinas (Route 868, Cataño)
        Escambron (Puerta de Tierra, San Juan)

Isla Verde (Route 187, Isla Verde)
Luquillo (Highway 3, Luquillo)
Seven Seas (Route 987, Fajardo)
Sun Bay (Route 997, Vieques)
Punta Santiago (Highway 3, Humacao)
Punta Guilarte (Highway 3, Humacao)
Punta Guilarte (Highway 3, Arroyo)
Cana Gora (Route 333, Guánica)
Boquerón (Route 101, Boquerón)
Añasco (Route 410, Añasco)
Cerro Gordo (Route 690, Vega Baja)
Sardinera (Route 698, Dorado)

Warning: Don't go walking along the beaches at night. Even if you find that secluded, hidden beach of your dreams, proceed with caution. On unguarded beaches you will have no way to protect yourself or your valuables should you be approached by a robber or mugger, which happens frequently.

BOATING & SAILING

The waters off Puerto Rico provide excellent boating in all seasons. For sailors, winds average 10 to 15 knots virtually year-round. Marinas provide facilities and services on a par with any in the Caribbean, and many have powerboats or sailboats for rent, crewed or bareboat charter.

Marinas include the **San Juan Bay Marina** (☎ 787/721-8062); **Marina Puerto Chico,** at Puerto Chico (☎ 787/863-0834); **Marina del Mar** at Palmas del Mar in Humacao (☎ 787/850-2065); and **Marina de Salinas** (☎ 787/752-8484) in Salinas. The Caribbean's largest and most modern marina, **Puerto del Rey** (☎ 787/860-1000), is located on the island's east coast in Fajardo.

Annual sailing regattas include the Copa Velasco Regatta for ocean racing, at Palmas del Mar in Humacao.

CAMPING

The island abounds in sandy beaches and forested hillsides suitable for erecting a tent. More protected and much safer are sites throughout the island where simple cabins, sometimes with fireplaces, are maintained by the **Recreational Development Company of Puerto Rico.** Although accommodations are bare-boned minimalist, the costs are much less than those charged by hotels. For more information and an application to rent one of the units, call ☎ 787/721-2800. It is better and safer to camp only in sites maintained by the government. Some of these are simple places where you erect your own tent, although they are outfitted with electricity and running water. Showers are communal. To stay at a campsite costs between $10 and $17 per night per tent.

Many sites offer very basic cabins for rent. Each cabin is equipped with a full bathroom, a stove, a refrigerator, two beds, and a table and chairs. However, most of your cooking will probably be tastier if you do it outside at one of the on-site barbecues. In nearly all cases you must provide your own sheets and towels.

The loveliest campsites in Puerto Rico include **Maricao,** deep in the cool mountains. Each cabin here comes with a fireplace at no extra charge. Or you might like to camp along or near a lovely beach. If so, the best sites are **Añasco** and **Humacao,** which are right on the beach. Añasco provides campsites; cabins and campsites are available at Humacao. **Arroyo** is another beach site offering both cabins and regular campsites. The most expensive site is at **Boquerón Beach.** These cabins are the most

---

Take Me Out to the *Beisbol* Game

Whereas the United States may claim baseball as its national pastime, the sport also has a long, illustrious history in Puerto Rico. Imported around the turn of the 20th century by plantation owners as a leisure activity for workers, *beisbol* quickly caught fire, and local leagues have produced such major-league stars as Roberto Alomar, Bernie Williams, and the late great Roberto Clemente.

A top-notch league of six teams—featuring many rising professionals honing their skills during the winter months—begins its season in October and plays in ballparks throughout the island. Many baseball fans from the U.S. mainland come down specifically to see these teams play. For a chance to see good baseball in a more intimate setting than is afforded in the major leagues, call **Professional Baseball of Puerto Rico** (☎ 787/765-6285) for information about professional games and, if available, a schedule.

---

luxurious in Puerto Rico; they come with air-conditioning, but they cost $109 per night for up to 6 people.

An official from one of the park departments will provide you with a map and detailed instructions about how to reach each of these sites. Additional information may be available from the **Parks and Recreation Association of Puerto Rico** (☎ 787/721-2800).

DEEP-SEA FISHING

The offshore fishing here is top-notch! Allison tuna, white and blue marlin, sailfish, wahoo, dolphin, mackerel, and tarpon are some of the fish that can be caught in Puerto Rican waters, where 30 world records have been broken.

Charter arrangements can be made through most major hotels and resorts. In San Juan, **Benitez Fishing Charters** sets the standard by which to judge other captains (see chapter 6). In Palmas del Mar, which has some of the best year-round fishing in the Caribbean, you'll find **Capt. Bill Burleson** (see chapter 10).

GOLF

Home to 13 golf courses, including 8 championship links, Puerto Rico justifiably is known as the "Scotland of the Caribbean." In fact, the 72 holes at the Hyatt resorts at Dorado offer the greatest concentration of golf in the Caribbean.

The courses at the **Hyatt Dorado Beach Hotel** and the **Hyatt Regency Cerromar** are among the 25 best created by Robert Trent Jones. Jack Nicklaus rates the challenging 13th hole at the Hyatt Dorado as one of the top 10 in the world. On the southeast coast, crack golfers consider holes 11 through 15 at the **Golf Club at Palmas del Mar** to be the toughest five successive holes in the Caribbean. At **Wyndham El Conquistador Resort and Country Club,** the spectacular $250 million resort at Las Croabas east of San Juan, the course's 200-foot changes in elevation provide panoramic vistas. At Palmer on the northeast coast, inexperienced golfers prefer the **Rio Mar Golf Course** to the more challenging courses at Dorado.

With the exception of the El Conquistador Resort and Country Club, these courses are open to the public. See chapter 10 for more details.

HIKING

The mountainous interior of Puerto Rico provides ample opportunities for hill climbing and nature treks. These are especially appealing because panoramas open at the least-expected moments, often revealing spectacular views of the faraway sea.

The most popular, most beautiful, and most spectacular trekking spots include **El Yunque,** the sprawling jungle maintained by the U.S. Forest Service, and the only rain forest on U.S. soil.

El Yunque is part of the **Caribbean National Forest,** lying a 30-minute drive east of San Juan. More than 250 species of trees and some 200 types of fern have been identified here. Some 60 species of birds inhabit El Yunque, including the increasingly rare Puerto Rican parrot. Such rare birds as the elfin wods warbler, the green mango hummingbird, and the Puerto Rican lizard-cuckoo live here.

Park rangers have clearly marked the trails that are ideal for walking. Our favorite, taking 2 hours for the round-trip jaunt, is called La Mina & Big Tree Trail, which is actually two trails combined. The La Mina Trail is paved and signposted, beginning at the picnic center adjacent to the visitor center and running parallel to La Mina River. It is named for gold once discovered on the site. After you reach La Mina Falls, the Big Tree Trail begins (also signposted). It winds a route through the towering trees of Tabonuco Forest until it approaches Route 191. Along the trail you might spot such native birds as the Puerto Rican woodpecker, the tanager, the screech owl, and the bullfinch.

Those with twice the time might opt for the El Yunque Trail, which takes 4 hours round-trip to traverse. This trail—signposted from El Caimitillo Picnic Grounds— takes you on a steep, winding path. Along the way you pass natural forests of sierra palm and palo colorado before descending into the dwarf forest of Mount Britton, which is often shrouded in clouds. Your major goal, at least for panoramic views, will be the lookout peaks of Roca Marcas, Yunque Rock, and Los Picachos. On a bright, clear day you can see all the way to the eastern shores of the Atlantic.

If you're not a hiker but you appreciate rain forests, there's an easy way out here. You can drive through the forest on Route 191, a tarmac road. This trail goes from the main highway of Route 3 penetrating deep into El Yunque. You can actually see ferns that grow some 120 feet tall, and at any minute you expect a hungry dinosaur to peek between the fronds looking for a snack—namely you. You're also treated to lookout towers offering panoramic views, waterfalls, picnic areas, and even a restaurant.

El Yunque is not the only forest reserve in Puerto Rico. Others range from coastal mangrove swamps teeming with bird life to densely forested palm groves in the high-altitude interior.

A lesser forest, but one that is still intriguing to visit, is the **Maricao Forest Reserve,** near the coffee town of Maricao. This forest is in western Puerto Rico, east of the town of Mayagüez. Take Route 105 east from Mayagüez to explore it. Trails are signposted here, and your goal might be the highest peak in the forest, Las Tetas de Cerro Gordo, at 2,625 feet. A panoramic view unfolds from here, including a spotting of the off-shore island of Mona. Nearly 50 species of birds live in this forest, including the Lesser Antillean pewee and the scaly naped pigeon. Nature watchers will delight to know that there are some 280 tree species in this reserve. Some 38 of the tree species are found only in Maricao.

North of Ponce, **Toro Negro Forest Reserve** (take Route 139) lies along the Cordillera Central, the cloud-shrouded Panoramic Route that follows the Cordillera Central as it goes from the southeast town of Yabucoa all the way to Mayagüez on the west coast. This 7,000-acre park, ideal for hikers, straddles the highest peak of the Cordillera Central in the very heart of Puerto Rico. A forest of lush trees, the reserve also contains the headwaters of several main rivers.

The lowest temperatures recorded on the island—some 40°F (4°C)—were measured at **Lake Guineo,** the island's highest lake, which lies within the reserve. The best trail to take here is a short, paved, and wickedly steep path on the north side of Route 143 going up to the south side of Cerro de Punta, which at 4,390 feet is the highest peak in Puerto Rico. Allow about half an hour for an ascent up this peak. Once at the top, you'll be rewarded with Puerto Rico's grandest view, sweeping across the lush interior from the Atlantic to the Caribbean coasts. Other peaks in the reserve also offer hiking possibilities.

For information about other forest reserves, specifically **Guánica State Forest** and the **Carite Forest Reserve,** refer to chapter 8 on Ponce, Mayagüez, and San Germán.

Equally suitable for hiking are the protected lands (especially the **Río Camuy Caves**) whose topography is characterized as "karst"—that is, limestone riddled with caves, underground rivers, and natural crevasses and fissures. Although these regions pose additional risks and technical problems for trekkers, some people prefer the opportunities they provide for exploring the territory both above and below its surface. See chapter 7 for details about El Yunque and the Río Camuy Caves.

A word of warning: When you hike in the tropics, you can quickly become dehydrated and also sustain more serious insect bites and sunburn than you would while hiking in more temperate climes. Take plenty of water and drink it frequently, wear a sun hat, and consider the advisability of long-sleeved shirts and sunscreen to protect yourself from heat exhaustion and sunstroke.

For more information about any of the national forest reserves of Puerto Rico, call the **Department of Sports & Recreation** at ☎ 787/721-2800.

NATURE TOURS

Lectures on wildlife and the environment are offered by the Commonwealth of Puerto Rico Department of Natural Resources, especially for scientists and students. Also, tours of the nature reserves and forests on the island can be arranged in advance. You need to specify the name of the reserve or forest you'd like to visit. For a description of the best of these forest reserves, refer to "Hiking," above. Contact the **Department of Natural Resources,** Forest, Reserves and Refuge Area, P.O. Box 5887, San Juan, PR 00906 (☎ **787/721-5495** for the reserve and refuge; 787/723-1717 for the forest).

Despite the lushness, forest reserves, rain forest, and plant, bird, and animal life here, nature-oriented clubs such as the Sierra Club and the Audubon Society do not have organized nature tours to Puerto Rico. On the other hand, the local **Tropix Wellness Tours** (☎ 787/268-2173; fax 787/268-1722) offers five major excursions, including the exploration of sea turtles' nesting sites in Culebra, the Phosphorescent Bay in Vieques, the Rio Camuy Cave system in Camuy, and the dry, desert-like forest in Guánica.

Its **Happy Turtle Tour,** or *la tortuga Feliz,* on Culebra includes a half-day kayaking/snorkeling expedition and a visit to the sea turtles' nesting sites during the spring/summer season. The cost includes 4 days and 3 nights of accommodations at a villa with a view and air-conditioning. The tour starts at Rivas Dominici Airport in Miramar, and interisland air transportation to Culebra Airport is included. Rates are $355 per person, based on double occupancy, and include continental breakfast, three boxed lunches, and equipment for escorted expeditions.

The **Caveman Tour,** or *Tour Cavernicola,* in Camuy includes an expedition through one of the world's largest underground cave river systems. Miles of natural waterways are surrounded by stalagmites, stalactites, sunless vegetation, and 20 species of marsupials. The tour includes 3 days and 2 nights of accommodations at the Parador Guajataca in Quebradillas. Rates are $279 per person, based on double occupancy, and include two full breakfasts, one full lunch, and equipment.

The **Express Tour** in Maricao includes a full-day hiking expedition in the mountains and natural spring-water pools of the area. The Express Tour costs $243 per person, including 3 days and 2 nights double occupancy at the Hacienda Juanita, a restored coffee plantation turned hotel.

The **Wet & Dry Tour** in Guánica includes two expeditions: a dry forest hike and kayaking in the clear waters of a mangrove swamp. Southwestern Puerto Rico is home to the world's largest remaining tract of tropical dry coastal forest. This part of the island also features miles of mangrove channel systems. Visitors can explore these waterways by kayak as they are led to secluded Puerto Rican beaches. The tour includes 4 days and 3 nights of accommodations at the Compamarina Hotel. Rates are $395 per person, based on double occupancy, and include three full breakfasts and equipment.

Tropix Wellness Tours will customize an itinerary for those traveling to Puerto Rico alone, or for groups of six or more. "Add-ons" to the fixed tours, such as body-rafting expeditions through underground cave rivers and hiking excursions, can also be arranged.

SCUBA DIVING & SNORKELING

The continental shelf, which surrounds Puerto Rico on three sides, is responsible for an abundance of coral reefs, caves, seawalls, and trenches for scuba diving and snorkeling.

Open-water reefs off the southeastern coast near **Humacao** are visited by migrating whales and manatees. Many caves are located near Isabela on the west coast. The **Great Trench,** off the island's south coast, is ideal for experienced open-water divers. Caves and the seawall at **La Parguera** are also favorites. **Vieques and Culebra islands,** off the east coast, have coral formations. ✪ **Mona Island,** off the west coast, offers unspoiled reefs at depths averaging 80 feet; seals are one of the attractions. Uninhabited islands, such as **Icacos,** off the northeastern coast near Fajardo, are also popular with both snorkelers and divers.

These sites are now within reach since many of Puerto Rico's dive operators and resorts offer packages that may include daily or twice-daily dives, scuba equipment, instruction, and excursions to the island's popular attractions.

In San Juan, the **Caribe Aquatic Adventures** offers an array of sailing, scuba, and snorkeling trips, as well as boat charters and fishing (see chapter 6). At the Doral Palmas del Mar Resort, **Coral Head Divers & Water Sports Center** offers daily two-tank open-water dives for certified divers, plus snorkeling trips to Monkey Island and Vieques (see chapter 10).

Elsewhere on the island, several other companies offer scuba and snorkeling instruction. We provide details in each section.

Because of its overpopulation, the waters around San Juan aren't the most ideal for **snorkeling.** In fact, the entire north shore of Puerto Rico fronts the Atlantic, where the waters are often turbulent. Windsurfers—not snorkelers—gravitate to the waves and surf in the northwest.

The most ideal conditions for snorkeling in Puerto Rico are along the shores of the remote islands of Vieques and Culebra (see chapter 11).

The best snorkeling on the main island is found near the town of **Fajardo,** to the east of San Juan and along the tranquil eastern coast.

The calm, glasslike quality of the clear Caribbean along the south shore also is ideal for snorkeling. The most developed tourist mecca here is the city of Ponce. Few rivers empty their muddy waters into the sea along the south coast, resulting in gin-clear waters offshore. You can snorkel off the coast without having to go on a boat trip. One good place is at **Playa La Parguera,** where you can rent snorkeling equipment from kiosks along the beach. This beach lies east of the town of Guánica, to the east of Ponce. Here tropical fish add to the brightness of the water, which is generally turquoise. The addition of mangrove cays in the area also makes La Parguera more of an allure for snorkelers. Another good spot for snorkelers is **Caja de Muertos** off the coast of Ponce. Here a lagoon coral reef boasts a large number of fish species.

SURFING

Puerto Rico's northwest beaches attract surfers from around the world. Called the Hawaii of the East, the island has hosted a number of international competitions. October through February are the best surfing months, but the sport is enjoyed in Puerto Rico from August through April. The most popular areas are from Isabela around Punta Borinquén to Rincón—with beaches such as Wilderness, Surfers, Crashboat, Los Turbos in Vega Baja, Pine Grove in Isla Verde, and La Pared in Luquillo. Surfboards are available at many water-sports shops.

International competitions held in Puerto Rico have included the 1968 and the 1988 World Amateur Surfing Championships, the annual Caribbean Cup Surfing Championship, and the 1989 and 1990 Budweiser Puerto Rico Surfing Challenge events.

TENNIS

Puerto Rico has approximately 100 tennis courts. Many are at hotels and resorts; others are in public parks throughout the island. Several *paradores* also have courts. A number of courts are lighted for nighttime play.

In San Juan, the **Caribe Hilton** and the **Condado Plaza Hotel & Casino** have tennis courts. Also in the area is a **public court** at the old navy base, Isla Grande, in Miramar. The entrance is from Avenida Fernández Juncos at bus stop 11. See chapter 6.

The twin **Hyatt Resorts Caribbean** at Dorado and Cerromar maintain a total of 21 courts between them. The **Tennis Center** at Palmas del Mar in Humacao, the largest in Puerto Rico, features 20 courts. See chapter 10.

WINDSURFING

Windsurfing is a popular water sport on Puerto Rico, with the sheltered waters of the Condado Lagoon in San Juan a favorite spot. Other sites include Ocean Park, Enseñada, Boquerón, Honda Beach, and Culebra. Puerto Rico hosted its first major windsurfing tournament, the Ray Ban Windsurfing World Cup, in 1989.

Throughout the island, many companies offering snorkeling and scuba diving also provide windsurfing equipment and instruction, and dozens of hotels have facilities on their own premises.

One of the best places to arrange for windsurfing in San Juan is at **Caribe Aquatic Adventures** (see chapter 6). Along the north shore, windsurfing is excellent at the beachfront of the Hyatt Dorado Beach Hotel, where the **Penfield Island Adventures** offers lessons and rentals (see chapter 7).

13 Tips on Choosing Your Accommodations

HOTELS & RESORTS

There is no rigid classification of Puerto Rican hotels. The word "deluxe" is often used—or misused—when "first class" might be a more appropriate term. Self-described first-class hotels often aren't. We've presented fairly detailed descriptions of the hotels in this book, so you'll get an idea of what to expect once you're here.

Even in the real deluxe and first-class properties, however, don't expect top-rate service and efficiency. The slow tropical pace is what folks mean when they talk about "island time." Also, "things" often don't work as well in the tropics as they do in some of the fancy resorts of California or Europe. You may even experience power failures.

Ask detailed questions when booking a room. Don't just ask to be booked into a certain hotel, but specify your likes and dislikes. There are several logistics of getting the right room in a hotel. Entertainment in Puerto Rico is often alfresco, so light sleepers obviously won't want a room directly over a steel band. In general, back rooms cost less than oceanfront rooms, and lower rooms cost less than upper-floor units. Therefore, if budget is a major consideration with you, opt for the cheaper rooms. You won't have a great view, but you'll pay less. Just make sure that it isn't next to the all-night drummers.

Transfers from the airport or the cruise dock are included in some hotel bookings, most often in a package plan but usually not in ordinary bookings. This is true of first-class and deluxe resorts but rarely of medium-priced or budget accommodations. Always ascertain whether transfers (which can be expensive) are included.

When using the facilities at a resort, make sure that you know exactly what is free and what costs money. For example, swimming in the pool is nearly always free, but you might be charged for use of a tennis court. Nearly all water sports cost extra, unless you're booked on some special plan such as a scuba package. Some resorts seem to charge every time you breathe and might end up costing more than a deluxe hotel that includes most everything in the price.

Some hotels are right on the beach. Others involve transfers to the beach by taxi or bus, so factor in transportation costs, which can mount quickly if you stay 5 days to a week. If you want to go to the beach every day, it might be wise to book a hotel on the Condado and not stay in romantic Old San Juan: you'll spend a lot of time and money transferring back and forth between your hotel and the beach.

Most hotels in Puerto Rico are on the windward side of the island, with lots of waves, undertow, and surf. If a glasslike smooth sea is imperative for your stay, you can book on the leeward or Caribbean side, which is better for snorkeling. That means the eastern shore of Puerto Rico and its southeast coast. The major centers here are the resort complex of Palmas del Mar and the "second city" of Ponce.

SPAS

The Penthouse spa—the best on the island—at the **El San Juan Hotel & Casino** has full amenities for men and women, including fitness evaluations, supervised weight-loss programs, aerobics classes, sauna, steam room, and massage. It's open 7 days a week, year-round. A daily fee for individual services is assessed. See chapter 5.

The Plaza Spa at the **Condado Plaza Hotel & Casino** features Universal weight-training machines, video exercycles, sauna, whirlpool, facials, and massages. See chapter 4.

The fitness center at the **Doral Palmas del Mar Resort** in Humacao features hydra-fitness exercise equipment, exercise programs, free-weight training, and computerized fitness evaluations. It's open 7 days a week. See chapter 10.

The Spa Caribe at the **Hyatt Regency Cerromar Beach** offers shape-up programs, including aerobics and "talking" Powercise machines, health evaluations, plus skin- and body-care treatments, such as massage facials. See chapter 7.

At the **Parador Baños de Coamo** in Coamo, there are therapeutic thermal springs—one hot, one cool. There are also two swimming pools (one for children) and a tennis court. It's open daily. See chapter 9.

What the Symbols Mean

First-time travelers to Puerto Rico may at first be confused by classifications on hotel-room rate sheets. We've used these same classifications in this guide. One of the most common rates is **MAP,** meaning Modified American Plan. Simply put, that means room, breakfast, and dinner, unless the room rate is quoted s eparately in a listing, and then it means only breakfast and dinner. **CP** means Continental Plan—that is, room and a light breakfast. **EP** is European Plan—room only. **AP,** American Plan, is the most expensive rate because it includes your room and three meals a day.

THE PUERTO RICAN GUESTHOUSE

An entirely different type of accommodation is the guesthouse, where Puerto Ricans themselves usually stay when they travel. Ranging in size from 7 to 25 rooms, they offer a familial atmosphere. Many are on or near the beach, some have pools or sundecks, and a number serve meals.

In Puerto Rico, however, the term *guesthouse* has many meanings. Some guesthouses are like simple motels built around swimming pools. Others have small individual cottages with their own kitchenettes, constructed around a main building in which you'll often find a bar and a restaurant serving local food. Some are surprisingly comfortable, often with private baths and swimming pools. You may or may not have air-conditioning. The rooms are sometimes cooled by ceiling fans, or by the trade winds blowing through open windows at night.

For value, the guesthouse can't be topped. Staying at a guesthouse, you can journey over to a big beach resort, using its seaside facilities for only a small charge. Although bereft of frills, the guesthouses we've recommended are clean and safe for families or single women. However, the cheapest ones are not places where you'd want to spend a lot of time because of their modest furnishings.

For further information, contact the **Puerto Rico Tourism Company,** 575 Fifth Ave., New York, NY 10017 (☎ **800/223-6530** or 212/586-6262).

PARADORES

In an effort to lure travelers beyond the hotels and casinos of San Juan's historic district to the tranquil natural beauty of the island's countryside, the Puerto Rico Tourism Company offers *paradores puertorriqueños*—charming country inns—which are comfortable bases for exploring the island's varied attractions. Vacationers seeking a peaceful idyll can also choose from several privately owned and operated guesthouses.

Using Spain's *parador* system as a model, the Puerto Rico Tourism Company established the *paradores* in 1973 to encourage tourism across the island. Each of the *paradores* is situated in a historic place or site of unusual scenic beauty and must meet high standards of service and cleanliness.

Some of the *paradores* are located in the mountains and others by the sea. Most have swimming pools, and all offer excellent Puerto Rican cuisine. Many are within easy driving distance of San Juan. To make a reservation at one of the *paradores,* call Paradores of Puerto Rico at ☎ **800/443-0266** in the United States (8am to noon and 1 to 4:30pm Atlantic time).

VILLAS & VACATION HOMES

You can often secure good deals in Puerto Rico by renting privately owned villas and vacation homes.

Many villas have a staff, or at least a maid who comes in a few days a week, and they also provide the essentials of home life, including bed linen and cooking paraphernalia. Condos usually come with a reception desk and are often comparable to life in a suite at a big resort hotel. Nearly all condo complexes have swimming pools (some have more than one).

Private apartments are rented either with or without maid service. This is more of a no-frills option than the villas and condos. The apartments may not be in buildings with swimming pools, and they may not have a front desk to help you. Among the major categories of vacation homes, cottages offer the most freewheeling way to live. Most cottages are fairly simple, many opening in an ideal fashion onto a beach, whereas others may be clustered around a communal swimming pool. Many contain no more than a simple bedroom together with a small kitchen and bath. For the peak winter season, reservations should be made at least 5 or 6 months in advance.

Dozens of agents throughout the United States and Canada offer these types of rentals (see "Rental Agencies," below, for some recommendations). You can also write to local tourist information offices, which can advise you on vacation home rentals.

Travel experts agree that savings, especially for a family of three to six people, or two or three couples, can range from 50 to 60% of what a hotel would cost. If there are only two in your party, these savings probably don't apply.

RENTAL AGENCIES

Agencies specializing in renting properties in Puerto Rico include:

Villas of Distinction, P.O. Box 55, Armonk, NY 10504 (☎ **800/289-0900** in the U.S. or 914/273-3331; fax 914/273-3387), is one of the best rental agencies offering "complete vacations," including airfare, rental car, and domestic help. Some private villas have two to five bedrooms, and almost every villa has a swimming pool.

Caribbean Connections Plus Ltd., P.O. Box 261, Trumbull, CT 06611 (☎ **203/ 261-8603;** fax 203/261-8295), offers many apartments, cottages, and villas in the Caribbean. Caribbean Connections specializes in island hopping with JetAir, and it offers especially attractive deals for U.S. West Coast travelers. This is one of the few reservations services whose staff has actually been on the islands, so members can talk to people from experience and not from a computer screen.

VHR, Worldwide, 235 Kensington Ave., Norwood, NJ 07648 (☎ **800/633-3284** or 201/767-9393; fax 201/767-5510), offers the most comprehensive portfolio of luxury villas, condominiums, resort suites, and apartments for rent in the Caribbean, including complete packages for airfare and car rentals. The company's more than 4,000 homes and suite resorts are handpicked by the staff, and accommodations are generally less expensive than comparable hotel rooms.

Hideaways International, 767 Islington St., Portsmouth, NH 03801 (☎ **800/ 843-4433** in the U.S. or 603/430-4433; fax 603/430-4444), provides a 144-page guide with illustrations of its accommodations in the Caribbean so that you'll get some idea of what you're renting. Most of its villas, which can accommodate up to three couples or a large family of about 10, come with maid service. You can also ask this travel club about discounts on plane fares and car rentals.

Villanet, 7200 34th Ave., NW, Seattle, WA 98117 (☎ **800/488-RENT** or 425/ 653-7733; fax 425/653-3866), maintains an inventory of several thousand properties, specializing in condos and villas with weekly rates ranging from $700 to $50,000. It arranges weekly or longer bookings. For their color catalog including prices, descriptions, and pictures, send $15, which will be applied to your next rental.

Sometimes local tourist offices will also advise you on vacation-home rentals if you write or call them directly.

Fast Facts: Puerto Rico

American Express   See "Fast Facts: San Juan," in chapter 3.

Area Code   The telephone area code for Puerto Rico is **787.** For calls on the island, the area code is not used.

ATM Networks   See "Money," earlier in this chapter.

Banks   All major U.S. banks have branches on Puerto Rico; their hours are from 8am to 2:30pm Monday through Friday and from 9:45am to noon on Saturday.

Business Hours   Regular business hours are Monday through Friday from 8am to 5pm. Shopping hours vary considerably. Regular shopping hours are Monday through Thursday and Saturday from 9am to 6pm. On Friday, stores have a long day: 9am to 9pm. Many stores also open on Sunday from 11am to 5pm.

Camera & Film   Nearly all well-known brands of film are sold on Puerto Rico. Rolls of film cost about what they do on the U.S. mainland. It's relatively easy to get film processed on the island, especially in San Juan. It's important to protect your camera not only from theft but also from saltwater and sand; furthermore, the camera can become overheated and any film it contains can be ruined if left in the sun or locked in the trunk of a car. For the best commercial camera stores in Puerto Rico, see "Fast Facts: San Juan," in chapter 3.

Car Rentals   See "Getting Around," earlier in this chapter.

Climate   See "When to Go," earlier in this chapter.

Currency   See "Money," earlier in this chapter.

Customs   See "Entry Requirements & Customs," earlier in this chapter.

Dentists & Doctors   Dental emergencies can be taken care of at the **San Juan Health Center,** 150 Avenida de Diego, Santurce (☎ **787/725-0202**). This center also handles medical emergencies within the Greater San Juan area.

Documents   See "Entry Requirements & Customs," earlier in this chapter.

Driving Rules   See "Getting Around," earlier in this chapter.

Drugs   A branch of the Federal Narcotics Strike Force is permanently stationed on Puerto Rico, where illegal drugs and narcotics are a problem. Convictions for possession of marijuana can bring severe penalties, ranging from 2 to 10 years in prison for a first offense. Possession of hard drugs, such as cocaine or heroin, can lead to 15 years or more in prison.

Drugstores   It's a good idea to carry enough prescription medications with you to last the duration of your stay. If you're going into the hinterlands, take along the medicines you'll need. If you need any additional medications, you'll find many drugstores in San Juan and other leading cities. One of the most centrally located pharmacies in Old San Juan is the **Puerto Rican Drug Co.,** Calle San

Paradores of Puerto Rico

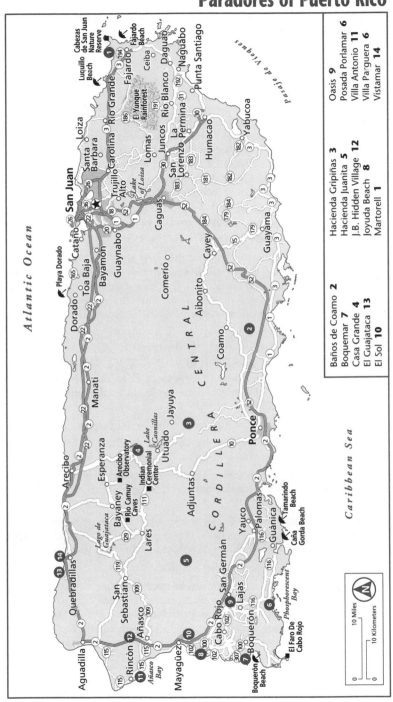

Baños de Coamo **2**
Boquemar **7**
Casa Grande **4**
El Guajataca **13**
El Sol **10**

Hacienda Gripiñas **3**
Hacienda Juanita **5**
J.B. Hidden Village **12**
Joyuda Beach **8**
Martorell **1**

Oasis **9**
Posada Porlamar **6**
Villa Antonio **11**
Villa Parguera **6**
Vistamar **14**

Francisco 157 (☎ 787/725-2202); it's open Monday through Saturday from 7:30am to 9:30pm and Sunday from 8am to 7:30pm.

Electricity   The electricity is 110 volts AC, as it is in the continental United States and Canada.

Embassies & Consulates   Since Puerto Rico is part of the United States, there is no U.S. embassy or consulate. Instead, there are branches of all the principal U.S. federal agencies. Canada has no embassy or consulate either. In case of a problem, citizens of the United Kingdom can call ☎ 787/721-5193 or 787/723-6355-to receive recorded directions to leave a message including their name, address, telephone number, and a brief description of their problem. A staff member will eventually return the call. Otherwise, there are no special provisions or agencies catering to British travel needs in Puerto Rico. There are no agencies serving Australian or New Zealand citizens.

Emergencies   In an emergency, dial 911. Or call the local **police** (☎ 787/ 343-2020), **fire department** (☎ 787/343-2330), **ambulance** (☎ 787/ 343-2550), or **medical assistance** (☎ 787/754-3535).

Health Care   Medical-care facilities on the island are on par with those in the United States, with excellent hospitals and clinics. Hotels can arrange for a doctor in case of an emergency. Most major U.S. health insurance plans are recognized, but it's advisable to check with your carrier or insurance agent in advance of your trip, since medical attention is very expensive. See "Health & Insurance," earlier in this chapter.

Holidays   See "When to Go," earlier in this chapter.

Hospitals   In a medical emergency, call 911. The following facilities maintain 24-hour emergency rooms: **Ashford Presbyterian Community Hospital,** 1451 Ashford Ave. (☎ 787/721-2160), and the **San Juan Health Center,** Avenida de Diego 150 (☎ 787/725-0202).

Information   See "Visitor Information," earlier in this chapter.

Internet Access   Public access to the Internet is available at some large-scale resorts; the staff often provides access from one of their own computers.

Language   English is understood at the big resorts and in most of San Juan. Out in the island, Spanish is still *numero uno.* See appendix B for basic English and Spanish words.

Liquor Laws   You must be 21 years of age to purchase liquor in stores or buy drinks in hotels, bars, and restaurants. If you are 21 or over but look younger, bring photo identification such as a driver's license that gives your date of birth.

Maps   See "Getting Around," earlier in this chapter.

Marriage Requirements   There are no residency requirements for getting married in Puerto Rico. You'll need parental consent if either of you is under 18. Blood tests are required, although a test conducted within 10 days of the ceremony on the U.S. mainland will suffice. A doctor must sign the license after an examination of the bride and groom. For complete details, contact the **Commonwealth of Puerto Rico Health Department,** Demographic Register, 26 Fernandez Juncos (P.O. Box 9342), San Juan, PR 00917 (☎ 787/767-9120, ext. 2302).

Newspapers & Magazines   The *San Juan Star,* a daily English-language newspaper, has been called the *"International Herald Tribune* of the Caribbean." It concentrates extensively on news from the United States. You can also pick up copies of *USA Today* at most news kiosks. If you read Spanish, you might enjoy *El Nuevo Día*, the most popular local tabloid. Few significant magazines are published on Puerto Rico, but *Time* and *Newsweek* are available at most newsstands.

Passports   See "Visitor Information," earlier in this chapter.

Pets   To bring your pet in, you must produce a health certificate from a mainland veterinarian and show proof of vaccination against rabies. Very few hotels allow animals, so check in advance. Many veterinarians are listed in the yellow pages of the local telephone book.

Postal Services   Since the U.S. Postal Service is responsible for handling mail on the island, the regulations and tariffs are the same as on the mainland. Stamps may be purchased at any post office, each of which is open Monday through Friday from 8am to 5pm. Saturday hours are from 8am to noon (closed Sunday). As on the mainland, you can purchase stamps at vending machines in airports, stores, and hotels. At press time, first-class letters to addresses within Puerto Rico, the United States, and its territories cost 33¢; postcards, 20¢. Letters and postcards to Canada both cost 48¢ for the first half-ounce. Letters and postcards to other countries cost 60¢ for the first half-ounce. But note: These rates will rise during the life of this edition.

Safety   Crime exists here as it does everywhere. Use common sense and take precautions. Muggings are commonplace on the Condado and Isla Verde beaches, so you might want to confine your moonlit beach nights to the fenced-in and guarded areas around some of the major hotels. The countryside of Puerto Rico is safer than San Juan, but caution is always the rule. Avoid small and narrow country roads and isolated beaches, either night or day.

Smoking   Antismoking regulation is less stringent than it is on the U.S. mainland. For example, anyone over 18 can smoke in any bar here. Smoking is permitted in restaurants, within clearly designated sections, but not necessarily everywhere. Most hotels have smoking and nonsmoking rooms.

Taxes   In addition to the government tax of 7% in regular hotels or 10% in hotels with casinos, some hotels add a 10% service charge to your bill. If they don't, you're expected to tip for services rendered. There is no airport departure tax.

Telephone, Telex & Fax   Coin-operated phones are found throughout the island, with a particularly dense concentration in San Juan. After depositing your coins, you can dial a seven-digit number at the sound of the dial tone. If you're calling long distance within Puerto Rico, add a 1 before the numbers. When you're placing a call to the U.S. mainland or to anywhere else overseas, preface the number with 011. An operator (or a recorded voice) will tell you how much money to deposit, although you'll probably find it more practical to use a calling card issued by such long-distance carriers as Sprint, AT&T, or MCI. Public phones that allow credit cards such as American Express, Visa, or MasterCard to be inserted or "swiped" through a magnetic slot are rare on the island. Most of these are located at the San Juan airport. Most phone booths contain printed instructions for dialing. Local calls are 10¢. Most Puerto Ricans buy phone cards valid for between 15 and 100 units. The 30-unit card costs $13.50; the 60-unit card, $27.50. The card provides an even less expensive and usually more convenient way of calling within Puerto Rico or to the U.S. mainland. They are for sale in most pharmacies and gift shops on the island.

Most hotels will send a telex or fax for you and bill the costs to your room, and in some cases, they'll even send a fax for a nonguest if you agree to pay a charge. Barring that, several agencies in San Juan will send a fax anywhere you want for a fee. Many are associated with print shops/photocopy stands. **Eagle Print,** 1229 F. D. Roosevelt Blvd., Puerto Nuevo, San Juan, PR 00920 (☎ **787/782-7830**), charges $2 per page for faxes sent to the U.S. mainland.

Time   Puerto Rico is on Atlantic standard time, which is 1 hour later than eastern standard time. Puerto Rico does not go on daylight saving time, however, so the time here is the same year-round.

Tipping   Tipping is expected here, so hand over the money as you would on the U.S. mainland. That usually means 15% in restaurants, except for fast-food places; 10% in bars; and 10% to 15% for taxi drivers, hairdressers, and other services, depending on the quality of the service rendered. Tip a porter, either at the airport or at your hotel, $1 per bag. Europeans and others may not like this method of compensation, but the U.S. government imposes income tax on wait staff and other service-industry workers whose income is tip-based according to the gross receipts of their employers; therefore, those workers could end up paying tax on a tip you didn't give them.

Visitor Information   See "Visitor Information," earlier in this chapter.

Water   See "Health & Insurance," earlier in this chapter.

Weights & Measures   There's a mixed bag of measurements in Puerto Rico. Because of its Spanish tradition, most weights (meat and poultry) and measures (gasoline and road distances) are metric. But because of the American presence, speed limits appear in miles per hour, and liquids such as beer are sold by the ounce.

Getting to Know San Juan   3

San Juan, the capital city, will introduce you to the commonwealth. All but a handful of visitors arrive here. This is the political base, economic powerhouse, and cultural center of the island, and home to about one-third of all Puerto Ricans.

The second-oldest city in the Americas (behind Santo Domingo in the Dominican Republic), this metropolis presents two completely different faces to the world. On one hand, the charming historic district, Old San Juan, is strongly reminiscent of the Spanish Empire. On the other, modern expressways outside the historic district cut through urban sprawl to link towering concrete buildings and beachfront hotels resembling those of Miami Beach.

Old San Juan is a 7-square-block area that was once completely enclosed by a wall erected by the Spanish with slave labor. The most powerful fortress in the Caribbean, this fortified city repeatedly held off would-be attackers. By the 19th century, however, it had become one of the Caribbean's most charming residential and commercial districts. Today it's a setting for restaurants and shops. Most of the major resort hotels are located nearby, along the Condado beachfront and at Isla Verde (see chapter 4).

1 Orientation

ARRIVING BY PLANE

Visitors from overseas arrive at **Luis Muñoz Marín International Airport** (☎ 787/791-1014), the major transportation center of the Caribbean. The airport is on the easternmost side of the city, rather inconvenient to nearly all hotels except the resorts and small inns at Isla Verde.

The airport offers an array of services, including a tourist information center, fast-food restaurants, barbershops and hairdressers, coin lockers to store luggage (particularly useful if you're visiting one of the smaller islands on a shuttle plane), bookstores, banks, money exchange kiosks, and even a bar (open daily from noon to 4pm), which offers a sampling of the best Puerto Rican rums in all their many hues and flavors.

GETTING FROM THE AIRPORT INTO THE CITY

BY TAXI   Dozens of taxis line up outside the airport to meet arriving flights, so you rarely have to wait. Fares can vary widely, depending on traffic conditions. If you're staying at one of the beachfront hotels along the Condado, the average fare from the airport is $13.

Although technically cab drivers should turn on their meters, more often than not they'll quote a flat rate before starting out. The rate system seems effective and fair, and if you're caught in impenetrable traffic, it might actually work to your advantage. The island's **Public Service Commission,** or PSC (☎ 787/756-1401), establishes flat rates between the Luis Muñoz Marín International Airport and major tourist zones as listed here: From the airport to any hotel in Isla Verde, the fee is $8; to any hotel in the Condado district, the charge is $12; and to any hotel in Old San Juan, the cost is $16. Normal tipping supplements of between 10 and 15% of that fare are appreciated.

BY MINIVAN OR LIMOUSINE   Be aware that a wide variety of vehicles at the San Juan airport call themselves *limosinas* (their Spanish name). One outfit whose sign-up desk is in the arrivals hall of the international airport, near American Airlines, is the **Airport Limousine Service** (☎ 787/791-4745). They offer minivan service from the airport to various San Juan neighborhoods for prices that are lower than what a taxi would charge. Whenever 8 to 10 passengers can be accumulated, the fare for transport, with luggage, to any hotel in Isla Verde is $2.50 per person; to the Condado, $3 per person; and to Old San Juan, $3.50 per person.

For conventional limousine service, **Bracero Limousine** (☎ 787/253-1133) offers upholstered cars with drivers that will meet you and your entourage at the arrivals terminal for luxurious, private transportation to your hotel. Transport to virtually anywhere in San Juan ranges from $85 to $105; whereas, transport to points throughout the island varies from $150 to $275, depending on the time and distance. Ideally, transport should be arranged in advance of your arrival, in which event a car and driver will be waiting for you near the arrivals terminal.

BY CAR   All the major car-rental companies have kiosks at the airport. Although it's possible to rent a car once you arrive, your best bet is to reserve one before you leave home. See the "Getting Around" section of chapter 2 for details.

To drive into the city, head west along Route 26, which becomes Route 25 as it enters Old San Juan. If you stay on Route 25 (also called Avenida Muñoz Rivera), you'll have the best view of the ocean and the monumental city walls.

Just before reaching the Capitol building, turn left between the Natural Resources Department and the modern House of Representatives office building. Go 2 blocks until you reach the intersection of Paseo de Covadonga, then take a right past the Treasury Building, and park your car in the Covadonga Parking Garage on the left. This garage is open 24 hours. A free shuttle-bus service loops the old town from here on two different routes.

BY BUS   Those with little luggage can take the T1 bus, which runs to the center of the city.

VISITOR INFORMATION
Tourist information is available at the **Luis Muñoz Marín Airport** (☎ 787/ 791-1014), daily from 9am to 5:30pm. Another office is at **La Casita,** Pier 1, Old San Juan (☎ 787/722-1709).

CITY LAYOUT
Metropolitan San Juan includes the old walled city on San Juan Island; the city center on San Juan Island, containing the Capitol building; Santurce, on a larger peninsula, which is reached by causeway bridges from San Juan Island (the lagoon-front section here is called Miramar); Condado, the narrow peninsula that stretches from

San Juan Island to Santurce; Hato Rey, the business center; Río Piedras, site of the University of Puerto Rico; and Bayamón, an industrial and residential quarter.

The Condado strip of beachfront hotels, restaurants, casinos, and nightclubs is separated from Miramar by a lagoon. Isla Verde, another resort area, is near the airport, which is separated from the rest of San Juan by an isthmus.

FINDING AN ADDRESS Finding an address in San Juan isn't always easy. You'll have to contend not only with missing street signs and numbers but also with street addresses that appear sometimes in English and at other times in Spanish. The most common Spanish terms for thoroughfares are *calle* (street) and *avenida* (avenue). When they are used, the street number will follow them; for example, the Gran Hotel El Convento is located at Calle del Cristo 100, in Old San Juan. Locating a building in Old San Juan is relatively easy, with the odd numbers on one side of the street and the even numbers on the other. The area is only 7 square blocks, so by walking around it's possible to locate most addresses.

STREET MAPS *Qué Pasa?*, the monthly tourist magazine distributed free by the tourist office, contains accurate, easy-to-read maps of San Juan and the Condado, pinpointing the major attractions.

Neighborhoods in Brief

OLD SAN JUAN This 7-square-block area is the most historic in the West Indies. Filled with Spanish colonial architecture and under constant restoration, it lies on the western end of an islet. It's encircled by water; on the north is the Atlantic Ocean, and on the south and west is the tranquil San Juan Bay. Ponte San Antonio bridge connects the old town with "mainland" Puerto Rico. Ramparts and old Spanish fortresses form its outer walls.

PUERTA DE TIERRA Translated as "gateway to -the land" or "gateway to the island," Puerta de Tierra lies just east of the old city walls of San Juan. This section of metropolitan San Juan is split by Avenida Ponce de León and interconnects the historic peninsula of Old San Juan with the Puerto Rican "mainland." The settlement, founded by freed black slaves, today functions as the island's administrative center and is the site of many military and government buildings, including the Capitol building and various U.S. naval reserves.

MIRAMAR This is an upscale residential neighborhood, across the bridge from Puerto de Tierra. Many yachts anchor in its waters on the bay side of Ponte Isla Grande, and some of the finest homes on Puerto Rico are found here. It's also the site of Isla Grande Airport, where you can board flights to the offshore islands of Vieques and Culebra.

CONDADO/SANTURCE The Condado is the glittering beachfront strip of San Juan—site of most of the major hotels. It's linked to Puerto de Tierra and Old San Juan by a bridge built in 1910. The greater neighborhood of Santurce, adjoining the Condado, was once the most exclusive in San Juan. However, now it's in sad decline.

OCEAN PARK Dividing the competitive beach resort areas of the Condado and Isla Verde, Ocean Park is a beachfront residential neighborhood that's sometimes plagued by flooding, especially during hurricanes. It used to be called the "wild and wooly" western fringe of the Condado, but it's completely built up today with houses that are smaller and more spread out than those within the Condado district. Beaches here are slightly less crowded than those at Condado or Isla Verde. Because of several gay guesthouses in the area, some of the beaches of Ocean Park attract male homosexuals.

San Juan Orientation

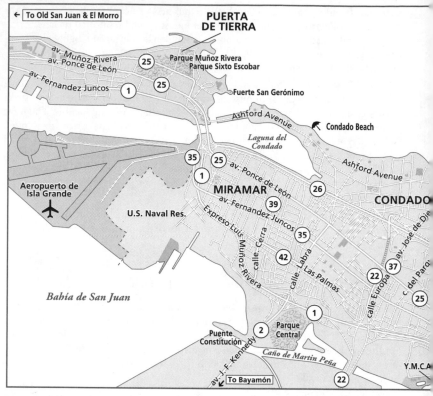

← To Old San Juan & El Morro

PUERTA DE TIERRA

av. Muñoz Rivera
av. Ponce de León
(25)
Parque Muñoz Rivera
Parque Sixto Escobar

av. Fernandez Juncos
(1) (25)
Fuerte San Gerónimo

Ashford Avenue
Condado Beach

Laguna del Condado

(35) (25) av. Ponce de León
(1)
MIRAMAR
(26)
CONDADO

Aeropuerto de Isla Grande

U.S. Naval Res.

av. Fernandez Juncos
(39)
Expreso Luis Muñoz Rivera
calle. Cerra
(35)

av. Jose de Die

(42)
calle. Labra
calle. Las Palmas

(22) (37)
calle Europa
c. del Parq
(25)

Bahía de San Juan

(1)

Parque Central

Puente Constitución
(2)
av. J. F. Kennedy
← To Bayamón
Caño de Martín Peña
(22)
Y.M.C.A

HATO REY   Santurce's loss was Hato Rey's gain. Situated to the south of the Martín Peña canal, this area today is the Wall Street of the West Indies, filled with many high-rises, a large federal complex, and many business and banking offices. Actually, it was once a marsh until landfill and concrete changed it forever.

RÍO PIEDRAS   South of both Hato Rey and Santurce, this is the site of the University of Puerto Rico and its student population. It's dominated by the landmark Roosevelt Bell Tower, named for Theodore Roosevelt who donated the money for its construction. The main thoroughfare is Paseo de Diego, site of a popular local market where produce is sold. The Agricultural Experimental Station of Puerto Rico maintains a botanical garden; there are many tropical plants here, including 125 species of palms.

BAYAMÓN   The San Juan sprawl has reached this once-distant southwestern suburb, which had been farmland before industry moved in and took over. Some 200,000 people and nearly 200 factories are now located in this geographically large district. Bus no. 46 from the center of San Juan runs out here. At Route 2, kilometer 6.4, in Guayanobo are the ruins of Caparra, the first colonial settlement on the island.

2 Getting Around

BY TAXI   Except for a handful of important, high-profile tourist routes, public taxis are metered within San Juan, or should be. Normal tipping supplements of between

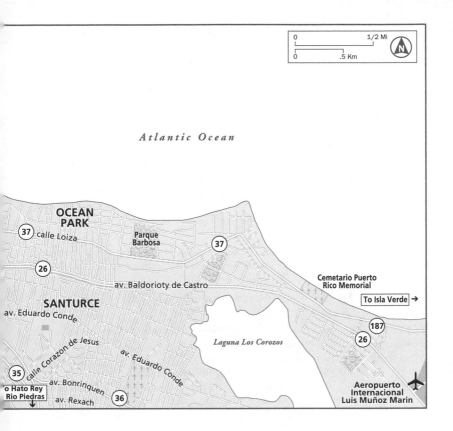

10 and 15% are appreciated. Passengers traveling between most other destinations within greater San Juan are charged by meter readings. The initial charge is $1, plus 10¢ for each one-tenth mile and 50¢ for every suitcase, with a minimum fare of $3. These rates apply to conventional *taxis turisticos,* which are usually white-painted vehicles with official logos on their doors. Owned by a medley of individual outfitters within San Juan, they maintain standards that are higher than those of the cheaper but more erratic and inconvenient *públicos,* which are described in chapter 2. Call the PSC to request information or to report any irregularities.

Taxis are invariably lined up outside the entrance to most of the island's hotels, and if not, a staff member can almost always call one for you. But if you want to arrange a taxi on your own, call the **Rochdale Cab Company** (☎ 787/721-1900) or the **Mejor Cab Company** (☎ 787/723-2460).

You'll have to negotiate a fare with the driver, usually at a flat rate, for trips to far-flung destinations within Puerto Rico.

BY BUS   The **Metropolitan Bus Authority** (☎ 787/729-1512 for route information) operates buses in the greater San Juan area. Bus stops are marked by upright metal signs or yellow posts reading PARADA. There's one bus terminal in the dock area and another at the Plaza de Colón. A typical fare is 25¢ to 50¢.

Most of the large hotels of the Condado and Isla Verde maintain an air-conditioned bus that makes free shuttle runs into Old San Juan. Clients are usually deposited at the Plaza de Colón. Public buses also make the run along the Condado, stopping at clearly designated bus stops placed near the major hotels. Public buses usually deposit their clients at the Plaza Colón and the main bus terminal across the street from the Cataño ferryboat pier. This section of Old San Juan is the starting point for many of the city's metropolitan bus routes.

Here are some useful, public bus routes: bus no. 2 goes from the Plaza de Colón along the Condado, eventually reaching the commercial section of San Juan, Hato Rey; bus no. A7 passes from Old San Juan to the Condado and goes on to Avenida Isla Verde; and no. T1 heads for Avenida de Diego in the Condado district, then makes a long run to Isla Verde and the airport.

BY TROLLEY   When youtire of walking around Old San Juan, you can board one of the free trolleys that run through the historic area. Departure points are the Marina and La Puntilla, but you can board along the route by flagging the trolley down (wave at it, and signal for it to stop) or by waiting at any of the clearly designated stopping points. Relax and enjoy the sights as the trolleys rumble through the old and narrow streets.

ON FOOT   This is the only way to explore Old San Juan. All the major attractions can easily be covered in a day. If you're going from Old San Juan to Isla Verde, however, you'll need to rely on public transportation.

BY RENTAL CAR   See "Getting Around" in chapter 2 for details—including some reasons why you *shouldn't* plan to drive in Puerto Rico.

BY FERRY   The *Agua Expreso* (☎ 787/788-1155) connects Old San Juan with the industrial and residential communities of Hato Rey and Cataño, across the bay. Ferries depart daily every 30 minutes from 6am to 9pm. The one-way fare to Hato Rey is 75¢, and the one-way fare to Cataño is 50¢. Departures are from the San Juan Terminal at the pier in Old San Juan. However, it's best to avoid rush hours since hundreds of locals who work in town use this ferry. Each ride lasts about 20 minutes.

Fast Facts: San Juan

Airport   See "Arriving by Plane," earlier in this chapter.

American Express   The agency is represented in San Juan by **Travel Network,** 1035 Ashford Ave., Condado (☎ **787/725-0960**). The office is open Monday through Friday from 9am to 1pm and 2 to 5pm, Saturday from 9am to noon.

Camera & Film   Both **Cinefoto** (☎ 787/753-7238) and **Rabola** (☎ 787/753-8778), located in the Plaza Las Americas Shopping Mall in Hato Rey, offer a wide variety of photographic supplies. Cinefoto is open Monday through Saturday from 9am to 9pm. Rabola is open Monday through Saturday from 9am to 9pm, Sunday from 11am to 5pm.

Car Rentals   See "Getting Around" in chapter 2. If you want to reserve after you've arrived in Puerto Rico, call **Avis** (☎ 787/791-2500), **Budget** (☎ 787/791-3685), or **Hertz** (☎ 787/791-0840).

Currency Exchange   The unit of currency is the U.S. dollar, so American travelers will not need this service. But for British and Canadian travelers, most banks will provide this service. You can also exchange money at the **Luis Muñoz Marín International Airport.** See also "Money" in chapter 2.

Drugstores   See "Pharmacies" below.

Great Discounts Through the LeLoLai VIP Program

For the $10 it will cost you to join Puerto Rico's ✪ **LeLoLai VIP** (Value in Puerto Rico) program, you can enjoy the equivalent of up to $250 in travel benefits. You'll get discounts on admission to folklore shows, guided tours of historic sites and natural attractions, lodgings, meals, shopping, activities, and more. Of course, most of the experiences linked to LeLoLai are of the rather touristy type, but it can still be a good investment.

With membership, the *paradores puertorriqueños,* the island's modestly priced network of country inns, give cardholders 10 to 20% lower room rates Monday through Thursday. Discounts of 10 to 20% are offered at many restaurants, from San Juan's toniest hotels to several *mesones gatronómicos,* government-sanctioned restaurants serving Puerto Rican fare. Shopping discounts are offered at many stores and boutiques, and, best yet, cardholders get 10 to 20% discounts at many island attractions.

The card also entitles you to free admission to some of the island's folklore shows. At press time, the pass included *Jolgorio,* presented every Wednesday at 8:30pm at the Caribe Terrace of the Caribe Hilton, although the specifics might change by the time you arrive in Puerto Rico.

For more information about this card, call ☎ 787/723-3135 or go to the El Centro Convention Center at Ashford Avenue on the Condado. Although you can call for details before you leave home, you can only sign up for this program once you reach Puerto Rico. Many hotel packages include participation in this program as part of their offerings.

Emergencies   In an emergency, dial 911. Or call the local **police** (☎ 787/343-2020), **fire department** (☎ 787/343-2330), **ambulance** (☎ 787/343-2550), or **medical assistance** (☎ 787/754-3535). Dental emergencies are handled at the **San Juan Health Center** at Avenida de Diego 150 in Santurce (☎ 787/725-0202).

Eyeglasses   Services are available at **Pearle Vision Express,** Plaza Las Americas Shopping Mall (☎ 787/753-1033). Hours are Monday through Saturday from 9am to 9pm and Sunday from 11am to 5pm.

Hospitals   **Ashford Presbyterian Community Hospital,** 1451 Ashford Ave. (☎ 787/721-2160), and the **San Juan Health Center,** Avenida de Diego 150 (☎ 787/725-0202), both maintain 24-hour emergency rooms.

Information   See "Visitor Information," earlier in this chapter.

Internet Access   Public access to the Internet is available at **Soapy's Station,** 111 Gilberto Concepción de Gracia, Old San Juan (☎ 787/289-0344), in an annex of the Wyndham Old San Juan Hotel & Casino.

Maps   See "City Layout," earlier in this chapter.

Pharmacies   One of the most centrally located pharmacies is the **Puerto Rican Drug Co.,** Calle San Francisco 157 (☎ 787/725-2202), in Old San Juan. It's open Monday through Saturday from 7:30am to 9:30pm and Sunday from 8am to 7:30pm. **Walgreen's,** 1130 Ashford Ave., Condado (☎ 787/725-1510), is open 24 hours a day.

Police   Call ☎ 787/343-2020 for the local police.

Post Office   In San Juan, the General Post Office is at 585 Roosevelt Ave. (☎ 787/767-3604). If you don't know your address in San Juan, you can ask that your mail be sent here "c/o General Delivery." This main branch is open Monday through Friday from 6am to 9pm, Saturday from 8am to 2pm. A letter from Puerto Rico to the U.S. mainland will arrive in about 4 days. See "Fast Facts: Puerto Rico," in chapter 2, for more information.

Rest Rooms   Rest rooms are not public facilities accessible from the street. It's necessary to enter a hotel lobby, cafe, or restaurant for access to a toilet. Fortunately, large-scale hotels are familiar with this situation, and someone looking for a *WC* usually isn't challenged during his or her pursuit.

Safety   At night, exercise extreme caution when walking along the back streets of San Juan, and don't venture onto the unguarded public stretches of the Condado and Isla Verde beaches at night. All these areas are favorite targets for muggings.

Salons   Most of San Juan's large resort hotels, including the Condado Plaza, the Marriott, and the Wyndham Old San Juan, maintain their own hair salons, catering to both men and women. All are very competent

Taxis   See "Getting Around," earlier in this chapter.

Telephone, Telex & Fax   Many public telephones are available at **World Service Telephone (AT&T),** Pier 1, Old San Juan (☎ 787/721-2520). To send a fax or telex, go to **Eagle Print,** 1229 F. D. Roosevelt Blvd., Puerto Nuevo (☎ 787/782-7830). For more information, see also "Fast Facts: Puerto Rico" in chapter 2.

Tourist Offices   See "Visitor Information," earlier in this chapter.

Transit Information   For information about bus routes in San Juan, call ☎ 787/729-1512.

Where to Stay in San Juan 4

Whatever your preferences in accommodations—a beachfront resort or a place in historic Old San Juan, sumptuous luxury or an austere, inexpensive base from which to see the sights—you can find a perfect fit in San Juan.

In addition to checking the recommendations listed here, you may want to contact a travel agent; there are package deals galore that can save you money and match you with an establishment that meets your requirements. See "Package Tours" in chapter 2.

Before even talking to a travel agent, refer to our comments about how to select a room in Puerto Rico. See "Hotels & Resorts" under "Tips on Choosing Your Accommodations" in chapter 2. You might also refer to comments under "Package Tours" in the same chapter, particularly if you're planning to book a deal with all your meals included.

Not all hotels here have air-conditioned rooms. We've pointed them out in the recommendations below. If air-conditioning is important to you, make sure "A/C" appears right after the number of units near the top of the listings.

If the beach is not important to you, and you prefer shopping and historic sights instead, then Old San Juan might be your preferred nest for the night. The high-rise resort hotels lie primarily along the Condado beach strip and the equally good sands of Isla Verde. The hotels along Condado and Isla Verde attract the cruise-ship and casino crowd. The hotels away from the beach in San Juan, in such sections as Santurce, are primarily for business clients.

TAXES & SERVICE CHARGES
All hotel rooms in Puerto Rico are subject to a 7 to 9% tax, which is not included in the rates given here. Most hotels also add a 10% service charge. When you're booking a room, it's always best to inquire about these added charges.

MAKING RESERVATIONS
You may make your reservations by telephone, mail, fax, and, in some cases, the Internet. If you're booking into a chain hotel, such as a Hilton, you can easily make your reservations by calling their toll-free phone numbers in many countries. We give the North American toll-free numbers in this book.

You can usually cancel a room reservation 1 week ahead of time and get a full refund. A few places will return your money on cancellations up to 3 days before the reservation date; others won't return any of your deposit, even if you cancel far in advance. It's best to clarify this issue when you make your reservation. If booking by mail, include a stamped, self-addressed envelope with your payment so that the hotel can easily send you a receipt and confirmation.

If you arrive without a reservation, begin your search for a room as early in the day as possible. If you arrive late at night and without a reservation, you may have to take what you can get, often in a price range much higher than you'd like to pay.

San Juan has become a year-round destination, and summers are no longer as tranquil as they used to be. Nonetheless, hotels still have lower occupancy from mid-April to mid-December. Off-season discounts, which can be substantial, are granted at the resort hotels during this slower period.

1 Old San Juan

Old San Juan is 1¹/₂ miles from the beach; choose a hotel here if you're more interested in shopping and attractions than you are in water sports.

EXPENSIVE

✪ El Convento. 100 Cristo St., San Juan, PR 00901. ☎ **800/468-2779** or 787/723-9020. Fax 787/721-2877. www.elconvento.com. E-mail: elconvento@ad.com. 58 units. A/C TV TEL. Winter $315–$375 double; from $500 suite. Off-season $200–$280 double; from $400 suite. AE, DC, DISC, MC, V. No parking available. Bus: Old Town Trolley.

Puerto Rico's most famous hotel had deteriorated into a shabby version of its former self, but it came majestically back to life when it was restored and reopened in 1997. Built in 1651 in the heart of the old city, it was the New World's first Carmelite convent, but over the years it played many roles from a dance hall to a flop house to a parking lot for garbage trucks. It first opened as a hotel in 1962.

Now restored at the cost of around $275,000 per room, El Convento offers one of the most charming and historic hotel experiences anywhere in the Caribbean. There is a concierge-style reception and check-in, and roomy accommodations on the third to fifth floors. The rooms include Spanish-style furnishings, elaborate paneling, and handmade terra-cotta floor tiles. Each unit contains double or twin beds, fitted with comfortable mattresses and fine linen, and such extras as VCRs, stereos, coffeemakers, irons, and ironing boards. The small bathrooms, with combination tubs and showers, contain scales, second phones, and hair dryers. Although the facilities aren't as diverse as those of some resorts on the Condado or in Isla Verde, this hotel's sweeping charm and Old Town location usually compensate.

Dining/Diversions: The lower two floors feature a collection of shops, bars, and restaurants. Breakfast is served in an outdoor garden terrace. There's also a rather sedate small-scale casino.

Amenities: Pool, whirlpool, indoor fitness center, massage

Wyndham Old San Juan Hotel & Casino. 100 Brumbaugh St., San Juan, PR 00901. ☎ **800/996-3426** or 787/721-5100. Fax 787/721-1111. www.wyndham.com. 240 units. A/C TV TEL. Winter $315–$365 double; from $575 suite. Off-season $225–$300 double; from $300 suite. AE, CB, DC, DISC, MC, V. Free parking; valet parking $15. Bus: A7.

Opened in 1997, this dignified nine-story waterfront hotel was conceived as part of a $100 million renovation of San Juan's port facilities. It has an unusual and desirable position between buildings erected by the Spanish monarchs in the 19th century and

Old San Juan Accommodations

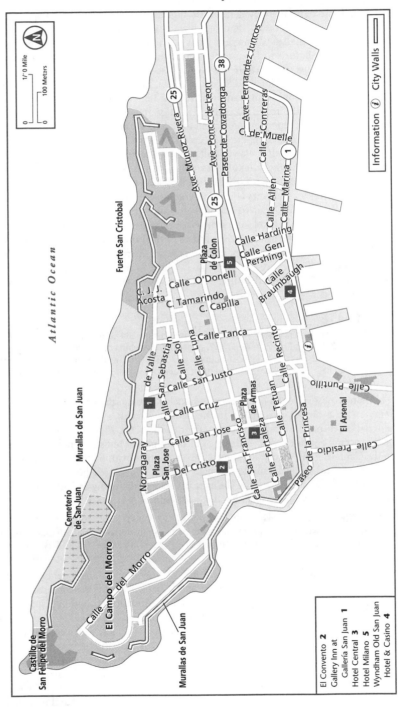

Atlantic Ocean

Fuerte San Cristobal

Castillo de
San Felipe del Morro

Cemeterio
de San Juan

Murallas de San Juan

Calle El Campo del Morro

Calle Campo del Morro

Murallas de San Juan

Norzagaray

Plaza
San Jose

Del Cristo

Calle San Jose

Calle Cruz

de Valle

Calle San Sebastian

Calle Sol

Calle Luna

Calle San Justo

Plaza
de Armas

Calle San Francisco

Calle Fortaleza

Calle Tetuan

C. J. J. Acosta

Calle O'Donell

C. Tamarindo

C. Capilla

Calle Tanca

Calle Harding

Plaza
de Colon

Calle Genl
Pershing

Calle
Braumbaugh

Calle Recinto

Calle

Calle Puntillo

Calle Presidio

El Arsenal

Paseo de la Princesa

Ave. Munoz Rivera

Ave. Ponce de Leon

Paseo de Covadonga

Ave. Fernandez Juncos

C. de Muelle

Calle de Contreras

Calle Allen

Calle Marina

25
25
38
1

5
4
1
3
2

Information ⓘ   City Walls

El Convento **2**
Gallery Inn at
    Galleria San Juan **1**
Hotel Central **3**
Hotel Milano **5**
Wyndham Old San Juan
    Hotel & Casino **4**

1/10 Mile
100 Meters

the city's busiest and most modern cruise-ship terminals. Most of the major cruise ships dock nearby, so this is a good choice if you want to spend time in San Juan before boarding a ship. On days when cruise ships pull into port, the hotel's lobby and bars are likely to be jammed with passengers stretching their legs after a few days at sea. Fortunately, the upper floors are closely attuned to hotel guests.

Although the pastel-colored building is modern, iron railings and exterior detailing convey a sense of colonial San Juan. Its triangular floor plan encircles an inner court-yard that floods light into the tasteful and comfortable bedrooms, each of which has two phone lines and a modem connection for laptop computers. Other than that, the smallish rooms lack character, although each comes with a comfortable mattress and a compact bathroom with a shower stall. Think of a typical Holiday Inn geared for business travelers instead of a luxury resort.

Dining/Diversions: About 80% of the lobby level is devoted to a 10,000-square-foot casino, with slot machines and poker and roulette tables. There's an upscale din-ing room (Restaurant Darseñas) that also functions as the breakfast area; it serves perfectly fine if unremarkable international cuisine with some regional specialties. Evening meals are more intimate than lunches, when the place takes on a somewhat businesslike edge. Two bar/lounges, one with live music, round out the entertainment.

Amenities: Room service (6:30am to 11:30pm), concierge, conference center. A rooftop pool, fully equipped health club, and whirlpool overlook the harbor and cruise-ship docks.

MODERATE

Gallery Inn at Galería San Juan. Calle Norzagaray 204–206, San Juan, PR 00901. ☎ **787/722-1808.** Fax 787/724-7360. www.thegalleryinn.com. E-mail: reservations@ galleryinn.com. 22 units. $145–$350 double; $270–$350 suite. Rates include continental breakfast. AE, MC, V. There are 6 free parking spaces, plus parking on the street. Bus: Old Town Trolley.

This hotel's location and ambience are unbeatable, though the nearest beach is a 15-minute ride away. Set on a hilltop in the Old Town, with a sweeping sea view, this unusual hotel contains a maze of verdant courtyards. In the 1700s, it was the home of an aristocratic Spanish family. Today, it's one of the most whimsically bohemian hotels in the Caribbean. All courtyards and rooms are adorned with hundreds of sculptures, silk screens, and original paintings, usually for sale. We suggest booking one of the least expensive doubles—even the cheapest units are fairly roomy and attractively fur-nished with good beds and small but adequate bathrooms.

Hotel Milano. Calle Fortaleza 307, San Juan, PR 00901. ☎ **787/729-9050.** Fax 787/722-3379. www.home.coqui.net\hmilano. E-mail: hmilano@coqui.net. 30 units. A/C TV TEL. $90–$150 double. Parking $15 per day in a nearby parking lot. AE, MC, V. Bus: Old Town Trolley.

Old Town's newest hotel was created in April 1999 within a 1920s warehouse. You'll enter a wood-sheathed lobby at the lower, less desirable end of Fortaleza Street before ascending to one of the clean, well-lit bedrooms. Despite its location in historic Old Town, there's nothing much charming about this place. The simple, modern rooms have cruise-ship–style decor and unremarkable views. The more expensive accommo-dations contain small refrigerators and jacks for laptop computers.

The building's fifth floor (the elevator goes only to the fourth floor) contains an alfresco Italian and Puerto Rican restaurant, the Panoramic, which has views of San Juan's harbor. It's open Tuesday through Sunday from 11am to 3pm and 6 to 10:30pm (until 11:30pm on Friday and Saturday), although there are more hip and more fash-ionable restaurants nearby, including Fussion (see chapter 5).

INEXPENSIVE

Hotel Central. Calle San José 202, San Juan, PR 00901. ☎ **787/722-2751.** 23 units. $55 double. MC, V. No parking. Bus: A7.

This is one of the most unusual hotels in the historic heart of Old San Juan, but it's definitely not for everyone. Its fans compare it to a rundown hotel that has staggered through revolutions, civil wars, and the changing tides of fashion. In fact, few other hotels on Puerto Rico will give you such a strong sense of nostalgia as will this battered remnant of another time. Originally built in the 1930s, it lies adjacent to the Old Town's plaza de Armas. Although the pleasures and distractions of the city's historic core lie all around, don't expect amenities of any kind in the rooms, which have ceiling fans and minimalist (and rather old) furnishings. Many also have creaky bathrooms. Rooms on the second floor have the tallest ceilings. All units need paint and attention, but in view of the low cost, no one minds living in a bit of a dump. The elevator hauling you upstairs, decoratively speaking, is really a mess. The nearest beach is a 20-minute ride away.

2 Puerta de Tierra

Stay in Puerta de Tierra only if you have a desire to be at either the Caribe Hilton or the Radisson Normandie, because when you stay there, you're sandwiched halfway between Old San Juan and the Condado, but you're not getting the advantages of staying right in the heart of either.

Caribe Hilton. Calle Los Rosales, San Juan, PR 00902. ☎ **800/HILTONS** in the U.S. and Canada or 787/721-0303. Fax 787/725-8849. www.caribehilton.com. E-mail: info@ CaribeHilton. com. 644 units. A/C MINIBAR TV TEL. Winter $320–$750 double. Off-season $230–$340 double. Year-round $450–$1,000 suite. Children 16 and under stay free in parents' room (maximum 4 people per room). AE, CB, DC, DISC, MC, V. Self-parking $10; valet parking $20. Bus: A7.

Because this beachfront hotel was the first Hilton ever built outside the U.S. mainland (in 1949), the Hilton chain considers it the most historically significant property within their organization. In the late 1990s, the chain bought it back from the local entrepreneurs who had been running it, closed it down, and poured rivers of money into an extensive renovation. The result, although not fully operational at press time, is one of the most up-to-date spa and convention hotels in San Juan.

The hotel has the only private beach on the island. And because of its location adjacent to a Spanish colonial fort, the ruinous Fort San Jerónimo, it's the only hotel in Puerto Rico to incorporate an antique naval installation into its gardens. Its large size (17 acres of parks and gardens) and sprawling facilities often attract conventions and tour groups. Only the Condado Plaza and the Hotel El San Juan rival it for nonstop activity. Rooms are housed in any of three separate subsections, ranging in height from 3 to 20 stories. Each was substantially upgraded in the late 1990s, and prices vary according to the amenities in your room and its exposure. Each has a larger-than-expected bathroom and all the modern conveniences you'd expect from a world-class chain.

Dining/Diversions: At press time, only two restaurants were operational, although you can expect about a half dozen after the 2000 renovations are finished. One of the most visible is Morton's of Chicago, a branch of the famous steak house. In the Caribe Terrace Bar, you can order the bartender's celebrated piña colada, once enjoyed by the likes of movie legends Joan Crawford and Errol Flynn. The 12,400-square-foot casino, adjacent to the lobby atrium, is open daily from noon to 4am, and features blackjack, craps, baccarat, roulette, and slot machines.

Amenities: Room service (6am to 1am), laundry/valet, baby-sitting, Spa Caribe, two freshwater swimming pools, health club, aerobics, beach activities, children's playground, playroom, six lighted tennis courts, business center.

Radisson Normandie. Avenida Muñoz-Rivera (at the corner of Calle Los Rasales), San Juan, PR 00902. ☎ **800/333-3333** in the U.S. or 787/729-2929. Fax 787/729-3083. 177 units. A/C TV TEL. Winter $250–$350 double; $550 suite. Off-season $165–$205 double; $450 suite. Rates include continental breakfast. AE, DC, MC, V. Outdoor parking $8. Bus B5, B21.

At press time, this hotel was only partially open because of renovations; it should be fully functional by summer 2000. This write-up is based on what is known at this time.

It isn't as well accessorized as its nearby competitor, the Hilton, but for a clientele of mostly business travelers, it doesn't really matter. The hotel first opened in 1939 and remains one of the purest examples of art deco architecture in Puerto Rico. Originally built for a Parisian cancan dancer by her tycoon husband, the building has a curve-sided design that was inspired by the famous French ocean liner, *Le Normandie.* The gardens are not particularly extensive, and the beach is unexceptional. But several multimillion-dollar renovations, most recently in 2000 after devastation by a 1998 hurricane, have given the place a conservative, vaguely historic charm. Bedrooms are tastefully outfitted. The lobby retains its original art deco zest, soaring upward into an atrium whose centerpiece is a bubbling aquarium.

Dining/Diversions: The hotel's most formal eatery is the Restaurant Normandie. Less elaborate is the Café-Bar Paris. There's a day bar beside the pool.

Amenities: Room service (7am to 11pm daily), hair salon for men and women, laundry, baby-sitting, a limited water-sports program, and a freshwater swimming pool that retains memories of scandalous Jazz Age parties.

3 Condado

This is where you'll find the city's best beaches. Once the Condado area was filled with the residences of the very wealthy, but all that changed with the construction of the Puerto Rico Convention Center. Private villas gave way to high-rise hotel blocks, restaurants, and nightclubs. The Condado shopping area, along Ashford and Magdalena avenues, has an extraordinary number of boutiques. There are good bus connections into Old San Juan, or you can take a taxi.

VERY EXPENSIVE

✪ **Condado Plaza Hotel & Casino.** 999 Ashford Ave., San Juan, PR 00907. ☎ **800/468-8588** in the U.S. or 787/721-1000. Fax 787/721-4613. www.williamshosp.com. 570 units. A/C MINIBAR TV TEL. Winter $340–$490 double; $450–$1,350 suite. Off-season $220–$385 double; $350–$925 suite. AE, CB, DC, DISC, MC, V. Valet parking $15. Bus: A7.

This is one of the busiest hotels on Puerto Rico, with enough facilities, restaurants, and distractions to keep a visitor occupied for weeks. Although not the most intimate of San Juan's hotels, it is the most prominent, set on a strip of beachfront at the beginning of the Condado. It's a favorite of business travelers, tour groups, and conventions, but also attracts independent travelers because of its wide array of amenities. The Hilton is its major rival, but we prefer this hotel's style and flair, especially after its recent $40 million overhaul. The original buff-colored structure is linked by an elevated passageway above Ashford Avenue to its annex, the Laguna Wing, which has its own lobby with direct access from the street.

All units have private terraces and are spacious, bright, and airy, fitted with deluxe beds and mattresses, either king-size or doubles, but most often twins. The good-size bathrooms contain thick towels and hair dryers. The complex's most deluxe section, the Plaza Club, has 80 units (including five duplex suites), a VIP lounge reserved exclusively for the use of its guests, and private check-in/check-out service.

The hotel is owned by the same consortium that owns the somewhat more upscale El San Juan Hotel & Casino (see below). Use of the facilities at one hotel can be charged to a room at the other.

Dining/Diversions: Only the El San Juan Hotel has a more dazzling array of dining options. This place is known for creating charming restaurants with culinary diversity that attract many local residents. The hotel's premier restaurant, a hot ticket on San Juan's dining scene, is Cobia, winner of several culinary awards thanks to its sophisticated blend of Pacific Rim and Caribbean dishes (see chapter 5). Other choices include Mandalay, which blends Chinese cuisine with a sushi bar and teppanyaki tables, and Las Palmas, a spot for warm-weather sandwiches and salads. Tony Roma's is a popular and durable restaurant selling succulent and greasy ribs, fried onions, and barbecue. And if you get hungry in the middle of the night, Max's Grill, adjacent to the casino, is an upscale 24-hour diner serving food like what you'd expect in a New York City deli. After dark, La Fiesta Lounge features live merengue and salsa.

Amenities: 24-hour room service, five pools, water sports, Plaza Spa, fitness center in the Laguna Wing, two lit Laykold tennis courts, fresh towels at beach and pools, laundry.

San Juan Marriott Resort & Stellaris Casino. 1309 Ashford Ave., San Juan, PR 00907. ☎ **800/464-5005** or 787/722-7000. Fax 787/722-6800. www.marriott.com/marriott/ SJUPR. E-mail: sjmarbc@tld.net. 538 units. A/C MINIBAR TV TEL. Winter $325–a$430 double; from $550 suite. Off-season $205 double; from $550 suite. AE, DC, DISC, MC, V. Parking $8. Bus: B21.

This 21-story landmark, next to one of the best beaches in the area, is the tallest building on the Condado. Marriott spent staggering sums to extensively renovate the hotel following a tragic fire in 1989. The current building packs in lots of postmodern style. If there's a flaw, it's the decor of the comfortable but bland bedrooms, with pastel colors that look washed out when compared to the rich mahoganies and jewel tones of the rooms in the rival Condado Plaza Hotel. Nonetheless, the units here boast one of the most advanced telephone networks on the island, carefully maintained security and fire-prevention systems, safes, and in-room VCRs. They're generally spacious, with good views of the water. Extras include two phones with voice mail, plus an iron and ironing board. Bathrooms have hair dryers, shower/tub combinations, and excellent plumbing.

Dining/Diversions: We suggest having only one dinner in-house (at Ristorante Tuscany; see chapter 5), then dining out for the rest of your stay, unless you want just a fresh salad or a sandwich. There's live music in the lobby every evening from 6 to 9pm; two bands perform here Thursday through Saturday from 9pm to 3am. La Vista offers buffet lunches and dinners, and a poolside grill serves tropical drinks, sandwiches, and salads. The Stellaris Casino, which isn't as glitzy as some of its competitors, is next to the main lobby.

Amenities: 24-hour room service, two tennis courts, two pools (whose mosaic bottoms glow luminously when viewed from the hotel's observatory-style 21st floor), a health club with many massage and spa treatments. Concierge, beauty salon, shopping kiosks, tour desk, car-rental facilities.

EXPENSIVE

Radisson Ambassador Plaza Hotel & Casino. 1369 Ashford Ave., San Juan, PR 00907. ☎ **800/468-8512** in the U.S. or 787/721-7300. Fax 787/782-5179. www.radisson.com. 320

units. A/C TV TEL. Winter $245–$275 double; $275–$385 suite. Off-season $220–$250 double; $250–$320 suite. AE, CB, DC, DISC, MC, V. Self-parking $6; valet parking $10. Bus: A7.

At the eastern edge of the Condado, a short walk from the beach, the Ambassador became competitive with its more glamorous neighbors after a local entrepreneur poured $40 million into its restoration in 1990. Since then, it has evolved into a competent but not particularly exciting hotel. What's missing (especially at these prices) are the resort amenities associated with the Hilton, the Condado Plaza, the Ritz-Carlton, and the El San Juan. Nor does this hotel have the sense of whimsy and fun that's so much a part of those dazzling competitors.

Accommodations are in a pair of towers, one of which is devoted to suites. The decor is inspired variously by 18th-century Versailles, 19th-century London, imperial China, and art deco California. However, in spite of the gaudy, glitzy overlay, know that the hotel used to be a Howard Johnson, a fact evident in the relatively small size of the standard rooms. Each unit has pay-per-view movies and a balcony with outdoor furniture. The beds, twins or doubles, are fitted with fine linen and quality mattresses, and the bathrooms have generous shelf space and a combination tub/shower.

Dining/Diversions: La Scala's northern Italian cuisine is the hotel's culinary highlight. The casino (open from 10am to 4am) has more slot machines than any other on the Condado, and a singer/pianist performs from a quiet corner bar. There are two bar/lounges, one with live local dance music.

Amenities: Room service (from 6:30am to 11pm), penthouse-level fitness and health club, beauty salon, rooftop pool, whirlpool, business center, baby-sitting, laundry, 24-hour concierge, VIP floors with extra amenities and enhanced services, a social programmer who offers a changing array of daily activities.

MODERATE

Best Western Hotel Pierre. Av. José de Diego 105, Condado, San Juan, PR 00914. ☎ 800/468-4549 or 787/721-1200. Fax 787/721-3118. 184 units. A/C TV TEL. Winter $136 double. Off-season $129 double. Extra person $15. Children 11 and under stay free in parents' room. Rates include continental breakfast. AE, DC, DISC, MC, V. Free parking. Bus: 22.

The high-rise "Lucky Pierre" has long been one of the San Juan's major bargains. It's 4 blocks from the beach and an easy drive to most major San Juan attractions if you rent a car. It's a small resort, with a large swimming pool and deck in a setting of palm trees. The bedrooms, although hardly grand, have recently been remodeled. Kids are welcome here, and baby-sitting can be arranged. Two restaurants, Metropol and La Petite, are moderately priced and serve a respectable cuisine. On-site services include laundry and valet, a beauty and barbershop, and room service from 5pm to midnight.

Condado Lagoon Days Inn. Calle Clemenceau 6, Condado, San Juan, PR 00907. ☎ 800/858-7407 or 787/721-0171. Fax 787/724-4356. 50 units. A/C TV TEL. Winter $119 double; $125–$150 suite. Off-season $109 double; $125–$150 suite. Rates include continental breakfast. Children 12 and under stay free in parents' room. AE, DC, MC, V. No parking available. Bus: A5.

This family-oriented hotel, remodeled in 1996, rises seven stories above a residential neighborhood across the street from Condado Beach. The accommodations are small and not particularly imaginative in their decor, but usually contain queen-size beds and a small refrigerator. Some rooms have sofas that convert into beds for children. There's a small swimming pool on the premises, a modest coffee shop near the lobby, room service, and maid service. Baby-sitting can be arranged. The bars, restaurants, and facilities of the Condado neighborhood are within walking distance.

Eastern San Juan Accommodations

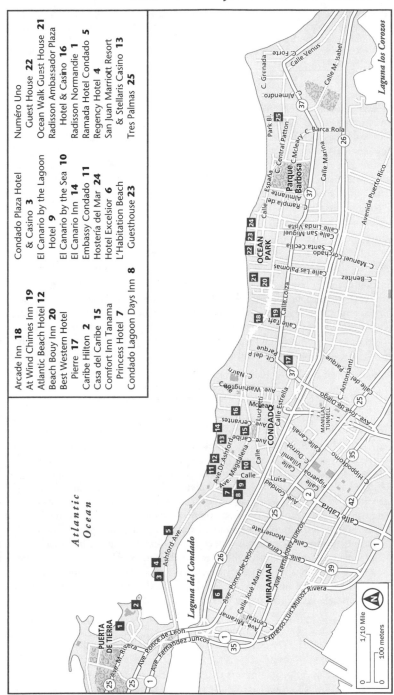

Arcade Inn **18**
At Wind Chimes Inn **19**
Atlantic Beach Hotel **12**
Beach Bouy Inn **20**
Best Western Hotel
  Pierre **17**
Caribe Hilton **2**
Casa del Caribe **15**
Comfort Inn Tanama
  Princess Hotel **7**
Condado Lagoon Days Inn **8**

Condado Plaza Hotel
  & Casino **1**
El Canario by the Lagoon
  Hotel **9**
El Canario by the Sea **10**
El Canario Inn **14**
Embassy Condado **11**
Hostería del Mar **24**
Hotel Excelsior **6**
L'Habitation Beach
  Guesthouse **23**

Numéro Uno
  Guest House **22**
Ocean Walk Guest House **21**
Radisson Ambassador Plaza
  Hotel & Casino **16**
Radisson Normandie **1**
Ramada Hotel Condado **5**
Regency Hotel **4**
San Juan Marriott Resort
  & Stellaris Casino **13**
Tres Palmas **25**

El Canario by the Lagoon Hotel. Calle Clemenceau 4, Condado, San Juan, PR 00907. ☎ **800/533-2649** in the U.S. or 787/722-5058. Fax 787/723-8590. www.canariohotels. com. E-mail: canariopr@aol.com. 40 units. A/C TV TEL. Winter $100–$110 double. Off-season $80–$90 double. Rates include continental breakfast and morning newspaper. AE, DC, DISC, MC, V. No parking available. Bus: B21 or C10.

A relaxing, informal European-style hotel, El Canario is in a quiet residential neighborhood just a short block from Condado Beach. This is one of the better B&Bs in the area, although it still charges affordable rates. The hotel is very much in the Condado style, which evokes Miami Beach in the 1960s. The bedrooms are generous in size and have balconies. Most have twin beds with firm mattresses. Bathrooms are sleek and contemporary, with generous towels and enough space to spread out your stuff. Extra amenities include an in-room safe and a complimentary tropical breakfast and morning newspaper. Free coffee is also available in the lobby. Hotel amenities include a tour desk and a self-service Laundromat; the staff can make arrangements for you to have access to a nearby health club. If the hotel doesn't have room for you, it can book you into its sibling properties, either El Canario Inn or El Canario by the Sea.

Embassy Condado. 1126 Sea View, Condado, San Juan, PR 00907. ☎ **787/725-8284.** Fax 787/725-2400. 14 units. A/C TV. Winter $95–$125 double; $145 suite. Off-season $55–$110 double; $115 suite. Extra person $10–$15. AE, MC, V. No parking available. Bus: A5.

Surrounded by a residential neighborhood, this two-story guesthouse sits on a quiet dead-end street about a block inland from the sands of Condado Beach. It offers a relaxed atmosphere—you could live in a swimsuit or shorts for your entire stay. The all-white bedrooms have rattan furniture and tropical accessories. Each has a kitchenette or access to one. The hotel features a rooftop sundeck with a view directly over the beach, plus a pool and a whirlpool. Maid service is included and baby-sitting can be arranged.

Ramada Hotel Condado. 1045 Ashford Ave., San Juan, PR 00907. ☎ **800/468-2040** or 787/723-8000. Fax 787/722-8230. 98 units. A/C MINIBAR TV TEL. Winter $220 double. Off-season $170 double. AE, DISC, MC, V. Parking $12. Bus: A7 or 21.

This standard hotel is right on the oceanfront in the heart of the Condado section. It lacks the style or facilities of some of its very expensive neighbors, but you can bask in the sun by the pool, have lunch or drinks on the sundeck, and dance the night away to live music in the Polo Lounge. The on-site Restaurant Papaya specializes in many Puerto Rican dishes, including *asopaos* (the local gumbo) often made with shrimp and lobster. A selection of seafood is featured nightly. Shopping, sights, and island nightlife are within walking distance or just a short ride away. The rooms are classified as standard, superior, or deluxe. The deluxe rooms are larger and open onto the beach; the superior rooms are slightly smaller and are on the upper floors overlooking the water. The standard rooms face the busy street and are smaller. All the bathrooms are well maintained and medium in size with adequate shelf space. The price seems rather high for what you get, but you must pay dearly for a beachfront Condado location, even though the shoreline adjacent to the hotel is rocky (head instead for the sandy beach at the Condado Plaza, a 5-minute walk away). Laundry service is available.

Regency Hotel. 1005 Ashford Ave., San Juan, PR 00907. ☎ **800/468-2823** in the U.S. or 787/721-0505. Fax 787/722-2909. 127 units. A/C TV TEL. Winter $185–$225 double; $295 suite. Off-season $145–$170 double; $220 suite. Rates include continental breakfast. AE, DC, MC, V. Parking $5. Bus: A7.

This modest choice occupies prime Condado real estate, although the beach here is approached through an underground parking garage. The generally spacious rooms aren't style-setters by any means, but most are comfortable and clean and are a good value for the tab-happy Condado district. Many are equipped with kitchenettes, and all of the suites contain fully equipped kitchens. Whether you like this hotel or not may depend on your room assignment: all rooms have balconies but not all face the ocean. Although the units are constantly being renovated, some are shabbier than others and of unequal quality. Discuss the rooms in detail with management before making reservations, and if possible, see the room before checking in. On the premises are a bar and the St. Moritz restaurant, a dining enclave with conservatively classic food. Although the hotel has its own small-scale freshwater pool, some guests prefer to do their swimming, gambling, dining, and drinking at the Condado Plaza next door.

INEXPENSIVE

Atlantic Beach Hotel. 1 Calle Vendig, Condado, San Juan PR 00907. ☎ **787/721-6900.** Fax 787/721-6917. 37 units. A/C TV TEL. Year-round $85–$115 double. AE, DC, MC, V. No parking available. Bus: A7.

This is the most famous gay hotel in Puerto Rico. Housed within a five-story sienna-colored building with vaguely art deco styling, the hotel is best known for its ground-floor indoor-outdoor bar—the most visibly gay bar in Puerto Rico. It extends from the hotel lobby onto a wooden deck about 15 feet above the sands of Condado beach. In the late 1990s, the owner—a long-time resident of Puerto Rico originally from the U.S. mainland—extensively upgraded the bedrooms. The units are simple, uncontroversial cubicles with stripped-down but serviceable and clean decor. Some are smaller than others, but few of the short-term guests seem to mind—maybe because the place can have the spirit of a house party. There's a whirlpool on the rooftop; an on-again, off-again, in-house restaurant; and the above-mentioned bar, an especially popular site every Sunday afternoon and evening. The top floor is devoted to a duplex penthouse with a soaring pyramid-shaped ceiling. The space was originally conceived as a disco that thrived throughout the 1970s and early 1980s.

○ **At Wind Chimes Inn.** 1750 Ashford Ave., Condado, San Juan, PR 00911. ☎ **800/ 946-3244** or 787/727-4153. Fax 787/726-5321. 13 units. A/C TV TEL. Winter $65–$95 double. Off-season $55–$85 double. Rates include continental breakfast. AE, DC, DISC, MC, V. Parking $5. Bus: B21 or A7.

This restored and renovated Spanish manor, 1 short block from the beach and 3¹⁄₂ miles from the airport, is one of the best guesthouses on the Condado. Upon entering a tropical patio, you'll find tile tables surrounded by palm trees and bougainvillea. There's plenty of space on the deck and a covered lounge for relaxing, socializing, and eating breakfast. Dozens of decorative wind chimes add melody to the daily breezes. The good-size rooms offer a choice of sizes, beds, and kitchens; all contain ceiling fans and air-conditioning. Beds have firm mattresses and bathrooms, and although small, are efficiently laid out. The inn has recently added a pool.

Casa del Caribe. Calle Caribe 57, San Juan, PR 00907. ☎ **787/722-7139.** Fax 787/725-3995. 13 units. A/C TV TEL. Winter $75–$125 double. Off-season $55–$85 double. Rates include continental breakfast. AE, DISC, MC, V. Parking $5. Bus: B21 or C10.

Don't expect the Ritz, but if you're looking for a bargain on the Condado (that's not on the beach), this is it. Formerly known as Casablanca, this renovated guesthouse was built in the 1940s, later expanded, then totally refurbished in 1995. It's on a shady side street just off Ashford Avenue, behind a wall and garden. A very Puerto Rican ambience has been created, with emphasis on Latin hospitality and comfort. The small but cozy guest rooms have ceiling fans and air-conditioners, and most feature original Puerto Rican art. The bedrooms are most inviting, with firm mattresses and efficiently organized bathrooms. The front porch is a social center for guests. You can also cook out at a barbecue area. The beach is a 2-minute walk away, and the hotel is also within walking distance of some megaresorts with glittering casinos.

Comfort Inn Tanama Princess Hotel. 1 Joffre St., Condado, San Juan, PR 00907. ☎ **888/ 826-2621** in the U.S. or 787/724-4160. Fax 787/724-4160 (same as phone). 113 units. A/C TV TEL. Winter $99 double. Off-season $85 double. Children 12 and under stay free in parents' room. Rates include continental breakfast. AE, DC, DISC, MC, V. Free parking. Bus: T1.

A seven-story white-painted structure, this recently expanded hotel has a desirable Condado location but without the towering prices of the grand resorts along the beach. Tanama is about a 2-minute walk from Condado Beach and is convenient to Old San Juan (a 15-minute drive) and the airport (a 20-minute drive). Most accommodations come with two double beds (ideal for families) and ceiling fans. Many open onto balconies with water views. It's about a 5-minute walk to major casinos at the Condado Plaza and San Juan Marriott hotels (see above). A fairly good restaurant serves a nouvelle cuisine, or you can walk to many nearby restaurants.

El Canario by the Sea. Av. Condado 4, Condado, San Juan, PR 00907. ☎ **787/722-8640.** Fax 787/725-4921. 25 units. A/C TV TEL. Winter $88–$114 double. Off-season $75–$85 double. AE, MC, V. No parking available. Bus: A7.

When compared to its newer and more stylish neighbors, such as the Marriott, this uncomplicated 1950s-era hotel looks almost like a period piece. But that's part of its charm. Come here for an absolute lack of pretension or resort-style services. The hotel's most extensive renovation occurred after Hurricane George (1998) ripped the place apart. Since then, the hotel has done a roaring business with repeat guests looking for something on the Condado that's relatively inexpensive. Cooled by ceiling fans, as well as air-conditioning, bedrooms range in size from small to medium and have a tropical resort aura; bathrooms are small but have adequate shelf space. There's no bar on the premises, and other than breakfast, no meals are served. But the location is midway between the Condado beachfront and the many restaurants of Ashford Avenue, a fact that will never leave a resident hungry.

El Canario Inn. 1317 Ashford Avenue, Condado, San Juan 00907. ☎ **787/722-3861.** Fax 878 787/722-0391. www.canariohotels.com. E-mail: CanarioPR@aol.com 25 units. A/C TV TEL. Winter $99–$114 double. Off-season $75–$85 double. AE, DC, MC, V. No parking available. Bus: C10.

Affiliated with El Canario by the Lagoon Hotel (see above), this little bed-and-breakfast originally built as a private home is one of the best values along the high-priced Condado strip. The location is just 1 block from the beach (you can walk there in your bathing suit). This well-established hotel lies directly on the landmark Ashford Avenue, center of Condado action, and is close to casinos, nightclubs, and many restaurants in all price ranges. Although surrounded by megaresorts, it is but a simple inn, with rather small but comfortable rooms and good maintenance by a helpful staff. You can relax on the hotel's patios or in the whirlpool area, which is surrounded by tropical foliage. There is no elevator.

4 Miramar

Miramar, a residential neighborhood, is very much a part of metropolitan San Juan, and a brisk 30-minute walk will take you where the action is. Regrettably, the beach is at least half a mile away.

Hotel Excelsior. Av. Ponce de León 801, San Juan, PR 00907. ☎ **800/298-4274** or 787/721-7400. Fax 787/723-0068. 140 units. A/C TV TEL. Winter $140–$153 double; $181 suite. Off-season $117–$130 double; $154 suite. Children under 10 stay free in parents' room; cribs free. AE, MC, V. Free parking. Bus: T1.

Handsome accommodations and good service are offered at this family-owned and operated hotel. The bedrooms have been completely refurbished; many have fully equipped kitchenettes, and all have hair dryers, two phones (one in the bathroom), and marble vanities. Included in the rates are shoe shines and transportation to the nearby beach, as well as parking in the underground garage or the adjacent parking lot. This hotel is known for its excellent maintenance and meticulous housekeeping.

The award-winning Augusto's Restaurant is open for lunch noon to 3pm Tuesday through Friday and for dinner 7 to 9:30pm Monday through Saturday; Café Miramar serves breakfast, lunch, and dinner, and is open 7am to 10pm daily. A cocktail lounge, an exercise room, and a beauty shop complete the hotel's facilities. Services include laundry and baby-sitting, plus limited room service.

5 Santurce & Ocean Park

Less fashionable (and a bit less expensive) than their nearest neighbors, Condado (to the west) and Isla Verde (to the east), Santurce and Ocean Park are wedged into a modern, not particularly beautiful neighborhood that's bisected with lots of roaring traffic arteries and commercial enterprises. Lots of sanjuaneros come here to work in the district's many offices and to eat in its many restaurants. Of the two, the coastal subdivision of Ocean Park is a bit more fashionable than landlocked Santurce, but with the beach never more than a 20-minute walk away, few of Santurce's residents seem to mind.

MODERATE

✪ **Hosterlá del Mar.** 1 Tapia St., Ocean Park, Santurce, San Juan, PR 00911. ☎ or fax **787/727-3302.** E-mail: hosteria@caribe.net. 24 units. A/C TV TEL. Winter $150 double; $175 apt. Off-season $98 double; $150 apt. Children 11 and under stay free in parents' room. AE, MC, V. No parking available. Bus: A5.

Lying a few blocks from the Condado casinos and a 3-minute walk from the beach are the white walls of this distinctive landmark. It's located between Isla Verde and Condado in a residential seaside community popular with locals looking for beach action on weekends. The hotel boasts medium-size ocean-view rooms. Those on the second floor have balconies; those on the first floor open onto patios. The guest-room decor is invitingly tropical; there are good beds, ceiling fans, and small but efficient bathrooms. There's no pool, but a full-service restaurant is known for its vegetarian, macrobiotic, and Puerto Rican plates, all freshly made. The place is simple, yet with its own elegance, and the hospitality is warm

L'Habitation Beach Guesthouse. Calle Italia 1957, Ocean Park, San Juan, PR 00911. ☎ **787/727-2499.** Fax 787/727-2599. 10 units. A/C MINIBAR TV. Winter $102–$111 double. Off-season $82–$91 double. Extra person $10. Rates include continental breakfast. AE, DISC, MC, V. Free parking. Bus: T1.

Formerly the Beach House, this small hotel sits on a tranquil tree-lined street with a sandy beach right in its backyard. Located only a few blocks from the Condado, this inn has a laid-back atmosphere. Good-size and well-maintained bedrooms have ceiling fans, comfortable beds, and fairly simple furnishings. The most spacious rooms are numbers 8 and 9, which also open onto ocean views. Chairs and beverage service are provided in a private beach area, and guests can enjoy breakfast alfresco. You can also eat or drink on the breezy patio overlooking the sea. Ask for one of the bar's special margaritas—after two you will feel no pain; after a third, the night is yours.

INEXPENSIVE

Arcade Inn. 8 Taft St., Santurce, Condado, PR 00911. ☎ **787/725-0668.** Fax 787/728-7524. 19 units. A/C TV. Winter $70–$80 double; $100 suite. Off-season $60–$70 double; $90 suite. MC, V. Free parking. Bus: T1 or 2.

The Arcade Inn was originally built as a private home in 1943 and was transformed into a simple hotel in 1948. But it didn't become well known until the late 1960s, when its reasonable rates began to attract families with children and college students traveling in groups. It's a stucco-covered building with vaguely Spanish colonial detailing on a residential street lined with similar structures. The accommodations each contain a small refrigerator and simple, slightly battered furniture. There's no swimming pool and few amenities on-site, but the beach is only a 5-minute walk away.

Beach Buoy Inn. 1853 McLeary, Ocean Park, San Juan, PR 00911. ☎ **800/221-8119** or 787/728-8119. Fax 787/268-0037. 15 units. A/C TV. Winter $65–$77 double; $80 efficiency. Off-season $60–65 double; $70 efficiency. Children 11 and under stay free in parents' room. Rates include continental breakfast. AE, MC, V. Free parking. Bus: A5 or A7.

About a block from the beach, this B&B deserves to be better known. This place is a comfortable, snug nest, and the staff is especially helpful and friendly. Its rooms are not decorated as nicely as those at the At Wind Chimes Inn (see above), but they're clean and decent. The efficiencies have two double beds or two twin beds. All units have color TV with cable, although many guests gather around the large TV in the lounge to watch basketball and football games. Some units have small refrigerators. There's daily maid service and free parking on the premises. It has no restaurant, bar, or pool, but many of these features are available nearby. You can enjoy the complimentary breakfast outdoors on the patio if you wish.

Numéro Uno Guest House. Calle Santa Ana 1, Santurce, San Juan PR 00911. ☎ **787/726-5010.** Fax 787/727-5482. 12 units. A/C TEL. May–Nov $60–$145 double. Dec–Apr $85–$185 double. Extra person $20. Rates include contiental breakfast. AE, DC, MC, V. No parking available. Bus: A5.

As a translation of its name implies, this is the best of the small-scale low-rise guesthouses in Ocean Park. It was originally built in the 1950s within a prestigious residential neighborhood adjacent to the wide sands of Ocean Park Beach. A massive renovation in 1999 transformed the placed into the closest thing in Ocean Park to the kind of stylish boutique hotel that you might find in an upscale California neighborhood. Much of this is thanks to the hardworking owner, Esther Feliciano, who cultivates within her walled compound a verdant garden, replete with splashing fountains, a small swimming pool, and manicured shrubbery and palms. Stylish-looking bedrooms contain white tile floors, wicker or rattan furniture, and comfortable beds and mattresses. Some repeat clients, many of whom are gay, refer to it as their fantasy version of a private villa beside a superb and usually convivial beach. There's a bar and a well-recommended restaurant on the premises. The staff can direct you to water-sports emporiums nearby for virtually any tropical water sport. Whereas it lacks the staggering diversity of the big hotels of the nearby Condado or Isla Verde, some guests value its sense of intimacy and small-scale charm.

Ocean Walk Guest House. 1 Atlantic Place, Ocean Park, San Juan, PR 09911. ☎ **787/728-0855.** Fax 787/728-6434. 45 units. TV. Winter $65–$105 double; $120–$130 suite. Off-season, $45–$75 double; $75–$85 suite. AE, MC, V. No parking available. Bus: A5 or A7.

Small-scale, informal, and congenially battered, this gay-friendly inn is set directly on the beach of Ocean Park. Originally built in the 1930s as an apartment building and converted into a guesthouse in the 1950s, it encompasses four separate concrete buildings, each accessorized with plants, fountains, a tiny swimming pool, and a somewhat inconvenient array of iron security gates. A restaurant, the site's social centerpiece, lies under a sunroof at the edge of the beach. Open to the breezes, it serves three meals a day and an ongoing roster of drinks. Staff is accommodating and friendly, catering to crowds that, although primarily gay, also include an occasional family with small children. Bedrooms are extremely simple, with much-used furniture, high ceilings, and few decorative accessories. The best asset of this place is its beach location; otherwise, expect a congenial summer-camp ambience and battered but serviceable amenities. Some of the rooms, but not all, have air-conditioning. Your host is long-time Puerto Rico resident Jim, a native of Chicago.

Tres Palma. 2212 Ocean Park Blvd., San Juan, PR 09913. ☎ **888/290-2076** in the U.S. or 787/727-4617. Fax 787/727-5434. www.trespalmasinn.com. E-mail: trespalm@coqui.net. 15 units. A/C TV TEL. Winter $69–$160 double. Off-season $59–$140 double. Extra person $15. Rates include continental breakfast. AE, MC, V. No parking available. Bus: A5 or A7.

Across the street from the ocean, this apartment-style guesthouse overlooks the surf. It's one of the best values for those seeking a beach vacation. Recently renovated, the hotel is really more like a B&B, lying between two main tourist destinations, the Condado to the west and Isla Verde to the east. If you don't want to swim in the ocean, try the hotel's pool in a secluded courtyard. You can also relax on the rooftop sundeck while soaking in the whirlpool. The medium-size bedrooms are simply but comfortably furnished, with rather standard motel items. Each guest room has a private entrance, ceiling fan, and most have a small refrigerator. Larger rooms also contain small kitchens.

6 Isla Verde

Beach-bordered Isla Verde is closer to the airport than the Condado and Old San Juan. The hotels here are farther from Old San Juan than those in Miramar, Condado, and Ocean Park. It's a good choice if you don't mind the isolation and want to be near fairly good beaches.

VERY EXPENSIVE

✪ **El San Juan Hotel & Casino.** 6063 Isla Verde Ave., San Juan, PR 00902. ☎ **800/ 468-2818** or 787/791-1000. Fax 787/791-0390. 389 units. A/C MINIBAR TV TEL. Winter $395–$595 double; from $1225 suite. Off-season $285–$480 double; from $975 suite. AE, DC, DISC, MC, V. Self-parking $8; valet parking $13. Bus: A7, M7, or T1.

One of the best hotels in Puerto Rico evokes Havana in its heyday. Built in the 1950s, it has been restored with an infusion of millions—some $80 million in 1997 and 1998 alone. It's a great choice for (well-to-do) families, with more activities for children than any other property on Puerto Rico.

The beachfront hotel is surrounded by 350 palms, century-old banyans, and gardens. Its 700-yard-long sandy beach is the finest in the San Juan area. The hotel's river pool, with its currents, cascades, and lagoons, evokes a jungle stream, and the lobby is the most opulent and memorable in the Caribbean. Entirely sheathed in red marble and hand-carved mahogany paneling, the public rooms stretch on almost endlessly.

The large, well-decorated units have intriguing touches of high-tech; each contains a dressing room, three phones, and a VCR. Bedrooms are the ultimate in luxury in San Juan with private safes and deluxe mattresses on the king or double beds. Bathrooms have all the amenities, from robes to hair dryers to thick towels; a few feature whirlpools. About 150 of the units are designed as comfortable bungalows and are in the outer reaches of the garden. Known as *casitas,* they include Roman tubs, atrium showers, and access to the fern-lined paths of a tropical jungle a few steps away. A 17-story $60 million wing with 120 luxury oceanfront suites was completed late in 1998.

Dining/Diversions: No other hotel in the entire Caribbean offers such a rich diversity of dining options and such high-quality food. Yamato, a Japanese restaurant, is one of the best at the hotel. Good Italian food is served at La Piccola Fontane. La Veranda Restaurant, near the beach, is open 24 hours, serving American and Caribbean food. Or you can promenade down a re-creation of a Hong Kong waterfront to a Chinese restaurant, Back Street Hong Kong. The Palm Restaurant is a branch of the fabled midtown Manhattan steak house. At the new rooftop Ranch Restaurant, you can chow down on barbecued ribs and chicken. Tequila Bar & Grill is known for its Mexican food, mighty margaritas, and sunset views. Finally, the main lobby now sports a trendy Cigar Bar (see "San Juan After Dark" in chapter 6). The in-house casino is open daily from noon to 4am.

Amenities: 24-hour room service, rooftop health club, Penthouse Spa, two pools, water sports, steam room, sauna, tennis court, table tennis, dry cleaning, baby-sitting, massage service. The supervised Kids Klub has daily activities ranging from face painting to swimming lessons—all for children 5 to 12. Scheduled to be finished in 2001 is an underground parking garage, plus four new tennis courts and a pro shop.

Ritz-Carlton San Juan Spa & Casino. 6961 State Rd., #187, Isla Verde, Carolina, PR 00979. ☎ **800/241-3333** or 787/253-1700. Fax 787/253-0700. www.ritzcarlton.com/location/caribbean/55.main.htm. 414 units. A/C MINIBAR TV TEL. Winter $519–$710 double. Off-season $439–$599 double. Suites from $885 year-round. AE, DC, DISC, MC, V. Valet parking $10. Bus: A7, M7, or T1.

Immediately after its opening in the late 1990s, the Ritz-Carlton took its place among the most spectacular deluxe hotels in Puerto Rico. Set on 8 acres of prime beachfront, within a 5-minute drive from the airport, it was designed to appeal to both business travelers and vacationers. Beautifully furnished guest rooms open onto ocean views or the gardens of nearby condos within this elite district. Rooms are very large and include excellent mattresses, fine linen, minibars, and data ports. The bathrooms are exceptionally plush, with stone sheathings, hair dryers, scales, bathrobes, and deluxe personal toiletries. Most contain separate facilities for tubs and showers. The preferred accommodations are in the 9th-floor Ritz-Carlton Club—accessible only by a key-activated elevator—which has a private lounge and personal concierge staff.

Dining/Diversions: The scope and diversity of dining here is second only to the El San Juan Hotel, but as for top-shelf dining facilities, the Ritz Carlton has no equal. The premier venue, the Vineyard Room, is one of the finest in San Juan (see review in chapter 5). The Grill Room with its replica of a Maine schooner and collection of fine antique porcelain, offers alfresco dining and ocean views; it specializes in Caribbean market buffets, but also offers an à la carte menu. The alfresco Ocean Bar and Grill has panoramic views of the beach and ocean, often complemented by a steel band. "The Bar," as it's called, is one of the most elegant drinking areas in the Caribbean. The comfortable and formal-looking Lobby Lounge, also with panoramic ocean views and live entertainment nightly, is especially noted for its afternoon tea. The hotel has the Caribbean's largest casino (see below).

Amenities: The 12,000-square-foot spa, one of the most sophisticated of its kind on Puerto Rico, with facilities that are surpassed only by the Golden Door at El Conquistador, has panoramic ocean views. It offers yoga, fitness programs, aerobics, and

Isla Verde Accommodations & Dining

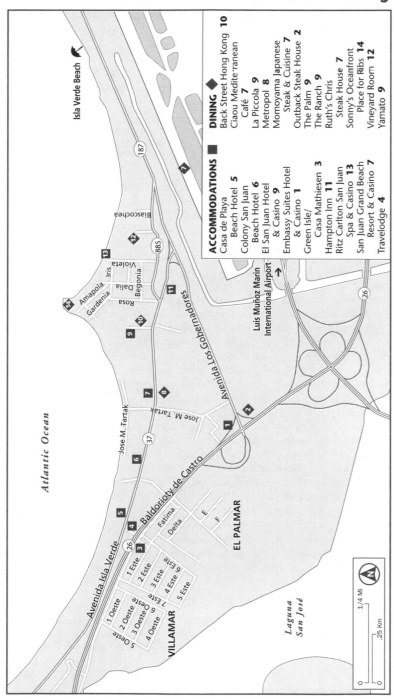

ACCOMMODATIONS ■

Casa de Playa
Beach Hotel **5**
Colony San Juan
Beach Hotel **6**
El San Juan Hotel
& Casino **9**
Embassy Suites Hotel
& Casino **1**
Green Isle/
Casa Mathiesen **3**
Hampton Inn **11**
Ritz Carlton San Juan
Spa & Casino **13**
San Juan Grand Beach
Resort & Casino **7**
Travelodge **4**

DINING ◆

Back Street Hong Kong **10**
Ciaou Mediterranean
Café **7**
La Piccola **9**
Metropol **8**
Momoyama Japanese
Steak & Cuisine **7**
Outback Steak House **2**
The Palm **9**
The Ranch **9**
Ruth's Chris
Steak House **7**
Sonny's Oceanfront
Place for Ribs **14**
Vineyard Room **12**
Yamato **9**

aqua-aerobics in the pool. Upstairs, there are 11 treatment rooms, where a tactful and alert staff offers facials, massages, manicures, pedicures, hydrotherapy, body wraps, and more. Healthful cuisine is available to serious spa-goers, too. Two lit tennis courts, twice-daily maid service, 24-hour room service, laundry service, baby-sitting, beauty salon, programs for children. There's also a 7,200-square-foot swimming pool. Arrangements can be made for golf, snorkeling, fishing, waterskiing, sailing, and horseback riding.

San Juan Grand Beach Resort & Casino. 187 Isla Verde Ave., Isla Verde, PR 00979. ☎ **800/443-2009** in the U.S. or 787/791-6100. Fax 787/791-8525. www.sjgrand.com. E-mail: sjgrand@coqui.net. 400 units. A/C TV TEL. Winter $325–$485 double; from $600 suite. Off-season $225–$395 double; from $445 suite. AE, DC, DISC, MC, V. Self-parking $8; valet parking $12. Bus: T1.

Opening right onto the sands of the beach, this 14-story hotel scalloped with half-moon balconies is today a formidable rival of the El San Juan Hotel next door. The Grand doesn't have the elaborate setting of the El San Juan, but it offers better service and maintenance. It benefited from a $15.2 million renovation, and carries under-stated luxury to a high level in both its public and private rooms. The hotel offers miles of public space and first-rate restaurants, enough attractions to keep many guests on site during most of their vacation. The staff goes all out to spoil you, and, although the place attracts high rollers to its casino, gambling is just one of the many activities here. Families are made to feel at home. It's a safe haven as security is the tightest on the beach, and guests feel sheltered in an all-encompassing womb.

Most of the comfortable, medium-size rooms have balconies and terraces, and taste-ful furnishings with a lot of pizzazz. All units have the same amenities but are priced differently based on exposure, the most expensive being on the top floor, even though they lack balconies. Extras include coffeemakers, second phones, irons and ironing boards, luxury beds with deluxe mattresses, and fine linen. Bathrooms have power showerheads, deep tubs, hair dryers, and scales. The most desirable units are in the Plaza Club, a minihotel within the hotel that sports a private entrance, concierge ser-vice, complimentary food and beverage buffets, and suite/spa and beach facilities.

Dining/Diversions: Dining within any of this hotel's five restaurants merits atten-tion. In fact, Giuseppe offers some of the beachfront's best northern Italian food, and Ruth's Chris Steak House serves the juiciest steaks in Puerto Rico. On the boardwalk, our personal favorite, Ciao, offers breakfast and light Mediterranean fare. In the lobby area is a teppanyaki and sushi bar. At the Grand Market buffet, you can buy a picnic basket for a day on the beach. The in-house nightclub offers revue-style spoofs of Hol-lywood legends and glittery, Vegas-inspired shows. The casino is also popular.

Amenities: The resort boasts the Caribbean's largest free-form swimming pool, complete with waterfalls, rockscapes, and a swim-up bar. Room service (6am to 2pm and 5pm to 2am), baby-sitting, laundry, limousine service, massage service, business center, scuba diving.

EXPENSIVE

Colony San Juan Beach Hotel. 2 Jose M. Tartak St., Isla Verde, Carolina, PR 00979. ☎ **888/265-6699** or 787/253-0100. Fax 787/253-0220. 83 units. A/C MINIBAR TV TEL. Winter $199–$282 double; $455 suite. Off-season $155–$199 double; $365 suite. AE, DC, DISC, MC, V. Self-parking free, valet parking $8. Bus: T1.

This well-designed branch of a Pittsburgh-based hotel chain opened in 1997, just across a quiet one-way street from the beach of Isla Verde and about 2 blocks from the gambling and nightlife facilities of some of Puerto Rico's most expensive hotels. In comparison, holidaymakers pay relatively reasonable rates here for comfortable

---

ⓘ Family-Friendly Accommodations

Caribe Hilton *(see p. 73)*   Children under 16 stay free in their parents' room at this deluxe hotel, which has two swimming pools and is situated in a 17-acre tropical park.

El San Juan Hotel & Casino *(see p. 83)*   This hotel, although expensive, offers more programs for children than any other hotel on Puerto Rico. Its supervised Kids Klub provides daily activities—ranging from face painting to swimming lessons—for children 5 to 12 years of age.

Hampton Inn *(see below)*   For families seeking the kind of lodging values found on the mainland, this new hotel is highly desirable, as many of its rooms have two double beds. There's also a beautiful swimming pool in a tropical setting. Suites have microwaves and refrigerators.

---

accommodations. The Colony features its own outdoor swimming pool, snack bar, and health club on its uppermost (10th) floor, as well as a pizzeria and a more upscale Italian trattoria (Maxim's) adjacent to its lobby. Well-furnished, moderate-size bedrooms contain safes for valuables and Nintendo games on their TVs. Some have balconies and more than half enjoy sea views.

Embassy Suites Hotel & Casino. 8000 Jose M. Tartak St., Isla Verde, Carolina, San Juan, PR 00979. ☎ **800/362-2779** or 787/791-0505. Fax 787/791-0555. 300 suites. A/C MINIBAR TV TEL. Winter $295–$350 1-bedroom suite; $550 2-bedroom suite; $700 presidential suite. Off-season $180 1-bedroom suite; $300 2-bedroom suite; $500 presidential suite. Rates include breakfast. AE, DC, MC, V. Self-parking $6; valet parking $10. Bus: T1.

The location is 2 blocks from the beach, and the hotel has its own water world, with waterfalls and reflecting ponds set against a backdrop of palms. As you enter, you're greeted with an aquarium, giving a tropical resort aura to the place. The suites are excellent, comfortably furnished, and roomy, with bedrooms separated from the living rooms. They also contain wet bars, a combination shower and tub bath, two phones, private safes, and dining tables. The most spacious suites are those with two double beds; otherwise, the units are furnished with king-size beds, and these latter accommodations are smaller. The best view of the water is from units above the third floor.

There is a swimming pool and a fitness center. Bedrooms contain cooking facilities with at least a refrigerator, microwave, and coffeemaker. You'll find a business center on the premises, and two restaurants, including the Embassy Grille, a low-key indoor/outdoor affair, and an independently managed Outback Steakhouse branch (see review in chapter 5). There's also a small-scale casino on the property.

MODERATE

Hampton Inn. 6530 Isla Verde Road., Isla Verde, Carolina, San Juan, PR 00979. ☎ **800/HAMPTON** or 787/791-8777. Fax 787/791-8575. 200 units. A/C TV TEL. Winter $164–$174 double; $184–$204 suite. Off-season $135–$145 double; $155–$175 suite. AE, MC, V. Free parking. Bus: T1.

Opened late in 1997, this chain hotel is set across the busy avenue from Isla Verde's sandy beachfront, far enough away to keep costs down but within a leisurely 10-minute walk to the casinos and nightlife. Two beige-painted towers, with four and five floors, hold the simple, clean, and comfortable bedrooms. There's no restaurant on the premises, no real garden, and other than a whirlpool and a swimming pool with a swim-up bar, very few facilities or amenities. Because of its reasonable prices and location, however, this Isla Verde newcomer could be a good choice.

Travelodge. Av. Isla Verde (P.O. Box 6007, Loiza Station), Santurce, San Juan, PR 00914. ☎ **800/578-7878** or 787/727-1300. Fax 787/727-7150. 92 units. A/C TV TEL. Winter $135 double; $175 suite. Off-season $93 double; $150 suite. AE, MC. No parking available. Bus: T1.

Rising eight stories above the busy traffic of Isla Verde, this chain hotel offers comfortable but small bedrooms furnished simply with bland, modern furniture. They're done in typical motel style, with small but serviceable bathrooms. Many guests carry a tote bag to the beach across the street, then hit the bars and restaurants of the expensive hotels nearby. There's only one restaurant (the Country Kitchen), one pool, and one bar (the Escort Lounge), which features live dance music every Wednesday through Saturday nights. In 1997, about a third of the hotel's rooms were renovated; more are set to be spruced up. Though it's simple and not very personal, this is a good choice for the money.

INEXPENSIVE

Casa de Playa Beach Hotel. 86 Isla Verde Ave., San Juan, PR 09979. ☎ **800/916-2272** or 8787/728-9779. Fax 787/727-1334. 21 units. A/C TV TEL. Winter $105 double; $160 suite. Off-season $80 double; $115 suite. Children 9 and under stay free in parents' room. Rates include continental breakfast. AE, DC, DISC, MC, V. No parking available. Bus: B21 or C10.

Jutting out over the sand on the mile-long Isla Verde beach, this bargain oasis is a find. If you're less interested in being in the center of San Juan than you are in spending time on the beach, check out this modest choice. The hotel consists of two 2-story peach-colored buildings, with a porch around the second floor and a small garden in front. Some rooms have small refrigerators. Furnishings are a bit modest and functional but comfortable nonetheless, with much-used but still firm mattresses. Rooms open onto tidily maintained, small bathrooms. Standard but inexpensive Italian food is served at a beach bar and restaurant, Fredo's. The staff will try to arrange babysitting. The hotel doesn't have everything—no pool, no room service—but the price is hard to beat in Isla Verde.

Green Isle/Casa Mathiesen. 36 Calle Uno, Villamar, Isla Verde, Pr 00979. ☎ **800/677-8860** or 787/726-8662. Fax 787/268-2415. 45 units. A/C TV TEL. Winter $97 double. Off-season $72 double. AE, MC, V. No parking available. Bus: A5.

Small, unassuming, and subject to the roar of the nearby traffic, this hotel stands across the busy avenue from the larger and much more expensive San Juan Grand Beach Resort & Casino. Each of the simple, low-slung accommodations contains its own kitchenette and simple, summery furniture. There are two small swimming pools, although most residents prefer to swim in the sea—the beach is a 5-minute walk. Dozens of cheap fast-food joints are nearby.

Where to Dine in San Juan

5

San Juan has the widest array of restaurants in the Caribbean. You can enjoy fine continental, American, Italian, Chinese, Mexican, and Japanese cuisines, to name a few. In recent years, many restaurants have shown a greater appreciation for traditional Puerto Rican cooking, and local specialties now appear on the menus of leading restaurants. Whenever possible, many chefs enhance their dishes with native ingredients.

Before searching for a restaurant, you should review "Puerto Rico's Exotic Bill of Fare" in appendix A.

Many of San Juan's best restaurants are in the resort hotels along the Condado and at Isla Verde. There has been a restaurant explosion in San Juan in the past few years, but many of the newer ones are off-the-beaten tourist path, and some have not yet achieved the quality found at many of the older, more traditional restaurants.

Local seafood is generally in plentiful supply, but no restaurant guarantees that it will have fresh fish every night, especially during winter when the sea can be too turbulent for local fishermen. In those cases, the chef has to rely on fresh or frozen fish flown in from Miami. If you want fresh fish caught in Puerto Rican waters, ask your waiter about the "catch of the day." Make sure he or she can guarantee that the fish was recently caught rather than resting for a while in the icebox.

Puerto Rico is ideal for picnicking year-round. The best place to fill a picnic basket is the **Repostería Kassalta** (see "Santurce & Ocean Park" below). Puerto Rican families often come to this cafeteria/bakery/deli to order delicacies for their Sunday outings.

The best places for a picnic are **Muñoz Marín Park,** along Las Américas Expressway, west of Avenida Piñero, and the **Botanical Gardens,** operated by the University of Puerto Rico in the Río Piedras section.

1 Best Bets

- **Best Wine List:** The luxurious **Vineyard Room** in the dazzling new Ritz-Carlton, 6961 State Road #187, Isla Verde (☎ 787/253-1700), holds forth with a refined California/Mediterranean cuisine. Some of its recipes have never been served in Puerto Rico before. Begin perhaps with cream of frog's leg soup flavored with sweet garlic petals, and go on to slow-roasted veal cheek with two types of beans. Desserts are as sumptuous as the setting. The Vineyard Room offers one of the island's finest wine lists.

- **Best Old Town Chef:** Acclaimed as one of Puerto Rico's finest chefs, Marisoll Hernández presides over **Chef Marisoll,** Calle del Cristo 202 (☎ 787/ 725-7454). *Gourmet* magazine—and some of the most savvy foodies in San Juan's Old Town—loves her imaginative dishes. She even makes soup aficionados out of those who usually aren't. Try her cream of exotic wild mushroom soup with an essence of black truffles or her butternut squash soup with crisp ginger.
- **Best Classic French Cuisine:** If you like classic French food, then head to **La Chaumière,** Calle Tetuán 367 (☎ 787/722-3330), in San Juan's Old Town. In back of the Tapía Theater, this two-story restaurant is intimate and inviting. The cuisine follows time-tested recipes of which Escoffier might have approved: onion soup, oysters Rockefeller, scallops Provençal, and a perfectly prepared rack of baby lamb Provençal.
- **Best Nuevo Latino Cuisine:** The **Parrot Club,** Calle Fortaleza 363 (☎ 787/ 725-7370), wows Old Town taste buds with its modern interpretation of Puerto Rican specialties. Even San Juan's mayor and the governor have made it their favorite. Husband-and-wife team Emilio Figueroa and Gigi Zafero not only borrow from a repertoire of Puerto Rican and Spanish recipes but even use Taíno and African influences in their cuisine. Their ceviche is the best in town, and their Créole-style flank steak is worth the trek from Condado Beach.
- **Best Japanese & Best Sushi Restaurant:** In San Juan's Old Town, **Yukiyú,** Calle Recinto Sur 311 (☎ 787/721-0653), pioneered a style of Japanese and Asian cuisine unfamiliar here. Locals learned to eat raw fish (sushi), and a few have even become addicted. Other than its sushi bar—acclaimed as the best in the Caribbean—a wide array of Japanese- and Asian-inspired dishes are available, including a delectable yellowfin tuna with teriyaki.
- **Best Burgers:** Patrons freely admit that **El Patio de Sam,** Calle San Sebastián 102 (☎ 787/723-1149), is not always on target with its main dishes. But they do agree on one thing: the hamburgers are the juiciest and most delectable in San Juan. The black-bean soup isn't bad either. The Old Town atmosphere is also intriguing—you almost expect to encounter Bogie and Bacall.
- **Best Asopao:** Soul food to Puerto Ricans, *asopao* is the regional gumbo made in as many different ways as there are chefs on the island. Some versions are too thick to be called soup, such as the seafood variety at **La Bombonera,** Calle San Francisco 259 (☎ 787/722-0658), in San Juan's Old Town, which is more like a stew. Another popular version of asopao includes pigeon peas, although the one with chicken is better known.
- **Best Creole Cuisine:** You'd have to go all the way to Madrid to find Spanish food as well prepared as it is at **Ramiro's,** Av. Magdalena 1106 (☎ 787/721-9049). The chefs take full advantage of fresh island produce to create an innovative cuisine. In fact, the style is New Créole, although its roots are firmly planted in Spain. Their fresh fish and char-grilled meats are succulent, and any dessert with their strawberry-and-guava sauce is a sure palate pleaser.
- **Best Local Cuisine:** Devoted to *la cocina criolla,* the term for the often starchy local cuisine, **Ajili Mójili,** 1052 Ashford Ave. (☎ 787/725-9195), features food that islanders might have enjoyed in their mama's kitchen. Try such specialties as *mofongos* (green plantains stuffed with veal, chicken, shrimp, or pork) or the most classic *arroz con pollo* (stewed chicken with saffron rice) in town.
- **Best Hotel Restaurant:** We concur with *San Juan City Magazine,* which hailed **Ristorante Tuscany** in the San Juan Marriott Resort, 1309 Ashford Ave. (☎ 787/722-7000), as the best hotel restaurant of 1997. Its standards continue to be maintained. The chef searches the markets for some of the best and freshest

ingredients to whip into succulent northern Italian cuisine that is smooth and refined to the palate. Some diners visit just to sample the gourmet pizzas from a wood-burning oven.

- **Best Italian Restaurant:** In El San Juan Hotel & Casino, **La Piccola Fontana,** 6063 Isla Verde Ave. (☎ 787/791-0966), takes you on a culinary tour of sunny Italy. Plate after plate of delectable northern Italian food is presented nightly—everything from grilled fillets of fresh fish to succulent pastas. Service is first-rate, the welcome warm.
- **Best View, Best Alfresco & Best Ribs:** It may seem like a lot of bests, but **Sonny's Oceanfront Place for Ribs,** in the Empress Oceanfront Hotel, 2 Amapola St. in Isla Verde (☎ 787/791-3083), delivers on all counts. Ribs are always tender, cooked to perfection, and flavored with savory sauces. The alfresco terrace overlooks the twinkling lights along the Isla Verde and Condado coastlines.
- **Best Late-Night Dining:** If you have hunger pangs late at night, forget the fast-food joints and head to **Amadeus,** Calle San Sebastián 106 in Old San Juan (☎ 787/722-8635). It offers Caribbean ingredients deftly handled with a nouvelle twist. And it does so Tuesday through Sunday until 2am. An attractive, trendy, generally young crowd arrives late to feast on the refined cuisine, enjoying such delights as Cajun-grilled mahimahi.
- **Best Family Meals:** Out in Isla Verde, **Ciaou Mediterranean Café,** in the San Juan Grand Beach Resort & Casino, 187 Isla Grande Ave. (☎ 787/791-5000), offers an excellent and reasonably priced menu. Many tables are placed on a private boardwalk adjacent to the beach. Pizza and pasta are enduringly favorite dishes here, although you can choose from a large selection of other Mediterranean fare.
- **Best Pizza:** At **Via Appia,** 1350 Ashford Ave. (☎ 787/725-8711), you'll think you're back in Italy rather than on the Condado. Try the special: a delectable blend of sausages, onions, mushrooms, pepperoni, green pepper, and bubbling cheese. Or sample a pizza with meatballs or one with vegetarian ingredients.
- **Best Sunday Brunch:** Both locals and American visitors flock to the **Caribe Hilton,** Calle Los Rosales (☎ 787/721-0303), for its delectable all-you-can-eat Sunday brunch. Good food, glamour, and live music are combined here. The freshly prepared seafood alone is worth the set price, which includes champagne.
- **Best Aphrodisiac Cuisine:** Take someone special to **Ostra Cosa,** 154 Calle Cristo (☎ 787/722-2672), for a night of romance. Even if you aren't in mood, the owner promises that you will be after consuming his dishes, which are "chock full of aphrodisiacs." All the food is guaranteed to enhance your performance in the bedroom.
- **Best Ice Cream:** On a cobble-covered street in Old San Juan, **Ben & Jerry's,** Calle del Cristo 61 (☎ 787/723-6313), is a block from the landmark cathedral, Catedral de San Juan, across from the entrance to the El Convento Hotel. This North American chain offers the best ice cream in San Juan. Any of the 32 flavors—10 of them low-fat—taste particularly good on hot steamy days, when their names, such as Chubby Hubby and Phish Food (the chocolate chunks are shaped like fish), seem especially ironic and/or flavorful, depending on your point of view. Servings cost $3 to $5, depending on size.
- **Best Drinks:** Even when we're in San Juan waiting for plane connections and have time available, we take a taxi to **Maria's,** Calle del Cristo 204 (☎ 787/721-1678), in Old San Juan, for the coolest and most original drinks in the city. More fresh fruit is consumed here every 5 minutes than Carmen Miranda ever wore on her hat. On a hot day, there is no finer place to enjoy a mixed-fruit frappé; a banana, pineapple, or chocolate frost; or an orange, papaya, or lime freeze. See chapter 6.

2 Old San Juan

VERY EXPENSIVE

❂ **Chef Marisoll.** Calle del Cristo 202. ☎ **787/725-7454.** Reservations required. Main courses $24–$32. AE, MC, V. Tues–Sat noon–2:30pm; Tues–Sun 7–10:30pm. Bus: A7, T1, or 2. CONTEMPORARY.

Marisoll Hernández is one of the top chefs of Puerto Rico. Trained in Hilton properties, including one in London, she broke away to become a restaurateur in the Old Town of San Juan. In a Spanish colonial building, with a courtyard patio for dining, her eight-table restaurant is warm and intimate. Service is low-key and slightly formal, though a bit distracted. Two of her soups were recognized by *Gourmet* magazine, including a cream of exotic wild mushrooms with an essence of black truffles and a butternut squash with crisp ginger. Caesar salads might appear garnished with duck or lobster. There's usually a catch of the day, such as dorado with a medley of sauces— whatever strikes the chef's fancy. You can also sample her risotto with shrimp, lobster, and scallops in a saffron sauce. A truly elegant and beautifully flavored tenderloin with foie gras is another specialty.

EXPENSIVE

Fussion. 327 Fortaleza. ☎ **787/721-7997.** Reservations recommended. Main-course pizza and pastas $9–$15. Fish and meat platters $19–$24. AE, MC, V. Mon–Sat 11am–3pm and 6–11:30pm, Sun 11am–4pm. Bus: Old Town Trolley. FRANCO-LATINO.

The best representative of the hip urban restaurants cropping up in Old Town, Fussion has the kind of allure you'd expect in Manhattan's Soho or Miami's South Beach. Designed to compete directly with the neighboring Parrot Club, this high-ceilinged space showcases an airy colonial building to its best advantage, thanks to oversized paintings by Puerto Rican luminary Carlos Davila Rinaldi and an animated bar crowd, composed of the young, the restless, and the emotionally unattached. The aim here is to provide sophisticated, fusion-style cuisine in a format familiar to urban hipsters. Menu items include ahi tuna–stuffed spring rolls; poached Anjou pears with cabrales cheese served with mesclun leaves and walnut-flavored vinaigrette; and a quirky but appealing roster of pizzas topped with duck meat, salmon, three kinds of cheeses, or vegetarian selections. Delectable entrees include mahimahi and red snapper with cucumber couscous and reductions of both red peppers and cilantro; fillets of cod wrapped in prosciutto; and a traditional version of roasted rack of lamb with mint sauce. Look for live music every Wednesday night beginning at 9pm.

Il Perugino. Calle del Cristo 105. ☎ **787/722-5481.** Reservations required. Main courses $23–$31. AE, MC, V. Daily 6:30–11pm. Bus: A7, T1, or 2. TUSCAN/UMBRIAN.

This is one of the most elegant Italian restaurants in San Juan, with a courtyard containing covered tables. It's located in a 270-year-old town house, a short walk uphill from Catedral de San Juan. The entrance is filled with dozens of photographs of owner/chef Franco Seccarelli with friends and well-known patrons, the most notable being Pavarotti. The space is painted in shades of ochre and umber, reminiscent of Perugia, Seccarelli's homeland. Dishes and flavors are perfectly balanced. Examples include shrimp salad (usually a mundane dish, but quite special here), scallop salad, perfectly marinated fresh salmon, veal entrecôte with mushrooms, and medallions of beef flavored with balsamic vinegar. In season, there's an emphasis on black and white truffles, although these ingredients can raise the dish price substantially. Want something adventurous? Try the black pasta with crayfish and baby eels.

◐ La Chaumière. Calle Tetuán 367. ☎ **787/722-3330.** Reservations required. Main courses $25–$28.50. AE, DC, MC, V. Mon–Sat 6pm–midnight. Closed July–Aug. Bus: Old Town Trolley. CLASSIC FRENCH.

The classic cuisine here has a loyal following of foodies. Just steps from the famous Tapia Theater, this restaurant has a cafe-style decor in a greenhouse setting. You might begin with a Marseilles-style fish soup or a hearty country pâté, then follow with a perfectly prepared rack of baby lamb Provençal, filet mignon with béarnaise sauce, magret of duckling, or Dover sole meunière. Or you might choose the tender chateaubriand for two. Old standbys include chitterling sausage with red wine sauce, veal Oscar, and oysters Rockefeller.

◑ Parrot Club. Calle Fortaleza 363. ☎ **787/725-7370.** Reservations not accepted. Main courses $9–$16 lunch, $9–$16 brunch, $16–$24 dinner. MC, V. Tues–Sun 11:30am–3pm and 6–11pm (until midnight Fri–Sat). Closed 2 weeks in July. Bus: A7, T1, or 2. MODERN PUERTO RICAN.

The hottest restaurant in Old San Juan is this bistro and bar serving a Nuevo Latino cuisine that blends traditional Puerto Rican cooking with Spanish, Taíno, and African influences, heightened by rich, contemporary touches. It's set in a neighborhood known as SOFO (South of Fortaleza Street), within a stately looking 1902 building that was originally a hair-tonic factory. Today, you'll find a cheerful-looking dining room, where you can sometimes spot Puerto Rico's governor or San Juan's mayor, and a verdant courtyard with tables for at least 200 diners scattered amid potted ferns, palms, and orchids. Live music, either Brazilian, salsa, or Latino jazz, is offered every weeknight and during the popular Sunday brunches.

Menu items are updated interpretations of old-fashioned Puerto Rican specialties. They include ceviche of halibut, salmon, tuna, and mahimahi marinated in lime juice and seasonings; delicious crab cakes; *criolla*-style flank steak; and pan-seared tuna served with a sauce made from dark rum and essence of oranges. Everybody's favorite drink is parrot passion, made from lemon-flavored rum, triple sec, oranges, and passion fruit.

◑ Yukiyú. Calle Recinto Sur 311. ☎ **787/721-0653.** Reservations recommended. Main courses $19.95–$34.95; fixed-price teppanyaki dinners $29.95–$38.95; sushi $2.95–$3.95 per piece. AE, DISC, MC, V. Mon–Fri noon–2:20pm and 5–11pm, Sat noon–2:20pm and 7–11pm; Sun 3:30–9pm. Bus: A7, T1, or 2. JAPANESE.

Traditional Japanese and other Asian cooking techniques are combined in this Old Town restaurant. Tabs can mount quickly at the sushi bar, acclaimed as the best in the Caribbean. Sushi is available at both lunch and dinner, but the teppanyaki grill at the front, where your own personal chef cooks your meal, is open only at dinner. The dining room itself is postmodern and monochromatic.

Against this backdrop, the various chefs tempt you with hibachi chicken or chicken with scallops and sesame seeds. You might begin with miso soup or steamed pork dumplings, then go on to a shrimp-and-vegetable tempura, or perhaps fillet of sole with capers. Fresh yellowfin tuna with teriyaki is a favorite, as is New York sirloin in teriyaki sauce.

MODERATE

Al Dente. Calle Recinto Sur 309. ☎ **787/723-7303.** Reservations recommended. Main courses $14–$18. AE, MC, V. Mon–Fri noon–2:30pm and 5–11pm, Sat noon–11pm. Bus: A7, T1, or 2. SICILIAN.

Located in the heart of Old San Juan, this unpretentious and well-established restaurant has a decor that evokes a trattoria in Palermo. Both the dress code and the

---

Take a Strong Coffee Break

A coffee break in Old San Juan might last an afternoon. *Taza* (cup) after *taza* of Puerto Rico's rich brew might make you desert Jamaican Blue Mountain coffee or Hawaiian Kona forever. By law, Puerto Rican coffeehouses must serve coffee made from homegrown beans, most often from the mountains in the center of the island.

For years we've taken our espresso—from early morning until our final "nightcap"—at **Cuatro Estaciones,** a rather ugly and completely nondescript kiosk at the end of the bustling Plaza de Armas (see the walking tour in chapter 6). You'll get a quick jolt from this tasty brew, which attracts local java heads day and night.

---

ambiance are relaxed and casual. You might sample the scallops on a bed of spinach sautéed in cream, or gnocchi with pesto, fettuccine maestro, ravioli (cheese or shrimp versions), or well-seasoned calamari. The chef also makes his own desserts, including cheesecake, tiramisu, and chocolate tortes. Nearly all dishes are genuinely satisfying, and the restaurant delivers quality food at a reasonable price. Brochettes of fresh tuna laced with pepper and Mediterranean herbs is an excellent choice.

✪ **Amadeus.** Calle San Sebastián 106 (across from the Iglesia de San José). ☎ **787/ 722-8635.** Reservations recommended. Main courses $10–$26. AE, MC, V. Mon 6pm–2am, Tues–Sun noon–2am (kitchen closes at midnight). Bus: M2, M3, or T1. CARIBBEAN.

Housed in a brick-and-stone building constructed in the 18th century by a wealthy merchant, Amadeus offers Caribbean ingredients with a nouvelle twist. The appetizers alone are worth the trip, especially the Amadeus dumplings with guava sauce and arrowroot fritters. The chef will even prepare a smoked salmon and caviar pizza. While receiving cordial service, you can enjoy dishes *de la tierra* (from the land) or *del mar* (from the sea), including a catch of the day. One zesty specialty is pork scallopini with sweet-and-sour sauce.

Amanda's Café. 424 Norzagaray. ☎ **787/722-0187.** Reservations not necessary. Main courses $10.75–$20. AE, MC, V. Thurs–Tues noon–1:30am. Bus: Old Town Trolley. MEXICAN.

The color scheme of turquoise and hot pink is appealingly garish. But if you're feeling a bit reckless after too many hours of shopping in Old San Juan, the earthiness might be just what you need. Come here for a sidewalk table and colorful daiquiris, which might make a continued exploration of Old Town seem beside the point. Food is presented as something of an afterthought to the drinks. The menu includes belly-busting platters of Mexican staples, as well as shrimp with garlic, stuffed chiles with tacos, a daily fish platter, and enchiladas (the Swiss version with peanuts and raisins is intriguing).

Café Zaguán. 359 Calle Tetuán at the Plaza Arturo Sotohano. ☎ **787/724-3359.** Reservations recommended for dinner on Fri–Sat; otherwise, not necessary. Lunch sandwiches and salads $3–$6; dinner main courses $15–$32. AE, MC, V. Mon–Sat 9:30am–4pm and 6–11pm, Sun 10am–6pm. Bus: Old Town Trolley. INTERNATIONAL.

A confusing thing about this restaurant is the layout of the long and narrow space—you won't know where you want to sit. New Jersey–born owners Billy and Diana Karmazyn have created a catch-all eatery that combines aspects of an indoor-outdoor cafe, a take-away sandwich shop, and a venue that becomes more formal after 6pm. Lunch features simple dishes such as club sandwiches, stir-fried tofu, and salads. Dinners,

Old San Juan Dining

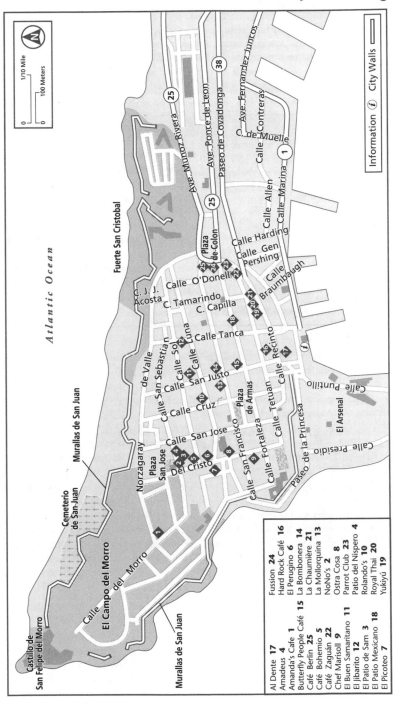

Atlantic Ocean

Fuerte San Cristóbal

Castillo de
San Felipe del Morro

Cemeterio
de San-Juan

Murallas de San Juan

El Campo del Morro

Calle del Morro

Murallas de San Juan

Murallas de San-Juan

Ave. Muñoz Rivera
Ave. Ponce de León
Paseo de Covadonga
Ave. Fernández Juncos

C. de Muelle
Calle de Contreras
Calle Marina

Calle Allen
Calle Harding

Plaza
de Colón

Calle Harding
Calle Gen
Pershing

Calle O'Donell
C. J. J.
Acosta
C. Tamarindo
C. Capilla

Calle
Braumbaugh

Calle Tanca
Calle Luna
Calle Sol
Calle San Sebastián
de Valle

Calle Recinto

Calle San Justo

Calle Tetuan

Calle Cruz

Plaza
de Armas

Calle San José
Norzagaray

Plaza
San José

Calle San Francisco

Calle Fortaleza

Del Cristo

Calle San Cristóbal

Paseo de la Princesa

Calle Presidio

El Arsenal

Calle Puntillo

1
38
25
25

Legend

Al Dente **17**
Amadeus **4**
Amanda's Cafe **1**
Butterfly People Café **15**
Café Berlin **25**
Café Bohemio **5**
Café Zaguán **22**
Chef Marisoll **9**
El Buen Samaritano **11**
El Jíbarito **12**
El Patio de Sam **3**
El Patio Mexicano **18**
El Picoteo **7**

Fussion **24**
Hard Rock Café **16**
El Perugino **6**
La Bombonera **14**
La Chaumière **21**
La Mallorquina **13**
NoNo's **2**
Ostra Cosa **8**
Parrot Club **23**
Patio del Nispero **4**
Rolando's **10**
Royal Thai **20**
Yukiyú **19**

Information (i)   City Walls

A Toothpick on Your Table

When you've had too many hotel meals or patronized too many first-class restaurants and want something authentic, head for **El Jibarito**, Calle Sol 280 (☎ 787/725-8375), where locals flock for food like their mamas used to make.

Don't be put off by the setting. We're not talking luxe here. Established in the mid-1970s by Pedro and his wife, Aïda, two self-professed *jibaros* (peasants), the restaurant is a dive complete with the mandatory fluorescent lighting, vinyl tablecloths, and even blinking Christmas bulbs (at any time of the year). The waiter, as one diner recently observed, is likely to take out his toothpick and lay it on your table as he scribbles down your menu selections for the evening. Even Sifredo, the restaurant's most visible assistant, claims to be a jibaro; he's both proud and amused by the word's hillbilly implications.

Stick to the simple dishes and you'll rarely go wrong here. We sampled the lamb stew on a recent occasion and found it perfectly seasoned and tender. Other specialties that have endured over time are the yellow rice with green beans and shredded pork, shrimp with garlic sauce, and several kinds of *mofongo*. The nicest part for last: your final tab, which is invariably inexpensive. Main courses range from $7 to $12.50, and American Express, Diners Club, MasterCard, and Visa are accepted. El Jibarito is open Monday through Thursday from 7am to 7pm, Friday and Saturday from 8:30am to 9pm.

---

however, show Billy's culinary training at other creative restaurants in Puerto Rico. His entrees include sesame-crusted tuna served with vegetable sushi rolls and spicy szechuan sauce, and pulled pork quesadillas with papaya salsa. Even more indigenous is *mangu-longo*, a Dominican–Puerto Rican dish incorporating plantains topped with sautéed shrimp and a wine-flavored cream sauce.

El Patio de Sam. Calle San Sebastián 102 (across from the Iglesia de San José). ☎ **787/ 723-1149.** Sandwiches, burgers, and salads $8.95–$9.50, platters $11–$25. AE, DC, DISC, MC, V. Sun–Thurs 11am–midnight, Fri–Sat 11am–1:30am. Bus: Old Town Trolley. AMERICAN/ PUERTO RICAN.

Established in 1953, this joint has survived several generations of clients, who come here for booze, burgers, Puerto Rican food, and dialogue. The setting includes an exterior space with tables that overlook a historic statue of Ponce de León and a well-known church, and a labyrinth of dark, smoked-stained inner rooms with high-beamed ceilings and lots of potted plants. Menu items are rib-sticking and substantial, not particularly subtle, foils for booze and beer. Examples include *pastel criollo* (plantains stuffed with ground beef and Creole spices), paella, grilled chicken and steak, black-bean soup, calamari, and codfish croquettes.

Ostra Cosa. 154 Calle Cristo. ☎ **787/722-2672.** Reservations recommended. Main courses $8–$25. AE, MC, V. Daily noon–10pm. Bus: Old Town Trolley. ECLECTIC/APHRODISIAC.

This is the most artfully promoted restaurant in San Juan, with a growing clientele who swears that the ambience here, with or without Viagra, is one of the most sensual and romantic in Old San Juan. It was created by a former advertising executive, Alberto Nazario, a lifestyle guru who mingles New Age thinking with good culinary techniques to promote love, devotion, and—perhaps—a heightened sexuality. Couples dine beneath a massive quenepe tree—waiters will tell you to hug the tree and make a wish—in a colonial courtyard surrounded by a 16th-century building that was once the home of the colony's governor. The atmosphere, enhanced by domesticated quail and chirping tree frogs, will make you feel far removed from the cares of the city. Featured foods are high in phosphorus, zinc, and flavor, designed to promote an "eat-up, dress-down experience." Many are laced with fresh basil, honey, avocados, or shellfish. The ceviche is superb, as are the grilled prawns.

Royal Thai. Calle Recinto Sur 315. ☎ **787/725-8401.** Reservations recommended. Main courses $15.95–$35.95. AE, MC, V. Mon–Sat noon–3pm and 6–11pm, Sun noon–3pm and 5–10pm. Bus: Old Town Trolley. THAI.

Thai cuisine arrived relatively late to Puerto Rico, long after it was a familiar sight in urban areas of the U.S. mainland. If you're an aficionado of the cuisine, this is as good as it gets anywhere on the island. The setting is a long and narrow room filled with Thai embroideries and sculpture, outfitted in tones of pink and blue. Menu items include some of the best duck in town, served in either a curry or a tamarind sauce; sea bass steamed with prawns and ginger or deep-fried with curry sauce; and a medley of sautéed seafood with brown sauce and cooking sherry. An excellent beginning is chicken with coconut milk.

INEXPENSIVE

Butterfly People Café. Calle Fortaleza 152. ☎ **787/723-2432.** Salads, sandwiches, and quiches $1.50–$7.95. AE, MC, V. Mon–Sat 10am–6pm. Bus: A7, T1, or 2. CONTINENTAL/ AMERICAN.

This rather cramped restaurant is on the second floor of a restored mansion next to the world's largest gallery devoted to butterflies. Wherever you look, thousands of framed butterflies will delight or horrify you (depending on how you feel about these beautiful insects). You can dine at one of the tables inside the cafe, which overlooks a courtyard. The cuisine is tropical and light European fare made with fresh ingredients. You might begin with gazpacho or vichyssoise, follow with quiche or one of the daily specials, and finish with chocolate mousse or the tantalizing raspberry chiffon pie with fresh raspberry sauce. A full bar offers tropical specialties such as piña coladas, fresh-squeezed Puerto Rican orange juice, and Fantasias, a frappé of seven fresh fruits.

Café Berlin. 407 Plaza Colón. ☎ **787/722-5205.** Main courses $11.95–$17.95. AE, MC, V. Mon–Fri 10am—10pm, Sat–Sun 8am–10pm. Bus: Old Town Trolley. INTERNATIONAL.

Other than the hardworking staff, there's very little about this place that's particularly Hispanic. What you'll get is a corner of Central Europe, identified by a *Jugendstil*-inspired sign, serving coffee, pastries, and a limited array of light platters, such as pasta, on tiny marbletop tables like what you'd expect in Vienna. Paintings, all of them for sale, are displayed on scarlet-colored walls, and lavishly caloric pastries are arranged behind glass display cases. More substantial, rib-sticking fare includes salmon in an orange- and garlic-flavored herb broth, scallops in a pesto sauce, or turkey breast Stroganoff.

Café Bohemio. In the El Convento Hotel, Calle del Cristo 100. ☎ **787/723-9200.** Reservations not necessary. Main courses $9.50–$14.50. AE, MC, V. Daily 11am–11pm. Bus: Old Town Trolley. INTERNATIONAL.

Accessible via a side entrance of the Old Town's most historic hotel, within a high-ceilinged room that evokes the 18th century, this genuinely popular singles bar attracts a congenial group of fans. Lots of people come just for a drink or to enjoy the live music presented every Tuesday through Friday beginning at 9:30pm. But if you're in the mood for a meal, you can order well-prepared versions of ceviche in tequila sauce, blackened calamari, cajun-crusted red snapper, or spinach and ricotta cheese crêpes. Pizzas and burgers are also available.

El Buen Samaritano. Calle Luna 255 (near San Justo St.). ☎ **787/721-6184.** Reservations not accepted. Platters and main courses $6–$15. No credit cards. Daily 7am–8 or 9pm. Bus: A5. PUERTO RICAN.

Only the most experimental foreign tourists would venture in here, despite the fact that its format provides lots of insights into the subculture of this thriving inner-city neighborhood. In fact, we have included this authentic little eatery to answer the often-posed question "Where do the locals dine?" It stands adjacent to the back door of city hall, near the corner of San Justo Street, on one of our favorite "backwater" streets of the historic Old Town. Almost no English is spoken, it's as Créole and ethnic as anything on the island, and it contains no more than four well-scrubbed tables in a setting Hemingway would have praised. Everything is predictably filling and starchy, including roast pork with yellow rice and beans or fillet of red snapper in pungent tomato sauce. The menu, which depends largely on whatever was available in the marketplace that morning, will be recited lethargically by a member of the family who owns this tiny hole-in-the-wall. Except during the midday crush, no one will mind if you opt for just a cup of thick Puerto Rican coffee, a beer, or a soda, which you'll consume beneath the high rafters of a building from the Old Town's dimly remembered colonial past.

El Patio Mexicano. 260 Calle Fortaleza. ☎ **787/723-5449.** Reservations not necessary. Main courses $7.50–$16.50. AE, DISC, MC, V. Mon–Sat 11:30am–11:30pm. Bus: Old Town Trolley. MEXICAN.

The owners proudly refer to their restaurant as a museum and art gallery that happens to serve excellent food. A tour of the premises reveals all the charm of a 19th-century country store in an isolated Mexican puebla. There's memorabilia commemorating folk heroes such as Francisco Villa, photographs of Mexican movie stars of the 1930s and 1950s, elaborately carved beams and columns, and handicrafts, which probably required months of labor by entire villages. The best way to begin is with a mango margarita in an absolutely enormous glass. The menu retains an allegiance to "pure" Mexican (not Tex-Mex) cuisine, as shown in such dishes as chicken breast with tamarind sauce and *enchiladas divorciadas* (divorced enchiladas), consisting of red and green enchiladas divided by a "fence" of refried beans. *Sopa trasca* is a rich broth laced with three kinds of meat, two kinds of cheeses, avocados, and sour cream. Meals are served on hand-painted Mexican stoneware. Every Thursday, live Mexican folk music is presented from 8 to 11pm.

El Picoteo. In the El Convento Hotel, Calle Cristo 100. ☎ **787/643-1597.** Reservations not necessary. Tapas $3.50–$12.50; main courses $6.50–$14. AE, MC, V. Tues–Sun noon–midnight. Bus: Old Town Trolley. SPANISH/PUERTO RICAN.

One of the island's most sought-after caterer's, Paula Paley operates this consistently popular gathering place. Surrounded by climbing bougainvillea and the thick masonry of Puerto Rico's most historic hotel, the outdoor setting is rich in Spanish colonial charm. Savor the ambience with a stiff drink, or perhaps a glass of wine or beer, and several *tapas,* the culinary specialty of Spain. These small-scale dishes seem to make wine or beer taste better. The many offerings include spicy *chorizo* sausages in red wine sauce; boiled potatoes and tuna marinated in vinegar; four kinds of empañadillas, including versions with lobster, beef, or thin-sliced Serrano ham; smoked chicken breast; and Galician-style octopus. Come here for a snack, a before-dinner meal, or— if you compose your meal with a variety of small plates—a feast.

Hard Rock Café. Calle Recinto Sur 253. ☎ **787/724-7625.** Burgers, sandwiches, and platters $6.99–$17.99. AE, DC, DISC, MC, V. Mon–Fri 11:30am–1:30am, Sat–Sun 10:30am–1:30am. Bus: Old Town Trolley. AMERICAN.

This is San Juan's most blatant example of gringo-derived cultural imperialism, but oddly enough, very few clients seem to mind. Set near the cruise-ship terminals on a historic avenue in the Old Town, it's loaded with memorabilia from the glory years of rock-and-roll and permeated with an engaging kind of friendliness. One dining room is devoted to the Beatles, complete with symbol-rich murals that only the most fervent fans can interpret. Check out the other "artifacts," which include a wig worn by Elton John and a jacket that once encased the torso of John Lennon. Standard menu items include barbecued ribs and pork sandwiches, chicken and rib combos, smoked pork chops and pastas; steaks, fiery chili, and a selection of well-stuffed sandwiches. On days when cruise ships pull into port (usually Tuesday and Sunday), the place is likely to be mobbed.

✪ **La Bombonera.** Calle San Francisco 259. ☎ **787/722-0658.** Reservations recommended. American breakfast $4–$6; main courses $6.55–$12.95. AE, DISC, MC, V. Daily 7:30am–8pm. Bus: M2, M3, or T1. PUERTO RICAN.

An exceptional value, this place has been offering homemade pastries, well-stuffed sandwiches, and endless cups of coffee since 1902. Its atmosphere evokes turn-of-the-20th-century Castile transplanted to the New World. The food is authentically Puerto Rican, homemade, and inexpensive, with regional dishes like rice with squid, roast leg of pork, and seafood *asopao*. For dessert, you might select an apple, pineapple, or prune pie, or one of many types of flan. Service is polite, if a bit rushed, and the place fills up quickly at lunchtime.

La Mallorquina. Calle San Justo 207. ☎ **787/722-3261.** Reservations not accepted at lunch, recommended at dinner. Dinner main courses $13.95–$25.95. AE, MC, V. Mon–Sat 11:30am–10pm. Closed Sept. Bus: A7, T1, or 2. PUERTO RICAN.

San Juan's oldest restaurant was founded in 1848 in a building that retains much of its original architectural character. Run by the same family, the Rojos, who have owned the place since around 1900, it contains an old-fashioned mahogany bar that fills most of one wall, and a valuable rounded wall clock made in 1860 by the Welsh and Spring Company (a name known to antique collectors). If you look carefully at the floor adjacent to the bar, you'll see the building's original gray and white marble flooring that the owners are laboriously restoring to its original condition, square foot by square foot. Lunches tend to attract local office workers; dinners are more cosmopolitan and leisurely, with many residents of the Condado and other modern neighborhoods selecting this place because of its old-world charm. Food has changed little over the decades, with special emphasis on *asopao* made with rice and either chicken, shrimp, or lobster and shrimp. *Arroz con pollo* (rice stewed with chicken) is almost as popular. Begin with either garlic soup or gazpacho, follow the entree with a flan, and you'll have enjoyed an authentically Puerto Rican meal. A favorite touch is the white cotton slipcovers draped over the cane-backed chairs. Visit here for tradition and good value rather than innovation.

NoNo's. Calle San Sebastián 100 (at Calle Cristo). ☎ **787/725-7819.** Hamburgers and main courses $4.25–$6.95. AE, MC, V. Daily 11am–3am; bar 11am–4am. Bus: A7, T1, or 2. AMERICAN/FAST FOOD.

In the heart of Old San Juan in a 2-century-old building overlooking Plaza San José, NoNo's brings stateside food to those eager for salads, mozzarella sticks, three-decker sandwiches, chicken-fried steaks, hamburgers (here called NoNo burgers), and onion rings. You'll sit beneath a beamed ceiling, near a large and accommodating bar where folks seem only peripherally interested in the food.

Patio del Nispero. In the Hotel El Convento, Calle Cristo 100. ☎ **787/723-9260.** Reservations not necessary. Sanwiches $8.50–$10; platters $14–$24. AE, DC, MC, V. Daily 11am–10pm. Bus: Old Town Trolley. INTERNATIONAL.

Surrounded by the soaring atrium of Old San Juan's most historic hotel, this restaurant provides a charming oasis of calm and quiet within a congested city. Pots of verdant plants thrive under the direct sunlight of the open sky, while big canvas umbrellas shield diners from the rain. No one will mind if you order just a drink (the daiquiris are excellent) or a cup of coffee while resting after a tour of the Old Town or the cathedral next door. But if you want food, consider fillet of red snapper with Créole sauce, chicken breast with chestnuts and mushrooms in cognac sauce, broiled veal chop with Marsala sauce, and a wide selection of desserts. Two evenings a week feature live music.

Rolandos. Calle de la Cruz 152. ☎ **787/724-1198.** Reservations recommended. Main courses $6.95–$16.95. AE, MC, V. Daily 11am–10pm. Bus: Old Town Trolley. PUERTO RICAN.

Despite its relative newness to the Old Town, this restaurant quickly became crowded with local office workers. It's set within a high-ceilinged Spanish colonial room with heavy beams and a black-and-white tiled floor. Flavorful food is served in generous portions to diners at tiny, claustrophobically close tables. You might be happiest here if you avoid the lunch-hour crush between 12:15 and 1:30pm, when the place is simply too crowded for comfort. Menu items are almost exclusively Puerto Rican, with nary a shred of international consciousness. Begin with a slice of *tortilla espagñol* (Spanish omelet), deep-fried calamari, or perhaps a steaming bowl of cream of green plantain soup. Follow this with codfish stew, fillet of red snapper, *mofongo relleño de camarones* (mashed green plantain stuffed with shrimp), or medallions of veal flavored with sherry.

3 Puerta de Tierra

Caribe Hilton. Calle Los Rosales. ☎ **787/721-0303.** Reservations recommended. All-you-can-eat buffet brunch $35.95 for adults, half price for children under 10. AE, DC, MC, V. Sun only 12:30–4pm. Bus: A7. INTERNATIONAL.

Every Sunday the Hilton's brunch captivates the imagination of island residents and U.S. visitors with its combination of excellently prepared food, glamour, and entertainment. There's a clown to keep the children amused, as well as live music on the bandstand for anyone who cares to dance. Champagne is included in the price. Food is arranged at several different stations: Puerto Rican dishes, seafood, paella, ribs, cold cuts, steaks, pastas, and salads. Afterward, you might like to stroll amid the boutiques and seafront facilities of this famous hotel.

4 Condado

VERY EXPENSIVE

La Scala. In the Radisson Ambassador Plaza Hotel & Casino, 1369 Ashford Ave. ☎ **787/ 721-7300.** Reservations recommended. Main courses $16.95–$36. AE, MC, V. Tues–Fri noon–3pm; daily 6–11pm. Bus: A7. NORTHERN ITALIAN.

One of the most sophisticated Italian restaurants in San Juan caters to discerning diners who appreciate the nuances of fine cuisine and service. The decor includes neutral colors, stucco arches, and murals. The menu lists just about the entire repertoire of northern Italian cuisine. You'll find a specialty version of Caesar salad, fresh mushrooms in garlic sauce, and a succulent half-melted version of fresh mozzarella in carozza. The fresh fish and seafood are flown in from New York and Boston. Specialties include halibut cooked in parchment, rigatoni with shiitake mushrooms and ricotta, and rack of lamb in a red wine sauce. Most meals here are memorable, and the cookery, for the most part, is creative and delicate. Service is attentive.

⚪ **Ramiro's.** Av. Magdalena 1106. ☎ **787/721-9049.** Reservations required in winter, recommended off-season. Main courses $25–$38. AE, DC, MC, V. Sun–Fri noon–3pm; Mon–Thurs 6:30–10:30pm, Fri–Sat 6:30–11pm, Sun 6–10pm. Bus: A7, T1, or 2. SPANISH/INTERNATIONAL.

In a half-century-old building near the Marriott Hotel, you'll find a refined cuisine and a touch of Old Spain. This restaurant prepares "New Créole" cooking, a style pioneered by owner and chef Jesús Ramiro. The menu is the most imaginative on the Condado. You might begin with breadfruit *mille-feuille* with local crabmeat and avocado. For your main course, any fresh fish or meat can be charcoal-grilled for you on request. Some of the latest menu specialties include paillard of lamb with spiced root vegetables and guava sauce, char-grilled black Angus steak with shiitake mushrooms, or grilled striped sea bass with citrus sauce. Among the many homemade desserts are caramelized mango on puff pastry with strawberry-and-guava sauce, and four kinds of chocolate.

EXPENSIVE

Ajili Mójili. 1052 Ashford Ave. (at the corner of Calle Joffre). ☎ **787/725-9195.** Reservations recommended. Main courses $16–$30. AE, MC, V. Mon–Fri 11:45am–3pm; Sun–Thurs 6–10pm, Fri–Sat 6–11pm. Bus: B21. PUERTO RICAN/CRÉOLE.

This restaurant is devoted exclusively to *la cucina criolla,* the starchy, down-home cuisine that developed on the island a century ago. It's set in the heart of the Condado's tourist strip, across from the convention center. Though the building housing is quite modern, look for artful replicas of crumbling brick walls à la Old San Juan and a bar that evokes Old Spain. The staff will willingly describe menu items in colloquial English. Locals come here for a taste of the food they enjoyed at their mother's knee, like *mofongos* (green plantains stuffed with veal, chicken, shrimp, or pork), *arroz con pollo* (stewed chicken with saffron rice), *medallones de cerdo encebollado* (pork loin sautéed with onions), *carne mechada* (beef rib eye stuffed with ham), and *lechon asado con maposteado* (roast pork with rice and beans). Wash it all down with an ice-cold bottle of local beer, such as Medalla.

Martino's. In the Diamond Palace Hotel & Casino, Av. Condado 55. ☎ **787/722-5256.** Reservations recommended. Main courses $16.50–$45. AE, DC, MC, V. Daily 5:30–11:30pm. Bus: A7. NORTHERN ITALIAN.

Martino's offers some of the finest service on the Condado and a classic Italian cuisine, centered primarily in the north of Italy, especially Lombardy. It's the domain of chef and owner Martin Acosta. His restaurant's picture windows open onto views of the Atlantic and the night lights of the Condado. Appetizers include hot seafood antipasti and Caesar and spinach salads. The Caesar salad is made tableside with real panache. For a main course you can order one of the homemade pasta dishes or choose from such appetizing dishes as seafood suprême, vitello Martino (with shrimp), gnocchi with cream sauce and Parmesan, and filet mignon Monnalisa, which is flambéed at your table. In fact, almost any dish can receive a tableside flambé if you want. Good and reasonably priced wines add to the dining pleasure.

⚪ **Pikayo.** In the Tanama Princess Hotel, 1 Calle Joffre. ☎ **787/721-6194.** Reservations recommended. Main courses $26–$32; fixed-price-price menus $58–$68. AE, DC, MC, V. Mon–Sat 6–10:30pm. Closed 2 weeks in Dec–Jan. Bus: T1. PUERTO RICAN/CAJUN.

This is an ideal place to go for the new generation of Puerto Rican cookery, with a touch of Cajun thrown in for spice and zest. This place not only keeps up with the latest culinary trends but often sets them, thanks to the inspired guidance of owner and celebrity chef Wilo Benet. Located on the lobby level of the Condado's Tanama

Princess Hotel, the dining room is outfitted in a minimalist, Japanese-inspired motif of grays and soft reds. Formal but not stuffy, and winner of more culinary awards than virtually any other restaurant in Puerto Rico, Pikayo specializes in the *criolla* cuisine of the colonial age, emphasizing the Spanish, Indian, and African elements in its unusual recipes. Appetizers include a dazzling array of taste explosions, including shrimp spring rolls with peanut sofrito sauce; crab cake with aïoli; and a ripe plantain, goat cheese, and onion tart. Main course delights feature charred rare yellowfin tuna with onion escabeche and red snapper fillet with sweet potato purée served with foie gras butter. Our favorite remains the grilled shrimp with polenta and a barbecue sauce made with guava.

Ristorante Tuscany. In the San Juan Marriott Resort, 1309 Ashford Ave. ☎ **787/ 722-7000.** Reservations recommended. Main courses $19.50–$29.25. AE, DC, DISC, MC, V. Daily 6–11pm. Bus: B21. NORTHERN ITALIAN.

This is the showcase restaurant of one of the most elaborate hotel reconstructions in the history of Puerto Rico, and the kitchen continues to rack up culinary awards. Notable entrees include grilled veal chops with shallots and a glaze of Madeira, and grilled chicken breast in cream sauce with chestnuts, asparagus, and brandy, surrounded with fried artichokes. The seafood selections are excellent, especially the fresh red snapper sautéed in olive oil, garlic, parsley, and lemon juice. The risottos prepared al dente in the traditional northern Italian style are the finest on the island, especially the one made with seafood and herbs. The cold and hot appetizers are virtual meals unto themselves, with such favorites as grilled polenta with sausages or fresh neck clams and mussels simmered in herb-flavored tomato broth.

MODERATE

Caruso. 1104 Ashford Ave. ☎ **787/723-6876.** Main courses $9.75–$23.50. AE, DC, MC, V. Daily 6–11pm. Bus: A5. ITALIAN.

Its decor and the brisk efficiency of its staff might remind you of a neighborhood trattoria in New York City, and, in fact, it's become the preferred neighborhood restaurant of many Condado residents who hail from New York. It's one of the most popular places around for pasta, because of its low prices and simple but down-to-earth food. Menu items include shrimp scampi, filet mignon, veal piccata, veal Marsala, and grilled fish of the day. If featured, the antipasti is a good bet, as is the carpaccio of salmon.

Cherry Blossom. In the San Juan Marriott Resort, 1309 Ashford Ave. ☎ **787/723-7300.** Reservations recommended. Main courses $11.75–$25.50 at lunch; $18.50–$29.50 at dinner. AE, DC, MC, V. Mon–Sat 12:30–3pm and 5:30–11pm, Sun 1–11pm. Bus: B21. JAPANESE.

Set on the street level of the San Juan Marriott, but with direct access to the busy pedestrian traffic of Ashford Avenue, this is one of the genuinely charming Japanese restaurants of the Condado. There are sections devoted to sushi, including a long bar where you can view the raw fish available that day, and to teppanyaki, where a corps of carefully trained chefs will fast-sear your meal on a sizzling griddle in front of you. The staff is charming, the food excellent.

Cobia. In the Condado Plaza Hotel, 999 Ashford Ave. ☎ **787/721-1000.** Reservations recommended. Main courses $18–$25. AE, DC, MC, V. Daily 5pm–midnight. Bus: A7. CARIBBEAN/PACIFIC RIM.

Set within the previously recommended hotel, just a short walk from one of the busiest casinos in San Juan, this restaurant presents a stylish, much-praised blend of Caribbean and Asian cuisine. The setting is an artfully contemporary room—with bubbling aquariums, maple trim, and comfortable chairs—which overlooks the glittering lights surrounding the nearby lagoon. Enjoy a drink at the bar outside before

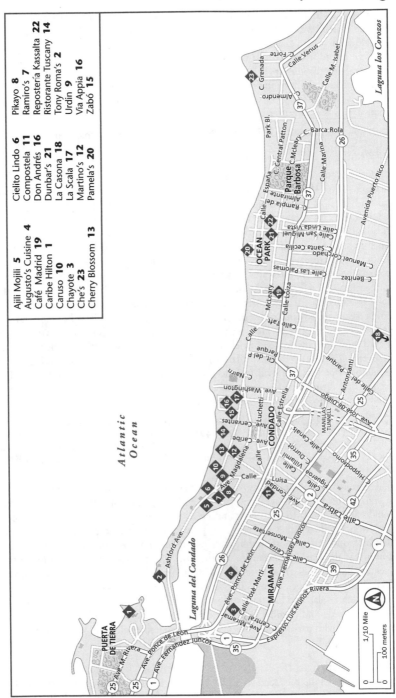

Ajili Mojili **5**
Augusto's Cuisine **4**
Café Madrid **19**
Caribe Hilton **1**
Caruso **10**
Chayote **3**
Che's **23**
Cherry Blossom **13**

Cielito Lindo **6**
Compostela **11**
Don Andrés **16**
Dunbar's **21**
La Casona **18**
La Scala **17**
Martino's **12**
Pamela's **20**

Pikayo **8**
Ramiro's **7**
Repostería Kassalta **22**
Ristorante Tuscany **14**
Tony Roma's **2**
Urdin **9**
Via Appia **16**
Zabó **15**

heading into dinner. There, menu items as developed by resident chef Phil Bellshaw include roasted West Indian pumpkin soup; cream of native root vegetable soup; pan-roasted salmon with cilantro-flavored risotto, smoked yellow pepper coulis, and black-bean salsa; and seafood paella with calamari, mojo chicken, pigeon peas, and chorizo sausage. Even the lobster at this place is likely to be served in ways you might not recognize, including a version with yucca *mofongo* and black-bean sofrito broth. One of the most enduringly popular desserts is chocolate-enriched *tres leches* with chocolate mousse and peanut butter brittle ice cream.

Urdin. Av. Magdalena 1105. ☎ **787/724-0420.** Reservations recommended. Main courses $18–$28. AE, MC, V. Sun–Fri noon–10:30pm, Sat 6–11pm. Bus: A7. PUERTO RICAN/INTERNATIONAL.

Urdin is proud of its reputation as one of the capital's bright young restaurants. It occupies a low-slung, stucco-covered house set near a slew of competitors. Inside, a fanciful decor of postmodern, Caribbean-inspired accents and metal sculpture brings a touch of Latino New York. Popularity has brought an unexpected development to this highly visible restaurant: the bar is almost more popular than the food. Consequently, you're likely to find the bar area jam-packed every day between 6 and 10pm. Cliquish, heterosexual, and fashionable, some of this crowd eventually gravitate toward the tables. Yes, that was Ricky Martin we spotted here one evening. Filled with authentic Spanish flavor that's not necessarily geared to the palates of timid diners, the food is innovative, flavorful, strong, and earthy. For starters, there are baby eels Bilbaina style or Castilian lentil soup. Main courses include fresh fillet of salmon in mustard sauce, fillet of fish "Hollywood style" (with onions, raisins, and mango slices served in white wine sauce), ostrich in red wine sauce (opinion at our table was divided over this choice), and rack of lamb with orange sauce. One always-pleasing dish is piquillo peppers stuffed with seafood mousse and black-olive sauce. Savvy locals finish their meal with a slice of sweet-potato cheesecake. The staff can diminish (if they're sulky) or enhance (if they're welcoming) a meal here.

⭐ **Zabó.** 14 Calle Candina (entrance via an alleyway on Ashford Ave. between Calles Washington and Cervantes). ☎ **787/725-9494.** Reservations recommended. Main courses $8.75–28 at lunch, $17.95–$28 at dinner. AE, MC, V. Tues–Fri noon–3pm, Sun noon–4pm; Tues–Wed 6–10pm, Thurs–Sat 6–11pm. Bus: A7. CREATIVE CARIBBEAN/MEDITERRANEAN/ASIAN.

This restaurant has gained citywide fame thanks to its blend of bucolic charm and superb, innovative food. It's set within a dignified, turn-of-the-20th-century villa that stands in contrast to the surrounding skyscrapers. The creative force here is owner/chef/culinary director Paul Carroll, who transformed the place from a simple deli into one of the most sought-after restaurants on the Condado. Items fuse the cuisines of the Mediterranean, the Pacific Rim, and the Caribbean into a menu that includes such dishes as blinis stuffed with smoked salmon and dill sauce or lobster medallions with ginger, thyme, and beurre blanc (white butter); carpaccio of salmon with mesclun salad and balsamic vinegar; and baked chorizo stuffed with mushrooms, sherry, paprika, and cheddar. The black-bean soup is among the very best in Puerto Rico, served with par-boiled cloves of garlic marinated in olive oil, which melt in your mouth like candy.

INEXPENSIVE

Cielito Lindo. 1108 Av. Magdalena. ☎ **787/723-5597.** Reservations recommended for dinner. Main courses $7.95–$16.50. AE, MC, V. Mon–Wed 11am–10:30pm, Thurs–Fri 11am–11:30pm, Sat 5–11pm. Bus: A7. MEXICAN.

One of the most likable things about this restaurant is the way it retains low prices and an utter lack of pretension despite the expensive Condado real estate that surrounds it. Something about it might remind you of a low-slung house in Puebla, Mexico, home of owner Jaime Pandal, who maintains a vigilant position from a perch at the cash register. Walls are outfitted with an intriguing mix of Mexican arts and crafts, and ads for popular tequilas and beer. None of the selections have changed since the restaurant was founded, a policy that long-term clients find reassuring. The place is mobbed, especially on weekends, with those looking for heaping portions of well-prepared, standardized Mexican food. Examples include fajitas of steak or chicken; strips of filet steak sautéed with green peppers and onions, covered with tomatoes and spicy gravy; enchiladas of chicken or cheese, covered with cheese and served with sour cream; and several kinds of tacos.

Don Andrés. 1350 Ashford Ave. ☎ **787/723-0222.** Reservations not necessary. Main courses $7.75–$16.75. AE, MC, V. Tues–Sat 11:30am–midnight, Sun–Mon 5pm–midnight. Bus: A7. MEXICAN.

Set on a prominent street corner in the Condado, the venue includes big tables, paper tablecloths, bright lights, and a connection with the busy street life of the Condado. Some of its panache derives from potent drinks (seven kinds of margaritas, each priced at $7), and live presentations of Mexican music every Thursday and Saturday from 7:30pm to midnight, and every Friday from 9:30pm to midnight. Standard menu items include tacos, nachos, enchiladas, chimichangas, and beef or chicken tortillas, all served with traditional garnishes. The owner, your host, is Armando (Andrés) Ramos.

Tony Roma's. In the Condado Plaza Hotel, 999 Ashford Ave. ☎ **787/721-1000,** ext. 2623. Reservations not accepted. Main courses $7.85–$20.. AE, MC, V. Daily noon–midnight. Bus: A7. BARBECUE.

Efficient and unpretentious, this is Puerto Rico's busiest branch of the international chain and one of the least expensive restaurants in the Condado. It's well appreciated for its spicy barbecued food (the honey barbecue is not as fiery). Menu items include a wide range of barbecued dishes, such as chicken and several varieties of ribs, as well as hamburgers and the famous Tony Roma onion ring loaf. The most expensive item in the house, a combination platter containing several kinds of ribs with all the fixings, is a meal in itself that's a particularly good value in this high-priced neighborhood.

Via Appia. 1350 Ashford Ave. ☎ **787/725-8711.** Pizza and main courses $8.95–$14.95. AE, MC, V. Mon–Fri 11am–11pm, Sat–Sun 11am–midnight. Bus: A5. ITALIAN.

A favorite of *sanjuaneros* visiting Condado for the day, Via Appia offers food that's sometimes praiseworthy. Its pizzas are the best in the neighborhood. The chef's signature pizza, Via Appia, is a savory pie made with sausages, onions, mushrooms, pepperoni, green peppers, cheese, and spices. Vegetarians also have a pizza to call their own (made with whole-wheat dough, eggplant, mushrooms, green peppers, onions, tomatoes, and cheese). There's even a pizza with meatballs. Savory pasta dishes, including baked ziti, lasagna, and spaghetti, are also prepared with several of your favorite sauces. All of this can be washed down with sangría. During the day, freshly made salads or sandwiches are also available.

5 Miramar

Augusto's Cuisine. In the Hotel Excelsior, 801 Av. Ponce de León, Miramar. ☎ **787/725-7700.** Reservations recommended. Main courses $25–$32; fixed-price menu $66–$100. AE, MC, V. Tues–Fri noon–3pm; Tues–Sat 7–9:30pm. Bus: B1. FRENCH/INTERNATIONAL.

With its European flair, this is one of the most elegant and glamorous restaurants in Puerto Rico. Austrian-born owner/chef Augusto Schreiner, assisted by a partly French-born staff, operates from a gray and green dining room set on the lobby level of a 15-story hotel in Miramar, a suburb near the island's main airport. Menu items are concocted from strictly fresh ingredients, including such dishes as lobster risotto; rack of lamb with aromatic herbs and fresh garlic; an oft-changing cream-based soup of the day (one of the best is corn and fresh oyster soup); and a succulent version of medallions of veal Rossini style, prepared with foie gras and Madeira sauce. The wine list is one of the most extensive on the island.

Chayote. In the Olimpo Hotel, Av. Miramar 603. ☎ **787/722-9385.** Reservations recommended. Main courses $16–$25. AE, MC, V. Tues–Fri Noon–2:30pm; Tues–Sat 7–10:30pm. Bus: 5. PUERTO RICAN/INTERNATIONAL.

Chayote's cuisine is among the most innovative in San Juan. It draws local business leaders, government officials, and film stars such as Sylvester Stallone and Melanie Griffith. It's an artsy, modern, basement-level bistro in a surprisingly obscure hotel (the Olimpo). The restaurant changes its menu every 3 months, but you might find appetizers like a yucca turnover stuffed with crabmeat and served with a mango and papaya chutney, or a ripe plantain stuffed with chicken and served with fresh tomato sauce. For a main dish, you might try red snapper fillet with citrus vinaigrette made of passion fruit, orange, and lemon. An exotic touch appears in the pork filet seasoned with dried fruits and spices in tamarind sauce and served with a green banana and taro root timbale. To finish off your meal, there's nothing better than the mango flan served with macerated strawberries.

✪ Compostela. Av. Condado 106. ☎ **787/724-6088.** Reservations required. Main courses $20–$34. AE, DC, MC, V. Mon–Fri noon–3pm; Mon–Sat 6:30–10:30pm. Bus: 2. SPANISH/PUERTO RICAN.

This restaurant offers formal service from a battalion of well-dressed waiters. Established by a Galician-born family, the pine-trimmed restaurant has gained a reputation as one of the best in the capital. The chef made his name on the roast peppers stuffed with salmon mousse. Equally delectable is duck with orange and ginger sauce or baby rack of lamb with fresh herbs. Of course, any shellfish grilled in brandy sauce is a sure winner. The chef also makes two different versions of paella, both savory. The wine cellar, comprised of some 10,000 bottles, is one of the most impressive in San Juan.

6 Santurce & Ocean Park

VERY EXPENSIVE

La Casona. Calle San Jorge 609 (at the corner of Av. Fernández Juncos). ☎ **787/727-2717.** Reservations required. Main courses $25–$45. AE, DC, MC, V. Mon–Fri noon–3pm; Mon–Sat 6–11pm. Bus: 1. SPANISH/INTERNATIONAL.

La Casona, in a turn-of-the-20th-century mansion surrounded by gardens, offers the kind of dining usually found in Madrid, complete with a strolling guitarist. The much-renovated but still charming place draws some of the most fashionable diners on Puerto Rico. Paella marinara, prepared for two or more, is a specialty, as is *zarzuela de mariscos* (seafood medley). Or you might select fillet of grouper in Basque sauce, octopus vinaigrette, osso buco (veal shanks), or rack of lamb. Grilled red snapper is a specialty, and you can order it with almost any sauce you want, although the chef recommends one made from olive oil, herbs, lemon, and pulverized toasted garlic. The cuisine here has both flair and flavor.

EXPENSIVE

✪ Pamela's. In the Numéro Uno Guest House, Calle Santa Ana 1. ☎ **787/726-5010.** Reservations recommended. Sandwiches and salads $8–$14; main-course platters $16–$35. AE, DC, MC, V. Mon–Sat noon–3pm and 7–10:30pm; Sun 11am–3pm and 7–10:30pm. Bus: A5. CARRIBBEAN FUSION.

A sense of cachet and style is very pronounced at this restaurant, a fact that's somewhat surprising considering its out-of-the-way location within a guesthouse on a residential street in Ocean Park. Part of its allure derives from a sophisticated blend of Caribbean cuisines (chef Michael Mastrianni refers to it as "Caribbean fusion") that mixes local ingredients, Puerto Rican flair, and the zest of a Greenwich Village restaurateur. Menu items include a salad that combines vine-ripened and oven-roasted tomatoes, each drizzled with roasted garlic and cilantro vinaigrette; club sandwiches stuffed with barbecued shrimp and cilantro-flavored mayonnaise; plantain-encrusted crab cakes with a spicy tomato-herb emulsion; and grilled island-spiced pork loin served with guava glaze and fresh local fruits. Beer or any of a wide array of party-colored drinks go well with this food.

INEXPENSIVE

Café Madrid. 100 Calle Loiza (at the corner of Calle Las Flores). ☎ **787/728-5250.** Reservations not accepted. Breakfast platters $2.25–$4; sandwiches $1.50–$3.25; lunch and dinner main courses $3.95–$7.95. No credit cards. Daily 6am–10pm. Bus: B5 or T1. PUERTO RICAN.

Come here to escape from the gloss and sheen of big-city, big-money tourism. Local residents promote this simple diner for its sense of workaday conviviality and low, low prices. Located on a narrow but busy street in a congested commercial neighborhood of Ocean Park, this joint has a battered facade with plastic lettering—signs that the inside is going to be very tacky. At first glance, that's partially true. But if you retain a sense of humor, you might begin to appreciate the Formica bar tops, rows of mismatched refrigerators, big-lettered menus over sizzling deep-fat fryers, and the kind of industrial accessories that Andy Warhol might have appreciated or even collected. It's been the domain of the Molina family since the 1930s, and the food has changed very little since then. Examples include roasted pork, sold either as a full-size meal platter or stuffed into a sandwich; several kinds of *asopao* and *carne frita* (fried meat); lasagna; and lots of empañadas. Roasted chicken, the signature dish, is an ongoing favorite.

Dunbar's. 1954 McLeary Ave. ☎ **787/729-2820.** Reservations not necessary. Burgers and sandwiches $8.50–$12.50. Main courses $9–$15. AE, DC, MC, V. Sun–Thurs 11:30am–midnight; Fri 11:30am–1am, Sat 5pm–1am. Bus A5 or A7 INTERNATIONAL.

Sprawling over at least five distinctly different dining and drinking areas, this is the busiest, most active, and most legendary bar and pub in Ocean Park. Painted an arresting shade of tangerine, it was established in 1982. The best way to navigate the labyrinth of Dunbar's is to wander through its various spaces: a large-screen TV room on the second floor attracts a macho, mostly North American crowd; a ground-floor pool room appeals to a deceptively affluent crowd of Spanish-speaking lawyers and doctors; and the various bars and cubbyholes ripple with possibilities for making friends or influencing your romantic destiny. Well-prepared menu items, each conceived by veteran chef, California-born Trent Eichler, pour out of the busy kitchens. Examples include thick sandwiches (Spanish chorizo sausage with roasted peppers is an ongoing favorite), omelets, pastas, and juicy steaks. French fries are made from vitamin-rich yams or conventional potatoes. Favorite drinks include (what else?) "Sex on the Beach" and lots of margaritas. Dunbar's was named, incidentally, after a particularly eccentric character in Joseph Heller's *Catch-22*.

Repostería Kassalta. Calle McLeary 1966. ☎ **787/727-7340.** Reservations not accepted. Full American breakfast $3.50–$5; soups $3.25–$4.75; sandwiches $3.50–$5; platters $4.75–$9. AE, DC, MC, V. Daily 6am–10pm. Bus: A5, A7, or T1. SPANISH/PUERTO RICAN.

This is the most widely known of San Juan's cafeteria/bakery/delicatessens. You'll enter a cavernous room flanked with sun-flooded windows and endless ranks of display cases filled with meats, sausages, and pastries appropriate to the season. Patrons line up to place their order at a cash register, then carry their selections, cafeteria style, to one of the many tables. Knowledge of Spanish is helpful but not essential. Among the selections are steaming bowls of Puerto Rico's best *caldo gallego*, a hearty soup laden with collard greens, potatoes, and sausage slices, served in thick earthenware bowls with hunks of bread. Also popular are Cuban sandwiches (sliced pork, cheese, and fried bread), steak sandwiches, a savory octopus salad, and an assortment of perfectly cooked omelets. Paella Valenciano is a Sunday favorite.

7 Punta Las Marias

Che's. Calle Caoba 35. ☎ **787/726-7202.** Reservations recommended for lunch, required for dinner. Main courses $13–$25. AE, DC, MC, V. Mon–Thurs noon–11pm, Fri–Sun noon–midnight. Bus: T1. ARGENTINE/ITALIAN/INTERNATIONAL.

Named after the Latino revolutionary Che Guevara, this place re-creates some of the color and drama of the Argentine pampas. It's about 2 miles east of Condado's resorts. Many of the specialties are grilled in the style preferred by cowherding gauchos. If you're not in the mood for highly seasoned flank steak or any of the grilled meats, you can choose from a variety of pastas and veal dishes. Meats are very tender here and well flavored.

8 Isla Verde

EXPENSIVE

The Palm. In El San Juan Hotel & Casino, 6063 Isla Verde Ave. ☎ **787/791-1000.** Reservations recommended. Main courses $18–$35, except lobster, which is priced by the pound and can easily cost $80 per serving. AE, DC, MC, V. Daily 6–10pm. Bus: A7, M7, or T1. STEAK/SEAFOOD.

The management of San Juan's most elegant hotel invited the Palm, a legendary New York steak house, to open a branch on the premises. The setting includes a stylish, masculine-looking saloon, where drinks are stiff, and a dining room with artfully simple linen-covered tables and caricatures of local personalities. If you've hit it big at the nearby casino, maybe you'll want to celebrate with the Palm's famous and famously pricey lobster (the lobster and all the shellfish can be shockingly expensive). Otherwise, there's a tempting number of options, all served in gargantuan portions: jumbo lump crabmeat cocktail, Caesar salad, lamb chops with mint sauce, grilled halibut steak, prime porterhouse steak, and steak "à la stone," which finishes cooking on a sizzling platter directly atop your table. One thing is certain—you'll never go hungry here.

La Piccola Fontana. In El San Juan Hotel & Casino, 6063 Isla Verde Ave. ☎ **787/ 791-0966.** Reservations required. Main courses $27.95–$39.95. AE, DC, MC, V. Daily 6pm–midnight. Bus: T1. NORTHERN ITALIAN.

Right off the luxurious Palm Court in the El San Juan Hotel, this restaurant takes classic northern Italian cuisine seriously and delivers plate after plate of delectable food. From its white linen to its classically formal service, it enjoys a fine reputation. The food is straightforward, generous, and extremely well prepared. You'll dine in one of two neo-Palladian rooms, where wall frescoes depict Italy's ruins and landscapes.

ⓗ Family-Friendly Restaurants

Caribe Hilton *(see p. 100)*   The Sunday brunch here—which is half price for children—is an all-you-can-eat buffet. There's even a clown on hand to keep the kids entertained

Hard Rock Café *(see p. 98)*   The local branch of this international chain is a sure-fire hit with kids. Despite the hype, the burgers are pretty good.

Butterfly People Café *(see p. 97)*   Children love eating lunch in this fantasy world of mounted butterflies. A favorite drink is Fantasia—a frappé made from seven fresh fruits

---

Menu items range from the appealingly simple (grilled fillets of fish or grilled veal chops) to more elaborate dishes (tortellini San Daniele, made with veal, prosciutto, cream, and sage; or *linguine scogliere,* with shrimps, clams, and seafood). Grilled medallions of filet mignon are served with braised arugula, Parmesan cheese, and balsamic vinegar.

Vineyard Room. In the Ritz-Carlton, 6961 State Road #187. ☎ 787/253-1700. Reservations required. Main courses $35; fixed-price menus $75–$85. AE, DC, MC, V. Oct–Mar Mon–Fri noon–2:30pm; year-round daily 6–11pm. Bus: A7, M7, or T1. CALIFORNIAN/ MEDITERRANEAN.

The finest restaurant in San Juan, this venue of haute cuisine has impeccable European credentials. French-born chef Philippe Trosche, a prize catch for the Ritz-Carlton, spearheads a staff of culinary luminaries. Select from such innovative appetizers as potato cannelloni filled with Caribbean lobster risotto or a summer salad of cavallion melon, Serrano ham, mozzarella, and olive pesto with ciabatta toast. The main courses are works of art: Nantucket sea bass with barley tapenade and black-olive sabayon, or apple-smoked rabbit with a cannellini bean mash. You might begin or end an experience here in the bar, a dark-paneled setting reminiscent of an Edwardian men's club in London. The wine-tasting menus, either four or five courses, are the best on the island.

MODERATE

Back Street Hong Kong. In El San Juan Hotel & Casino, 6063 Isla Verde Ave. ☎ 787/ 791-1000, ext. 1758. Reservations recommended. Main courses $17.95–$28.95. AE, MC, V. Mon–Sat 6pm–midnight, Sun 1pm–midnight. Bus: M4 or T1. MANDARIN/SZECHUAN/ HUNAN.

Head down a re-creation of a backwater street in Hong Kong—reconstructed from its original home at the 1964 New York World's Fair—to enter one of the best Chinese restaurants in the Caribbean. This spot consistently serves good food, filled with fragrance and flavor. Beneath a soaring redwood ceiling, you can enjoy pineapple fried rice served in a real pineapple, a version of scallops with orange sauce, Szechuan beef with chicken, or a Dragon and Phoenix (lobster mixed with shrimp).

Momoyama Japanese Steak and Cuisine. In the San Juan Beach Resort & Casino, 187 Isla Grande Ave. ☎ 787/791-8883. Reservations recommended. Fixed-price lunches $6.95–$13.95; lunch and dinner main courses $16.95–$29.95. AE, DC, MC, V. Mon–Fri noon–3pm and 5:30–11:30pm, Sat 5:30–11pm, Sun 1–11:30pm. Bus: A7, M7, or T1. JAPANESE.

Few other restaurants in Isla Verde are as indelibly associated with one dish: sushi pizza. The subject of rave reviews, it's made by deep-frying compressed rice into something akin to a pizza shell, which is layered with rows of salmon or tuna and garnished with fish roe, shaved ginger, and make-your-eyes-water wasabi mustard. If you prefer your food cooked, there are several teppanyaki tables, where food is fast-cooked in front of you as part of a highly theatrical culinary show. Choices include chicken teriyaki with shrimp, soy-and-ginger chicken with filet mignon, and several kinds of tempura.

Outback Steak House. In the Embassy Suites Hotel & Casino, 8000 José M. Tartak St. ☎ **787/791-4679.** Reservations not accepted. Main courses $14–$23. AE, MC, V. Mon–Thurs 5:30–10:30pm, Fri–Sat 5:30pm–midnight, Sun 2–10pm. Bus: T1. STEAK.

This Puerto Rican branch of the two-fisted, Australian-themed restaurant chain occupies a dark-paneled room with booths positioned around a prominent bar area. Here you can study memorabilia devoted to the Land Down Under while ordering such drinks as a genuinely delicious Wallabee Darn. There's a simple steak-and-potato-with-salad special priced at $11, a cost-conscious meal in itself. But more appealing are some of the chain's signature dishes, such as a Blooming Onion (a batter-dipped deep-fried onion that fans out from its platter like a demented lotus and tastes delicious with beer); at least four kinds of steaks, including filet mignon; fish, including mahimahi and salmon; and our favorite of the lot, Alice Springs chicken, a breast of chicken layered with bacon, mushrooms, and cheese, and served with honey-mustard sauce and french fries.

The Ranch. In El San Juan Hotel & Casino, 6063 Isla Verde Ave. ☎ **787/791-1000.** Reservations recommended at dinner Fri–Sat; otherwise, not necessary. Main courses $16.25–$34.25. AE, DC, DISC, MC, V. Daily 5:30–11pm (until midnight Fri–Sat). Bus: A7, M7, or T1. AMERICAN/STEAK.

When the very posh El San Juan Hotel carved out a space for this irreverent, tongue-in-cheek eatery on its top (10th) floor, it was viewed as a radical departure from an otherwise grand collection of in-house restaurants. The result is likely to make you smile, especially if you have roots anywhere west of Ohio. You'll be greeted with a hearty "Howdy, partner" and the jangling of spurs from a crew of denim-clad cowboys as you enter a replica of a corral in the North American West. Banquettes and bar stools are upholstered in faux cowhide; the decor is appropriately macho and rough-textured, and even the cowgirls on duty are likely to lasso anyone they find particularly appealing. The cowboys sing as they serve your steaks, barbecued ribs, country-fried steaks, Tex-Mex fajitas, and enchiladas. Food that's a bit less beefy includes seared red snapper with a cilantro-laced *pico de gallo* sauce. And if you want to buy a souvenir pair of cowboy spurs, you'll find an intriguing collection of western accessories and uniforms for sale outside. Consider beginning your meal with any of 20 kinds of tequila cocktails at the Tequila Bar, which lies a few steps away on the same floor. Big margaritas come in at least a half-dozen varieties, and platters of Tex-Mex food cost from $13.75 to $18.75 each. Especially succulent are soft-shell crabs layered in a pyramid with blue and yellow tortillas.

Ruth's Chris Steak House. In the San Juan Grand Beach Resort and Casino, 187 Isla Grande Ave. ☎ **787/253-1717.** Reservations recommended. Main courses $18.95–$35. AE, DC, MC, V. Daily 6pm–midnight. Bus: A7, M7, or T1. STEAK.

This Puerto Rican branch of one of the most famous steak-house chains in the world presents macho food in its simplest, least subtle form. It obsessively focuses on big drinks and big steaks, grilled in the simplest possible way—usually just with salt, pepper, and a brush-over of butter. These are served within two dark blue, mahogany-trimmed dining rooms, separated by a saloon-style bar. Beaming from a strategic point on the bar's wall is a portrait of corporate matriarch and single mother Ruth Fertel.

Her biography is part of the chain's corporate lore: in the 1960s she mortgaged her house to establish her first restaurant; later she linked her destiny with a crowd of smart investors.

Consider preceding your meal with one of several kinds of martinis, each served in an oversized goblet and packing a wallop stronger than a Nebraska steer. If you're genuinely hungry, you might begin with barbecued shrimp, mushrooms stuffed with crabmeat, or seared ahi tuna with a ginger, mustard, and beer sauce. If you're not overwhelmingly hungry, opt for a salad as an appetizer, since portions are large, two-fisted, and very filling. Steaks are as good as they get, the finest of the Middle West cattle country. Examples include rib eyes, veal chops, porterhouse, New York strips, filet mignons, and T-bones. There's also roasted chicken, lobster, and a fresh catch of the day. Potato side dishes come in seven different preparations—the au gratin version is particularly rich and cheesy. The variety and preparation of vegetables is rather surprisingly limited, each prepared in the simplest possible way. In direct opposition to this is a very urbane and cosmopolitan wine list priced from affordable to stratospheric, and including about 20 wines sold by glass.

Yamato. In El San Juan Hotel & Casino, 6063 Isla Verde Ave. ☎ **787/791-1000.** Reservations recommended. Sushi $2.25–$3 per piece; sushi and teppanyaki dinners $24–$40. AE, MC, V. Daily 6pm–midnight. Bus: A7, M7, or T1. JAPANESE.

The artfully simple decor shows the kind of modern urban minimalism that you might expect in an upscale California restaurant. Separate sections offer conventional seating at tables; at a countertop within view of a sushi display; or at seats around a hot grill where chefs shake, rattle, and sizzle their way through a fast but elaborate cooking ritual. Many visitors include at least some sushi with an entree such as beef sashimi with tataki sauce, shrimp tempura with noodle soup, filet mignon or chicken with shrimp or scallops, or several kinds of rice and noodle dishes.

INEXPENSIVE

✪ **Ciaou Mediterranean Café.** In San Juan Grand Beach Resort & Casino, 187 Isla Grande Ave. ☎ **787/791-5000.** Reservations recommended for dinner. Breakfast $5–$8; pizzas and salads $7.95–$16.95; main courses $15.95–$24.95. AE, DC, MC, V. Bus: A7, M7, or T1. MEDITERRANEAN.

In its own informal and breezy way, this is the most charming restaurant in Isla Verde. Draped with bougainvillea and set directly on the sands of the beach, it acts as both a barrier and a bridge between the hotel and the busy beach of Isla Verde. As such, the place is as likely to attract hotel guests as locals, who stroll in from the nearby condominiums. The establishment's visual centerpiece is an open-air kitchen set within the confines of an oval-shaped bar. Here, a crew of cheerfully animated chefs mingle good culinary technique with Latino theatricality. They are led by Xandra Lopez, one of the few female head chefs in Puerto Rico. More private are any of the tables placed, Portofino style, on a sinuously curved private boardwalk along the beach. Pizzas and pastas are enduringly popular here, but more appealing are such dishes as seafood salad, in which shrimp, scallops, calamari, peppers, onions, and lime juice create something you might have expected in the south of Italy. The Greek-style squid *(kalamarakia tiganita)* is battered and deep-fried, served with ratatouille and spicy marinara sauce. The Provençal-style rack of lamb comes with ratatouille, polenta, and Provençal herbs. The mixed grill of seafood evokes Marseille, thanks to its roe-enhanced *aïoli* and couscous. Overall, the place is chic, charming, and popular—one of our enduring favorites.

✪ **Metropol.** Av. Isla Verde. ☎ **787/791-4046.** Reservations not necessary. Main courses $5.50–$28.90. AE, MC, V. Daily 11am–7pm. Bus: A7, M7, or T1. CUBAN/PUERTO RICAN/INTERNATIONAL.

This is part of a restaurant chain known for serving the island's best Cuban food, although the chefs prepare a wide range of dishes. Metropol is the happiest blend of Cuban and Puerto Rican cuisine we've ever had. The black-bean soup is among the island's finest, served in the classic Havana style with a side dish of rice and chopped onions. Endless garlic bread accompanies most dinners, likely to include Cornish game hen stuffed with Cuban rice and beans or perhaps marinated steak topped with a fried egg (reportedly Castro's favorite). Smoked chicken or chicken-fried steak are also heartily recommended; portions are huge. Plantains, yucca, and all that good stuff accompany most dishes. Finish with a choice of thin or firm custard. Most dishes are at the low end of the price scale.

✪ **Sonny's Oceanfront Place for Ribs.** In the Empress Oceanfront Hotel, 2 Amapola St. ☎ **787/791-3083.** Main courses $7.95–$29.95. AE, DC, DISC, MC, V. Daily 8am–11pm. Bus: M8 or T1. AMERICAN.

Overlooking the sea and the hotel's terraced swimming pool, this restaurant opens onto one of San Juan's best nighttime views, made more glamorous by the glittering lights from the resorts. The cuisine is unpretentious and guaranteed to satisfy hunger pangs for American-style burgers. Several types of barbecued ribs are among the island's most flavorful, always cooked to perfection and seasoned with the most savory of sauces. You can also order pastas and barbecued chicken. More formal dishes include surf and turf, catch of the day, or lobster. Most items are served with the house version of coleslaw and beans.

Exploring San Juan   6

The Spanish began to settle in the area now known as Old San Juan around 1521. At the outset, the city was called Puerto Rico ("Rich Port"), and the whole island was known as San Juan.

The streets are narrow and teeming with traffic, but a walk through Old San Juan—in Spanish, *El Viejo San Juan*—is like a stroll through 5 centuries of history. You can do it in less than a day (see "Walking Tour: Old San Juan," below). In this historic 7-square-block area of the western side of the city, you can see many of Puerto Rico's chief sightseeing attractions and do some shopping along the way.

On the other hand, you may want to just plop yourself down on the sand with a tropical drink, or get outside and play. See section 3 of this chapter for details on all the beaches and active sports in the San Juan area.

Suggested Itineraries

In case you would like to drag yourself away from the beach, here are some suggestions about how to see San Juan.

If You Have 1 Day

To make the most of a short stay, head immediately for Old San Juan for an afternoon of sightseeing and shopping. You should definitely schedule a visit inside El Morro Fortress. Try to spend 2 hours at Condado Beach. Enjoy a Puerto Rican dinner at a local restaurant, listen to some salsa music, and enjoy a rum punch before retiring for the night.

If You Have 2 Days

On your first day, spend the morning shopping and sightseeing in Old San Juan. Schedule interior visits to El Morro Fortress and San Juan Cathedral, then relax on Condado Beach for the rest of the day. Enjoy a Puerto Rican dinner and some local music before retiring.

On your second day, spend the morning exploring El Yunque rain forest, a lush 28,000-acre site east of San Juan. Schedule 2 or 3 hours at nearby Luquillo Beach, the finest on Puerto Rico. Buy lunch from one of the open-air kiosks. Return to San Juan for the evening, attending either a folk-culture show (if available) or a Las Vegas–style revue. Visit the casinos for some action before retiring.

1 Seeing the Sights

Although we have outlined a walking tour of Old San Juan later in this chapter, here is an introduction to some of the sights mentioned there, as well as others you may want to seek out yourself.

FORTS

✪ **Castillo San Felipe del Morro.** At the end of Calle Norzagaray. ☎ **787/729-6960.** Admission $2 adults, $1 ages 13–17, free for children 12 and under. Daily 9am–5pm. Bus: A-5, B-21, or B-40.

Called "El Morro," this fort stands on a rocky promontory dominating the entrance to San Juan Bay. Constructed in 1540, the original fort was a round tower, which can still be seen deep inside the lower levels of the castle. More walls and cannon-firing positions were added, and by 1787, the fortification attained the complex design you see today. This fortress was attacked repeatedly by both the English and the Dutch.

The National Park Service protects the fortifications of Old San Juan, which have been declared a World Heritage Site by the United Nations. With some of the most dramatic views in the Caribbean, you'll find El Morro an intriguing labyrinth of dungeons, barracks, vaults, lookouts, and ramps. Historical and background information is provided in a video in English and Spanish. The nearest parking is the underground facility beneath the Quincentennial Plaza at the Ballajá barracks (Cuartel de Ballajá) on Calle Norzagaray. Sometimes park rangers lead hour-long tours for free, although you can also visit on your own. With the purchase of a ticket here, you don't have to pay the admission for Fort San Cristóbal (see below) if you visit during the same day.

✪ **Fort San Cristóbal.** In the northeast corner of Old San Juan (uphill from Plaza de Colón on Calle Norzagaray). ☎ **787/729-6960.** Admission $2 adults, $1 ages 13–17, free for children 12 and under. Daily 9am–5pm. Bus: A-5, B-21, or B-40; then the free trolley from Covadonga station to the top of the hill.

This huge fortress, begun in 1634 and reengineered in the 1770s, is one of the largest ever built in the Americas by Spain. Its walls rise more than 150 feet above the sea, a marvel of military engineering. San Cristóbal protected San Juan against attackers coming by land as a partner to El Morro, to which it is linked by a half-mile of monumental walls and bastions filled with cannon-firing positions. A complex system of tunnels and dry moats connects the center of San Cristóbal to its "outworks," defensive elements arranged layer after layer over a 27-acre site. You'll get the idea if you look at the scale model on display. Like El Morro, the fort is administered and maintained by the National Park Service. Be sure to see the Garita del Diablo, or the Devil's Sentry Box, one of the oldest parts of San Cristóbal's defenses, and famous in Puerto Rican legend. The devil himself, it is said, would snatch away sentinels at this lonely post at the edge of the sea. In 1898, the first shots of the Spanish-American War in Puerto Rico were fired by cannons on top of San Cristóbal during an artillery duel with a U.S. Navy fleet. Sometimes park rangers lead hour-long tours for free, although you can visit on your own.

Fort San Jerónimo. Calle Rosales, east of the Caribe Hilton, at the entrance to Condado Bay. ☎ **787/724-5477.** Free admission. Wed–Sat 9am–3pm. Bus: T1.

Completed in 1608, this fort was damaged in the English assault of 1797. Reconstructed in the closing year of the 18th century, it has now been taken over by the Institute of Puerto Rican Culture. Anyone wanting to see the view from the inside must call the Caribe Hilton; security here will open the gate to let you inside, but a special request has to be made.

CHURCHES

Capilla de Cristo. Calle del Cristo (directly west of Paseo de la Princesa). Free admission. Tues 10am–2pm. Bus: Old Town Trolley.

Cristo Chapel was built to commemorate what legend says was a miracle. In 1753, a young rider lost control of his horse in a race down this very street during the fiesta of St. John's Day and plunged over the precipice. Moved by the accident, the secretary of the city, Don Mateo Pratts, invoked Christ to save the youth, and he had the chapel built when his prayers were answered. Today it's a landmark in the old city and one of its best-known historical monuments. The chapel's gold and silver altar can be seen through its glass doors. Since the chapel is open only 1 day a week, most visitors have to settle for a view of its exterior.

Catedral de San Juan. Calle del Cristo 153 (at Caleta San Juan). ☎ **787/722-0861.** Free admission. Daily 8:30am–4pm. Bus: Old Town Trolley.

The spiritual and architectural centerpiece of Old San Juan, as you see it in its present form, was begun in 1540 as a replacement for a thatch-roofed chapel that was blown apart by a hurricane in 1529. Chronically hampered by a lack of funds and a recurring series of military and weather-derived disasters, it slowly evolved into the gracefully vaulted, Gothic-inspired structure you see today. Among the many disasters to hit this cathedral are the following: In 1598, the Earl of Cumberland led the British Navy in a looting spree, and in 1615, a hurricane blew away its roof. In 1908, the body of Ponce de León was disinterred from the nearby Iglesia de San José and placed in a marble tomb near the transept, where it remains today (see the box in appendix A for more about Ponce de León). The cathedral also contains the wax-covered mummy of St. Pio, a Roman martyr persecuted and killed for his Christian faith. The mummy has been encased in a glass box ever since it was placed here in 1862. To the right of the mummy is a bizarre wooden replica of Mary with four swords stuck in her bosom. After all the looting and destruction over the centuries, the cathedral's great treasures, including gold and silver, are long gone, although many beautiful stained-glass windows remain. The cathedral faces Plaza de las Monjas (the Nuns' Square), a shady spot where you can rest and cool off.

Iglesia de San José. Plaza de San José, Calle del Cristo. ☎ **787/725-7501.** Free admission. Church and Chapel of Belém, Mon–Wed and Fri 7am–3pm, Sat 8am–1pm. Currently closed for renovations; call to check status. Bus: Old Town Trolley.

Initial plans for this church were drawn in 1523, and Dominican friars supervised its construction in 1532. Both the church and its monastery were closed by decree in 1838, and the property was confiscated by the royal treasury. Later, the Crown turned the convent into a military barracks. The Jesuits restored the badly damaged church. This was the place of worship for Ponce de León's descendants, who are buried here under the family's coat of arms. The conquistador, killed by a poisoned arrow in Florida, was interred here until his removal to the Catedral de San Juan in 1908.

Although badly looted, the church still has some treasures, including *Christ of the Ponces,* a carved crucifix presented to Ponce de León, four oils by José Campéche, and two large works by Francisco Oller. Campeche was the leading Puerto Rican painter of the 18th century, and Oller was Puerto Rico's stellar artist of the late 19th and early 20th centuries. Many miracles have been attributed to a painting in the Chapel of Belém, a 15th-century Flemish work called *Virgin of Bethlehem.*

Look for the statue of Ponce de León in the adjoining plaza—it was made from melted-down British cannons captured during Sir Ralph Abercromby's unsuccessful attack on San Juan in 1797.

The church is currently closed for extensive renovations; check its status before heading here.

MUSEUMS

Many of the museums in Old San Juan close for lunch between 11:45am and 2pm, so schedule your activities accordingly if you intend to museum-hop.

Felisa Rincón de Gautier Museum. Caleta de San Juan 51 at Recinto Oeste. ☎ 787/ 723-1897. Admission free. Mon–Fri 9am–4pm. Bus: Old Town Trolley.

The most heralded woman of modern Puerto Rico served as the mayor of San Juan for 22 consecutive years, between 1946 and 1968. The museum that commemorates her memory is in a 300-year-old building a few blocks downhill from San Juan's cathedral, near one of the medieval gates (La Puerta San Juan) that pierce the walls of the Old City. The interior is devoted to the life and accomplishments of Felisa Rincón de Gautier (1897–1994), and proudly displays some of her personal furniture and artifacts, as well as 212 plaques, 308 certificates of merit, 11 honorary doctorates, and 113 symbolic keys to other cities, such as Gary, Indiana, and Perth Amboy, New Jersey. Her particular areas of influence included child welfare and elementary education. Photographs show her with luminaries that include everyone from Eleanor Roosevelt to the pope. The oldest of nine children, and daughter of a local lawyer and a schoolteacher, she shouldered the responsibilities of rearing her younger siblings after the death of her mother when she was 12. Today, the museum illuminates Doña Felisa's life as well as the reverence in which Puerto Ricans hold their most celebrated political matriarch. As such, it's a quirky, intensely personalized monument that combines a strong sense of feminism with Puerto Rican national pride.

Museo de Arte e Historia de San Juan. Calle Norzagaray 150. ☎ 787/724-1875. Free admission. Wed–Sun 10am–5pm. Bus: B-21 to Old San Juan terminal; then a trolley car from the terminal to the museum.

Located in a Spanish colonial building at the corner of Calle MacArthur, this cultural center was the city's main marketplace in the mid-19th century. Local art is displayed in the east and west galleries, and audiovisual materials reveal the history of the city. Sometimes major cultural events are staged in the museum's large courtyard. English- and Spanish-language audiovisual shows are presented Monday through Friday every hour on the hour from 9am to 4pm.

Museo de las Américas. Cuartel de Ballajá. ☎ 787/724-5052. Free admission. Tues–Fri 10am–4pm, Sat–Sun 11am–5pm. Bus: Old Town Trolley.

One of the major new museums of San Juan, Museo de las Américas showcases the artisans of North, South, and Central America, featuring everything from carved figureheads from New England whaling ships to dugout canoes carved by Carib Indians in Dominica. It is unique in Puerto Rico and well worth a visit. Also on display is a changing collection of paintings by artists from throughout the Spanish-speaking world, some of which are for sale, and a permanent collection called "Puerto Rican Santos," which includes a collection of carved, wooden saints donated by Dr. Ricardo Alegría.

Museo del Indio. Calle San José (at the corner of Calle Luna). ☎ 787/721-2864. Free admission. Tues–Sat 8am–4pm. Bus: T1.

This museum is housed in a 250-year-old colonial building. Its cramped and airless rooms open onto a colonial courtyard. Exhibits include a modest collection of petroglyphs, maps celebrating the geography and diversity of the Americas, and a not particularly exciting collection of glassed-in exhibits. This is not a major museum, but a possible detour if you're shopping in the neighborhood.

Old San Juan Attractions

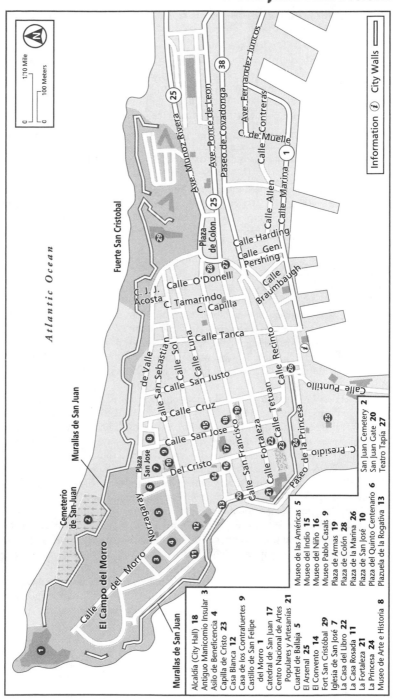

Atlantic Ocean

Fuerte San Cristobal

Cemeterio de San-Juan

Murallas de San Juan

El Campo del Morro

Calle del Morro

Norzagaray

Plaza San Jose

de Valle

Calle San Sebastián

Calle Sol

Calle Luna

Calle San Justo

Calle Tanca

C. J. J. Acosta

Calle O'Donell

C. Tamarindo

C. Capilla

Calle Braumbaugh

Calle Gen! Pershing

Calle Harding

Plaza de Colon

Calle Allen

Calle Marina

Calle Contreras

C. de Muelle

Ave. Ponce de Leon

Paseo de Covadonga

Ave. Fernandez Juncos

Ave. Muñoz Rivera

Calle Cruz

Calle San Jose

Del Cristo

Calle San Francisco

Calle Fortaleza

Calle San José

Calle Tetuan

Calle Recinto

Calle Puntillo

Paseo de la Princesa

C. Presidio

Information *i* City Walls

Murallas de San Juan

Alcaldía (City Hall) **18**	Museo de las Américas **5**
Antiguo Manicomio Insular **3**	Museo del Indio **15**
Asilo de Beneficencia **4**	Museo del Niño **16**
Capilla de Cristo **23**	Museo Pablo Casals **9**
Casa Blanca **12**	Plaza de Armas **19**
Casa de los Contrafuertes **9**	Plaza de Colón **28**
Castillo de San Felipe del Morro **1**	Plaza de la Marina **26**
Catedral de San Juan **17**	Plaza de San José **10**
Centro Nacional de Artes Populares y Artesanías **21**	Plaza del Quinto Centenario **6**
Cuartel de Ballajá **5**	Plazuela de la Rogativa **13**
El Arsenal **25**	San Juan Cemetery **2**
El Convento **14**	San Juan Gate **20**
Fort San Cristóbal **29**	Teatro Tapia **27**
Iglesia de San José **7**	
La Casa del Libro **22**	
La Casa Rosada **11**	
La Fortaleza **21**	
La Princesa **24**	
Museo de Arte e Historia **8**	

117

Museo Pablo Casals. Plaza de San José, Calle San Sebastián 101. ☎ **787/723-9185.** Admission $1 adults, 50¢ children. Tues–Sat 9:30am–5:30pm. Bus: T1.

Adjacent to Iglesia de San José, this museum is devoted to the memorabilia left to the people of Puerto Rico by the musician Pablo Casals. The maestro's cello is here, along with a library of videotapes (played upon request) of some of his festival concerts. This small 18th-century house also contains manuscripts and photographs of Casals. The annual Casals Festival draws worldwide interest and internationally known performing artists; it's held during the first 2 weeks of June.

Museum of History, Anthropology and Art. Av. Ponce de León, Río Piedras Campus. ☎ **787/764-0000,** ext. 2452. Free admission. Mon–Fri 9am–4:15pm, Sat–Sun 9am–3:15pm. Closed holidays. Take the bus marked RÍO PIEDRAS from Plaza de Colón in Old San Juan to stop 36.

Here you'll find good collections of paintings by Puerto Rican artists, including Francisco Oller (late 19th and early 20th centuries) and José Campéche, the first important artist of the country (18th century). There's also a large collection of pre-Columbian Puerto Rican native artifacts from the Ingeri, sub-Taíno, and Taíno civilizations.

HISTORIC SIGHTS

In addition to the forts and churches listed above, you may want to see the following:

San Juan Gate, Calle San Francisco and Calle Recinto Oeste, built around 1635, just north of La Fortaleza, several blocks downhill from the cathedral, was the main point of entry into San Juan if you arrived by ship in the 17th and 18th centuries. The gate is the only one remaining of the several that once pierced the fortifications of the old walled city. The San Juan Gate was one of six heavy wooden doors cut into the walls. For centuries it was closed at sundown to cut off access to the historic old town. Bus: T1.

Plazuela de la Rogativa, Caleta de las Monjas, is a little plaza with a statue of a bishop and three women commemorating one of Puerto Rico's most famous legends. In 1797, from across San Juan Bay at Santurce, the British held the Old Town under siege. However, that same year they mysteriously sailed away. Later, the commander claimed he feared that the enemy was well prepared behind those walls—he apparently saw many lights and believed them to be reinforcements. Some people believe that those lights were torches carried by women in a *rogativa,* or religious procession, as they followed their bishop. An artfully stylized bronze statue of a bishop, trailed by a trio of torch-bearing women, was donated to the city on its 450th anniversary. Bus: T1.

The **city walls** around San Juan were built in 1630 to protect the town against both European invaders and Caribbean pirates. The city walls that remain today were once part of one of the most impregnable fortresses in the New World and even today are an engineering marvel. Their thickness averages 20 feet at the base and 12 feet at the top, with an average height of 40 feet. At their top, notice the balconied buildings that served for centuries as hospitals and also residences of the island's various governors. Between Fort San Cristóbal and El Morro, bastions were erected at frequent intervals. The walls come into view as you approach from San Cristóbal on your way to El Morro. Bus: T1.

San Juan Cemetery, Calle Norzagaray, officially opened in 1814 and has since been the final resting place for many prominent Puerto Rican families. The circular chapel, dedicated to Saint Magdalene of Pazzis, was built in the 1860s. Aficionados of old graveyards can wander among marble monuments, mausoleums, and statues, marvelous examples of Victorian funereal statuary. However, since there are no trees, or any form of shade here, it would be best not to go exploring in the noonday sun. In any case, be careful—the cemetery is often a venue for illegal drug deals and can be dangerous. Bus: T1.

Alcaldía (City Hall). Calle San Francisco. ☎ **787/724-7171,** ext. 2391. Free admission. Mon–Fri 8am–4pm. Closed holidays. Bus: Old Town Trolley.

The City Hall, with its double arcade flanked by two towers resembling Madrid's City Hall, was constructed in stages from 1604 to 1789. Still in use, this building today contains a tourist information center downstairs plus a small art gallery on the first floor.

Casa Blanca. Calle San Sebastián 1. ☎ **787/724-4102.** Admission $2. Tues–Sat 9am–noon and 1–4:30pm. Bus: Old Town Trolley.

Ponce de León never lived here, although construction of the house—built in 1521, 2 years after his death—is sometimes attributed to him. The work was ordered by his son-in-law, Juan García Troche. The parcel of land was given to Ponce de León as a reward for services rendered to the Crown. Descendants of the explorer lived in the house for about $2^1/_2$ centuries until the Spanish government took it over in 1779 for use as a residence for military commanders. The U.S. government also used it as a home for army commanders. On the first floor, the **Juan Ponce de León Museum** is furnished with antiques, paintings, and artifacts from the 16th through the 18th centuries. In back is a garden with spraying fountains, offering an intimate and verdant respite from the monumental buildings of Old San Juan.

Casa de los Contrafuertes (House of the Buttresses). Plaza de San José, Calle San Sebastián 101. ☎ **787/724-5477.** Free admission. Tues–Sat 8:30am–4:30pm. Bus: Old Town Trolley.

Adjacent to the Museo de Pablo Casals, this thickly buttressed building is believed to be the oldest residence remaining in El Viejo San Juan. The complex also contains a **pharmacy museum,** which documents the history of a 19th-century pharmacy in the town of Cayey. Even if you're not a specialist, this museum is fascinating and fun if only to see what was acceptable as cures for what ailed you back in those days. Upstairs you'll find a **graphic arts museum,** displaying prints and paintings by local artists.

El Arsenal. La Puntilla. ☎ **787/724-0700.** Free admission. Wed–Sun 8:30am–4:30pm. Bus: Old Town Trolley.

The Spaniards used a shallow craft to patrol the lagoons and mangroves in and around San Juan. Needing a base for these vessels, they constructed El Arsenal in the 19th century. It was at this base that they staged their last stand, flying the Spanish colors until the final Spaniard was removed in 1898, at the end of the Spanish-American War. Changing art exhibitions are held in the building's three galleries.

La Casa del Libro. Calle del Cristo 255. ☎ **787/723-0354.** Free admission. Tues–Sat 11am–4:30pm. Bus: Old Town Trolley.

This restored 19th-century house shelters a library and museum devoted to the arts of printing and bookmaking, with examples of fine printing, which date back 5 centuries, and some illuminated medieval manuscripts.

La Fortaleza. Calle Fortaleza, overlooking San Juan Harbor. ☎ **787/721-7000,** ext. 2211. Free admission. 30-minute tours of the gardens and building (conducted in English and Spanish) given Mon–Fri, every hour 9am–4pm. Bus: T1.

The office and residence of the governor of Puerto Rico is the oldest executive mansion in continuous use in the western hemisphere, and it has served as the island's seat of government for more than 3 centuries. Yet, its history goes back further, to 1533, when construction began on a fortress to protect San Juan's Spanish settlers during raids by Carib tribesmen and pirates. The original medieval towers remain, but as the edifice was subsequently enlarged into a palace, other modes of architecture and ornamentation were also incorporated, including baroque, Gothic, neoclassical, and Arabian. La Fortaleza has been designated a national historic site by the U.S. government. Informal but proper attire is required.

Teatro Tapía. Av. Ponce de León. ☎ **787/721-0169.** Access limited to tickets holders at performances (see "San Juan After Dark"). Bus: Old Town Trolley.

Standing across from the Plaza de Colón, this is one of the oldest theaters in the western hemisphere, built about 1832. In 1976, a restoration returned the theater to its original appearance. Much of Puerto Rican theater history is connected with the Tapía, named after the island's first prominent playwright, Alejandro Tapía y Rivera (1826 to 1882). Various productions—some musical—are staged here throughout the year, representing a repertoire of drama, dance, and cultural events.

HISTORIC SQUARES

In Old San Juan, **Plaza del Quinto Centenario** (or Quincentennial Plaza, in English) overlooks the Atlantic from atop the highest point in the city.

A striking and symbolic feature of the plaza, which was constructed as part of the 1992 through 1993 celebration of the 500th anniversary of the discovery of the New World, is a sculpture that rises 40 feet from the plaza's top level. The monumental totemic sculpture in black granite and ceramics symbolizes the earthen and clay roots of American history and is the work of Jaime Suarez, one of Puerto Rico's foremost artists. From its southern end, two needle-shaped columns point skyward to the North Star, the guiding light of explorers. Placed around the plaza are fountains, other columns, and sculpted steps that represent various historic periods in Puerto Rico's 500-year heritage.

Quincentennial Plaza is at the hub of a group of some of the most significant and impressive structures dating from colonial times. Clear and sweeping views extend from the plaza to El Morro Fortress at the headland of San Juan Bay and to the Dominican Convent and San José Church, a rare New World example of true Gothic architecture. Asilo de Beneficencia, a former indigents' hospital dating from 1832, occupies a corner of El Morro's entrance and is now the new home of the Institute of Puerto Rican Culture. Adjacent to the plaza stands the Cuartel de Ballajá, built in the mid-19th century as the Spanish army headquarters and still the largest edifice in the Americas constructed by Spanish engineers; it houses the Museum of the Americas.

Centrally located, Quincentennial Plaza is one of modern Puerto Rico's respectful gestures to its colorful and lively history. It is a perfect introduction for visitors seeking to discover the many rich links with the past in Old San Juan.

Once named St. James Square, or Plaza Santiago, **Plaza de Colón** in the heart of San Juan's Old Town is bustling and busy, reached along the pedestrian mall of Calle Fortaleza. The square was renamed Plaza de Colón to honor the 400th anniversary of the explorer's so-called discovery of Puerto Rico. Of course, it is more politically correct today to say that Columbus explored or came upon an already inhabited island. He certainly didn't discover it. But when a statue here, perhaps the most famous on the island, was erected atop a high pedestal, it was clearly to honor Columbus, not to decry his legacy.

You Paid What?

47,000 hotels, 700 airlines,
50 rental car companies. And a few
million ways to save money.

Travelocity.com
A Sabre Company

Go Virtually Anywhere.

AOL Keyword: Travel

Travelocity® and Travelocity.com are trademarks of Travelocity.com LP and Sabre® is a trademark of an affiliate of Sabre Inc.
© 2000 Travelocity.com LP. All rights reserved.

Will you have enough stories to tell your grandchildren

©2000 Yahoo! Inc.

Yahoo! Travel

DO YOU
YAHOO!
?

PARKS & GARDENS

Administered by the University of Puerto Rico, **Jardín Botánico,** Barrio Venezuela at the intersection of routes 1 and 847 in Río Piedras (☎ 787/763-4408), is a lush tropical garden with some 200 species of vegetation. You can pack a picnic lunch and bring it here if you choose. The orchid garden is exceptional, and the palm garden is said to contain some 125 species. Footpaths blaze a trail through heavy forests opening onto a lotus lagoon. Admission is free. It's open daily from 8am to 4:30pm. Take bus 19 to reach it.

Muñoz Rivera Park, Avenida Ponce de León (☎ 787/724-4430), is affiliated with Luis Muñoz Marín Park (see below), with which it is frequently confused. This green space is administered by the Park Trust of Puerto Rico (☎ 787/763-0613). More closely linked to central San Juan than to the suburbs, it's a rectangular, seaward-facing park that was built about 50 years ago to honor Luis Muñoz Rivera, the Puerto Rican statesman, journalist, and poet. It's filled with picnic areas, wide walks, shady trees, landscaped grounds, and recreational areas. Its centerpiece (El Pabellon de la Paz) is sometimes used for cultural events and expositions of handicrafts. Admission is free, and the park is open 24 hours. Take the Los Américas Expressway to Avenida Piñero, then head west until you reach the entrance; or take bus A1.

Luis Muñoz Marín Park, Avenida Piñero, at Alto Rey (☎ 787/751-3353), is administered by the Park Trust of Puerto Rico, and is the best-known, most frequently visited children's playground in Puerto Rico—although it has equal appeal to adults. Conceived as a verdant oasis in an otherwise crowded urban neighborhood, it's a fenced-in repository of swings, jungle gyms, and slides set amid several small lakes. Here you'll also find an incomparable view of San Juan. A small-scale cable car carries passengers aloft at 10-minute intervals for panoramic views of the surrounding landscape ($1.25 per person). Open Wednesday through Sunday from 8:30am to 5pm. Entrance for pedestrians is free, although parking costs $4 per vehicle. By public transportation, take bus A1 to Río Piedras, then switch to bus 52.

Parque Central Municipio de San Juan, Calle Cerra (☎ 787/722-1646), was inaugurated in 1979 for the Pan-American Games. This mangrove-bordered park covers 35 acres and lies southwest of Miramar. Joggers appreciate its labyrinth of trails, tennis players come to use the courts, and all kinds of city dwellers stroll to relieve the pressures of urban life. Admission for pedestrians is free, although parking costs 75¢. Open Monday through Thursday from 6am to 10pm, Friday from 6am to 9pm, Saturday and Sunday from 6am to 6pm. Take bus A1 to reach it.

SIGHTSEEING TOURS

If you want to see more of the island but you don't want to rent a car or manage the inconveniences of public transportation, perhaps an organized tour is for you.

Castillo Sightseeing Tours & Travel Services, 2413 Calle Laurel, Punta La Marias, Santurce (☎ 787/791-6195), maintains offices at some of the capital's best-known hotels, including the Caribe Hilton, San Juan Marriott Resort, and El San Juan Grand. Using six of their own air-conditioned buses, with access to others if demand warrants it, the company's tours include pickups and drop-offs at hotels as an added convenience.

One of the most popular half-day tours departs most days of the week between 8:30 and 9am, lasts 4 to 5 hours, and costs $32 per person. Leaving from San Juan, it tours along the northeastern part of the island to El Yunque Rain Forest.

The company also offers a city tour of San Juan that departs daily at 1 or 1:30pm. The 4-hour trip costs $32 per person and includes a stopover at the Bacardi Rum Factory, where you're treated to a complimentary rum drink. The company also operates full-day snorkeling tours to the reefs near the coast of a deserted island off Puerto Rico's eastern edge aboard one of two sail and motor-driven catamarans. With lunch, snorkeling gear, and piña coladas included, the full-day (7:45am to 5pm) excursion goes for $69 per person.

Few cities of the Caribbean lend themselves so gracefully to walking tours. You can always embark on these on your own, stopping and shopping en route (see "Walking Tour: Old San Juan," below).

ESPECIALLY FOR KIDS

Puerto Rico is one of the most family-friendly islands in the Caribbean, and many hotels offer family discounts. Programs for children are also offered at a number of hotels, including day and night camp activities and baby-sitting services. Trained counselors at these camps supervise children as young as 3 in activities ranging from nature hikes to tennis lessons, coconut carving, and sand-sculpture contests.

Teenagers can learn to hip-hop dance Latino style with special salsa and merengue lessons, learn conversational Spanish, indulge in water sports, take jeep excursions, or scuba dive in some of the best diving locations in the world.

The best kiddies program is offered at **El San Juan Hotel & Casino** (see chapter 4), where camp activities are presented to children between the ages of 5 and 12. Counselors design activities according to the interests of groups of up to 10 children. Kids Klub members receive a T-shirt, membership card, and three "Sand Dollars" for use in the game room or at a poolside restaurant. The daily fee of $28 includes lunch.

Another worthy choice is the **Condado Plaza Hotel & Casino** (see chapter 4), where the daily Camp Taíno offers a regular program of activities and special events for children ages 5 to 12. The $25-per-child fee includes lunch. The hotel also has a toddlers' pool, and the kids' water slide in its main pool starts in a Spanish-style castle turret. For teenagers, the hotel has a video game room, a tennis court, several putting greens, and various organized activities.

Children should love **El Morro Fortress** (see "Forts," above), since it looks just like the castles they have seen on TV and at the movies. On a rocky promontory, El Morro is filled with dungeons and dank places and also has lofty lookout points for viewing San Juan Harbor.

Luis Muñoz Marín Park (see "Parks & Gardens," above) is one of the best places to take your children for a picnic. It has the most popular children's playground in Puerto Rico. It's filled with landscaped grounds and recreational areas—lots of room for fun in the sun.

Museo del Niño (Children's Museum). Calle del Cristo 150. ☎ **787/722-3791.** Admission $2.50. Tues–Thurs 9am–3:30pm, Fri 9am–5pm, Sat–Sun 12:30–5pm. Bus: Old Town Trolley.

In the late 1990s, the city of San Juan turned over one of the most desirable buildings in the colonial zone—a 300-year-old villa directly across from the city's cathedral—to a group of sociologists and student volunteers. Jointly, they created the only children's museum in Puerto Rico, with mixed results. Through interactive exhibits, children learn simple lessons, such as the benefit of brushing teeth or recycling aluminum cans, or the value of caring properly for pets. Staff members include lots of student volunteers who play either one-on-one or with small groups of children. Nothing here is terribly cerebral, and nothing will necessarily compel you to return. But it does provide a playtime experience that some, but not all, children will remember fondly for several weeks.

Plaza Acuatica. Las Américas Expressway, opposite Plaza de las Américas, Hato Rey. ☎ **787/754-9800.** Admission $12.95, $8.95 for children under 11 (activities are extra). Feb–May Sat–Sun 10am–6pm; June–Aug daily 10am–6pm; Sept Sat–Sun 10am–6pm. Closed Oct–Jan. Bus: V21 from Old San Juan.

This water park is an outdoor amusement area that the whole family can enjoy. Activities range from water slides and "rapids" to miniature golf. There are also dining facilities.

Time Out Family Amusement Center. Plaza de las Américas, Las Américas Expressway at Roosevelt Ave., Hato Rey. ☎ **787/753-0606.** Free admission (activities are extra). Sun–Thurs 9:30am–10pm, Fri–Sat 9:30am–11:30pm. Bus: V21 from Old San Juan.

This is the most popular venue for family outings on Puerto Rico. On weekends, seemingly half of the families in the city show up. It has a large variety of electronic games for children and adults alike, but there are no rides.

Walking Tour: Old San Juan

Start: Plaza de la Marina.
Finish: Fort San Cristóbal.
Time: 2 hours (not counting stops).
Best times: Any sunny day between 7am and 6pm.
Worst times: When several cruise ships are in port simultaneously.

The streets are narrow and teeming with traffic, but a walk through Old San Juan (in Spanish, *El Viejo San Juan*) is like a stroll through 5 centuries of history. Beneficiary of millions of dollars' worth of restoration since the early 1970s, Old San Juan is one of the world's most potent reminders of the power and grandeur of the Spanish Empire. This tour follows an itinerary that begins at a point just to the west of San Juan's cruise piers and then encircles the perimeter of some of the best-preserved fortifications built by the Spaniards during the 16th and 17th centuries. En route, it will pass beneath the governor's historic mansion, La Fortaleza, and encircle the Casa Blanca—ancestral home of the Ponce de León family—before ending at a point beyond the entrance of one of the most fiercely guarded fortresses of the colonial age, Fort San Cristóbal.

Begin your walking tour near the post office, amid the taxis, buses, and urban congestion of:

1. **Plaza de la Marina,** a sloping, many-angled plaza situated at the eastern edge of one of San Juan's showcase promenades—Paseo de la Princesa. This 19th-century paseo was an esplanade where the Spanish colonial gentry once strolled while enjoying the balmy Caribbean air.

Towering royal palms shade the broad esplanade, now paved with brick. On the paseo's west side overlooking the sea, a large bronze fountain, *Raices* (Roots), sculpted in 1992 by the Spanish artist Luís Sanguino, depicts the Amerindian, African, and Spanish origins of Puerto Rico as human figures with dolphins cavorting at their feet. Viewed from afar, the entire ensemble looks like a caravel being steered out to sea by dolphins, setting its course for the 21st century. On the paseo's east side stand five allegorical pieces on the island's heritage sculpted by José Buscaglia also in 1992. This work is said to symbolize the various epochs that Puerto Rico has undergone in the past 5 centuries—from the coming of the Spanish conquistadores to the beginning of Puerto Rico's role as a U.S. protectorate.

A gazebo serves light seafood dishes, salads, and the island's famed rich coffee. Outdoor tables with umbrellas allow parents to keep an eye on their children who may be enjoying the playground nearby. More than 20 trees were planted to shade the tables. Criollo dishes are also available from food carts with colored awnings.

Walk westward along Paseo de la Princesa, past heroic statues and manicured trees until you reach:

2. La Princesa, the gray-and-white building on your right, which served for centuries as one of the most feared prisons in the Caribbean. Today it houses the offices of the Puerto Rico Tourism Company and an exhibit of work by Puerto Rican artists since the 1950s. Gallery hours are Monday through Friday from 9am to noon and 1 to 4pm, with no admission charged. In front of La Princesa stands a sculpture of one of the island's most beloved leaders, Doña Felisa Gautier, mayor of San Juan from 1946 to 1968.

Continue walking westward to the base of the heroic fountain near the edge of the sea. Turn to your right and follow the seaside promenade as it parallels the edge of the:

3. City Walls, once part of one of the most impregnable fortresses in the New World. See "Historic Sights," above.

Continue walking between the sea and the base of the city walls until the walkway goes through the walls at the:

4. San Juan Gate, at Calle San Francisco and Recinto del Oeste, built around 1635, as the main point of access from the wharves to the colony's interior. See "Historic Sights," above.

Now that you're inside the once-dreaded fortifications, turn immediately right and walk uphill along Calle Recinto del Oeste. The wrought-iron gates at the street's end, which will probably be guarded by a pair of attendants, lead to:

5. La Fortaleza, the centuries-old residence of the Puerto Rican governor, located on Calle La Fortaleza. See "Forts," above.

Now retrace your steps along Calle Recinto del Oeste, walking first downhill and then uphill for about a block until you reach Caleta de las Monjas. Fork left until you see a panoramic view and a contemporary statue marking the center of:

6. Plazuela de la Rogativa, where the statue on this small square commemorates a time in 1797 when British soldiers mistook a religious procession for the arrival of Spanish reinforcements and fled. See "Historic Sights," above.

Now, continue westward, passing between a pair of urn-capped gateposts. You'll be walking parallel to the crenellations of the 17th-century city walls. The cool, tree-shaded boulevard will fork (take the right-hand fork) and pass just above the pink walls of:

7. La Casa Rosada, a graceful villa built in 1812 for leaders of the Spanish army. It cannot be visited. Continue climbing the steeply inclined cobble-covered ramp to its top. Walk westward across the field toward the neoclassical gateway of a fortress believed impregnable for centuries, the:

8. Castillo de San Felipe del Morro ("El Morro"), whose fortress walls were designed as part of a network of defenses that made San Juan *La Ciudad Murada* (the Walled City). See "Forts," above.

After your visit, with El Morro behind you, retrace your steps through the sunlit, treeless field to the point you stood at when you first sighted the fortress. Walk down the Calle del Morro past the:

Walking Tour—Old San Juan

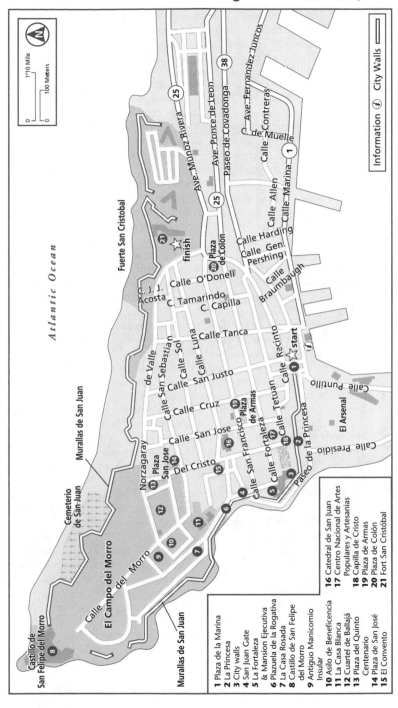

1 Plaza de la Marina
2 La Princesa
3 City walls
4 San Juan Gate
5 La Fortaleza & Mansion Ejecutiva
6 Plazuela de la Rogativa
7 La Casa Rosada
8 Castillo de San Felipe del Morro
9 Antiguo Manicomio Insular
10 Asilo de Beneficencia
11 La Casa Blanca
12 Cuartel de Ballajá
13 Plaza del Quinto Centenario
14 Plaza de San José
15 El Convento
16 Catedral de San Juan
17 Centro Nacional de Artes Populares y Artesanías
18 Capilla de Cristo
19 Plaza de Armas
20 Plaza de Colón
21 Fort San Cristóbal

Information (i)   City Walls

125

9. **Antiguo Manicomio Insular,** whose construction was decreed by the Spanish king in 1854 as an insane asylum. Converted to a U.S. army barracks after the Spanish-American War, it has functioned since 1965 as the Puerto Rican Academy of Fine Arts. Iron fences of grace and elegance protect a pair of court-yards centered around splashing fountains. Walk parallel to the facade of this former asylum, turning right at an unmarked street that passersby might tell you is the Calle de Beneficias. Further on, notice the stately neoclassical building (painted buff with fern-green trim) on your right. It's the:

10. **Asilo de Beneficencia ("Home for the Poor"),** which dates from the 1840s. It has two attractive interior patios, an austere dignity, and usually an echoing silence. Today, it houses the administrative offices of the Institute of Puerto Rican Culture, with several changing exhibition galleries, plus an interesting room filled with pre-Columbian artifacts. The galleries are open Wednesday through Friday from 9am to 4:30pm, Saturday and Sunday from 11am to 6pm. The little museum of pre-Columbian artifacts can be visited Tuesday from 9am to 7pm and Wednesday through Sunday from 9am to 5pm. For more information, call ☎ 787/724-0700.

Continue walking uphill to the small, formal, and sloping plaza at the street's top. On the right-hand side, within a trio of buildings, is:

11. **Casa Blanca,** which was built by the son-in-law of Juan Ponce de León as the great conquistador's island home (he never actually lived here). See "Historic Sights," above.

After your visit, exit by the compound's front entrance and walk downhill, retracing your steps for a half block, heading toward the massive and monumental tangerine-colored building on your right, the:

12. **Cuartel de Ballajá,** the 19th-century military barracks of Ballajá, which once housed troops from Spain along with their wives and children, in a setting evocative of the most austere and massive monasteries of Old Spain. It is still the largest edifice in the Americas constructed by Spanish engineers. It was declared a National Historic Monument in 1954. On the building's second floor is the **Museo de las Américas** (see "Museums," above).

After your visit, exit through the barrack's extremely narrow eastern door, where you'll immediately spot one of the most dramatic modern plazas in Puerto Rico, the:

13. **Plaza del Quinto Centenario,** a terraced tribute to the European colonization of the New World, and one of the most elaborate and formal piazzas in Puerto Rico.

Now, walk a short block to the southeast to reach the ancient borders of the:

14. **Plaza de San José,** whose center is dominated by a heroic statue of Juan Ponce de León, which was cast from an English cannon captured during a naval battle in 1797. Around the periphery of the square, notice three important sites: the Museo de Pablo Casals, whose exhibits honor the life and work of the Spanish-born cellist who adopted Puerto Rico as his final home (see "Museums," above); the Casa de los Contrafuertes (House of the Buttresses), which is adjacent to the Museo de Pablo Casals (see "Historic Sights," above); and the Iglesia de San José, where the conquistador's coat of arms hangs above the altar (see "Churches," above). Established by the Dominicans in 1523, this church is one of the oldest places of Christian worship in the New World.

☕ **TAKE A BREAK**   Plaza de San José is home to at least three prominent bars and restaurants, all of which serve beer, coffee, or a simple meal. They include El Patio de Sam and a supremely informal tavern, NoNo's, where local night owls occupy virtually every nook and bar stool, especially after sundown (see chapter 5). Also appealing is El Boquerón, operating out of a narrow storefront midway between the two.

Now exit from the plaza's southwestern corner and walk downhill along one of the capital's oldest and best-known streets, Calle del Cristo (also known as Calle Cristo). Two blocks later, at the corner of Calle las Monjas, you'll find the venerable walls of:

15. El Convento, which originally was conceived as a convent in the 17th century but functioned for many decades as one of the few hotels within the old city (see the recommendation in chapter 4). Across the street from El Convento lies the island's most famous church and spiritual centerpiece, the:

16. Catedral de San Juan, a distinguished landmark that in recent years has been restored to its original Spanish beauty. See "Churches," above.

Now walk 2 more blocks southward along Calle del Cristo, through one of the most attractive shopping districts in the Caribbean. After passing Calle Fortaleza, look on your left for the:

17. Centro Nacional de Artes Populares y Artesanías, a popular arts and crafts center that belongs to the Institute of Puerto Rican Culture. See "Shopping," below.

After your visit, continue to the southernmost tip of Calle del Cristo (just a few steps away) to the wrought-iron gates that surround a chapel no bigger than an oversized newspaper kiosk, the:

18. Capilla de Cristo, its altar dedicated to the "Christ of Miracles." See "Churches," above.

Now retrace your steps about a block along the Calle del Cristo, walking north. Turn right along Calle Fortaleza. One block later, turn left onto Calle de San José, which leads to the site of the capital's most symmetrical and beautiful square:

Plaza de Armas, a broad and open Spanish-style plaza that was the original main square of Old San Juan and the very hub of the city. It has a lovely fountain with 19th-century statues representing the four seasons. In times gone by, families with unmarried daughters would parade around the square. It was a proper way for fully chaperoned young women to catch the eye of young, available men. The plaza is bordered by the Calles San Francisco, Fortaleza, San José, and Cruz. Two important buildings flanking this square are the neoclassic Intendencia (which houses certain offices of the U.S. State Department) and San Juan's City Hall, or Alcaldía. Relax on one of the benches if you choose, before leaving the square eastward along Calle San Francisco.

☕ **TAKE A BREAK   La Bombonera,** Calle San Francisco 259 (☎ 787/ 722-0658), offers take-away baked goods, as well as sandwiches, spicy platters of Puerto Rican food, and endless cups of richly scented coffee. No one will mind if you just order something to drink, but if you want lunch, the portions are copious and inexpensive. It's rather informal; the place bustles, but no one goes away hungry.

After your pick-me-up, continue your promenade eastward along the length of Calle San Francisco. It will eventually deposit you beside the traffic, parked cars, and open-air conviviality of the very large:

19. Plaza de Colón, with its stone column topped with a statue of Christopher Columbus. See "Historic Squares," above. To the side of the square is the Tapía Theater, which has been restored to its original 19th-century elegance (see "Historic Sights," above).

Continue along Calle San Francisco to the intersection with Calle de Valle, and follow the signs to:

20. Fort San Cristóbal, built as part of the string of fortifications guarding one of Spain's then-most-valuable colonies. Today, like its twin, El Morro, it is maintained by the National Park Service and can be visited throughout the day. See "Forts," above.

2 Nearby Attractions

Called "the Cathedral of Rum," the **Bacardi Distillery** at Route 888, kilometer 2.6 at Cataño (☎ 787/788-1500), is the largest of its kind in the world. Reached by taking a ferry across San Juan Bay (50¢ each way), the distillery produces 100,000 gallons of rum daily. Free 45-minute guided tours take place Monday through Saturday from 9:30am to 3:30pm. Complimentary rum drinks are offered at the beginning of the tour, and a well-stocked gift shop sells a wide assortment of handsome items, from T-shirts to duffel bags. Naturally, you can purchase Bacardi rums here at prices that are slightly more reasonable than those at home. Some rums available are not sold on the U.S. mainland and make unusual gifts.

Upon entering the first floor, you'll get a glimpse of what rum production was like a century ago, including oak barrels used in the aging process and an old sugar-cane wagon. On the fifth floor you'll enter the Hall of Rum with a collection of beverages made by the corporation over a period of years. You'll then witness "the birth of rum"—the fermentation processes of molasses (it takes 100 gallons of molasses to produce one barrel of rum).

At the end of the tour you'll visit the Bacardi Family Museum, documenting the family's history, and you can watch a short video about the bottling process. Afterward, you can stroll through the beautiful grounds overlooking Old San Juan.

3 Diving, Fishing, Tennis & Other Outdoor Pursuits

Active vacationers will have a wide choice of things to do in San Juan, from beaching to windsurfing. The beachside hotels, of course, offer lots of water-sports activities (see chapter 4).

THE BEACHES

Some public stretches of shoreline around San Juan are overcrowded, especially on Saturday and Sunday; others are practically deserted. If you find that secluded, hidden beach of your dreams, proceed with caution. On unguarded beaches you'll have no way to protect yourself or your valuables should you be approached by a robber or mugger, which has been known to happen. For more information about the island's many beaches, call the **Department of Sports and Recreation** (☎ 787/724-2500).

All beaches on Puerto Rico, even those fronting the top hotels, are open to the public. Public bathing beaches are called *balnearios* and charge for parking and for use of facilities, such as lockers and showers. Public beaches shut down on Monday; if Monday is a holiday, the beaches are open for the holiday but close the next day, Tuesday. Beach hours are from 9am to 5pm in winter, to 6pm off-season. Major public beaches in the San Juan area have changing rooms and showers; Luquillo also has picnic tables.

Famous with beach buffs since the 1920s, ✪ **Condado Beach** put San Juan on the map as a tourist resort. Backed up by high-rise hotels, it seems more like Miami Beach than any other in the Caribbean. From parasailing to sailing, all sorts of water sports can be booked at kiosks along the beach or at the activities desk of the various hotels. There are also plenty of outdoor bars and restaurants when you tire of the sands. Condado is especially busy wherever a high-rise resort is located. People-watching seems to be a favorite sport along these golden strands.

A favorite of sanjuaneros themselves, golden-sand **Isla Verde Beach** is also ideal for swimming, and it, too, is lined with high-rise resorts à la Miami Beach. Many luxury condos are on this beachfront. Isla Verde has picnic tables, so you can pick up the makings of a lunch and make it a day at the beach. This strip is also good for snorkeling because of its calm, clear waters, and many kiosks will rent you equipment. Isla Verde Beach extends from the end of Ocean Park to the beginning of a section called Boca Cangrejos. The best beach at Isla Verde is at the Hotel El San Juan. Most sections of this long strip have separate names, such as El Alambique, which is often the site of beach parties, and Punta El Medio, bordering the new Ritz-Carlton, also a great beach and very popular even with the locals. If you go past the luxury hotels and expensive condos behind the Luís Muñoz Marín International Airport, you arrive at the major public beach at Isla Verde. Here you'll find a *balneario* with parking, showers, fast-food joints, and water-sports equipment. The sands here are whiter than the golden sands of the Condado, and are lined with coconut palms, sea-grape trees, and even almond trees, all of which provide shade from the fierce noonday sun.

One of the most attractive beaches in the Greater San Juan area is **Ocean Park,** a mile of fine gold sand in a neighborhood east of Condado. This beach attracts both young people and a big gay crowd. Access to the beach at Ocean Park has been limited recently, but the best place to enter is from a section called El Ultimo Trolley. This area is ideal for volleyball, paddleball, and other games. The easternmost portion, known as Punta Las Marias, is best for windsurfing. The waters at Ocean Park are fine for swimming, although they can get rough at times.

Rivaling Condado and Isla Verde beaches, ✪ **Luquillo Public Beach** is the grandest in Puerto Rico and one of the most popular. It's 30 miles east of San Juan near the town of Luquillo. Here you'll find a mile-long half-moon bay set against a backdrop of coconut palms. This is another of the dozen or so *balnearios* of Puerto Rico. Saturday and Sunday are the worst times to go, as hordes of *sanjuaneros* head here for fun in the sun. Water-sports kiosks are available, offering everything from windsurfing to sailing. Facilities include lifeguards, an emergency first-aid station, ample parking, showers, and toilets. You can easily have a local lunch here at one of the beach shacks offering cod fritters and tacos.

SPORTS & OUTDOOR PURSUITS
BIKE RENTALS
Much favored by the dozens of holidaymakers pedaling up and down the Condado, **Hot Dog Bicycles,** 1024 Ashford Ave. (☎ **787/721-0623**), rents big-geared mountain bikes for $15 a day. Fortunately for the neighborhood's noise pollution, they don't rent mopeds or motor scooters. The best places to bike are along Ashford Avenue (in Condado), Calle Loiza (between Condado and Ocean Park), and Avenida Baldorioty de Castro (in Santurce). Other streets in this area may be too congested. Similarly, because of the traffic, biking in Old San Juan is not recommended.

CRUISES

For the best cruises of San Juan Bay, go to **Caribe Aquatic Adventures** (see "Scuba Diving," below). Bay cruises start at $20 per person.

DEEP-SEA FISHING

It's top-notch! Allison tuna, white and blue marlin, sailfish, wahoo, dolphin (mahimahi), mackerel, and tarpon are some of the fish that can be caught in Puerto Rican waters, where 30 world records have been broken. Charter arrangements can be made through most major hotels and resorts.

Capt. Mike Benitez, who has chartered out of San Juan for more than 40 years, is one of the most qualified sport-fishing captains in the world. (Past clients include Jimmy Carter.) **Benitez Fishing Charters** can be contacted directly at P.O. Box 9066541, Puerto de Tierra, San Juan, PR 00906 (☎ **787/723-2292** until 9pm). The captain offers a 45-foot air-conditioned deluxe Hatteras, the *Sea Born.* Fishing tours for parties of up to six cost $450 for a half-day excursion and $750 for a full day, with beverages and all equipment included.

GOLF

A 45-minute drive east from San Juan on the northeast coast takes you to Palmer and its 6,145-yard ✪ **Rio Mar Golf Course** (☎ **787/888-8811**). Inexperienced golfers prefer this course to the more challenging and more famous courses at Dorado (see chapter 7), even though trade winds can influence your game along the holes bordering the water, and occasional fairway flooding can present some unwanted obstacles. Greens fees are $140 before 2pm, $90 after 2pm. A gallery of 100 iguanas also adds spice to your game at Rio Mar.

HEALTH CLUBS

If your hotel doesn't have a gym or health spa of its own, consider working the kinks out of your muscles at **Muscle Factory,** 1302 Ashford Ave., Condado (☎ **787/ 721-0717**). It's air-conditioned, well equipped, and popular with residents of the surrounding high-rent district. Entrance costs $10 per visit, $35 for 5 days, or $45 for a week. Hours are Monday through Thursday from 6am to 10pm, Friday from 6am to 9pm, Saturday from 9am to 6pm, and Sunday from 10am to 2pm.

HORSE RACING

Great thoroughbreds and outstanding jockeys compete year-round at **El Comandante,** Av. 65 de Infantería, Route 3, kilometer 15.3, at Canovanas (☎ **787/ 724-6060**), Puerto Rico's only racetrack, a 20-minute drive east of the center of San Juan. Post time varies from 2:15 to 2:45pm on Monday, Wednesday, Friday, Saturday, and Sunday. Entrance to the clubhouse costs $3, although no admission is charged for the grandstand.

RUNNING

The cool, quiet, early morning hours before 8am are a good time to jog through the streets of Old San Juan. Head for the wide, sweeping thoroughfares adjacent to the fortress of San Felipe del Morro and then the fortress of San Cristóbal, whose walls jut upward from the flat ground. You might join Puerto Rico's governor, a dedicated runner, in making several laps around the seafront Paseo de la Princesa at the base of his home, La Fortaleza.

Finally, if you don't mind heading out into the island a bit from your base in Old San Juan, you might opt for a run through the palm trees of the Parque Central, near

Calle Cerra and Route 2 in Santurce. Condado's Ashford Avenue is a busy site for morning runners as well.

SCUBA DIVING

In San Juan, the best outfitter is **Caribc Aquatic Adventures,** P.O. Box 9024278, San Juan Station, San Juan, PR 00902 (☎ **787/724-1882** or 787/281-8858), which operates a dive shop in the rear lobby of the Radisson Normandie Hotel, open daily 8am–4pm. The company offers diving certification from both PADI and NAUI as part of 40-hour courses priced at $465 each. A resort course for first-time divers costs $97. Also offered are local daily dives in the waters close to San Juan, as well as the option of traveling farther afield into waters near the reefs of Puerto Rico's eastern shore. If time permits, we recommend a full-day dive experience; if time is limited, many worthy dive sites lie closer to San Juan and can be experienced in a half day.

SNORKELING

Snorkeling is better in the outlying portions of the island instead of in overcrowded San Juan. But if you don't have time to explore greater Puerto Rico, you'll find that most of the popular beaches, such as Luquillo and Isla Verde, have pretty good visibility and kiosks renting equipment. Snorkeling equipment generally costs $15. If you're on your own in the San Juan area, one of the best places is the San Juan Bay marina near the Caribe Hilton.

Water-sports desks at the big San Juan hotels at Isla Verde and Condado can generally make arrangements for instruction and equipment rental and can also lead you to the best places for snorkeling, depending on where you are in the sprawling metropolis. If your hotel doesn't offer such services, you can also contact **Caribe Aquatic Adventures** (see "Scuba Diving," above), which caters to both snorkelers and scuba divers. Other possibilities for equipment rentals are at **Caribbean School of Aquatics,** Taft No. 1, Suite 10F, in San Juan (☎ **787/728-6606**), and **Mundo Submarino,** Laguna Gardens Shopping Center, Isla Verde (☎ **787/791-5764**).

SPAS & FITNESS CENTERS

The fitness centers at the following hotels are open only to hotel guests. On the other hand, spa treatments are open to all, and prices are standardized. See chapter 4 for details about the hotels and resorts.

Massages may vary from $55 to $140 per hour, with another $15 for aromatherapy. Facials range from $155 to $200, depending on how deep and how thorough you want the treatment. Special clay and seaweed beauty masks range from $105 to $140, with body scrubs costing from $55 to $140. Standard manicures are $35 to $85, with pedicures costing $65 to $85.

The grandest and largest spa in Puerto Rico is at the **Ritz-Carlton** (☎ **800/ 241-3333** or 787/253-1700). This 12,000-square-foot, elegant marble-and-stone building provides panoramic ocean views to accompany self-improvement therapies and fitness activities, such as yoga, aerobics, and aqua-aerobics. Upstairs, there are 11 treatment rooms, offering facials, massage, manicures, pedicures, hydrotherapy, and body wraps, among other treatments.

The Spa at the **Caribe Hilton & Casino** (☎ **800/HILTONS** or **787/721-0303**) offers Universal and Nautilus weight machines, aerobics and yoga classes, treadmills, aerobicycles, massage, herbal wraps, loofah body polishes, and facials.

The Plaza Spa at the **Condado Plaza Hotel & Casino** (☎ **800/468-8588** or 787/721-1000) features Universal weight training machines, video exercycles, sauna, whirlpools, and facials and massage.

The Penthouse Spa at **El San Juan Hotel & Casino** (☎ 800/468-2818 or 787/791-1000) offers fitness evaluations, supervised weight-loss programs, aerobics classes, a sauna, a steam room, and massage.

The Spa Caribe at the **Hyatt Regency Cerromar Beach** (☎ 800/233-1234 or 787/796-1234) offers shape-up programs including aerobics and "talking" Powercise machines and health evaluations, plus skin and body care treatments such as massage, facials, and loofah polish.

TENNIS

In San Juan, courts can be found at the **Caribe Hilton & Casino,** Puerta de Tierra (☎ 787/721-0303), open daily 7am–6pm, and the **Condado Plaza Hotel & Casino,** 999 Ashford Ave. (☎ 787/721-1000), open daily 6am–9pm. Nonguests can use these courts if they make reservations. There are also 17 public courts, lit at night, at **San Juan Central Municipal Park,** at Calle Cerra (exit on Route 2; ☎ 787/722-1646), open daily. Fees are $3 an hour from 8am to 6pm, going up to $4 per hour from 6 to 10pm.

WINDSURFING

A favorite spot is the sheltered waters of the Condado Lagoon in San Juan. Throughout the island, many of the companies that provide snorkeling and scuba-diving equipment also offer windsurfing equipment and instruction, and dozens of hotels have facilities on their premises. Two such hotels are the Condado Plaza Hotel (☎ 800/468-8588 in the U.S. or 787/721-1000), where beginners can learn to windsurf on the quiet waters of a sheltered lagoon, and El San Juan Hotel (☎ 800/468-2818 or 787/791-1000), where experienced windsurfers can skim along the waters of the open ocean. For more information, call the hotels directly.

4 Shopping

Because Puerto Rico is a U.S. commonwealth, American citizens don't pay duty on items brought back to the mainland. And you can still find great bargains on Puerto Rico, where the competition among shopkeepers is fierce. Even though the U.S. Virgin Islands are duty free, you can often find far lower prices on many items in San Juan than on St. Thomas.

The streets of Old Town, such as Calle San Francisco and Calle del Cristo, are the major venues for shopping. Note, however, that most stores in Old San Juan are closed on Sunday.

Native handicrafts can be good buys, including needlework, straw work, ceramics, hammocks, and papier-mâché fruits and vegetables, as well as paintings and sculptures by Puerto Rican artists (see "Puerto Rican Handicrafts" in appendix A). Among these, the carved wooden religious idols known as *santos* (saints) have been called Puerto Rico's greatest contribution to the plastic arts and are sought by collectors. For the best selection of *santos,* head for Galeria Botello, Olé, or Puerto Rican Arts & Crafts (see "Gifts & Handicrafts," below).

Puerto Rico's biggest and most up-to-date shopping mall is **Plaza Las Americas,** in the financial district of Hato Rey, right off the Las Americas Expressway. This complex, with its fountains and modern architecture, has more than 200 mostly upscale shops. The variety of goods and prices is about comparable to that of large stateside malls.

ANTIQUES

El Alcazar. Calle San José 103. ☎ **787/723-1229.**

Established in 1986 by retired career officers with the U.S. Army and the U.S. State Department, this is the largest emporium of antique furniture, silver, and art objects in the Caribbean. The best way to sift through the massive inventory is to begin at the address listed above, on Calle San José between Calle Luna and Calle Sol, and ask the owners, Sharon and Robert Bartos, to guide you to the other three buildings that are, literally, stuffed with important art and antiques. Each shop lies within a half block of the organization's headquarters, and each is within a historic building of architectural or historic importance (public areas of several large Puerto Rican hotels contain furnishings acquired here). Hint: For antique silver, crystal, delicate porcelain, glittering chandeliers, Russian icons, and objects of religious devotion such as *santos*, look first at the organization's above-mentioned headquarters. Some of the objects, especially the 1930s-era dining room sets, whose chair backs are composed of wood medallions held in place by woven canes or wicker, derive from Puerto Rico. The majority of the objects, however, are culled from estates and galleries throughout Europe.

ART

Galería Botello. Calle del Cristo 208. ☎ **787/723-2879.**

A contemporary Latin American art gallery, Galería Botello is a living tribute to the late Angel Botello, one of Puerto Rico's most outstanding artists. Born after the Spanish Civil War in a small village in Galicia, Spain, he fled to the Caribbean and spent 12 years in Haiti. His paintings and bronze sculptures, evocative of his colorful background, are done in a style uniquely his own. This galería is his former colonial mansion home, which he restored himself. Today it displays his paintings and sculptures, showcases the works of many outstanding local artists, and offers a large collection of Puerto Rican antique *santos*.

Galería Palomas. Calle del Cristo 207. ☎ **787/725-2660.**

This and the also-recommended Galería Botello are the two leading art galleries of Puerto Rico. Here find works by some of the leading painters in Latin America. Prices range from $75 to $35,000, and exhibits are rotated every 2 to 3 weeks. The setting is a 17th-century colonial house. Of special note are works by such local artists as Homer, Moya, and Alicea.

Haitian Souvenirs. Calle San Francisco 206. ☎ **787/723-0959.**

In spite of its name, this is the best store in San Juan specializing in Haitian art and artifacts. Its walls are covered with framed versions of primitive Haitian landscapes, portraits, crowd scenes, and whimsical visions of jungles where lions, tigers, parrots, and herons take on quasi-human personalities and forms. Most paintings range from $35 to $350, although you can usually bargain them down a bit. Look for the brightly painted wall hangings crafted from sheets of metal. Also look for satirical metal wall hangings, brightly painted, representing the *tap-taps* (battered public minivans and buses) of Port-au-Prince. They make amusing and whimsical souvenirs of a trip to the Caribbean.

Magia Artefactos. Calle del Cristo 99. ☎ **787/724-8764.**

Set across the street from the side entrance to El Convento Hotel, about a block uphill from the cathedral, this creatively disorganized art gallery has better and more interesting work than its nearby competitors. Most of the objects were crafted by San Juan native Manolo Díaz, whose art studies in Italy contributed to his zeal for incorporating architectural remnants into his sculptures. Especially poignant are montages that combine battered shutters from colonial buildings with *santos* (statues of the saints) carved by Puerto Rican artisans.

BOOKS

Bell, Book & Candle. 102 de Diego Ave., Santurce. ☎ **787/728-5000.**

For travel guides, maps, and just something to read on the beach, head here. It is a large, general-interest bookstore that carries fiction and classics in both Spanish and English, plus a huge selection of postcards.

The Bookstore. Calle San José 255. ☎ **787/724-1815.**

This is the leading choice in the Old Town, with the largest selection of titles. It sells a number of books on Puerto Rican culture as well as good maps of the island.

BUTTERFLIES (MOUNTED)

Butterfly People. Calle Fortaleza 152. ☎ **787/723-2432.**

Butterfly People is a gallery and cafe (see chapter 5) in a handsomely restored building in Old San Juan. Butterflies, sold here in artfully arranged boxes, range from $20 for a single mounting to thousands of dollars for whole-wall murals. The butterflies are preserved and will last forever. The dimensional artwork is sold in limited editions and can be shipped worldwide. Most of these butterflies come from farms around the world, some of the most beautiful hailing from Indonesia, Malaysia, and New Guinea. Tucked away within the same premises is **Malula Antiques.** Specializing in tribal art from the Moroccan sub-Sahara and Syria, it contains a sometimes-startling collection of primitive and timeless crafts and accessories.

CARNIVAL MASKS

La Calle. 105 Fortaleza. ☎ **787/725-1306.**

Every Puerto Rican knows that the best, and cheapest, place to buy brightly painted carnival masks *(vejigantes)* is in Ponce, where the tradition of making them from papier mâché originated. But if you can't spare the time for a side excursion to Ponce, this store in Old San Juan stocks one of the most varied inventories of *vejigantes* in the Puerto Rican capital. Depending on their size and composition (some include coconut shells, gourds, and flashy metal trim), they range from $12 to $2,400 each. Side-by-side with the pagan-inspired masks, you'll find a well-chosen selection of paintings by talented local artists, priced from $250 to $2,000 each.

CIGARS

Club Jibarito. 202 Calle Cristo. ☎ **787/724-7797.**

This is the retail outlet of a Puerto Rican–based manufacturer of genuinely excellent cigars. Here you can select from the Jibarito cigars that are proudly displayed within one of the best-designed humidors in town. Overall it's our favorite cigar emporium in San Juan, with a polite staff and lots and lots of class.

CLOTHING & BEACHWEAR

Casa Marriot. Calle Tanca 255. ☎ **787/722-0444.**

For more than 50 years, businessmen of San Juan have been coming here for a wide selection of mostly English, tropical-weight fabrics. For a suit, most North American men require from 3^{1}/$_{2}$ to 4 yards of fabric, priced from $12.95 to $110 a yard, plus another 2¹/₂ yards of lining, priced around $5 a yard. The helpful staff can direct you to any of several local tailors, who will charge from $250 to $350 to whip that fabric into a suit.

Lindissima Shop. Calle Fortaleza 300. ☎ **787/721-0550.**

This outlet offers a collection for women of contemporary sportswear and dresses for both daytime and evening. If you lack an outfit for a formal evening aboard ship, you are likely to find it here.

London Fog. Calle del Cristo 156. ☎ **787/722-4334.**

The last thing you need in steamy San Juan is a winter overcoat or parka, but the prices at this London Fog factory outlet are usually so low that a purchase is well worth it. Prices are often between 30 and 35% less than those at many retail stores on the U.S. mainland. Men's, women's, and children's garments are displayed on two floors of a colonial house.

Mrs. and Miss Boutique. Calle Fortaleza 154. ☎ **787/721-2668.**

The most visible article available within this shop is "the magic dress" for $115. Crafted in Morocco of a silky-looking blend of rayon and cotton, it comes in 10 different colors or patterns and can be worn 11 different ways. (A saleswoman will show you how.) The shop also stocks sarongs for $9.95 and long dresses, sometimes from Indonesia, that begin at only $25. There's a second branch of this shop at 252 Fortaleza (☎ **787/721-2668**), with basically the same merchandise.

Nono Maldonado. 1051 Ashford Ave. ☎ **787/721-0456.**

Named after its owner, a Puerto Rico–born designer who worked for many years as the fashion editor of *Esquire* magazine, this is one of the most fashionable and upscale haberdashers in the Caribbean. Selling both men's and women's clothing, it contains everything from socks to dinner jackets, as well as ready-to-wear versions of Maldonado's twice-a-year collections. Both ready-to-wear and couture are available here. Although this is the designer's main store (midway between the Condado Plaza and the Ramada Hotel), there is also a Maldonado boutique in El San Juan Hotel in Isla Verde.

Polo Ralph Lauren Factory Store. Calle del Cristo 201. ☎ **787/722-2136.**

It's as stylish and carefully orchestrated as anything you'd expect from one of North America's leading clothiers. Even better, its prices are often 35 to 40% less than the cost in retail stores on the U.S. mainland. You can find even greater discounts on irregular or slightly damaged garments, but inspect them carefully before buying. The store occupies two floors of a pair of colonial buildings, with one upstairs room devoted to home furnishings. Men's sizes larger than a 42 waist are almost never in stock.

W. H. Smith. In the Condado Plaza Hotel, 999 Ashford Ave. ☎ **787/721-1000,** ext. 2094.

This outlet sells mostly women's clothing, everything from bathing suits and beach attire to jogging suits. For men, there are shorts, bathing suits, and jogging suits. There's also a good selection of books and maps.

COFFEE & SPICES
Spicy Caribbee. Alle Cristo 154. ☎ **787/725-4690.**

This shop has the best selection of Puerto Rican coffee, which is gaining an increasingly good reputation among aficionados. It also has the Old Town's best array of hot spicy sauces of the Caribbean.

DECORATIVE ACCESSORIES

DMR (Designs & Museum Reproductions). La Cochera Building, 204 Calle Luna.
☎ **787/722-4181.**

In Old San Juan, this is the finest outlet for the serious shopper in search of home
furnishings styled in the West Indian fashion. The selection is ideal for a vacation
home near the beach, and includes such offerings as island paintings and mahogany
veranda chairs.

El Alcázar. 103 Calle San José. ☎ **787/723-1229.**

Here you can find decorative items from almost any part of the world, maybe even
remote Tibet. It's like wandering in your grandfather's attic—assuming he was an
ancient mariner with a taste for the exotic. Since the treasure trove of merchandise is
always changing, drop in for a surprise.

Goa. Calle Luna 152 at the Calle Cruz. ☎ **787/721-7669.**

Decorators on the lookout for rare and unusual objects consider this shop a dream
come true. The inventory is one of the most imaginative in Puerto Rico. Among other
places, objects hail from Afghanistan, Indonesia, Morocco, India, Brazil, Thailand,
and the Philippines. Exotic birdcages, sub-Saharan tables and chairs, and porcelain
vases covered in Arabic calligraphy are only some of the wonderful and sometimes
weird objects stocked here.

Xian Imports. Calle de la Cruz 153. ☎ **787/723-2214.**

Set within a jumbled, slightly claustrophobic setting, you'll discover porcelain, sculptures, paintings, and Chinese furniture, much of it antique. Island decorators favor
this spot as a source for unusual art objects.

GIFTS & HANDICRAFTS

Bared & Sons. Calle Fortaleza 65 (at the corner of Calle San Justo). ☎ **787/724-4811.**

Now in its fourth decade, this is the main outlet of a chain of at least 20 upper-bracket
jewelry stores on Puerto Rico. There's a worthy inventory of gemstones, gold,
diamonds, and wristwatches on the street level, which does a thriving business with
cruise-ship passengers. But the real value of this store lies one floor up, where a monumental collection of porcelain and crystal is on display in claustrophobic proximity.
It's a great source for hard-to-get and discontinued patterns (priced at around 20% less
than at equivalent stateside outlets) from Christofle, Royal Doulton, Wedgwood,
Limoges, Royal Copenhagen, Lalique, Lladró, Herend, Baccarat, and Daum.

Centro Nacional de Artes Populares y Artesanías. Calle Cristo 253. ☎ **787/722-0621.**

Many stores in San Juan sell tourist junk passed off as handicrafts. But at this center,
run by the Institute of Puerto Rican Culture, the quality of craft work is high. It is a
superb repository of native crafts, many of which are for display only but others of
which are for sale. Housed in a colonial building, this shop scans the island for artisans still practicing time-treasured crafts and doing so with considerable skill. The
prices aren't always cheap but the quality is high.

El Artesano. Calle Fortaleza 314. ☎ **787/721-6483.**

If your budget doesn't allow for an excursion to the Andes, head for this shop. You'll
find Mexican and Peruvian icons of the Virgin Mary; charming depictions of fish and
Latin American birds in terra-cotta and brass; all kinds of woven goods; painted cup-
boards, chests, and boxes; and mirrors and Latin dolls.

El Cundeamor. Fortaleza 105, Old San Juan. ☎ **787/721-5921.**

The inventory includes high-quality trays and serving dishes made from an intricately detailed aluminum-pewter alloy, often from Mexico. There's also a lot of silver jewelry, from Indonesia and Mexico, much of it adaptable to either modern or old-fashioned clothing.

Galería Bóveda. Calle del Cristo 209. ☎ **787/725-0263.**

This long, narrow space is crammed with exotic jewelry, clothing, greeting cards with images of life in Puerto Rico, some 100 handmade lamps, antiques, Mexican punched tin and glass, and art nouveau reproductions, among other items.

Olé. Calle Fortaleza 105. ☎ **787/724-2445.**

Browsing this store is a learning experience. Even the standard Panama hat takes on new dimensions. Woven from fine-textured *paja* grass and priced from $20 to $1,000, according to the density of the weave, the hats are all created the same size, then blocked—by an employee on site—to fit the shape of your head. Dig into this store's diverse inventory to discover a wealth of treasures—hand-beaten Chilean silver, Peruvian Christmas ornaments, Puerto Rican *santos*—almost all from Puerto Rico or Latin America.

Puerto Rican Arts & Crafts. Calle Fortaleza 204. ☎ **787/725-5596.**

Set in a 200-year-old colonial building, this unique store is one of the premier outlets on the island for authentic artifacts. Of particular interest are papier-mâché carnival masks from Ponce, whose grotesque and colorful features were originally conceived to chase away evil spirits. Taíno designs inspired by ancient petroglyphs are incorporated into most of the sterling silver jewelry sold here. There's an art gallery in back, with silk-screened serigraphs by local artists. The outlet has a gourmet Puerto Rican food section with items like coffee, rum, and hot sauces for sale. A related specialty of this well-respected store involves the exhibition and sale of modern replicas of the Spanish colonial tradition of *santos,* which are carved and sometimes polychromed representations of the Catholic saints and the infant Jesus. Priced from $44 to $225 each, and laboriously carved by artisans in private studios around the island, they're easy to pack in a suitcase because the largest one measures only 12 inches from halo to toe.

JEWELRY

Barrachina's. Calle Fortaleza 104 (between Calle del Cristo and Calle San José). ☎ **787/725-7912.**

The birthplace, in 1963, of the piña colada (an honor co-claimed by the staff at the Caribe Hilton), Barrachina's is a favorite of cruise-ship passengers. It offers one of the largest selections of jewelry, perfume, cigars, and gifts in San Juan. There's a patio for drinks where you can order (what else?) a piña colada. There is also a Bacardi rum outlet (bottles cost less than stateside but the same as at the Bacardi distillery), a costume jewelry department, a gift shop, and a section for authentic silver jewelry, plus a restaurant.

Gaston Bared Jewelry. Calle Fortaleza 154 (at Calle San José. ☎ **787/722-2172.**

This is an offshoot of the above-recommended Bared and Sons, but with a more contemporary inventory. This shop also has a branch at Calle Fortaleza 208 (same phone) that sells Murano crystal, Hummel and Lladró figurines, watches (including Omega, Seiko, and Tissot), and colored gemstones, such as amethysts, set into gold and silver settings.

The Gold Ounce. Plaza los Muchachos, Calle Fortaleza 201. ☎ **787/724-3102.**

This is the direct factory outlet for the oldest jewelry factory on Puerto Rico, the Kury Company. Most of the output is shipped stateside. Don't expect a top-notch jeweler here: many of the pieces are produced in endless repetition. But don't overlook the place for 14-karat-gold ornaments. Some of the designs are charming, and prices are about 20% less than those at retail stores on the North American mainland. In addition, the outlet has opened an art store, called **Arts and More** (☎ 787/725-2997), featuring regional works, plus a cigar store called **The Cigar Shop.**

Joyería Riviera. Calle La Cruz 205. ☎ **787/725-4000.**

This emporium of 18-karat gold and diamonds is the island's leading jeweler. Adjacent to Plaza de Armas, the shop has an impeccable reputation. Its owner, Julio Abislaiman, stocks his store at such diamond centers as Antwerp, Tel Aviv, and New York. This is the major distributor of Rolex watches on Puerto Rico. Prices range from $150 into the tens of thousands of dollars—at these prices, it's a good thing you can get "whatever you want," according to the owner.

Piercing Pagoda. 203 Calle Fortaleza. ☎ **787/725-1765.**

There's nothing Puerto Rican or glamorous about this branch of a large U.S. chain. But if you're in the market for a gold or silver chain, or perhaps a pendant or set of earrings, the sales here could be worth a detour. Be alert that some displays feature 10-karat gold rather than the more preferable, and expensive, 14- or 18-karat.

200 Fortaleza. Calle Fortaleza 200 (at the corner of Calle La Cruz). ☎ **787/723-1989.**

Known as a leading cost-conscious place to buy fine jewelry in Old San Juan, this shop has 14-karat Italian gold chains and bracelets that are measured, fitted, and sold by weight. You can purchase watches or beautiful gems in modern settings in both 14- and 18-karat gold. The store recently expanded its collection to include 18-karat, emerald, ruby, diamond, and pearl jewelry, along with platinum bridal jewelry.

Yas Mar. Calle Fortaleza 205. ☎ **787/724-1377.**

This shop sells convincing, glittering fake diamonds for those who don't want to wear the real thing. It also stocks real diamond chips, emeralds, sapphires, and rubies.

LACE & LINENS
Linen House. Calle Fortaleza 250. ☎ **787/721-4219.**

This unpretentious store specializes in napery, bed linens, and lace and has the island's best selection. Some of the more delicate pieces are expensive, but most are moderate in price. Inventories include embroidered shower curtains selling for around $35 each, and lace doilies, bun warmers, placemats, and tablecloths that seamstresses took weeks to complete. Some astonishingly lovely items are available for as little as $30. The aluminum/pewter serving dishes have beautiful Spanish-colonial designs. Prices here are sometimes 40% lower than those on the North American mainland.

LEATHER & EQUESTRIAN ACCESSORIES
Lalin Leather Shop. Avda. Piñero 1617, Puerto Nuevo, San Juan. ☎ **787/781-5305.**

Although it lies in an out-of-the-way suburb (Puerto Nuevo), about 2 miles south of San Juan, this is the best and most comprehensive cowboy and equestrian outfitter in Puerto Rico, probably in the entire Caribbean. Here you'll find all manner of boots, cowboy hats, and accessories. More important, however, is the wide array of saddles and bridles, some from Colombia, some from Puerto Rico, priced from a cost-conscious

$89 to as much as $1,200. Even the highest-priced items cost a lot less than their U.S. equivalents, so if you happen to have a horse or pony on the U.S. mainland, a visit here might be worth your while. If you decide to make the rather inconvenient pilgrimage, you won't be alone. Regular clients come from as far away as Iceland, the Bahamas, and New York. Everything can be shipped.

Leather & Pearls. Calle Tanca 252 (at the corner of Calle Tetuán). ☎ **787/724-8185.**

Majorca pearls and fine leather garments (bags, shoes, suitcases, briefcases, and accessories) are sold here from manufacturers that include Gucci and Fendi. Also look for leather goods from the same Iberian enterprise that brings you Lladró porcelain. A relative newcomer to the field of leather goods, they've impressed consumers with their quality and pizzazz.

MARKETS
Plaza del Mercado. Calle Dos Hermanos at Calle Capitol, Santurce. ☎ **787/723-8022.**

If you'd like an old-fashioned Puerto Rican market, something likely to be found in a small South American country, visit this offbeat curiosity. In a West Indian structure, the central market is filled with "botanicas" hawking everything from medicinal herbs to Puerto Rican bay rum. Here is your best chance to pick up some patchouli roots. What are they used for? In religious observances and to kill unruly cockroaches. Incidentally, there are some little cantinas here offering very typical Puerto Rican dishes, including roast pork. And you can also order the best mango banana shakes on the island.

SOUVENIRS
Planet Hollywood. Calle Tanca 259. ☎ **787/729-9410.**

If you happen to be a collector of rock-and-roll memorabilia, you might be interested in acquiring a T-shirt, baseball cap, pair of boxer shorts, or some other kind of commemorative souvenir from this gift shop. Ironically, there's no Planet Hollywood bar or restaurant here, as the Puerto Rico branch hasn't yet been built. (Indeed, that may never happen.)

5 San Juan After Dark

San Juan nightlife comes in all varieties. From the vibrant performing arts scene to street-level salsa or the casinos, discos, and bars, there's plenty of entertainment available almost any evening.

Qué Pasa, the official visitor's guide to Puerto Rico, lists cultural events, including music, dance, theater, film, and art exhibits. It's distributed free by the tourist office.

THE PERFORMING ARTS
Centro de Bellas Artes. Av. Ponce de León 22. ☎ **787/724-4747,** or 787/725-7334 for the ticket agent. Tickets $13–$65; 50% discounts for seniors. Bus: 1.

In the heart of Santurce, the Performing Arts Center is a 6-minute taxi ride from most of the Condado hotels. It contains the Festival Hall, Drama Hall, and the Experimental Theater. Some of the events here will be of interest only to Spanish speakers; others attract an international audience.

Teatro Tapía. Av. Ponce de León. ☎ **787/721-0169.** Tickets $15–$38, depending on the show. Bus: Old Town Trolley.

Standing across from Plaza de Colón and built about 1832, this is one of the oldest theaters in the western hemisphere (see "Historic Sights," earlier in this chapter).

Productions, some musical, are staged throughout the year and include drama, dances, and cultural events. You'll have to call the box office (open Monday through Friday from 9am to 6pm) for specific information.

THE CLUB & MUSIC SCENE

Babylon. In El San Juan Hotel & Casino, 6063 Isla Verde Ave., Isla Verde. ☎ **787/791-1000.** Cover $10, free for residents of El San Juan Hotel. Wed–Sat 9:30pm–3am. Bus: A7, T1, or 2.

Modeled after an artist's rendition of the once-notorious city of Mesopotamia, this nightclub is designed in the form of a circle, with a central dance floor and a wrap-around balcony where onlookers and voyeurs—a 25-to-45 age group—can observe the activities on the floor below. Equipped with one of the best sound systems in the Caribbean, its location within the most exciting hotel in San Juan allows guests the chance to visit the hotel's bars, its intricately decorated lobby, and its casino en route.

Café Matisse. Ashford Ave. ☎ **787/723-7910.** Cover (Fri–Sat only) $3.

Although it serves platters of food and defines part of its venue as a restaurant, this establishment is best known as a bar where live music—often salsa—is usually part of the ambience. Overall, the site is best known for its conviviality, sense of Big Apple cool, and hot music that makes every red-blooded Latino want to dance, dance, dance. It's open Tuesday through Saturday from 5pm to 2am or later, depending on the crowd.

Laser. Calle del Cruz 251. ☎ **787/725-7581.** Cover $6–$10.

Set in the heart of the old town near the corner of Calle Fortaleza, this disco is especially crowded when cruise ships pull into town. Once inside, you can wander over the three floors of its historic premises, listening to whatever music happens to be hot in New York at the time, with lots of additional Latino merengue and salsa thrown in as well. Depending on the night, the age of the crowd varies, but in general it's the 20s, 30s, and even 40s set. Usually, it's open daily from 8pm to 4am. Women enter free after midnight on Saturday.

THE BAR SCENE

Unless otherwise stated, there is no cover charge at the following bars.

Bar "El Columbus." Plaza Colón (204 Calle O'Donnell). No phone.

This appealing local spot is a battered bastion of another era, where countertops are crafted from Formica and a blaring TV fills in any conversational gaps. You'll get the feeling that this neighborhood bar has survived gentrification in much the style as it did 25 years ago.

Cigar Bar. El San Juan Hotel & Casino, 6063 Isla Verde Ave., Carolina. ☎ **787/791-1000.**

The Palm Court Lobby at this elegant hotel boasts an impressive cigar bar, with a magnificent repository of the finest stogies in the world. Although the bar is generally filled with visitors, some of San Juan's most fashionable men—and women too—can be seen puffing away in this chic rendezvous while sipping a cognac.

Fiesta Bar. In the Condado Plaza Hotel & Casino, 999 Ashford Ave. ☎ **787/721-1000.**

This bar lures in a healthy mixture of local residents and hotel guests, usually the post-35 set. The margaritas are appropriately salty, the rhythms are hot and Latin, and the free admission usually helps you forget any losses you might have suffered in the nearby casinos.

Birth of the Piña Colada

When actress Joan Crawford tasted the piña colada at what was then the Beach-combers Bar in the **Caribe Hilton,** Calle Los Rosales (☎ 787/721-0303), she claimed it was "better than slapping Bette Davis in the face."

This famous drink is the creation of bartender Ramon "Monchito" Marrero, now retired, who was hired by the Hilton in 1954. He spent 3 months mixing, tasting, and discarding hundreds of combinations until he felt he had the right blend. Thus, the frothy piña colada was born. It's been estimated that some 100 million of them have been sipped around the world since that fateful time.

Monchito never patented his formula and doesn't mind sharing it with the world. Still served at the Hilton, here is his not-so-secret recipe:

> 2 ounces light rum
> 1 ounce coconut cream
> 1 ounce heavy cream
> 6 ounces fresh pineapple
> 1/2 cup crushed ice
> Pineapple wedge and maraschino cherry for garnish

Pour rum, coconut cream, cream, and pineapple juice in blender. Add ice. Blend for 15 seconds. Pour into a 12-ounce glass. Add garnishes.

Maria's. Calle del Cristo 204. ☎ 787/721-1678.

Forget the tacky decorations. This is the town's most enduring bar, a favorite local hangout and a prime target for Old Town visitors seeking Mexican food and sangría. The atmosphere is fun, and the tropical drinks include piña coladas and frosts made of banana, orange, and strawberry, as well as the Puerto Rican beer, Medalla. Open daily from 10:30am to 3am.

Palm Court. In El San Juan Hotel & Casino, 6063 Isla Verde Ave., Isla Verde. ☎ 787/791-1000.

This is the most beautiful bar on the island—perhaps in the entire Caribbean. Most of the patrons are hotel guests, but rich-heeled locals make up at least a quarter of the business at this fashionable rendezvous. Set in an oval wrapped around a sunken bar area, amid marble and burnished mahogany, it offers a view of one of the world's largest chandeliers. After 9pm on Monday through Saturday, live music, often salsa and merengue, emanates from an adjoining room (El Chico Bar).

Shannon's Irish Pub. Calle Bori 496, Río Piedras. ☎ 787/281-8466.

Ireland and its ales meet the tropics at this pub with a Latin accent. A sports bar with TV monitors and high-energy rock-and-roll, it's the regular watering hole of many university students. There's live music Wednesday through Sunday—everything from rock to jazz to Latin. There are pool tables, and a simple cafe serves inexpensive lunches Monday through Friday. A $3 cover charge is sometimes imposed for a special live performance.

Violeta's. Calle Fortaleza 56 (2 blocks from the Gran Hotel Convento). ☎ 787/723-6804.

Stylish and comfortable, Violeta's occupies the ground floor of a 200-year-old beamed house. Because of its location in the old town, the bar draws an equal mix of visitors

Barhopping

More than any other place in the Caribbean, San Juan has a nightlife that success-fully combines New York hip with Latino zest and the music of the Spanish tropics. For a no-holds-barred insight into what this means, head for a pair of holes in the wall on a street immediately adjacent to the El Convento Hotel, a few steps from San Juan's Cathedral.

El Batey, 101 Calle del Cristo (no phone), and **Don Pablo,** 103 Calle del Cristo (no phone), which both charge between $2 and $2.75 per beer, are battered side-by-side hangouts with a clientele that might remind you of the characters in *East of Eden.* (In the 1980s, a Hollywood director selected these spots as the set for a Central American drug den, much to the amusement of the regular clientele.) Whereas El Batey's music remains firmly grounded in the rock-and-roll classics of the 1970s, with a scattering of Elvis Presley hits, Don Pablo prides itself on cutting-edge music that's continually analyzed by the counterculture aficionados who hang out here. El Batey is open daily from 2pm to 6am; Don Pablo, daily from 8pm to 4am.

Along with the dark and smoky **Bohemia,** just across the street in the cellar of El Convento Hotel, 100 Calle del Cristo (☎ 787/722-9020), these bars are hip hangouts for late-night dialogues.

In another part of the old city, near the lower end of Calle Fortaleza, are two radically different hangouts. The Latin-style **Douglas' Pub,** Calle Tanca 301 (☎ 787/721-9658), serves an array of vaguely hallucinogenic cocktails, which fuel the high-testosterone level of the mostly male, mostly straight, clientele. Open daily from 1pm to 4am, and run by nightlife entrepreneur Douglas Marin, it charges from $2.50 to $2.75 for a beer, and around $6.50 for any of about 40 mind-altering cocktails. If you want to play pool, climb to the loft-style second floor, where seven pool tables draw an animated crowd at 50¢ a game.

Virtually across the street from Douglas' Pub is the much more stylish and sedate **Café Tabac,** Calle Fortaleza 262 (☎ 787/725-6785). Inspired by a cafe in

and locals, usually in their 20s and 30s. Sometimes a pianist performs at the oversized grand piano. An open courtyard out back provides additional seating for sipping margaritas or other drinks.

Zabó. 14 Calle Candina. (entrance is via an alleyway on Ashford Avenue between Calles Washington and Cervantes.) ☎ 787/725-9494.

Among San Juan's young, restless, and unattached, this place is more famous for its bar than its restaurant. The bar is divided into two separate spaces, the more popular being a cottage-like outbuilding—open Tuesday through Friday from 5pm to midnight—on the grounds of a turn-of-the-20th-century villa. Lots of charm derives from the attractive crowd, stiff drinks such as cosmopolitans and martinis ($6.50 each), and live music every Wednesday night from 8 to 11:45pm. Some nights, depending on the operating hours of the restaurant, the bar crowd moves into the restaurant's entrance vestibule, a cozy spot for mingling.

HOT NIGHTS IN GAY SAN JUAN

Straight folks are generally welcome in each of these gay venues, and many local couples show up for the hot music and dancing. Local straight boys who show up to cause trouble are generally ushered out quickly. Unless otherwise stated, there is no cover.

1930s Havana, and cooked by ceiling fans that slowly spin air down onto potted palms and leather sofas, it specializes in fine cigars, Puerto Rican coffee, and a sophisticated array of drinks. These include around 40 kinds of martinis, each priced at $8, as well as aged cognacs, ports, and rums. It's open Monday through Saturday from noon to midnight (to 2am on Friday and Saturday). Appetizers, priced from $9.50 to $14, include pâtés, smoked fish, cheeses, and shrimp; desserts, priced from $6 to $10, are also available. A well-chosen roster of cigars costs from $4 to $20 each.

If you'd like to continue your barhopping, we have some other offbeat selections. These include **Hijos de Borinquén,** Calle San José at Calle San Sebastián (no phone), a nostalgic bar that evokes Puerto Rico in the 1950s with its checkered floor and posters of palm trees. The Puerto Rican beer Medalla is the drink of choice.

You might also stumble into **Carli Café Concierto,** 206 Calle Tetuán (☎ 787/725-4927), off Plazoleta Rafael Carrión. This is one of the Old Town's best spots for drinking margaritas and watching the world go by. You'll see everything from old widows dressed in black to bikini-clad tourists fresh off the cruise ships.

You can also stop in at **Aquí Se Puede,** 50 Calle San Justo (☎ 787/724-4448), which has excellent tapas and tropical fruit drinks.

One of the best places for people-watching is **Quatro Estaciones,** Plaza de Armas (no phone), a snack bar in the heart of one of Old Town's most bustling squares. It remains open 24 hours.

If you're still walking in the early hours of the morning, stop in at **El Farolito,** 277 Calle Sol (no phone). This small bar, decorated with old paintings of drunks, opens at noon and doesn't seem to close until dawn has long split the sky. The drink of choice here is coco frío with rum.

Beach Bar. On the ground floor of the Atlantic Beach Hotel, 1 Calle Vendig. ☎ 787/721-6900.

This is more crowded and animated than its competitor, the Hurricane Bar (see below) across the street. It's the site of a hugely popular Sunday afternoon gathering, which gets really crowded beginning around 4pm and stretches into the wee hours. There's an open-air bar protected from rain by a sloping rooftop and a space atop the seawall with a panoramic view of the Condado beachfront. Drag shows occasionally take place on the terrace. The bar is open daily from 11am to at least 1am.

Cups. 1708 Calle San Mateo, Santurce. ☎ 787/268-3570.

Set in a Latino tavern, the premises are valued as the only place in San Juan that caters almost exclusively to lesbians. Men of any sexual persuasion aren't particularly welcome. The scene reminds many lesbians of a tropical version of one of the bars they left behind at home. Although the club is open Wednesday through Sunday from 7pm to 4am, entertainment such as live music or cabaret is presented only on Wednesday at 9pm, Friday at 10pm, and Sunday at 8pm.

Eros. 1257 Ponce de León, Santurce. ☎ 787/725-9494. Cover $3–$5.

This is a two-level nightclub catering exclusively to the city's growing gay population. Patterned after the dance emporiums of New York, but on a smaller scale, the club has cutting-edge music and bathrooms that are among the most creative in the world. Here, wall murals present fantasy-charged, eroticized versions of ancient Greek and Roman gods. Regrettably, only one night a week (Wednesday) is devoted to Latino music; on other nights, the music is equivalent to what you'd find in the gay discos of either Los Angeles or New York City. Open Wednesday through Sunday from 10pm to 3 or 4am.

Hurricane Bar. 2 Calle Vendig. ☎ **787/725-2025.**

The bar is named in honor of the tropical storm that swept away its predecessor. This gay male hangout functions in tandem with the above-mentioned Beach Bar, which lies just across the dead-end street. Under new management by a team of entrepreneurs from Georgia and San Juan, it attracts a crowd that's a bit more sedate than the one that converges at the Beach Bar. It's open daily from 11am to 1am.

CASINOS

Many visitors come to Puerto Rico on package deals and stay at one of the posh hotels at the Condado or Isla Verde just to gamble.

The casino generating all the excitement today is the 18,500-square-foot **Casino at the Ritz-Carlton,** 6961 State Rd., Isla Verde (☎ **787/253-1700**), the largest in Puerto Rico. It combines the elegant decor of the 1940s with tropical fabrics and patterns. This is one of the plushest and most exclusive entertainment complexes in the Caribbean. You almost expect to see Joan Crawford—beautifully frocked, of course—arrive on the arm of Clark Gable. It features traditional games such as blackjack, roulette, baccarat, craps, and slot machines.

One of the splashiest of San Juan's casinos is at the **Wyndham Old San Juan Hotel & Casino,** Calle Brumbaugh 100 (☎ **787/721-5100**), where five-card stud competes with some 240 slot machines and roulette tables. You can also try your luck at the **Caribe Hilton** (one of the better ones), Calle Los Rosales (☎ **787/721-0303**), **El San Juan Hotel & Casino** (one of the most grand), 6063 Isla Verde Ave. (☎ **787/ 791-1000**), or the **Condado Plaza Hotel & Casino,** 999 Ashford Ave. (☎ **787/ 721-1000**). As in European casinos, there are no passports to flash or admissions to pay.

COCKFIGHTS

A brutal sport not to everyone's taste, cockfights are legal in Puerto Rico. The most authentic are in Salinas, a town on the southern coast with a southwestern ethos, which has *galleras,* or rings, for cockfighting. But you don't have to go all the way there to see a match. About three fights per week take place at the **Coliseo Gallistico,** Route 37, kilometer 1.5, Isla Verde. Call ☎ **787/791-6005** for the schedule and to order tickets, which cost $8, $10, $15, or $25, depending on your seat.

Side Trips from San Juan 7

Within easy reach of San Juan's cosmopolitan bustle are superb attractions and natural wonders. With San Juan as your base, you can explore the island by day, and still return in time for a final dip in the ocean and an evening on the town.

About 90 minutes west of San Juan is the world's largest radar/radio-telescope, Arecibo Observatory. After touring this awesome facility, you can travel west to nearby Río Camuy for a good look at marvels below ground. Here you can plunge deep into the subterranean beauty of a spectacular cave system carved over eons by one of the world's largest underground rivers.

Prefer to stay closer to San Juan? Virtually on the city's doorstep, only 18 miles to the west, is the Dorado resort, home of the famed Hyatt Dorado and Hyatt Regency Cerromar beach hotels. Both properties open onto beautiful white sandy beaches. If you want to avoid the congestion of the Condado's high-rise hotels, consider a beach holiday here. Both Hyatts are family-friendly.

Just 35 miles east of San Juan is the Caribbean National Forest, the only tropical rain forest in the U.S. National Park System. Named by the Spanish for its anvil-shaped peak, "El Yunque" receives more than 100 billion gallons of rainfall annually. If you have time for only one side trip, this is it. Waterfalls, wild orchids, giant ferns, towering tabonuco trees, and sierra palms make El Yunque a photographer's and hiker's paradise. Pick up a map and choose from dozens of trails graded by difficulty, including El Yunque's most challenging—the 6-mile-long El Toro Trail to the peak. New at El Yunque is El Portal Tropical Center. With 10,000 square feet of exhibit space, plazas, and patios, this facility greatly expands the recreational and educational programs available to visitors. La Coca Falls and an observation tower are just off Route 191.

Visitors can combine a morning trip to El Yunque with an afternoon of swimming and sunning on tranquil Luquillo Beach. "Luquillo" is a Spanish adaptation of Yukiyu, the god believed by the Taínos to inhabit El Yunque. Soft white sand, shaded by coconut palms and the blue sea, makes this Puerto Rico's best-known beach. Take a picnic or sample local specialties from the kiosks.

1 Arecibo & Camuy

41–47 miles W of San Juan

ATTRACTIONS

Dubbed "an ear to heaven," the ✪ **Arecibo Observatory** (☎ **787/878-2612**) contains the world's largest and most sensitive radar/radio-telescope. The telescope features a 20-acre dish, or radio mirror, set in an ancient sinkhole. It's 1,000 feet in diameter and 167 feet deep, and allows scientists to monitor natural radio emissions from distant galaxies, pulsars, and quasars, and to examine the ionosphere, the planets, and the moon using powerful radar signals. Used by scientists as part of the Search for Extraterrestrial Intelligence (SETI), this is the same site featured in the movie *Contact* with Jodie Foster. This research effort speculates that advanced civilizations elsewhere in the universe might also communicate via radio waves. The 10-year, $100 million search for life in space was launched on October 12, 1992, the 500-year anniversary of the New World's discovery by Columbus.

Unusually lush vegetation flourishes under the giant dish—ferns, wild orchids, and begonias. Assorted creatures like mongooses, lizards, and dragonflies have also taken refuge there. Suspended in outlandish fashion above the dish is a 600-ton platform that resembles a space station.

Tours at $3.50 are available at the observatory Wednesday through Friday from noon to 4pm, Saturday and Sunday from 9am to 4pm. There's a souvenir shop on the grounds. The observatory is a 90-minute drive west of San Juan, outside the town of Arecibo. From Arecibo, it's a 35-minute drive via routes 22, 134, 625, and 635 (the site is signposted).

Río Camuy Cave Park is 1 hour and 20 minutes west of San Juan on Route 129, at kilometer 18.9 (☎ **787/898-3100**), and contains the third-largest underground river in the world. It runs through a network of caves, canyons, and sinkholes that have been cut through the island's limestone base over the course of millions of years. Known to the pre-Columbian Taíno peoples, the caves came to the attention of speleologists in the 1950s. They were opened to the public in 1986.

Visitors first see a short film about the caves, then descend into the caverns in open-air trolleys. The trip takes you through a 200-foot-deep sinkhole and a chasm where tropical trees, ferns, and flowers flourish, along with birds and butterflies. The trolley then goes to the entrance of Clara Cave of Epalme, one of 16 in the Camuy caves network, where visitors begin a 45-minute walk, viewing the majestic series of rooms rich in stalagmites, stalactites, and huge natural "sculptures" formed over the centuries. The park has added the Tres Pueblos Sinkhole and the Spiral Sinkhole to its slate of attractions.

The caves are open Tuesday through Sunday from 8am to 4pm. Tickets are $10 for adults, $7 for children 2 to 12, and $5 for seniors. Parking is $2. For more information, phone the park.

WHERE TO DINE

The closest place for food is the Parador La Casa Grande in Utuado, a little mountain town south of Arecibo (see "Paradores of Western Puerto Rico," in chapter 9).

2 Dorado (The Hyatt Resorts)

18 miles W of San Juan

Dorado—the name itself evokes a kind of magic—is a world of luxury resorts and villas that unfolds along the north shore of Puerto Rico. The elegant ✪ **Hyatt Dorado Beach Hotel** and the newer, larger ✪ **Hyatt Regency Cerromar Beach Hotel** sit on the choice white-sand beaches here.

The site was originally purchased in 1905 by Dr. Alfred T. Livingston, a Jamestown, New York, physician, who developed it as a 1,000-acre grapefruit and coconut plantation. Dr. Livingston's daughter, Clara, widely known in aviation circles and a friend of Amelia Earhart, owned and operated the plantation after her father's death. It was she who built the airstrip here.

GETTING THERE

If you're driving from San Juan, take Highway 2 west to Route 693 north to Dorado (trip time: 40 min.). Otherwise, call **Dorado Transport Corp,** which occupies an office on the site shared by the Hyatt hotels (☎ **787/796-1234**). Using 18-passenger minibuses, they offer frequent shuttle service between the Hyatt Hotels and the San Juan airport. They operate at frequent intervals, daily between 11am and 10pm. The fare is $15 per person, but a minimum of three passengers must make the trip for the bus to operate.

Once you're in Dorado, you can get around via the shuttle bus that travels between the two hotels every 30 minutes during the day.

OUTDOOR ACTIVITIES

If you feel like doing something more energetic than lounging on the beautiful beachfront here, the Hyatt resorts (see below) both offer their guests a wide array of beachside water-sports activities. In fact, the Hyatt Regency Cerromar Beach Hotel has the world's longest freshwater **swimming pool.** Nonguests cannot use the swimming pools here, though they can use the facilities of the Penfield Island Adventures, for which they have to pay (see below for details).

With 72 holes, the Hyatt Resorts (☎ **787/796-1234**) offer the greatest number of **golf** options in the Caribbean. The Robert Trent Jones, Sr.–designed courses are among the finest anywhere. The two original courses—east and west (☎ **787/796-8961**), both of which are associated with the Hyatt Dorado Beach Resort—were carved out of a jungle and offer tight fairways bordered by trees and forests, with lots of ocean holes. The somewhat newer and less noted north and south courses (☎ **787/796-8915**), which fall under the jurisdiction of the Hyatt Regency Cerromar, feature wide fairways with well-bunkered greens and an assortment of lakes, water traps, and tricky wind factors. Each of the four has a 72 par. The longest course is the south course at 7,047 yards.

Guests of the Hyatt hotels get preferred tee times and lower fees than nonguests. For the north and south courses, Hyatt guests pay $65 for greens fees, while nonguests are charged $85. At the east and west courses, Hyatt guests are charged $110 for greens fees, rising to $160 for nonguests. Golf carts at any of the courses rent for $20, whether you play 9 or 18 holes. All four courses maintain separate pro shops, each with a bar and snack-style restaurant. Both are open daily from 7am until dusk.

The Hyatt resorts of **Dorado** and **Cerromar** (☎ 787/796-1234) have the best **tennis** in Puerto Rico, with a total of 15 courts between them. The charge is $15 an hour, rising to $18 from 6 to 10pm. Lessons are available for $60 per hour. Nonguests can't use the courts, however.

The best place for water sports is on the island's north shore along the well-maintained beachfront of the Hyatt Dorado Beach Hotel, near the 10th hole of the hotel's famous east golf course. Here, **Penfield Island Adventures** (☎ 787/796-1234, ext. 3200, or 787/796-2188) offers 90-minute **windsurfing lessons** for $60; board rentals cost $50 per half day. Well supplied with a wide array of Windsurfers, including some designed specifically for beginners and children, the school benefits from the almost uninterrupted flow of the north shore's strong, steady winds and an experienced crew of instructors. A **kayaking/snorkeling** trip (☎ 787/796-4645), departing daily at 9:15am and 11:45am, and lasting 1½ hours, costs $45. Two-tank boat **dives** go for $119 per person. **Waverunners** can be rented for $60 per half hour for a single rider, and $75 for two riders. A **Sunfish** rents for $45 for 1 hour, $65 for 2 hours.

WHERE TO STAY

The two Hyatt hotels in Dorado sprawl across the former Livingston estate, which now bristles with palms, pine trees, and purple bougainvillea, all fronting a 2-mile stretch of sandy ocean beach. The two side-by-side 18-hole championship golf courses designed by Robert Trent Jones are their big draw.

✪ **Hyatt Dorado Beach Resort & Casino.** Dorado, PR 00646. ☎ **800/233-1234** in the U.S. or 787/796-1234. Fax 787/796-6560. www.hyatt.com/pages/d/dorado.html. 298 units, 17 casitas. A/C MINIBAR TV TEL. Winter $495–$655 double; $785 casita for 2. Off-season $170–$325 double; $385–$450 casita for 2. MAP (mandatory in winter) $65 extra per day for adults, $35 extra per day for children. AE, DC, DISC, MC, V.

While the Cerromar (see below) is more like a conventional resort hotel, the Dorado Beach's low-rise buildings sprawl across a former plantation, amidst palms, pine trees, purple bougainvillea, all within a short walk of a 2-mile sandy beach. Its fans appreciate the emphasis on natural landscaping. Families interested in massive facilities and sports-oriented programs gravitate to the Cerromar Beach; those interested in a more peaceful, relaxing ambience cast their vote for the Dorado Beach. We like it better than the Cerromar, especially since a shuttle bus runs back and forth between the two resorts every half hour, allowing you to use the Cerromar's fabulous pool area even if you stay here.

Hyatt has spent millions on improvements. The renovated guest rooms have marble bathrooms and terra-cotta floors throughout. Accommodations are available on the beach or in villas tucked in and around the lushly planted grounds. They're fairly spacious, with a lot of extras such as irons and ironing boards. Bathrooms have everything from hair dryers to bathrobes, thick towels to power showers. The *casitas* are a series of private beach or poolside houses.

Dining/Diversions: Breakfast can be taken on your private balcony, and lunch on an outdoor ocean terrace. Dinner is served in a three-tiered main dining room where you can watch the surf. Hyatt Dorado chefs have won many awards, and the food at the hotel restaurants is among the most appealing in the Caribbean. The Beach Grill and Pro Shop are for casual meals. And don't forget the casino.

Amenities: Two 18-hole championship golf courses designed by Robert Trent Jones, Sr. (see below); seven all-weather tennis courts; a full-service spa; two pools; children's camp; one of the best windsurfing schools in Puerto Rico; 24-hour room service; baby-sitting; laundry/dry cleaning.

Hyatt Regency Cerromar Beach Hotel. Dorado, PR 00646. ☎ **800/233-1234** or 787/796-1234. Fax 787/796-4647. www.hyatt.com/pages/c/cerroa.html. 506 units. A/C MINIBAR TV TEL. Winter $350–$480 double; from $770 suite. Spring and fall $245–$325 double; from $570 suite. Summer $190–$230 double; from $435 suite. MAP (breakfast and dinner) $65 extra for adults, $35 extra for children. AE, DC, DISC, MC, V.

Near the more elegant Hyatt Dorado Beach Hotel, the bustling Cerromar stands on its own beach and boasts a wealth of sports facilities and resort amenities. The name *Cerromar* is a combination of two Spanish words—*cerro* (mountain) and *mar* (sea)—and true to its name, it's surrounded by mountains and ocean. Approximately 22 miles west of San Juan, the high-rise hotel shares the 1,000-acre former Livingston estate with the Dorado, so guests can enjoy the Robert Trent Jones, Sr., golf courses and other facilities at the next-door hotel; a shuttle bus runs back and forth between the two resorts every half hour. This property is more action-packed than the Dorado Beach, and attracts more convention groups and families with kids.

All rooms have first-class appointments and are well maintained; most have private balconies. All rooms have honor bars, in-room safes, and good mattresses. Bathrooms are equipped with thick towels and power showers; the Regency Club units also have robes and hair dryers.

Dining/Diversions: The outdoor Swan Café has three levels connected by a dramatic staircase; some tables overlook a lake populated by swans and flamingos. Other dining choices include Sushi Wong's and the hotel's pride and joy, Medici's. The Flamingo bar offers a wide, open-air expanse overlooking the sea and the water playground. The resort also has a casino and dance club.

Amenities: The water playground contains the world's longest freshwater swimming pool: a 1,776-foot-long fantasy pool with a riverlike current in five connected free-form pools. It takes 15 minutes to float from one end of the pool to the other. There are also 14 waterfalls, tropical landscaping, a subterranean whirlpool, water slides, walks, bridges, and a children's pool. A full-service spa and health club provide services for all manner of body and skin care, including massage. In addition to tennis courts and two golf courses, there's a children's day camp for ages 3 to 12, open year-round and known as Camp Hyatt. Room service is available 24 hours a day, and there's laundry/dry cleaning and baby-sitting.

WHERE TO DINE

El Malecón. Rte. 693, km 8.2. ☎ **787/796-1645.** Reservations not necessary. Main courses $8–$35.95. AE, MC, V. Daily 11am–11pm. PUERTO RICAN.

If you'd like to discover an unpretentious local place serving good Puerto Rican cuisine, then head for El Malecón, a simple concrete structure one minute from a small shopping center, which you pass on your way from the Hyatt hotels. It has a cozy family ambience and is especially popular on weekends. Some members of the staff speak English, and the chef is best with fresh seafood, which most diners order. The chef might also prepare a variety of items not listed on the menu. Most of the dishes are at the lower end of the price scale (see above); only the lobster is expensive.

Steak Co. In the Hyatt Regency Cerromar. ☎ **787/796-1234,** ext. 3240. Reservations required. Main courses $28–$38. AE, DC, DISC, MC, V. Daily 6:30–9:30pm. STEAK/NORTHERN ITALIAN.

This is the best of the three upscale restaurants in the two Hyatt hotels. Frequented by an upscale, usually well-dressed clientele, it occupies a soaring two-story room, which can be observed from the lobby above through plate-glass windows. While enjoying well-conceived cuisine, diners have views of venerable trees draped in Spanish moss, a landscaped pond, and a waterfall. The best steaks and prime ribs in this part of

Puerto Rico are served here—tender and grilled or cooked to your specifications. Most dishes are accompanied by large, perfectly baked (not soggy) potatoes and great sourdough bread. In the highly unlikely possibility you have room for dessert, you'll be glad you do.

3 El Yunque

25 miles E of San Juan

The rain forest of El Yunque (see "The Natural Environment," in appendix A) is a major attraction in Puerto Rico. Part of the Caribbean National Forest, this is the only tropical forest in the U.S. National Forest Service system. The 28,000-acre preserve was given its status by President Theodore Roosevelt.

GETTING THERE

This side trip will take you through some of Puerto Rico's most stunning natural .scenery and small towns, such as Trujillo Alto, Gurabo, Fajardo, Naguabo Beach, Humacao, Yabucoa, San Lorenzo, and Caguas.

From Condado, signs point the way southeast to Route 1. Near Río Piedras on your right, Route 3 is the famous highway that most motorists take to visit Luquillo Beach and El Yunque Rain Forest. Route 1 naturally blends into Route 3, which is sometimes called "Avenida 65 de Infantera" after the Puerto Rican regiment that fought in World War II and the Korean War.

At the intersection of Route 3 and Route 181, head south toward Trujillo Alto. South of Trujillo Alto, connect with Route 851, which continues until it comes to an intersection with Route 941. At this point, get on Route 941, which runs in a southwesterly direction. Along 941, and to your right, you'll come to **Lake of Loíza,** surrounded by mountains. You may see local farmers (*jíbaros*) riding horses laden with produce going to or from the marketplace. (Lake of Loíza is not to be confused with the northern coastal town of Loíza, which is known for its music and African heritage.)

Leave the town by heading east along Route 30. Before you approach the town of Juncos, signs point the way to Route 185, which will lead you to the small town of Lomas. Continue north along Route 185, following the signs to the major artery of Route 3. Allow a leisurely hour of driving time for this trek after having left the lake.

Once you have connected with Route 3, take it east toward El Yunque and then turn right (south) onto Route 191, which climbs up into the forest surrounding El Yunque's peak and that of its taller sibling, El Toro. You are now in the Caribbean National Forest, the most scenic, panoramic, and dramatic part of the eastern drive through Puerto Rico.

After viewing the lake, continue on Route 941, which now swings in a southeasterly direction through Puerto Rico's tobacco country to Guarbo. You'll know that you're nearing the town from the sweet aroma of drying tobacco leaves. Part of the town of Gurabo is set on the side of a mountain, and the streets consist of steps.

Leave Gurabo by heading east on Route 30. Near Juncos, turn left onto Route 185 north, follow it up through Lomas, and then get on Route 186 south. This road offers views of the ocean beyond the mountains and valleys. At this point, you'll be driving through the lower section of the Caribbean National Forest; the vegetation is dense, and you'll be surrounded by giant ferns. The brooks descending from the mountains become waterfalls on both sides of the road.

At this point, you can begin your exploration of the rain forest.

EXPLORING EL YUNQUE

Encompassing four distinct forest types, El Yunque is home to 240 species of tropical trees, flowers, and wildlife. More than 20 kinds of orchids and 50 varieties of ferns share this diverse habitat with millions of tiny tree frogs, whose distinctive cry of *coquí* (pronounced ko-*kee*) has given them their name. Tropical birds include the lively, greenish blue, red-fronted Puerto Rican parrot, once nearly extinct and now making a comeback. Other rare animals include the Puerto Rican boa, which grows to 7 feet. (It is highly unlikely that you will encounter a boa. The few who have are still shouting about it.)

El Yunque is the best of Puerto Rico's 20 forest preserves. The forest is situated high above sea level, with the peak of El Toro rising to 3,532 feet. You can be fairly sure you'll be showered upon, since more than 100 billion gallons of rain fall here annually. However, the showers are brief and there are many shelters. On a quickie tour, many visitors reserve only a half day for El Yunque. But it's unique and deserves at least a daylong outing.

El Yunque is the most popular spot in Puerto Rico for hiking; for a description of our favorite trails, see "Hiking" in chapter 2. The **Department of Natural Resources Forest Service** (☎ 787/724-8774) administers some aspects of the park, although for the ordinary hiker, more useful information may be available at **El Yunque Catalina Field Office,** near the village of Palma, beside the main highway at the forest's northern edge (☎ 787/888-5670). The staff can provide material about hiking routes, and, with 10 days' notice, help you plan overnight tours in the forest. If you reserve in advance, the staff will also arrange for you to take part in 2-hour group tours, costing $35 per person.

El Portal Tropical Forest Center, Route 191, Rio Grande (☎ 787/888-1880), an $18 million exhibition and information center, has 10,000 square feet of exhibition space. Three pavilions offer exhibits and bilingual displays. The actor Jimmy Smits narrates a documentary called "Understanding the Forest." The center is open daily from 9am to 5pm, charging an admission of $3.

WHERE TO STAY

Ceiba Country Inn. Road no. 977, km 1.2 (P.O. Box 1067), Ceiba, PR 00735. ☎ 787/885-0471. Fax 787/885-0471. 9 units. A/C TEL. $70 double. Extra person $5. Rate includes breakfast. AE, DISC, MC, V.

If you're looking for an escape from the hustle and bustle of everyday life, then this is the place for you. This small, well-maintained bed-and-breakfast is located on the easternmost part of Puerto Rico near the Roosevelt Road's U.S. naval base (you must rent a car to reach this little haven in the mountains). El Yunque is only 15 miles away, San Juan 35 miles to the west. The rooms are on the bottom floor of a large, old family home. All have private bathrooms; each unit also contains a small refrigerator. They are decorated in a tropical motif with flowered murals on the walls painted by a local artist. For a quiet evening cocktail, you may want to visit the small lounge on the second floor.

WHERE TO DINE

We recommend the dining and drinking facilities within the Westin Rio Mar (see below), which sits very close to the entrance to El Yunque.

4 Luquillo Beach

31 miles E of San Juan

✪ **Luquillo Beach** is the island's best and most popular public stretch of sand. From here, you can easily explore El Yunque Rain Forest.

GETTING THERE

If you are driving, pass the San Juan airport and follow the signs to "Carolina." This leads to Route 3, which travels east toward the fishing town of Fajardo, where you'll turn north to Las Croabas. To reach the Westin, the area's major hotel, follow signs to El Yunque, then signs to the Westin.

Private limousine from the San Juan airport costs $225 per carload to the Westin Rio Mar Beach Resort, Country Club & Ocean Villas. A taxi will cost approximately $70. Hotel buses make trips to and from the San Juan airport, based on the arrival times of incoming flights, for $27.50 per person, each way for transport to El Conquistador; $23 per person, each way, to the Westin.

HITTING THE BEACH

Luquillo Public Beach, Puerto Rico's finest, is palm dotted and crescent-shaped, opening onto a lagoon with calm waters and a wide, sandy bank. It's very crowded on weekends but much better during the week. There are lockers, tent sites, showers, picnic tables, and food stands selling a sampling of the island's *frituras* (fried fare), especially cod fritters and tacos.

You can also snorkel and skin dive among the living reefs with lots of tropical fish. Offshore are coral formations and spectacular sea life—eels, octopuses, stingrays, tarpon, big puffer fish, turtles, nurse sharks, and squid, among other sea creatures.

The best people to take you diving are at the **Dive Center** at the Westin Rio Mar Beach Resort, Country Club & Ocean Villas (☎ **787/888-6698**). This is one of the largest dive centers in Puerto Rico, a PADI five-star facility with two custom-designed boats that usually take no more than 6 to 10 divers. Snorkeling and skin diving costs $65, with an advanced open water certification going for $295. Otherwise, a two-tank dive goes for $115. Equipment rentals are also available. The beach is open Tuesday through Sunday from 9am to 5pm. It is closed Monday. If Monday is a holiday, the beach opens Monday and closes Tuesday.

WHERE TO STAY

Trinidad Guest House. 6A Ocean Dr., Luquillo, PR 00773. ☎ **787/889-2710.** Fax 787/ 889-4520. 10 units (6 with bathroom). TV. $64.20 double without bathroom; $80.25 double with bathroom; $101 triple with bathroom. Rates include breakfast. AE, MC, V. At km 36.2 along Rte. 3, turn toward the shore, then turn left and drive 4 short blocks.

Until recently, ever since the Martorell family arrived from Spain in 1800, this had been their family homestead. For decades it was one of the best-known *paradores* of Puerto Rico, called Parador Martorell. The location a half block from Luquillo Beach was its major asset. In 1999, the Martorells departed. The former *parador* is still basically the same place—only the name has changed. When you arrive, you'll enter an open courtyard, which suffices for alfresco outings since there are no grounds. Breakfast always features plenty of fresh-picked fruit and homemade breads and compotes. The main reason for staying here is Luquillo Beach, which has shady palm groves, crescent beaches, coral reefs for snorkeling and scuba diving, and a surfing area. All the rooms are small and all units are air-conditioned; insist on one of them if you book here.

Westin Rio Mar Beach Resort, Country Club & Ocean Villas. 6000 Rio Mar Blvd. (19 miles east of Luis Muñoz Marín International Airport, with entrance off Puerto Rico Hwy. 3), Rio Grande, PR 00745. ☎ **800/WESTIN-1** or 787/888-6200. Fax 787/888-6600. www.westinriomar.com. 600 units. A/C MINIBAR TV TEL. Double $395–$625; suite for two $525–$2,000. AE, CB, DC, DISC, MC, V.

Marking Westin's debut in the Caribbean, this $180 million, 481-acre resort opened in 1996 onto a relatively uncrowded neighbor (Rio Mar Beach) of the massively popular Luquillo Beach, a 5-minute drive away. (El Yunque Rain Forest is only a 15-minute drive from here.) One of the three largest hotels in Puerto Rico, it was designed to compete with the Hyatt hotels at Dorado and El Conquistador, with which it's frequently compared. More than either of those competitors, however, the Westin is a good example of a mega-hotel that focuses its marketing efforts on corporate conventions, of which you're likely to see several during your time here.

The majority of the accommodations are located in the resort's centerpiece, a seven-story Spanish/Caribbean–style building whose U-shaped floor plan opens onto the sea. The surrounding landscape includes several artificial lakes set amid tropical gardens. More than 60% of the guest rooms look out over palm trees to the Atlantic. Other units open onto the mountains and forests of nearby El Yunque National Park. Throughout, the style is Spanish hacienda with nods to the surrounding jungle, incorporating unusual art and sculpture. Bedrooms are spacious, with balconies or terraces, good mattresses, irons and ironing boards, and coffeemakers. Bathrooms are equally luxurious.

At press time, the Westin was completing construction of the Ocean Villas, scheduled to open in October 2000. These 58 luxury suites will feature one, two, or three bedrooms; full kitchens; living rooms; and balconies in two 5-story structures, located steps away from the main resort. The facility will also have two swimming pools, a fine dining restaurant, and "preferential" concierge services.

Dining/Diversions: You'll never go hungry here. The resort boasts 12 restaurants and lounges, everything from Marbella (a relatively casual indoor/outdoor all-day restaurant) to Palio, an Italian gourmet spot that serves the most elegant food in the most formal setting. There's also a beachfront grill and bar, a lobby bar with prolonged bouts of live merengue and salsa, and a 6,500-square-foot casino.

Amenities: The resort encompasses the Rio Mar Country Club, site of two important golf courses. The older of the two, the Ocean Course, was designed by George and Tom Fazio as part of the original resort, and as such, has been a staple on Puerto Rico's professional golf circuit since the 1960s. In 1997, Westin opened the property's second 18-holer, the slightly more challenging River Course, which is the first Greg Norman–designed course in the Caribbean. Par for both courses is 72. Thirteen tennis courts, a beach club with equipment rentals, a health club with aerobics classes, a spa offering massage and other treatments, 24-hour room service, and laundry/dry cleaning are available. The Iguana Kid's Club keeps children 4 to 12 amused during morning and evening sessions. The activities staff will help you arrange any sport or activity, including nearby horseback riding, hiking, deep-sea fishing, sailing, and boating.

WHERE TO DINE

Brass Cactus. In the Condominio Complejo Turistico, Rte. 3 Marginal. ☎ **787/889-5735.** Reservations not necessary. Sandwiches $7.50–$10.75. Main courses $14.75–$22.75. MC, V. Mon–Fri 11am–midnight, Sat–Sun 11am–2am. AMERICAN.

On a service road adjacent to Route 3 at the western edge of Luquillo, within a boxy-looking concrete building in need of repair, is one of the town's most popular bar/restaurants. Permeated with a raunchy, no-holds-barred spirit, this amiable spot has thrived since the early 1990s, when it was established by an Illinois-born bartender who outfitted the interior with gringo memorabilia. Drinks are stiff and the crowd looks tougher than it is, tending to calm down whenever food and drink are brought out. Menu items include king crab salad; tricolor tortellini laced with chicken and shrimp; several kinds of sandwiches and burgers; and platters of churrasco, T-bone steaks, chicken with tequila sauce, barbecued pork, and fried mahimahi.

Palio. In the Westin Rio Mar Beach Resort, Country Club & Ocean Villas. ☎ **787/888-6000.** Reservations recommended. Main courses $28–$38. AE, DC, MC, V. Nov–June daily 6–11pm; May–Oct Tues–Sat 6–11pm. INTERNATIONAL.

This richly decorated restaurant is the premier dining outlet of the region's largest and splashiest hotel. The Westin chain has poured time and energy into making this a showcase of the resort's creativity. Although most of the ingredients have to be flown in, the cuisine is excellent. A certain attachment to culinary tradition doesn't preclude a modern approach to the cookery. Dishes we've sampled have a superbly aromatic flavor and are beautifully presented and served. The sophisticated menu includes potato and sage gnocchi; rack of American lamb; fresh Maine lobster; center-cut veal chops stuffed with fresh mozzarella, tomatoes, and avocado, and served with grappa-laced mashed potatoes; and baby free-range chicken, spit-roasted, and served with rosemary jus.

Sandy's Seafood Restaurant and Steak House. Calle Fernandez Garcia 276, ☎ **787/ 889-5765.** Reservations recommended. Main courses $8–$32. AE, DISC, MC, V. Daily 11am–between 9:30 and 11pm, depending on business. PUERTO RICAN/SEAFOOD.

The concrete–and–plate-glass facade is less obtrusive than that of other restaurants in town, and the cramped, Formica-clad interior is far from stylish. Nonetheless, Sandy's is one of the most famous restaurants in northeastern Puerto Rico, thanks to the wide array of luminaries—U.S. and Puerto Rican political figures, mainstream journalists, beauty pageant winners, and assorted slumming rich—who travel from as far away as San Juan to dine here. Set about a block from the main square of the seaside resort of Luquillo, it was founded in 1984 by Miguel (Mike) Angel, a.k.a. Sandy. The proprietor usually directs operations from a perch within a narrow, aggressively simple bar that flanks one side of the respectable but far-from-cutting-edge dining room. The only decoration includes photographs of previous clients and rows of papaya set out to ripen on the bar top.

One end of the room contains a refrigerated display case loaded with whatever fish and shellfish have been hauled in from off the coast of Vieques. Platters, especially the daily specials, are huge—so copious, in fact, that they're discussed with fervor by competitors and clients alike. Examples include fresh shellfish, served on the half-shell; *asopaos;* four kinds of steak; five different preparations of chicken, including a delicious version with garlic sauce; four kinds of gumbos; paellas; a dozen preparations of lobster; even jalapeño peppers stuffed with shrimp or lobster. Pitchers of sangría or beer make worthy accompaniments. Side orders include french fries, fried or mashed ripe plantains, mashed cassava, rice and beans, and baked potatoes. Desserts are kept as simple as possible, usually only flan, a pastry of the day, and ice cream.

Ponce, Mayagüez & 8
San Germán

For those who want to see a less urban side of Puerto Rico, Ponce, on the south shore, and Mayagüez and San Germán, on the west coast, offer a variety of places to stay, and each makes a good center for sightseeing. From either Mayagüez or Ponce you can take a side trip to historic San Germán, site of Puerto Rico's second-oldest city with the oldest church in the New World.

Founded in 1692, Ponce is Puerto Rico's second-largest city and has received much attention because of its inner-city restoration. It is home to the island's premier art gallery.

Puerto Rico's third-largest city, Mayagüez, is a port located about halfway down the west coast. It may not be as architecturally remarkable as Ponce, but it's a fine base for exploring some sights and enjoying some very good beaches.

1 Ponce

75 miles SW of San Juan

"The Pearl of the South," Ponce was named after Loíza Ponce de León, great-grandson of Juan Ponce de León. Founded in 1692, it is today Puerto Rico's principal shipping port on the Caribbean. The city is well kept and attractive, as reflected by its many plazas, parks, and public buildings. A suggestion of a provincial Mediterranean town lingers in its air. Look for the *rejas,* or framed balconies, on the handsome colonial mansions.

Timed to coincide with 1992's 500th anniversary celebration of Christopher Columbus's voyage to the New World, a $440 million renovation began to bring new life to this once-decaying city. The streets are lit with gas lamps and lined with neoclassical buildings, just as they were a century ago. Horse-drawn carriages clop by, and strollers walk along sidewalks edged with pink marble. Thanks to the restoration, Ponce now recalls the turn of the 20th century, when it rivaled San Juan as a wealthy business and cultural center.

ESSENTIALS
GETTING THERE   American Eagle (☎ 800/433-7300) offers two daily flights between San Juan and Ponce (flight time: 35 min.) for $85 to $176 round-trip, depending on the ticket. However, prices are known to fluctuate, so call for last-minute details.

If you're driving, take Route 1 south to Highway 52, then continue south and west to Ponce. Allow at least 1¹/₂ hours.

VISITOR INFORMATION The **Ponce Municipal Tourist Office** has a kiosk inside the Parque de Bombas, on Plaza de Las Delicias (see below). If you find it temporarily unstaffed, go across the street to the second floor of the Citibank Building, where the administrative offices are located (☎ **787/843-0465**).

GETTING AROUND The town's inner core is small enough that everything can be visited on foot. Taxis provide the second-best alternative.

SEEING THE SIGHTS

Most visitors go to Ponce to see the city's architectural restoration. Calle Reina Isabel, one of the city's major residential streets, is a virtual textbook of the different Ponceño styles, ranging from interpretations of European neoclassical to Spanish colonial. The neoclassical style here often incorporates balconies, as befits the warmer climate, and an extensive use of pink marble. The "Ponce Créole" style, a term for Spanish colonial, includes both exterior and interior balconies. The latter have a wall of tiny windows that allows sunlight into the patio.

With partial funding from the governments of Puerto Rico and Spain, Ponce has restored more than 600 of its 1,000 historic buildings. Many are on streets radiating from the stately Plaza Las Delicias (Plaza of Delights). On Isabel, Reina, Pabellones, and Lolita Tizol streets, electrical and telephone wires have been buried, replica 19th-century gas lamps installed, and sidewalks trimmed with the distinctive, locally quarried pink marble. Paseo Atocha, one of Ponce's main shopping streets, is now a delightful pedestrian mall with a lively street festival on the third Sunday of every month. Paseo Arias, or Callejon del Amor (Lover's Alley), is a charming pedestrian passage between two 1920s bank buildings, Banco Popular and Banco Santander, on Plaza Las Delicias, where outdoor cafe tables invite lingering. Two monumental bronze lions by Spanish sculptor Victor Ochoa guard the entrance to the old section of the city.

In addition to the attractions listed below, the weekday **marketplace** at calles Atocha and Castillo is colorful, and the historic **La Perla Theater** and the **Serrallés rum distillery** are worth visits. Perhaps you'll want to simply sit in the plaza, watching the Ponceños at one of their favorite pastimes—strolling about town.

Cathedral of Our Lady of Guadalupe. Calle Concordia/Calle Union. ☎ **787/842-0134.** Free admission. Mon–Fri 6am–3:30pm, Sat–Sun 6am–noon and 3–8pm.

In 1660, a rustic chapel was built on this spot on the western edge of the Plaza de Las Delicias, and since then fires and earthquakes have razed the church repeatedly. In 1919, a team of priests collected funds from local parishioners to construct the Doric- and Gothic-inspired building that stands here today. Designed by architects Francisco Porrato Doría and Francisco Trublard in 1931, and featuring a pipe organ installed in 1934, it remains an important place for prayer for many of Ponce's citizens. The cathedral, named after a famous holy shrine in Mexico, is the best-known church in southern Puerto Rico.

✪ El Museo Castillo Serralles. El Vigía 17. ☎ **787/259-1774.** Admission $3 adults, $2 seniors over 62, $1.50 children under 16. Tues–Sun 9:30am–5:30pm. The roads leading to the museum are a confusing labyrinth of run-down, unnamed residential streets, so it's best to take a taxi; the fare is about $4 each way from the center of town.

Two miles north of the center of town is the largest and most imposing building in Ponce, constructed high on El Vigía Hill (see below) during the 1930s by the Serralles family, owners of a local rum distillery. One of the architectural gems of Puerto Rico, it is the best evidence of the wealth produced by the turn-of-the-20th-century sugar boom. Guides will escort you through the Spanish Revival house with .Moorish and Andalusian details. Highlights include panoramic courtyards, a baronial dining room, a small cafe and souvenir shop, and a series of photographs showing the tons of earth that were brought in for the construction of the terraced gardens.

El Vigía Hill. At the north end of Ponce. Take a taxi; from the Plaza de Las Delicias; the ride will cost about $4.

The city's tallest geologic feature, El Vigía Hill dominates Ponce's northern skyline. Its base and steep slopes are covered with a maze of 19th- and early 20th-century development. Once you reach the summit, you'll see the soaring Cruz del Vigía (Virgin's Cross). Built in 1984 of reinforced concrete to replace a 19th-century wooden cross in poor repair, this modern 100-foot structure bears lateral arms measuring 70 feet long and an observation tower (accessible by elevator), from which you can see all of the natural beauty surrounding Ponce.

The cross commemorates Vigía Hill's colonial role as a deterrent to contraband smuggling. In 1801, on orders from Spain, a garrison was established atop the hill to detect any ships that might try to unload their cargoes tax-free along Puerto Rico's southern coastline.

◯ Museo de Arte de Ponce. Av. de Las Américas 25. ☎ **787/848-0505.** Admission $4 adults, $1 children under 12. Daily 10am–5pm. Follow Calle Concordia from Plaza de Las Delicias 1¹/₂ miles south to Av. de Las Américas.

Donated to the people of Puerto Rico by Luís A. Ferré, a former governor, this, museum has the finest collection of European and Latin American art in the Caribbean. The building itself was designed by Edward Durell Stone (who also designed the John F. Kennedy Center for the Performing Arts in Washington, D.C.) and has been called the "Parthenon of the Caribbean." Its collection represents the principal schools of American and European art of the past 5 centuries. Among the nearly 400 works on display are exceptional pre-Raphaelite and Italian baroque paintings. Visitors will also see artworks by other European masters, as well as Puerto Rican and Latin American paintings, graphics, and sculptures. On display are some of the best works of the two "old masters" of Puerto Rico, Francisco Oller and José Campéche. The museum also contains a representative collection of the works of the old masters of Europe, including Gainsborough, Velázquez, Rubens, and van Dyck. The museum is best known for its pre-Raphaelite and baroque paintings and sculpture—not only from Spain, but from Italy and France as well. Both the Whitney in New York and the Louvre in Paris have borrowed from its collection. Temporary exhibitions are also mounted here.

Museum of the History of Ponce (Casa Salazar). Calle Reina Isabel 51–53 (at Calle Mayor). ☎ **787/844-7071.** Admission $3 adults, $1.50 seniors, $1 children. Mon and Wed–Fri 10am–5pm, Sat–Sun 10am–6pm.

Opened in the Casa Salazar in 1992, this museum traces the history of the city from the time of the Taíno peoples to the present. Interactive displays help visitors orient themselves and locate other attractions. The museum has a conservation laboratory, library, souvenir and gift shop, cafeteria, and conference facilities.

Casa Salazar ranks close to the top of Ponce's architectural treasures. Built in 1911, it combines neoclassical and Moorish details, while displaying much that is typical of the Ponce decorative style: stained-glass windows, mosaics, pressed-tin ceilings, fixed jalousies, wood or iron columns, porch balconies, interior patios, and the use of doors as windows.

Museum of Puerto Rico Music. Calle Isabel 50. ☎ **787/848-7016.** Free admission. Wed–Sun 9am–noon and 1–4pm.

This museum showcases the development of Puerto Rican music, with displays of Indian, Spanish, and African musical instruments that were played in the romantic danza, the favorite music of 19th-century Puerto Rican society, as well as the more African-inspired bomba and plena styles. Also on view are memorabilia of composers and performers.

Parque de Bombas. Plaza de Las Delicias. ☎ **787/284-4141.** Free admission. Wed–Mon 9:30am–6pm.

Constructed in 1882 as the centerpiece of a 12-day agricultural fair intended to promote the civic charms of Ponce, this building was designated a year later as the island's first permanent headquarters for a volunteer fire-fighting brigade. It has an unusual appearance—it's painted black, red, green, and yellow. A tourist information kiosk is situated inside the building (see "Visitor Information," above).

❂ Teatro la Perla. At Calle Mayor and Calle Christina. ☎ **787/843-4080.**

This theater, built in the neoclassical style in 1864, remains one of the most visible symbols of the economic prosperity of Ponce during the mid-19th century. Designed by Juan Bertoli, an Italian-born resident of Puerto Rico who studied in Europe, it was destroyed by an earthquake in 1918, and rebuilt in 1940 according to the original plans; it reopened to the public in 1941. It is noted for acoustics so clear that microphones are unnecessary. After an extensive restoration completed in 1990, the theater is now the largest and most historic in the Spanish-speaking Caribbean. Everything from plays to concerts to beauty pageants takes place here.

NEARBY ATTRACTIONS

The oldest cemetery in the Antilles, the **Tibes Indian Ceremonial Center** is on Route 503 at kilometer 2.7 (☎ 787/840-2255). Bordered by the Rio Portuguéz and excavated in 1975, it contains some 186 skeletons, dating from A.D. 300, as well as pre-Taíno plazas from A.D. 700. The site also includes a re-created Taíno village, seven rectangular ball courts, and two dance grounds. The arrangement of stone points on the dance grounds, in line with the solstices and equinoxes, suggests a pre-Columbian Stonehenge. Here you'll also find a museum, an exhibition hall that presents a documentary about Tibes, a cafeteria, and a souvenir shop. The museum is open Wednesday through Sunday from 9am to 4:30pm. Admission is $2 for adults, $1 for children. Guided tours in English and Spanish are conducted through the grounds.

   Hacienda Buena Vista, Route 10, kilometer 16.8 (☎ 787/848-7020 or 787/ 722-5882), is a 30-minute drive north of Ponce. Built in 1833, it preserves an old way of life, with its whirring waterwheels and artifacts of 19th-century farm production. Once it was one of the most successful plantations on Puerto Rico, producing coffee, corn, and citrus. It was a working coffee plantation until the 1950s, and 86 of the original 500 acres are still part of the estate. The rooms of the hacienda have been furnished with authentic pieces from the 1850s. Tours, lasting 2 hours, are conducted Wednesday through Sunday at 8:30am, 10:30am, 1:30pm, and 3:30pm (in English only at 1:30pm). Reservations are required. Tours cost $5 for adults, $2 for children. The hacienda lies in the small town of Barrio Magüeyes, on Route 10 between Ponce and Adjuntas.

HIKING & BIRD WATCHING IN GUÁNICA STATE FOREST

Heading directly west from Ponce, you reach ❂ **Guánica State Forest** (☎ 787/ 724-3724), a setting that evokes Arizona or New Mexico. Here you will find the best-preserved subtropical ecosystem on the planet. The Cordillera Central cuts off the rain coming in from the heavily showered northeast, making this a dry region of cacti -and bedrock, a perfect film location for one of those old-fashioned western movies.

It's also ideal country for birders. Some 50% of all of the island's terrestrial bird species can be seen in this dry and dusty forest. You might even spot the Puerto Rican emerald-breasted hummingbird. A number of migratory birds often stop here. The most serious ornithologists seek out the Puerto Rican nightjar, a local bird that was believed to be extinct until one was sighted. Now it's estimated that there are nearly a thousand of them. UNESCO has named Guánica a World Biosphere Reserve. Some 750 plants and tree species grow in the area.

To reach the forest, take Route 334 northeast of Guánica to the heart of the forest. There's a ranger station here that will give you information about hiking trails. The booklet provided by the ranger station outlines 36 miles of trails through the four forest types. The most interesting is the mile-long **Cueva Trail,** which gives you the most scenic look at the various types of vegetation. You might even encounter the endangered bufo lemur toad, once declared extinct but found to still be jumping in this area.

Walking Tour: Ponce

Start: Plaza de Las Delicias.
Finish: Plaza de Las Delicias.
Time: 90 minutes, excluding coffee breaks, museum visits, and shopping stops.

The downtown revitalization of Ponce has required more money and generated more publicity than that of any other city (after San Juan) on Puerto Rico. Your tour of this Caribbean showplace begins on the eastern edge of the town's main square, the Plaza de Las Delicias (also known as Plaza Muñoz Rivera). Within the symmetrical borders of this main square, you'll see the red-and-black–striped, clapboard facade of the town's most frequently photographed building. (Red and black, incidentally, are the colors of the city's flag.)

Note the Victorian gingerbread and the deliberately garish colors of the:

1. **Parque de Bombas (Old Municipal Fire House),** which housed the fire department before it moved into more modern quarters in another part of the city. You can still see a handful of bright .red fire engines parked inside.

On the plaza's opposite side, adjacent to Calle Concordia/Calle Union is the:

2. **Cathedral of Our Lady of Guadalupe,** the best-known church in southern Puerto Rico. Its alabaster altars were commissioned by an ex-governor of Puerto Rico in the late 1960s in Burgos, Spain; there will almost certainly be parishioners at prayer inside.

As you leave the cathedral, notice the many impeccably clipped trees ringing the perimeter of the plaza. Identified as Indian laurels, they were planted between 1906 and 1908 and are one of the botanical triumphs of Ponce. Clipped manually into topiary forms and carefully groomed by a master gardener, they are well worth a second or third glance. The elaborate iron lampposts nearby date from 1916.

Across Calle Concordia from the main entrance to the cathedral is one of Ponce's most famous houses, the:

3. **Casa Armstrong-Poventud,** a paneled and ornately crafted building that was once the home of a wealthy Scottish-born banker. The Poventud family moved in after the Armstrongs. Today, it's a cultural center.

Note that at this western border of the Plaza de Las Delicias, street signs might identify it as Plaza de Getou. Regardless of what the plaza is called, turn right on exiting Casa Armstrong-Poventud and walk southward beneath the Indian laurels. On the square's southern edge, you'll see one of the most historic buildings of Ponce, restored to reflect its original function during Spanish colonial days, the:

4. **Casa Alcaldía (City Hall),** standing on the site of an 18th-century monastery. This building was erected in 1840 as a general assembly, and then it served as the civic jail until 1905. Speeches by Theodore Roosevelt (in 1906), Herbert Hoover (in 1931), and Franklin D. Roosevelt (in 1934) were delivered from its central second-floor balcony to crowds assembled below. George Bush visited the building in 1987. The clock set into the tower was imported from London in 1877, and a tour of the baronial street-level interior reveals a memorial plaque dedicated to the fallen American dead (Second Wisconsin Regiment) during the Spanish-American War. A few paces farther, you'll see a galleried courtyard that formerly served as prisoners' cells. The building's main courtyard was used for public executions. In City Hall, other plaques make clear that the city of Ponce was named not after Juan Ponce de León, but rather after de León's great-grandson, Loíza Ponce de León, one of the town's early civic leaders.

Note across from the entrance to City Hall (in the town's main square) one of the most beautiful fountains of Puerto Rico, the:

5. **Lion Fountain,** crafted from marble and bronze and modeled after a famous fountain in Barcelona, Spain. It was made for the 1939 New York World's Fair and later purchased by the mayor of Ponce.

Continue your walk along the southern edge of the square. Note the way the plaza has "chopped corners" (broadly rounded 45-degree corners rather than 90-degree perpendicular corners). They were designed this way for increased visibility by the Spanish armies as a deterrent to civil unrest and the contraband trade that flourished here during their regime. Ponce is said to have the only large square on Puerto Rico designed with such a feature.

As you cross Calle Marina/Calle Commercio, which borders the southeastern edge of the square, look to your right to the faraway beaux arts:

6. **Centro Historíco,** painted a creamy shade of white. Originally built in 1922, this landmark served as the town's casino until it was closed in the mid-1960s. Today it houses government agencies and is not open to the public, although it can be admired from the outside. Nearer and more spectacular are two banks flanking the southeastern edge of the square, the:

7. **Banco de Santander** and **Scotia Bank,** both adorned with intricate stained-glass windows, art nouveau detailing, and dozens of unusual architectural features. The alleyway separating the two banks, Callejon Amor, is lined with African tulip trees planted to evoke the romantic spirit of a couple in love. This is also the site of public concerts held every Sunday between 8 and 9pm by classical orchestras or dance bands.

Proceed eastward along Calle Cristina, which funnels into the main square directly opposite the red-and-black–sided fire station. At the next cross street, diagonal to where you're standing, you'll see the:

8. **Memorial to Don Domingo,** dedicated to Don Domingo ("Cocolia") Cruz, longtime leader of Ponce's municipal band and one of the best-known musicians from Ponce. He died in 1934.

Turn left at Calle Mayor and admire the neoclassical facade of the largest and most historic theater in the Caribbean, the:

Walking Tour—Ponce

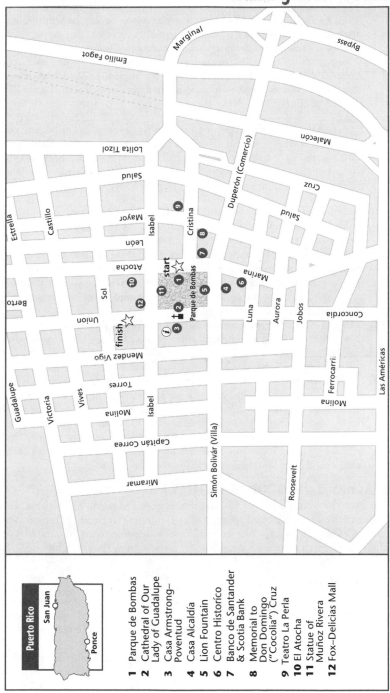

Puerto Rico

San Juan

Ponce

1 Parque de Bombas
2 Cathedral of Our Lady of Guadalupe
3 Casa Armstrong–Poventud
4 Casa Alcaldía
5 Lion Fountain
6 Centro Histórico
7 Banco de Santander & Scotia Bank
8 Memorial to Don Domingo ("Cocolía") Cruz
9 Teatro La Perla
10 El Atocha
11 Statue of Muñoz Rivera
12 Fox–Delicias Mall

9. Teatro La Perla, graced by six classical columns (see "Seeing the Sights," above). Depending on the time of day and the season, the lobby of this theater may be open for a quick look at the interior decoration.

Now continue walking northward along Calle Mayor to the first intersection (Calle Isabel). To your right stands a Moorish-inspired building known as the Casa Salazar (Salazar House), which accommodates a branch of the Puerto Rican Museum of History.

☕ **TAKE A BREAK**   Copious cups of coffee, assorted ice creams, and sandwiches are offered to tired pedestrians and talkative neighbors at the **Café Tomas/ Café Tompy,** Calle Isabel at the corner of Calle Mayor (☎ **787/840-1965**). Divided into less formal and more formal sections, it is open daily from 7am to midnight. For more information, see "Where to Dine," below.

After this break, walk westward along Calle Isabel until you reach the edge of the previously explored Plaza de Las Delicias. From the square's northeastern corner stretches:

10. El Atocha, the city's main shopping street. Stroll along its broad borders, noting the Spanish-inspired turn-of-the-20th-century architecture, the cast-iron benches, and the many police guards who ensure the street's tranquility. After your shopping, return to the main square and walk westward along its northern edge. Note, within the confines of the square is:

11. Statue of Muñoz Rivera, a memorial to one of Puerto Rico's best-known politicians (1898 to 1980), who helped Puerto Ricans become U.S. citizens after a career of political lobbying.

Proceeding along the edge of the square, note the:

12. Fox-Delicias Mall, one of the city's most alluring watering holes and shopping enclaves. Originally built in 1931 as a movie theater, its pink walls are excellent examples of art deco architecture in Puerto Rico. In crumbling disrepair, the theater was transformed into a disco during the 1960s. In 1989, the government of Spain earmarked funds for the restoration of this building to its original celluloid glamour. Today this mall contains an array of shops, nightclubs, and cafes, a good place for refreshment at the end of your stroll.

BEACHES & OUTDOOR ACTIVITIES

Ponce is a city—not a beach resort—and should be visited mainly for its sights. There is little in the way of organized sports, but a 10-minute drive west of Ponce will take you to ✪ **Playa de Ponce,** a long strip of white sand opening onto the tranquil waters of the Caribbean. This beach is usually better for swimming than the Condado in San Juan.

AT THE BEACH

La Guancha is a sprawling compound of publicly funded beachfront that has no equivalent anywhere else in Puerto Rico. Located 3 miles south of Ponce's cathedral, it has a large parking lot, a labyrinth of boardwalks, and a saltwater estuary with moorings for hundreds of yachts and pleasure craft.

A tower, which anyone can climb free of charge, affords high-altitude vistas of the active beach scene. La Guancha is a relatively wholesome version of Coney Island with a strong Hispanic accent and vague hints of New England.

On hot weekends, the place is mobbed with thousands of families who listen to recorded merengue and salsa. Lining the boardwalk are at least a dozen emporiums purveying beer, party-colored drinks, high-calorie snacks, and souvenirs. Weather permitting, this free beach is good for a few hours' diversion at any time of the year.

An offbeat and isolated adventure will take you to **Coffin Island,** an uninhabited key that's covered with mangrove swamps and ringed with worthwhile beaches. **Island Adventures,** c/o Rafi Vega, La Guancha (☎ 787/616-8568), will haul day-trippers there at a cost of $20 per person for a full-day beachgoer's outing (without snorkeling equipment). If you want to go snorkeling, the same full-day excursion, with the use of snorkeling equipment included, is $35 per person. Advance reservations (which you can make yourself, or leave to the desk staff of whatever hotel you opt for in Ponce) are necessary, as most of this outfit's excursions don't leave unless there are a predetermined number of participants.

Scuba divers can go to the best dive sites along the southern coast with **Gregory's Dive Center** (☎ 787/840-6424). The center can also make arrangements for fishing and sailing in the Ponce area.

The city owns two **tennis complexes,** one at Poly Deportivos, with nine hard courts, and another at Rambla, with six courts. Both are open from 9am to 10pm daily and are lighted for night play. You can play free, but you must call to make a reservation. For information, including directions on how to get there, call the **Secretary of Sports** at ☎ 787/840-4400.

To play golf, you have to go to **Aquirre Golf Course,** Route 705, Aquirre (☎ 787/853-4052), 30 miles east of Ponce (take Highway 52). This nine-hole course, open from 7:30am to sunset daily, charges $15 greens fees Monday through Friday, going up to $18 on weekends and holidays. Another course, **Club Zeportivo,** Carretera 102, kilometer 15.4, Barrio Jogudas, Cabo Rojo (☎ 787/254-3748), lies 30 miles west of Ponce. This course is a nine-holer, open daily from 7am to 5pm. Greens fees are $30 daily.

CARITE FOREST PRESERVE

In southeastern Puerto Rico, lying off the Ponce Expressway near Cayey, **Carite** is a 6,000-acre reserve with a dwarf forest that was produced by the region's high humidity and moist soil. From several peaks there are panoramic views of Ponce and the Caribbean Sea. On one peak is Nuestra Madre, a Catholic spiritual meditation center that permits visitors to stroll the grounds. Fifty species of birds live in the Carite Forest Reserve, which also has a large natural pool called Charco Azul. A picnic area and campgrounds are shaded by eucalyptus and royal palms. The forest borders a lake of the same name. Entrances to the forest are signposted from the town of Cayey, which itself is reached after an hour's drive from either Ponce or San Juan.

SHOPPING

If you feel a yen for shopping in Ponce, head for the **Fox-Delicias Mall,** at the intersection of Calle Reina Isabel and Plaza de Las Delicias, the city's most innovative shopping center. Among the many interesting stores is **Regalitos y Algo Mas,** located on the upper level. It specializes in unusual gift items from around Puerto Rico. Look especially for the Christmas tree ornaments, crafted from wood, metal, colored porcelain, or bread dough, and for the exotic dolls displayed by the owners. Purchases can be shipped anywhere in the world.

At the mall, the best outlet for souvenirs and artisan work is **El Palacio del Coquí Inc.** (☎ 787/841-0216), whose name means palace of the tree frog. This is the place to buy the grotesque masks (viewed as collectors' items) that are used at carnival time. Ask the owner to explain the significance of these masks.

Wet & Dry: A Hiking & Kayaking Tour

Southwestern Puerto Rico is the site of the world's largest remaining tract of tropical, dry, coastal forest, much of it preserved in Guánica State Forest. In contrast, this part of the island also features miles of mangrove channel systems. Visitors can visit this unusual terrain with **Tropix Wellness Tours** (☎ **787/268-2173;** fax 787/268-1722), whose "Wet and Dry Tour" includes two expeditions: a "dry" forest hike in Guánica State Forest and "wet" paddles through the mangroves by kayak. Visits to secluded beaches at sunset are included.

The 4-day, 3-night tour costs from $525 per person, double occupancy, including accommodations at the Copamarina Hotel, continental breakfast, and equipment for the escorted expeditions.

Utopía, Calle Isabel 78 (Plaza de Las Delicias; ☎ **787/845-8742**), conveniently located a few steps from the cathedral, has the most imaginative and most interesting selection of gift items and handicrafts in Ponce. Prominently displayed are *vegigantes,* brightly painted carnival masks inspired by carnival rituals and crafted from papier mâché. In Ponce, where many of these masks are made, they sell at bargain prices of between $5 and $500, depending on their size. Other items include cigars, pottery, clothing, and jewelry; gifts imported from Indonesia, the Philippines, and Mexico; and rums from throughout the Caribbean. Julio and Carmen Aguilar are the helpful and enthusiastic owners, who hail from Ecuador and Puerto Rico, respectively.

Galeria Taller Artistas del Sur, Calle Concordia at Calle Luna (☎ 787/ 813-2861), presents frequently changing expositions of some of the most creative artwork in southern Puerto Rico. Virtually every artist represented here comes from the island's southern tier. The place is partially staffed by student volunteers from local art schools, so you might get a sense of bureaucratic confusion, thanks to a visible lack of strong administration. Despite that, you might fall in love with one of the artworks, which usually range in price from $30 to $5,000. The place is open Wednesday through Sunday from 10am to 5pm.

WHERE TO STAY
EXPENSIVE

✪ Ponce Hilton and Casino. 1150 Av. Caribe (P.O. Box 7419), Ponce, PR 00732. ☎ **800/ HILTONS** in the U.S. and Canada, or 787/259-7676. Fax 787/259-7674. www.hiltons.com. 153 units. A/C MINIBAR TV TEL. $230 double; $495 suite. Extra person $20. AE, CB, DC, DISC, MC, V. Self-parking $4.50; valet parking $10.

This is the most glamorous hotel in southern Puerto Rico. On an 80-acre tract of land right on the beach, at the western end of Avenida Santiago de los Caballeros, the hotel is about a 5-minute (7-mile) drive from the center of Ponce. Designed like a miniature village, with turquoise-blue roofs, white walls, and lots of tropical plants, ornamental waterfalls, and gardens, it welcomes conventioneers and individual travelers alike. Spacious accommodations include ceiling fans, terraces or balconies, fine linen, and quality mattresses. The ground-floor rooms are the most expensive.

Dining/Diversions: The food is the most sophisticated on the south coast of Puerto Rico. Chefs use only the freshest ingredients, combined with imagination. The wait staff seems to have an extensive knowledge of the menu and will guide you through some exotic dishes—of course, you'll find familiar fare, too. The more glamorous of the hotel's two restaurants, La Cava, has some of the most intricate and thoughtful cuisine around. The less formal La Terraza specializes in buffets, which are often lavish. The cocktail lounge, El Bohemio, offers sunset-colored drinks and live music every evening. The hotel's casino, an appropriately glittery showcase, is open daily from noon to 4am.

Amenities: Lagoon-shaped pool ringed with gardens, business center, fitness center, video arcade, bike rentals, playground, summer camp for children; water sports available. Room service (from 7am to midnight), laundry, baby-sitting (if arranged in advance).

MODERATE

Meliá. Calle Cristina 2, Ponce, PR 00731. ☎ **800/742-4276** in the U.S. or 787/842-0260. Fax 787/841-3602. www.home.coqui.net/melia. E-mail: melia@coqui.net. 78 units. A/C TV TEL. $80–$100 double. Rates include continental breakfast. AE, DC, MC, V. Parking $3.

A city hotel with southern hospitality, the Meliá, which has no connection with the Meliáinternational hotel chain, often attracts businesspeople. The location is a few steps away from the Cathedral of Our Lady of Guadalupe and from the Parque de Bombas (the red-and-black firehouse). Although this old and somewhat tattered hotel was long ago outclassed by the more expensive Hilton, many people prefer to stay here for its old-time atmosphere. The lobby floor and stairs are covered with Spanish tiles of Moorish design. The small rooms are comfortably furnished and pleasant enough, and most have a balcony facing busy Calle Cristina or the old plaza. In some rooms, the mattresses are a bit tired, but others are new. Bathrooms are tiny. Breakfast is served on a rooftop terrace with a good view of Ponce, and Mark's Restaurant thrives under separate management (see below). You can park your car in the lot nearby.

Ponce Inn. Rte. 1, km 123.5, Mercedita, Ponce, PR 00715. ☎ **800/329-7466** or 787/841-1000. Fax 787/841-2560. 62 units. A/C TV TEL. $112 double; $121 suite. Rates include continental breakfast. AE, DC, MC, V. Free parking.

A 15-minute drive east of Ponce on Highway 52, opposite the Interamerican University, this hotel opened in 1989. Its modest bedrooms are conservative and comfortable, equipped with contemporary furnishings. The prices appeal to families with children. Facilities include a courtyard swimming pool, a children's wading pool, a whirlpool, a coin-operated laundry, an international restaurant, a bar/disco, and ice and vending machines for sodas and snacks.

INEXPENSIVE

Guest House Colonial. Calle Marina 9181, Ponce, PR 00731. ☎ and fax **787/843-7585.** 4 units. A/C TV. $70 for up to 2 occupants; $100 for up to 4 occupants; $130 for up to 6 occupants. MC, V.

This is the quirkiest and most unpredictably charming guesthouse in town. Ponce-born Roberto Porrata is the creative force behind this place, which was built in the 1880s as -the private home of a family linked to Puerto Rico's governor. The servants' quarters and stables have since been incorporated into a rambling compound in the heart of Ponce's historic core, a few blocks from the cathedral. Accommodations are rather oddly organized into a labyrinth of high-ceilinged spaces, some with antiques, some absolutely bare of furnishings. Expect a Spartan-looking collection of furniture, more space than you might have expected, and antique walls bare of ornamentation. Bathrooms are functional but not plush. Don't expect a conventional hotel if you opt to lodge here. The place evokes a bizarre but strangely appealing departure from the norm—an anachronism from the past maintained by liberal-thinking people with some very modern points of view.

The guesthouse has a restaurant in the courtyard and a bar under a lean-to in the garden. Many of the clients are either gay or gay-friendly, especially on Sunday afternoon when the site blossoms into a counterculture and convivial party with a life of its own. Main courses in the restaurant range from $8 to $25—of special note is the chef's version of lobster *asopao*. The restaurant is open daily, or whenever the chef feels like cooking, from 9am to 10:30pm.

Hotel Belgica. Calle Villa 122, Ponce, PR 00731. ☎ **787/844-3255.** Fax 787/844-6149. 21 units. A/C TV. $50–$60 double. MC, V.

In the hands of a skilled decorator with a large bankroll, this Spanish colonial mansion from around 1911 could be transformed into a very chic bed-and-breakfast. Until then, however, you'll be faced with a combination of historic charm and modern junkiness, overseen by a brusque staff. You might find this cost-conscious spot wonderful or horrible, depending on your point of view and room assignment. The most appealing accommodations are nos. 8, 9, and 10, which are spacious and have balconies that hang over the Calle Villa, a few steps from Ponce's cathedral square. This venue is for roughing it, backpacker style. No meals of any kind are served, but several cafes in the neighborhood fill in the breach.

WHERE TO DINE
EXPENSIVE

✪ **La Cava.** In the Ponce Hilton, 1150 Av. Caribe. ☎ **787/259-7676.** Reservations recommended. Main courses $25–$28. AE, DC, DISC, MC, V. Daily noon–3pm and 6:30–10:30pm. INTERNATIONAL.

With a design that resembles a 19th-century coffee plantation, this is the most appealing and elaborate restaurant in Ponce. There's a sense of antique charm, a well-trained staff, and a champagne and cigar bar where the bubbly sells for around $6 a glass. The well-prepared menu items change every 6 weeks, but might include duck foie gras with toasted brioche, Parma ham with mango, cold poached scallops with mustard sauce, fricassee of lobster and mushrooms in a pastry shell, grilled lamb sausage with mustard sauce on a bed of couscous, or a sophisticated seafood grill. Dessert could be a black-and-white soufflé or a trio of tropical sorbets.

✪ **Mark's at the Meliá.** In the Meliá Hotel, Calle Cristina. ☎ **787/842-0260.** Reservations recommended. Main courses $18–$28; lunch $12–$28. AE, DC, MC, V. Wed–Sat noon–3pm and 6–10:30pm, Sun noon–6pm. INTERNATIONAL.

Restaurant excitement in Ponce is generated by Mark and Melody French, who took over what was once a rather dull restaurant in this landmark hotel. This elegantly appointed setting provides a showcase for Mark's classical cookery, which uses fresh local ingredients, and Melody's expertise in wine and service. At lunch, you can be tantalized by tostone skins with plantains, or tempura jumbo shrimp with an Oriental salad. Soups are likely to feature cream of pumpkin, followed by such main dishes as corn-crusted red snapper with a yucca purée. At night, you get the best French signature dishes in Ponce, including roast rack of lamb with a mint crust, country veal chop flavored with horseradish, and duck breast with summer berries. Spectacular desserts include vanilla flan layered with rum sponge cake and topped with caramelized banana.

MODERATE

El Ancla. Av. Hostos Final 9, Playa Ponce. ☎ **787/840-2450.** Main courses $12–$35. AE, DC, MC, V. Sun–Thurs 11am–10pm, Fri–Sat 11am–midnight. PUERTO RICAN/SEAFOOD.

Ponce Accommodations & Dining

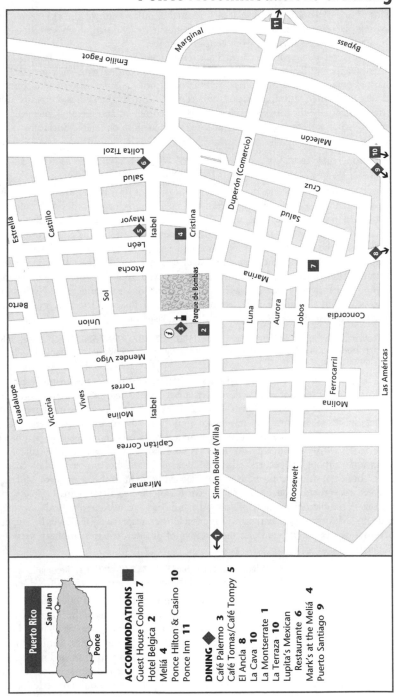

Puerto Rico

San Juan

Ponce

ACCOMMODATIONS ■
Guest House Colonial **7**
Hotel Belgica **2**
Meliá **4**
Ponce Hilton & Casino **10**
Ponce Inn **11**

DINING ◆
Café Palermo **3**
Café Tomas/Café Tompy **5**
El Ancla **8**
La Cava **10**
La Montserrate **1**
La Terraza **10**
Lupita's Mexican
  Restaurante **6**
Mark's at the Meliá **4**
Puerto Santiago **9**

167

This is one of Ponce's best restaurants, located 2 miles south of the city center on soaring piers that extend out over the surf from the rocky coastline. As you dine, the sound of the sea rises literally from beneath your feet.

Menu items are prepared with real Puerto Rican zest and flavor. An old favorite here is red snapper stuffed with lobster and shrimp, served either with fried plantain or mashed potatoes. Other specialties are fillet of salmon in caper sauce, and a seafood medley of lobster, shrimp, octopus, and conch. Most of the dishes are reasonably priced, especially the chicken and conch. One corner of the menu is reserved for lobster, which tops the price scale. The side orders are also delectable, including crab-meat rice or yucca in garlic.

La Montserrate. Sector Las Cucharas, Rte. 2. ☎ **787/841-2740.** Main courses $15–$22. AE, DC, DISC, MC, V. Daily 11am–10pm. PUERTO RICAN/SEAFOOD.

Beside the seafront, in a residential area about 4 miles west of the town center, this restaurant draws a loyal following from the surrounding neighborhood. A culinary institution in Ponce since it was established 20 years ago, it occupies a large, airy, modern building divided into two different dining areas. The first of these is slightly more formal than the next. Most visitors, however, head for the large room in back, where windows on three sides encompass a view of offshore islands. Specialties, concocted from the catch of the day, might include octopus salad, four different kinds of *asopao,* a whole red snapper in Créole sauce, or a selection of steaks and grills. Nothing is innovative, but the cuisine is typical of the south of Puerto Rico, and it's a family favorite. The fish dishes are better than the meat selections.

La Terraza. In the Ponce Hilton, Av. Caribe 1150. ☎ **787/259-7676.** Lunch buffet $18; dinner buffet $28. AE, DC, DISC, MC, V. Daily 12:30–3:30pm and 6:30–10:30pm. INTERNATIONAL.

This is one of the best restaurant values in Ponce. During the design phase of the Ponce Hilton, a team of architects and restaurateurs devoted lots of attention to this restaurant's layout and traffic flows. The result is a space with one of the most appealing buffets in Ponce. Featuring an impressive array of salads, soups, breads, meats, fish, and desserts, they're more formal and elaborate, and a bit more expensive, at dinner than at the self-service lunches. At dinner, a wait staff will bring your main course to your table, although appetizers, salads, desserts, and garnishes are retrieved by clients at the buffet. A different theme is emphasized every night of the week, with Monday devoted to variations on traditional Puerto Rican *mofongos* (plantains layered with various combinations of meat or seafood), and Tuesday, Wednesday, and Thursday featuring Mexican fajitas, barbecued ribs, and lobster, respectively. Friday is fish night, Saturday is steak, and Sunday is most festive of all, devoted to Caribbean versions of paella.

Puerto Santiago. Paseo Tablado, La Guancha. ☎ **787/840-7313.** Reservations not necessary. Main courses $17–$25. MC, V. Tues–Sun noon–10:30pm. INTERNATIONAL.

This is the best restaurant at La Guancha. Occupying the ground floor of the compound's most impressive tower, this spot is immediately adjacent to the longest stretch of boardwalk. Here, within a nautical-style room reminiscent of a seaside bar on Cape Cod, you can order a well-prepared seafood meal with all the fixings. Shrimp comes with garlic or saffron-flavored butter sauce, or in crêpes covered in melted mozzarella cheese; lobster can be served in at least seven different ways; and virtually any seafood can be ladled over heaping platters of pasta. Local fish comes Louisiana style (blackened), with crabmeat sauce or beurre blanc (white butter) sauce, or simply grilled with lemon. There's a limited list of beef and chicken dishes, but in light of the many varieties of fish and shellfish, almost everyone orders seafood. Either before or after your meal, consider a trek upstairs to La Terrazza, our favorite music bar (recommended below).

INEXPENSIVE

Café Palermo. Calle Union 3. ☎ **787/812-3873.** Reservations not necessary. Tapas $3.75–$5; main courses $8.50–$12. MC, V. Tues–Sat 11am–midnight, Sun 3pm–midnight. ITALIAN/PUERTO RICAN.

Set on the main square of Ponce, opposite the entrance to the cathedral, this small but charming bar and restaurant derives its creative force from Argentina-born owner Ricardo Cabral. The paneled, air-conditioned interior is a welcome relief from the city's downtown, and as such, does a brisk bar business with local shoppers and sightseers throughout the afternoon and evening. Many clients come just for a beer and a *ración* of tapas, but if you're looking for a meal, consider heaping portions of such good-tasting menu items as ravioli, spaghetti, Caesar salad, lasagna, beef Milanese, and breaded chicken cutlets. Thursday, Friday, and Saturday nights, beginning at 9pm, a live guitarist plays music evocative of Argentina, Italy, and Spain, which draws an animated nightlife crowd.

Café Tomas/Café Tompy. Calle Isabel at Calle Mayor. ☎ **787/840-1965.** Lunch $6–$18; dinner $7–$20. AE, MC, V. Restaurant daily 11:30am–midnight. Cafe daily 7am–midnight. PUERTO RICAN.

The more visible and busier section of this establishment functions as a simple cafe for neighbors and local merchants. On plastic tables often flooded with sunlight from the big windows, you can order coffee, sandwiches, or cold beer, perhaps while relaxing after a walking tour of the city.

The family-run restaurant is more formal. The discreet entrance is adjacent to the cafe on Calle Isabel. Here, amid a decor reminiscent of a Spanish *tasca* (tapas bar), you can enjoy such simply prepared dishes as salted filet of beef, beefsteak with onions, four kinds of *asopao,* buttered eggs, octopus salads, and yucca (similar to cassava) croquettes.

Lupita's Mexican Restaurante. Calle Reina Isabel 60. ☎ **787/848-8808.** Reservations recommended. Main courses $8–$12; platters for 2, $12–$30. AE, DC, MC, V. Sun–Thurs 11am–11pm, Fri–Sat 11am–2am. MEXICAN.

Lending a note of lighthearted fun to the city, this is the only Mexican restaurant in Ponce. Set in a 19th-century building and its adjoining courtyard, a short walk from Ponce's main square, it's the creative statement of Hector de Castro, who traveled throughout Mexico to find the elaborate fountains and the dozens of chairs and decorative accessories that fill these premises. The trompe l'oeil murals on the inside (featuring desert scenes in an amusing surrealism) were painted by the owner's sister, Flor de Maria de Castro.

A well-trained staff serves blue and green margaritas (frozen or unfrozen) and a wide array of other tropical drinks. Any of these might be followed by Mexican dishes cooked in cholesterol-free vegetable oil. Specialties include tortilla soup, taco salads, grilled lobster tail with tostones, seafood fajitas, and burritos, tacos, and enchiladas with a wide choice of fillings. A mariachi band plays on Friday. Lupita is an affectionate nickname for Guadalupe, the patron saint of both Mexico and the city of Ponce.

PONCE AFTER DARK

La Terrazza, above the Puerto Santiago Restaurant (☎ **787/840-7313**), is the most whimsical bar at La Guancha, the board-laced beachfront of Ponce. Part of the appeal is its location at the top of an open-sided watchtower. The owners define it as "a music pub," and as such, its collection of CDs rivals that of a sophisticated dance club in New York. Come here for an insight into what's hip with the young and restless of Puerto Rico's "second city." The venue is friendly, the drinks stiff, and if you're hungry, there's a short list of food items that includes fried calamari and lobster empañadas. Hours are Wednesday, Thursday, and Sunday from noon to 10pm, Friday and Saturday from noon to 2am. There is no cover charge.

2 Mayagüez

98 miles W of San Juan, 15 miles S of Aguadilla

The largest city on the island's west coast, Mayagüez is a port whose elegance and charm reached its zenith during the mercantile and agricultural prosperity of the 19th century. Most of the town's stately buildings were destroyed in a horrific earthquake in 1918, and today the town is noted more for its industry than its aesthetic appeal.

Although a commercial city—not a tourist resort—Mayagüez is a convenient stopover for those exploring the west coast. (The Best Western Mayagüez Resort & Casino draws most tourists here.) If you want a windsurfing beach, you have to head north of Rincón, or if you want a more tranquil beach, you can drive south from Mayagüez along Route 102 to Boquerón.

Nevertheless, Mayagüez is still identified as the honeymoon capital of Puerto Rico, partly because of the lush and beautiful vegetation that grows here and partly because of a peculiarly romantic 16th-century legend. It is said that local farmers often kidnapped young Spanish sailors who had stopped at Mayagüez for provisions en route to South America. There was a scarcity of eligible bachelors in Mayagüez, and the farmers kidnapped the young sailors in hopes of providing their daughters with husbands and their farms with overseers. However, it's anyone's guess whether this was good or bad luck.

Although the town itself dates from the mid-18th century, the area around it has figured in European history since the time of Christopher Columbus, who landed nearby in 1493. Today, in the gracious plaza at the town's center, a bronze statue of Columbus stands atop a metallic globe of the world.

Famed for the size and depth of its harbor (the second-largest on the island), Mayagüez was built to control the **Mona Passage,** a route essential to the Spanish Empire when Puerto Rico and the nearby Dominican Republic were vital trade and defensive jewels in the Spanish crown. Today this waterway is notorious for the destructiveness of its currents, the ferocity of its sharks, and the thousands of boat people who arrive illegally from either Haiti or the Dominican Republic, both on the adjacent island of Hispaniola.

Queen Isabel II of Spain recognized Mayagüez's status as a town in 1836. Her son, Alfonso XII, granted it a city charter in 1877. Permanently isolated from the major commercial developments of San Juan, Mayagüez, like Ponce, has always retained its own distinct identity.

Today the town's major industry is tuna packing; in fact, 60% of the tuna consumed in the United States is packed here. It is also an important departure point for deep-sea fishing and is the bustling port for exporting agricultural produce from the surrounding hillsides. Once the needlework capital of Puerto Rico, it still has women who create fine embroidery and drawn-thread work, industries that were brought to Puerto Rico centuries ago from Spain- and Hapsburg-controlled Holland and Belgium.

ESSENTIALS

GETTING THERE   **American Eagle** (☎ 800/433-7300) flies from San Juan to Mayagüez two times a day Monday through Friday, three times a day on weekends (flying time: 40 min.). Depending on restrictions, round-trip passage ranges from $124 to $176 per person.

Taxis meet arriving planes. If you take one, negotiate the fare with the driver first—cabs are unmetered here.

There are branches of **Avis** (☎ 787/833-7070), **Budget** (☎ 787/832-4570), and **Hertz** (☎ 787/832-3314) at the Mayagüez airport.

If you're driving from San Juan, head either west on Route 2 (trip time: $2^1/_2$ hrs.) or south from San Juan on the scenic Route 52 (trip time: 3 hr.). Route 52 offers easier travel.

VISITOR INFORMATION   Mayagüez doesn't have a tourist information office. If you're starting out in San Juan, inquire there before you set out (see "Visitor Information" under "Orientation" in chapter 3).

EXPLORING THE AREA: SURFING BEACHES & TROPICAL GARDENS

Along the western coastal bends of Route 2, north of Mayagüez, lie the best **surfing beaches** in the Caribbean. Surfers from as far away as New Zealand come to ride the waves. You can also check out panoramic **Punta Higüero** beach, nearby on Route 413, near Rincón. For more information, see "Rincón," below.

South of Mayagüez is ✪ **Boquerón Beach,** one of the island's best, with a wide strip of white sand and good snorkeling conditions.

For golfers, the **Best Western Mayagüez Resort & Casino** at Mayagüez (☎ 787/ 832-3030) makes arrangements for guests to play a nine-hole course at a nearby country club.

Mayagüez's chief attraction is the ✪ **Tropical Agriculture Research Station** (☎ 787/831-3435). It's located on Route 65, between Post Street and Route 108, adjacent to the University of Puerto Rico at Mayagüez campus and across the street from the **Parque de los Próceres** (Patriots' Park). At the administration office, ask for a free map of the tropical gardens, which have one of the largest collections of tropical plant species intended for practical use, including cacao, fruit trees, spices, timbers, and ornamentals. The grounds are open Monday through Friday from 7am to 5pm, charging no admission.

Mayagüez is the jumping-off point for visits to unique **Mona Island,** the "Galápagos of the Caribbean." See the box below for details.

Not far from Mayagüez is **Maricao.** You can reach it by taking Route 105 west and then driving north on Route 120. The town is colorful and rather small. On the outskirts, look for a sign that reads **LOS VIVEROS** (The Hatcheries); then take Route 410. Here, the Commonwealth Department of Agriculture hatches as many as 25,000 fish for stocking Puerto Rican freshwater lakes and streams.

Go back to Maricao to Route 120 south up to kilometer 13.8 until you reach the **Maricao State Forest** picnic area, located 2,900 feet above sea level. The observation tower provides a panoramic view across the green mountains up to the coastal plains. Continue on Route 120 across the forest to the town of Sabana Grande (Great Plain). Route 2 will then take you to the town of San Germán. (See below.)

Mona Island: The Galápagos of Puerto Rico

Off Mayagüez, the unique island of Mona teems with giant iguanas, three species of endangered sea turtles, red-footed boobies, and countless other sea birds. It features a tabletop plateau with mangrove forests and cacti, giving way to dramatic 200-foot-high limestone cliffs that rise above the water and encircle much of Mona.

A bean-shaped pristine island with no hotels, Mona is a destination for the hardy pilgrim who seeks the road less traveled. A pup tent, backpack, and hiking boots will do fine if you plan to forego the comforts of civilization and immerse yourself in nature. Snorkelers, spelunkers, biologists, and eco-tourists find much to fascinate them in Mona's wildlife, mangrove forests, coral reefs, and complex honeycomb, which is the largest marine-originated cave in the world. There also are miles of secluded white-sand beaches and palm trees.

Uninhabited today, Mona was for centuries the scene of considerable human activity. The pre-Columbian Taíno Indians were the first to establish themselves here. Later, pirates used it as a base for their raids, followed by guano miners who removed the rich crop fertilizer from Mona's caves. Columbus landed in Mona on his 1494 voyage, and Ponce de León spent several days here en route to becoming governor of Puerto Rico in 1508. The notorious pirate Captain Kidd used Mona as a temporary hideout.

Mona can be reached by organized tour from Mayagüez. Camping is available at $1 per night. Everything needed, including water, must be brought in, and everything, including garbage, must be taken out. For more information, call the Puerto Rico Department of Natural Resources at ☎ **787/724-3724.**

Encantos Ecotours (☎ **787/272-0005**) offers bare-boned but ecologically sensitive camping tours to Mona Island at sporadic intervals that vary according to the demand of clients who are interested. The experience includes ground transport to and from San Juan, sea transport departing from Cabo Rojo, use of camping and snorkeling gear, all meals (expect the equivalent of K rations cooked over a campfire), and fees. A package of 3 nights and 4 days of outdoor life, which comes with its share of discomforts and inconveniences, sells for around $600.

WHERE TO STAY

Best Western Mayagüez Resort & Casino. Rte. 104 (P.O. Box 3629), Mayagüez, PR 00709. ☎ **888/689-3030** or 787/832-3030. Fax 787/834-3475. www.mayaguezresort. com. E-mail: sales@mayaguezresort.com. 148 units. A/C MINIBAR TV TEL. $145–$175 double; $250 suite. AE, MC, V. Parking $4.50.

In 1995, this former Hilton was bought by a consortium of local investors, who poured $5.5 million into an extensive renovation. Since its reopening in 1996, the hotel has benefited more than ever from its redesigned casino, country club format, and position on 20 acres of tropical gardens at the northern approach to the city, 3 miles from the airport. The carefully landscaped grounds are an adjunct of the nearby Mayagüez Institute of Tropical Agriculture. There are five species of palm trees, eight kinds of bougainvillea, and numerous species of rare flora, set adjacent to the institute's collection of tropical plants, which range from a pink torch ginger to a Sri Lankan cinnamon tree.

The hotel's well-designed bedrooms open onto views of the swimming pool, and many units have private balconies. Guest rooms tend to be small, but have good beds and mattresses. Bathrooms have hair dryers, makeup mirrors, thick towels, and scales.

Dining/Diversions: For details about El Castillo, the hotel's restaurant, see "Where to Dine," below. The hotel functions as the major entertainment center of Mayagüez. Its casino has free admission and is open daily from noon to 4am. You can drink and dance at the Victoria Lounge Wednesday through Sunday from 8:30pm to 3am; entrance is also free.

Amenities: Olympic-size pool, children's pool, playground, whirlpool, minigym, three tennis courts, room service (from 6:30am to 11pm), laundry, baby-sitting. Deep-sea fishing, skin diving, surfing, and scuba diving can be arranged. A golf course is a 30-minute drive from the hotel.

Holiday Inn & Tropical Casino. 2701 Rte. 2, km 149.9, Mayagüez, PR 00680-6328. ☎ 800/HOLIDAY in the U.S. and Canada, or 787/833-1100. Fax 787/833-1300. www.holiday-inn.com. 151 units. A/C TV TEL. $109.50–$152 double; $210–$260 suite. AE, DC, MC, V.

This six-story hotel competes directly with the Best Western Mayagüez Resort & Casino, though we like the Best Western better. It's set 2 miles north of Mayagüez's city center, behind a parking lot and a well-maintained lawn that's no match for the dramatically landscaped Best Western. The Holiday Inn is contemporary, clean, and comfortable, however, and has a marble-floored, high-ceilinged lobby; an outdoor swimming pool with its own waterside bar; and a big, glittery casino. Bedrooms are comfortably but functionally outfitted in motel style; they've recently been refurbished. The hotel's social center is Holly's Café, an airy, stylish place that's open daily for breakfast, lunch, and dinner.

Hotel Parador El Sol. Calle Santiago Riera Palmer, 9 Este, Mayagüez, PR 00680. ☎ 787/834-0303. Fax 787/265-7567. 52 units. A/C TV TEL. $60–$85 double; $80–$105 triple. Rates include continental breakfast. AE, DC, MC, V.

This hotel from around 1970 provides some of the most reasonable and hospitable accommodations in this part of Puerto Rico, although it's far more geared to the business traveler than to the tourist, with no-frills furnishings. Central to the shopping district and to all highways, 2 blocks from the landmark Plaza del Mercado in the heart of the city, this six-floor restored hotel offers up-to-date facilities that include cable TV, a standard restaurant, and a swimming pool.

NEARBY PLACES TO STAY

✪ **Hotal Paradores Joyuda Beach.** Rte. 102, km 11.7, Cabo Rojo, PR 00623. ☎ 787/851-5650. Fax 787/255-3750. 41 units. A/C TV TEL. $90–$95 double. Two children under 12 stay free in parents' room. AE, MC, V. Follow Rte. 102 south of Mayagüez to Joyuda.

Built on the beach in scenic Cabo Rojo in 1989, this is little more than an average motel with standard furnishings, but it's a convenient and reasonably priced stopover nevertheless. From here you can easily head to El Combate Beach and the Cabo Rojo Wildlife Refuge. Tennis and golf are just 5 minutes away, and sport-fishing charters, as well as windsurfing and canoeing, can also be arranged. The hotel is often a favorite of Puerto Rican honeymooners.

Parador Hacienda Juanita. Rte. 105, km 23.5 (P.O. Box 777), Maricao, PR 00606. ☎ 800/443-0266 for reservations only, or 787/838-2550. Fax 787/838-2551. 21 units. $120–$126 double. Children under 12 stay free in parents' room. Rates include breakfast and dinner. AE, MC, V. Free parking.

Named after one of its long-ago owners, a matriarch named Juanita, this pink stucco building was originally constructed in 1836 as part of a coffee plantation. Situated 2 miles west of the village of Maricao, beside Route 105 heading to Mayagüez, it has a long veranda and a living room furnished with a large-screen TV and decorated with antique tools and artifacts of the coffee industry. Relatively isolated, it's surrounded by only a few neighboring buildings and the jungle. The Luis Rivera family welcomes visitors and serves drinks and meals in their restaurant. There's a swimming pool, billiards table, and Ping-Pong table on the premises. The bedrooms are simple and rural, with ceiling fans, rocking chairs, and rustic furniture. None of the rooms has TV or air-conditioning (ceiling fans suffice in the cool temperatures in this high-altitude place.

WHERE TO DINE

El Castillo. In the Best Western Mayagüez Resort & Casino, Rte. 104. ☎ **787/832-3030.** Breakfast buffet $11.25; Mon–Sat lunch buffet lunch $14; Sun brunch buffet $21.95; main courses $17.30. AE, MC, V. Daily 6:30am–11pm. INTERNATIONAL/PUERTO RICAN.

This is the best-managed large-scale dining room in western Puerto Rico, as well as the main restaurant for the largest hotel and casino in the area. Known for its generous lunch buffets, it serves only à la carte items at dinner, including seafood stew served on a bed of linguine with marinara sauce; grilled salmon with mango-flavored Grand Marnier sauce; and fillets of sea bass with a cilantro, white wine, and butter sauce. Steak and lobster are served on the same platter, if you prefer. The food has real flavor and flair, and isn't typical, bland hotel fare.

MAYAGÜEZ AFTER DARK

El Casino. At the Best Western Mayagüez Resort & Casino, Rte. 104. ☎ **787/832-3030.** No cover.

The completely remodeled casino with the adjoining Player's Bar is the only casino in Mayagüez. Try your luck at blackjack, dice, slot machines, roulette, and minibaccarat. It's open daily from noon to 4am.

Victoria's Lounge. In the Best Western Mayagüez Resort & Casino, Rte. 104. ☎ **787/ 831-7575.**

The music's hot and most likely merengue or salsa, originating from New York or Los Angeles, or even San Juan. Live music is presented at varying times Thursday through Saturday from 8pm to 3:30am. There's no cover except on special occasions like Valentine's Day.

Veranda Terrace. In the Best Western Mayagüez Resort & Casino, Rte. 104. ☎ **787/ 831-7575.**

On a large and airy covered terrace that opens to a view of a manicured tropical garden, this is a relaxing and soothing place for a cocktail. The bartenders specialize in rum-based concoctions that seem to go well with the hibiscus-scented air. Open daily from 10:30am to 1:30am.

3 San Germán

104 miles SW of San Juan, 34 miles W of Ponce

Only an hour's drive from Ponce or Mayagüez and the beaches of the southern coast, and just over 2 hours from San Juan, San Germán, Puerto Rico's second-oldest town, is a little museum piece. It was founded in 1512 and destroyed by the French in 1528.

Mayagüez

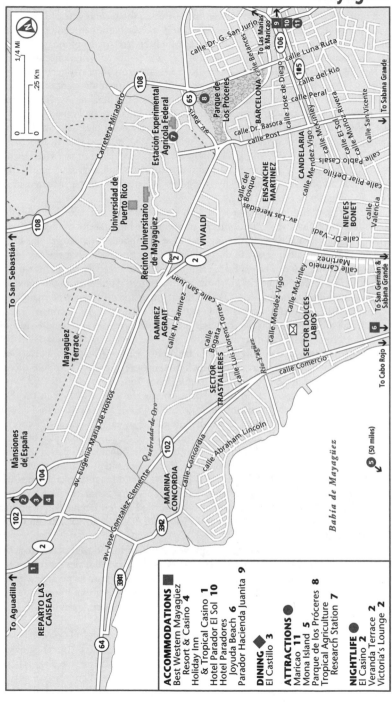

ACCOMMODATIONS ■
Best Western Mayagüez
  Resort & Casino 4
Holiday Inn
  & Tropical Casino 1
Hotel Parador El Sol 10
Hotel Paradores
Joyuda Beach 6
Parador Hacienda Juanita 9

DINING ◆
El Castillo 3

ATTRACTIONS ●
Maricao 11
Mona Island 5
Parque de los Próceres 8
Tropical Agriculture
  Research Station 7

NIGHTLIFE ●
El Casino 2
Veranda Terrace 2
Victoria's Lounge 2

Rebuilt in 1570, it was named after Germain de Foix, the second wife of King Ferdinand of Spain. Once the rival of San Juan, San Germán harbored many pirates who pillaged the ships that sailed off the nearby coastline. Indeed, many of today's residents are descended from the smugglers, poets, priests, and politicians who once lived here.

Although the pirates and sugar plantations are long gone, the city retains colorful reminders of its Spanish colonial past. Flowers brighten some of the patios here as they do in Seville. Also, as in a small Spanish town, many of the inhabitants stroll through the historic zone in the early evening. Nicknamed "Ciudad de las Lomas," or City of the Hills, San Germán boasts verdant scenery that provides a pleasant backdrop to a variety of architectural styles—Spanish colonial (1850s), criollo (1880s), neoclassical (1910s), art deco (1930s), and international (1960s)—depicted in the gracious old-world buildings lining the streets. So significant are these buildings that San Germán is only the second Puerto Rican city (the other is San Juan) to be included in the National Register of Historic Places.

The city's 249 historical treasures are within easy walking distance of one another. Regrettably, you must view most of them from the outside. If some of them are actually open, count yourself fortunate, as they have no phones, keep no regular hours, and are staffed by volunteers who rarely show up. Also, be aware that the signage for the historic buildings can be confusing and many of the streets in the old town tend to run one way. Most of the city's architectural treasures lie uphill from the congested main thoroughfare (Calle Luna). We usually try to park on the town's main street (Carretera 102, which changes its name within the borders of San Germán to Calle Luna), and then proceed on foot through the city's commercial core before reaching the architectural highlights described below.

One of the most noteworthy churches in Puerto Rico is ✪ **Iglesia Porta Coeli (Gate of Heaven),** which sits atop a knoll at the eastern end of a cobble-covered square, the Parque de Santo Domingo. Dating from 1606, in a style inspired by the Romanesque architecture of northern Spain, this is the oldest church in the New World. Restored by the Institute of Puerto Rican Culture, and sheathed in a layer of salmon-colored stucco, it contains a museum of religious art with a collection of ancient santos, the carved figures of saints that have long been a major part of Puerto Rican folk art. Look for the 17th-century portrait of St. Nicholas de Bari, the French Santa Claus. Inside, the original palm-wood ceiling and tough ausobo-wood beams draw the eye upward. Other treasures include early choral books from Santo Domingo, a primitive carving of Jesus, and 19th-century Señora de la Monserrate Black Madonna and Child statues. Admission costs $1 for both adults and children. It's open Wednesday through Sunday from 9am to 4:30pm. Call ☎ 787/264-4258 for more information.

Less than a hundred feet downhill from the church, at the bottom of the steps that lead from its front door down to the plaza below, is the **Casa Morales** (also known as the **Tomás Vivoni House,** after its architect), San Germán's most popular and widely recognized house. Designed in the Edwardian style, with wraparound porches, elaborate gables, and elements that might remind you of a Swiss chalet, it was built in 1913, reflecting the region's turn-of-the-century agrarian prosperity.

The long and narrow, gently sloping plaza that prefaces the Iglesia Porta Coeli is the Parque de Santo Domingo, one of San Germán's two main plazas. Street signs also identify the plaza as the Calle Ruiz Belvis. Originally a marketplace, the plaza is paved with red and black cobblestones, and bordered with cast-iron benches and portrait busts of prominent figures in the town's history. This plaza merges gracefully with a second plaza, which street signs and maps identify as the Plaza Francisco Mariano

Quiñones, the Calle José Julian Acosta, or the Plaza Principal. Separating the two plazas is the unused **Viejo Alcaldía (Old Town Hall)**. Built late in the 19th century, it's awaiting a new vision, perhaps as a museum or public building. It's closed to the public.

San Germán's most impressive church—and the most monumental building in the region—is **San Germán de Auxerre** (☎ 787/892-1027), which rises majestically above the western end of the Plaza Francisco Mariano Quiñones. Designed in the Spanish baroque style and painted yellow, it was built in 1573 in the form of a simple chapel with a low-slung thatch roof. Its present grandeur is the result of at least five subsequent enlargements and renovations. Much of what you see today is the result of a rebuilding in 1688 and a restoration in 1737 that followed a disastrous earthquake. Inside, are three naves, ten altars, three chapels, and a belfry that was rebuilt in 1939 following an earthquake in 1918. The central chandelier, made from rock crystal and imported from Barcelona in 1866, is the largest in the Caribbean. The pride of the church is the trompe l'oeil ceiling, which was elaborately restored in 1993. A series of stained-glass windows with contemporary designs were inserted during a 1999 restoration. The church can be visited daily from 7am to 7:30pm.

There is a handful of lesser sights near the town's two main squares. They include the **Farmacia Martin,** a modern pharmacy that's incongruously set within the shell of a graceful but battered art deco building at the edge of the Parque Santo Domingo (22 Calle Ruiz Belvis; ☎ 787/892-1122). They also include a cluster of battered and dilapidated clapboard-sided houses that line the southern side of the Calle Dr. Ueve, which rambles downhill from its origin at the base of the Iglesia Porta Coeli. The most important house is no. 66, the **Casa Acosta y Fores.** Also noteworthy is **Casa Juán Perichi,** a substantial-looking structure at the corner of the Calle Dr. Ueve and the Parque Santo Domingo, nearly adjacent to the Port Coeli. Both houses were built around 1917 of traditional wood construction and are viewed as fine examples of Puerto Rican adaptations of Victorian architecture. Regrettably, both are seriously dilapidated, although that might change as San Germán continues the slow course of its historic renovations.

To the side of the Auxerre church is the modern, cement-sided **Public Library,** Calle José Julia Acosta (☎ 787/892-3240), where you might be tempted to duck into its air-conditioned interior for a glance through the stacks and periodicals collection. It's open Monday through Thursday from 8am to 8:30pm, Friday from 8am to 6pm, and Saturday from 8am to 1pm and from 2 to 4:30pm. Behind the Auxerre church is at least one masonry-fronted town house whose design might remind you of southern Spain (Andalusia), especially when the flowers in the window boxes add splashes of color.

WHERE TO STAY & DINE

Parador El Oasis. Calle Luna 72, San Germán, PR 00683. ☎ 787/892-1175. Fax 787/892-1156. 52 units. A/C TV TEL. $70 double. Extra person $10. Children 11 and under stay free in parents' room. AE, DC, DISC, MC, V.

Although not state of the art, this hotel has a hardworking staff and appealing doses of Spanish colonial charm. If you'd like an anchor in this quaint old town, far removed from the beaches, it's a fine place to stay. A three-story building constructed around a pool and patio area, the hotel originated in the late 1700s as a privately owned mansion. With its mint green walls and white wicker furniture, some of the grace remains. The older rooms, positioned close to the lobby, show the wear and tear of the years, but are still preferred by some. More modern rooms, located in the back, are plain and functional yet clean and more spacious than the older units. Three of the units have private balconies. The hotel sits on the town's crowded main street, about 2 blocks from the historic churches described above.

The in-house restaurant is not the most imaginative choice in town, but it emerges year after year as the most reliable and consistent in the area. It's open Tuesday through Sunday from 11am to 2:30pm and 6 to 10pm. Main courses cost from $11 to $17, and include empañadillas, platters of Créole-style corn sticks and cheese balls, tender-loin wrapped in bacon, steaks layered with ham and cheese, and combination platters of steak and red snapper.

Western Puerto Rico 9

The scenery of western Puerto Rico can vary from a terrain evoking the Arizona desert to a dense blanket of green typical of Germany's Back Forest. In the interior you'll discover such attractions as the Taíno Indian Ceremonial Ball Park, Río Camuy Cave Park, Arecibo Observatory (see chapter 7), and the karst district. Along the west and south coasts, you'll find white sandy beaches, world-class surfing conditions, and numerous towns and attractions. If you choose to spend the night, there are outstanding hotels to choose from, as well as a few noteworthy paradores, a chain of government-sponsored, privately operated country inns.

The waters of the Atlantic northwest coast tend to be rough, ideal for surfers but not always good for swimming. Much of the area is taken over with karst terrain, a reference to cliffs and caves that dot the landscape, along with forest-tufted haystack hills and root-draped sinkholes. The best karst landscape is found at Río Abajo Forest, directly to the south of the city of Arecibo. Here, you'll find pine, mahogany, and teak plantations.

Some eight centuries ago, the Taíno Indians inhabited this western part of Puerto Rico, using it as a site for recreation and worship. Stone monoliths, some decorated with petroglyphs, remain as evidence of that long-ago occupation.

1 Rincón

100 miles W of San Juan, 6 miles N of Mayagüez

North of Mayagüez, on the westernmost point of the island, lies the small fishing village of Rincón in the foothills of La Cadena mountains. It's not a sightseeing destination unto itself, but surfers from as far away as New Zealand say the area's reef-lined beaches, off Route 2 between Mayagüez and Rincón, are the best in the Caribbean. Surfers are particularly attracted to the beach at **Punta Higuero,** on Route 413, which ranks among the finest surfing spots in the world. During winter, uninterrupted swells from the North Atlantic form perfect waves averaging 5 to 6 feet in height, with ridable rollers sometimes reaching 15 to 25 feet.

Endangered humpback whales also winter here, attracting a growing number of whale watchers. The lighthouse at El Faro Park is a great place to spot these mammoth mammals.

And many nonsurfers visit Rincón for only one reason: the Primavera Hotel, not only one of the finest hotels in Puerto Rico, but one of the best in the entire Caribbean.

ESSENTIALS

GETTING THERE   American Eagle (☎ 800/433-7300 or 787/749-1747) flies from San Juan to Mayagüez, the nearest airport, four times daily (flying time: 40 min.). Taxis meet planes arriving from San Juan. Because they're unmetered, you should negotiate the fare at the outset with your driver. For car rentals, see "Essentials" in the Mayagüez section, in chapter 8.

If you're driving from San Juan, travel either west on Route 2 (trip time: 2 hr.) or south from San Juan on scenic Route 52 (trip time: 3¹/₂ hr.). We recommend Route 52.

VISITOR INFORMATION   There is no tourist information office in Rincón. Inquire in San Juan before heading here (see "Visitor Information" under "Orientation" in chapter 3).

SURFING & OTHER OUTDOOR PURSUITS

In spite of its claim as the windsurfing capital of the Caribbean, there are very definite dangers in the waters off Rincón. In November 1998, three surfers (two from San Juan, one from the U.S. mainland) drowned in unrelated incidents offshore at Maria's Beach. These deaths are often cited as evidence of the dangerous surf that has misled some very experienced surfers. Local water-sports experts urge anyone who's considering surfing at Rincón to ask a well-informed local for advice. When the surf is up and undertows and riptides are particularly strong, losing a surfboard while far offshore seems to be one of the first steps to eventually losing your life.

Windsurfing is best from November to April. The best beaches for surfing lie from Borinquén Point south to Rincón. There are many surfing outfitters along this strip, the best of which is **West Coast Surf Shop,** 2 E. Muñoz Rivera at Rincón (☎ 787/823-3935).

West Coast Charters, located in the Marina at Rincón (☎ 787/823-4114), offers a number of options for fun in the water, ranging from whale watching and other fun cruises to renting diving or fishing equipment. Expeditions are arranged to Desecho Island Reef, one of the best reefs in the Caribbean for snorkeling and diving. Desecho Island is an uninhabited island 13¹/₂ miles offshore. A Federal Wildlife Preserve, it consists of 360 acres. The highest point rises 715 feet. The outfitter also attracts lots of sports fishermen in search of tuna, grouper, marlin, wahoo, and dolphin (the fish, not the mammal). Fishermen are taken out for a half day aboard a fully equipped boat, with a licensed and experienced charter captain. A snorkeling trip costs $35, a one-tank scuba dive $85. A half-day fishing charter is $400 per boat, including the guide. Whale-watching trips are often arranged from December to March.

Another good scuba outfitter is **Taíno Divers,** Black Eagle Marina at Rincón (☎ 787/823-64229), which offers local boat charters along with scuba and snorkeling trips. Other activities include whale-watching expeditions and sunset cruises. Fees are $85 for a one-tank dive, $475 for a half-day fishing boat rental, and $25 per person for a 2-hour sunset cruise.

The most visible and sought-after whale-watching panorama in Rincón is **Parque El Faro de Rincón (Rincón's Lighthouse Park),** which lies on El Faro Point peninsula at the extreme western tip of town. Within its fenced-in perimeter are pavilions selling souvenirs and snack items, rows of binoculars offering 25¢ views, and a stately looking lighthouse built in 1921. The park is at its most popular from November to

Western Puerto Rico & the Southwest Coast

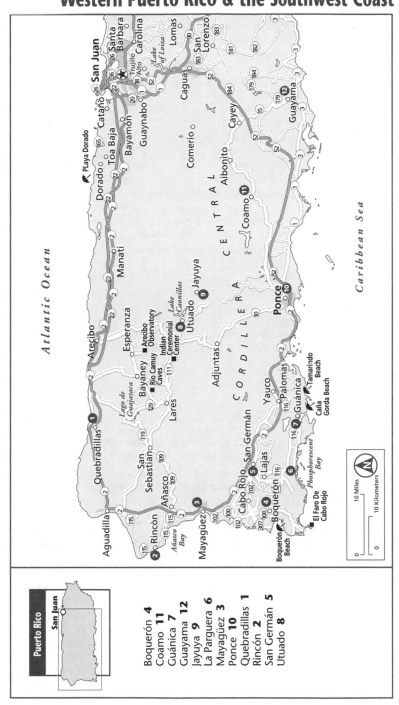

Atlantic Ocean

Caribbean Sea

San Juan
Santa Barbara
Lomas
Carolina
Lake of Loíza
San Lorenzo
Trujillo Alto
Caguas
Guaynabo
Cataño
Bayamón
Toa Baja
Guayama **12**
Cayey
Comerío
Aibonito
Coamo **11**
Coamo
Playa Dorado
Dorado
Manatí
Arecibo
Esperanza
Arecibo Observatory
Lake Caonillas
Jayuya
Jayuya **9**
Indian Ceremonial Center **8**
Utuado
CENTRAL CORDILLERA
Ponce
Ponce **10**
Bayaney
Río Camuy Caves
Lares
Adjuntas
Lago de Guajataca
Quebradillas **1**
San Sebastián
Yauco
Palomas
Tamarindo Beach
Guánica **7**
Caña Gorda Beach
Aguadilla
Rincón
Rincón **2**
Añasco
Añasco Bay
Mayagüez
Mayagüez **3**
San Germán
Cabo Rojo
San Germán **5**
Lajas
Boquerón **4**
Phosphorescent Bay
La Parguera **6**
Boquerón Beach
El Faro De Cabo Rojo

N

10 Miles
10 Kilometers

0
0

Puerto Rico

San Juan

Boquerón **4**
Coamo **11**
Guánica **7**
Guayama **12**
Jayuya **9**
La Parguera **6**
Mayagüez **3**
Ponce **10**
Quebradillas **1**
Rincón **2**
San Germán **5**
Utuado **8**

March for whale watching and in January and February for surfer gazing. The park is locked every evening between midnight and 7am. Otherwise, you're free to promenade with the locals any time you like.

If you get hungry, the park's snack bar is called **Restaurant El Faro,** Barrio Puntas, Carretera 413, kilometer 3.3 (no phone). It's open Monday through Friday from 9am to 7:30pm, Saturday from 9am to midnight, and Sunday from 9am to 8pm. Platters of American and Puerto Rican food, including *mofongos,* steaks, and burgers, cost from $12.95 to $18.95 each.

Adjacent to this park is the site of an old reactor dome, parts of which are still radioactive. Nonetheless, Puerto Rico plans to turn it into the island's first museum devoted to nuclear energy. The dome once housed an experimental reactor known as "Bonus," for Boiling Nuclear Superheater. It operated from 1964 to 1968, but was shut down because it wasn't cost-efficient. If plans go according to schedule, the museum will open around 2001, and is expected to draw 100,000 visitors annually to Rincón. The director of the plant claims that visitors will be exposed to radiation five times less than federal standards allow, about the same as standing outside in the tropical sun. Although the government insists there is no safety threat, ecologists have yet to be won over.

Punta Borinquén Golf Club, Route 107 (☎ **787/890-2987**), 2 miles north of Aquadilla's center, across the highway from the city's airport, was originally built by the U.S. government as part of the Ramey Air Force base. Today, its 18 holes are a public golf course, open daily from 7am to 6:30pm. Greens fees cost $20 for an all-day pass; a golf cart that can carry two passengers rents for $24 for 18 holes, or $12 for 9 holes. Clubs can be rented for $10 per set. The clubhouse contains a bar and a simple restaurant.

WHERE TO STAY
VERY EXPENSIVE

✪ **Horned Dorset Primavera Hotel.** Rte. 429 (P.O. Box 1132), Rincón, PR 00677. ☎ **800/633-1857** or 787/823-4030. Fax 787/823-5580. www.relasichateau.fr. 31 units. A/C. Winter $430 double; $530–$850 suite. Off-season $280 double; $420–$650 suite. MAP (breakfast and dinner) $80.45 per person extra. AE, MC, V. Children under 12 not accepted.

This is the most sophisticated hotel on Puerto Rico, and one of the most exclusive and elegant small properties anywhere in the Caribbean. It was built on the massive breakwaters and seawalls erected by a local railroad many years ago. Guests here enjoy a secluded, semiprivate beach.

The hacienda evokes an aristocratic Spanish villa, with wicker armchairs, hand-painted tiles, ceiling fans, seaside terraces, and cascades of flowers. This is really a restful place. Accommodations are in a series of suites that ramble uphill amid lush gardens. The decor is tasteful, with four-poster beds and brass-footed tubs in marble-sheathed bathrooms. Rooms are spacious and luxurious, with Persian rugs over tile floors, queen sofa beds in sitting areas, deluxe mattresses, and fine linen. Bathrooms are equally roomy and luxurious, with hair dryers and thick towels. Eight suites are located in the separate Casa Escondida villa, set at the edge of the property. Some of these units have private pools; others offer private verandas or sundecks.

Dining/Diversions: The hotel's restaurant is one of the finest on Puerto Rico (see "Where to Dine," below). There's a bar open throughout the day that serves delectable rum punches. Guitarists and singers often perform during cocktail and dinner hours.

Amenities: The best hotel library on Puerto Rico, pool, deep-sea fishing, room service (at breakfast and lunch only), concierge, laundry, massage, limousine and touring services. A gym, tennis courts, golf, and scuba diving are available nearby.

INEXPENSIVE

Lazy Parrot. Rd. 430, km 4.1. Barrio Puntas, Rincón, PR 00677. ☎ **800/294-1752** or 787/823-5654. Fax 787/823-0224. www.layzparrot.com. E-mail: lazyparrotinn@una.com. 7 units. A/C TV TEL. $85 double. AE, MC, V.

Set within an unlikely inland neighborhood, far from any particular view of the sea, this place has a better-than-average restaurant and clean, well-organized bedrooms. Each is comfortable albeit not overly large, with light-grained and durable furnishings that might seem appropriate for the bedroom of a high-school senior in a suburb on the U.S. mainland. Bathrooms are simple, functional, and workable, but not at all plush. It was built as a private home in the 1970s, then transformed into the inn you see today. The place is just as well known for its restaurant as it is for its rooms. Meals are served in an open-sided aerie on the building's uppermost floor. For more on this, refer to "Where to Dine."

Parador Villa Antonio. Rte. 115, km 12.3 (P.O. Box 68), Rincón, PR 00677. ☎ **800/443-0266** in the U.S. or 787/823-2645. Fax 787/823-3380. www.villa-antonio.com. E-mail: pva@villa-antonio.com. 55 units. A/C TV TEL. $80.25–$107 double. DC, MC, V.

Ilia and Hector Rúiz offer apartments by the sea in this privately owned and run *parador.* The beach outside is nice, but it's not kept as clean as it should be by the local authorities. (We've seen litter here.) Facilities include a children's playground, game rooms, two tennis courts, and a pool. Surfing and fishing can be enjoyed just outside your front door, and you can bring your catch right into the cottage and prepare a fresh seafood dinner in your own kitchenette (there's no restaurant). Be aware that the air-conditioning doesn't work properly, and, in general, better maintenance is needed. Nonetheless, this is a popular destination for Puerto Rican families who crowd in on the weekends. The motel-like rooms have balconies or terraces and small bathrooms. Furnishings are well used but offer reasonable comfort.

Villa Cofresi. Road #115, km 12.3, Rincón, PR. 00677. ☎ **787/823-2450.** Fax 787/823-1770. 52 units. A/C TV TEL. $95 double; $140 suite with kitchen. AE, DC, MC, V.

Set about a mile south of Rincón's center, this is a clean, family-run hotel with a view of the beach. Thanks to the three adult children of the Caro family, the place is better managed than many of its competitors. Bedrooms are comfortable and airy, with well-chosen furniture that might remind you of something in southern Florida. Each has a white tile floor, a refrigerator, and in most cases, two double beds. The two units that tend to sell out long in advance are nos. 47 and 55, which have windows opening directly onto the sea. On the premises are a small swimming pool and a bar, which is a focal point for leisurely cocktails throughout the day and early evening.

The in-house restaurant, La Ana de Cofresi, is named after the ship that was captained by the region's most famous 18th-century pirate, Roberto Cofresi. Hand-painted murals highlight some of his adventures. Open Monday through Friday from 5 to 10pm, Saturday and Sunday from noon to 10pm; it charges $8 to $30 for well-prepared main courses that are likely to include fish consommé, four kinds of *mofongo*, breaded scampi served either with Créole sauce or garlic, and very good steaks, including a 12-ounce New York sirloin.

A NEARBY PLACE TO STAY & DINE IN AGUADA

✪ **J. B. Hidden Village Hotel.** Carretera 2, Intersection 4416, km 1, Punta Nueve, Barrio Piedras Blancas, Sector Villarrubia, Aguada, PR 00602. ☎ **787/868-8686.** Fax 787/868-8701. 40 units. A/C TV TEL. $82 double; $119–$129 suite. AE, MC, V.

Named after the initials of its owners (Julio Bonilla, his wife, Jinnie, and their son, Julio, Jr.), this well-maintained and isolated hotel opened in 1990. Half a mile east of

Aguada, on a side street running off Route 4414, it's nestled into a valley between three forested hillsides, almost invisible from the road. The hotel is a quiet and simple refuge to vacationers who enjoy exploring the area's many beaches. There are two restaurants on the premises (one with a view looking out over a neighboring ravine), a small swimming pool, and a bar. Each comfortable bedroom offers views of the pool.

WHERE TO DINE
VERY EXPENSIVE

✪ **Horned Dorset Primavera.** In the hotel of the same name, Rte. 429. ☎ **787/823-4030.** Reservations recommended. Fixed-price dinners $64 for 5 courses, $88 for 11 courses. AE, MC, V. Daily noon–2:30pm and 7–9:30pm. FRENCH/CARIBBEAN.

This is the finest restaurant in western Puerto Rico, with a romance and an allure that are so unique that diners sometimes travel from San Juan for an intimate dinner. It's the southern extension of an award-winning restaurant in Leonardsville, New York. The name derives from a species of sheep that's a lot more comfortable in chilly upstate New York than in the Caribbean tropics. A masonry staircase sweeps from the garden to the second floor, where soaring ceilings and the atmosphere of a private villa await you.

The menu, which changes virtually every night, is likely to include chilled parsnip soup, fricassee of wahoo with wild mushrooms, grilled loin of beef with peppercorns, and medallions of lobster in an orange-flavored beurre-blanc (white butter) sauce. The grilled breast of duckling with bay leaves and raspberry sauce is delectable. The chef might serve dorado (mahimahi) grilled and offered with a ginger-cream sauce on a bed of braised Chinese cabbage, or delicious grilled squab with tarragon sauce. This restaurant can pleases even the most discriminating palates.

MODERATE

✪ **The Landing.** Carretera 413 (Interior), Barrios Puntas/Playa Antonio. ☎ **787/823-3112.** Reservations recommended for dinner Fri–Sat. Burgers and sandwiches $5.75–$8.25; platters $15.75–$28.75. AE, MC, V. Sun–Thurs 11:30am–midnight. Fri–Sat 11am–2am. INTERNATIONAL.

This is the most substantial of the many bars in Rincón, with a popularity so widespread that it's likely to attract as many as 800 clients on a Friday or Saturday night. The setting, which looks like a stylish private house, is adjacent to a beach favored by a cadre of devoted surfers. Its focal point is a sprawling bar where popular drinks include an M&M ($5 each)—loosely defined as a piña colada capped with layers of both light and dark rum. Edwin Nault, a former dental technician from Boston, is the competent entrepreneur who runs this place. Menu items include fried calamari, scampi, T-bone steaks, jerk chicken, churrasco, barbecued ribs, stuffed chicken breasts, and lobster kebabs. The view of Rincón's legendary surf, complete with dozens of surfers trying their luck on the the deep blue, is panoramic.

INEXPENSIVE

Calypso Café. Maria's Beach. No phone. Reservations not accepted. Burgers and simple platters $5–$7. No credit cards. Daily noon–2am. AMERICAN.

Set on a bend in the road between the Black Eagle Marina and the lighthouse (El Faro de Rincón), this sometimes charming bar attracts many of Rincón's young singles. One of the simplest drinking emporiums in the region, it consists of a roof, a fiesta-colored balustrade, and a collection of surfers, many from New York, New Jersey, and Florida. Maria's Beach, a well-known surfer's hangout, is a few steps away. A deejay or live band performs every Friday and Saturday night. The ambience might remind you of a latter-day remake of *The Endless Summer*.

Panaderia/Cafeteria Calvache. Rte 115, km 9. ☎ **787/823-6658.** Reservations not necessary. Breakfast, lunch, or dinner platters $2–$6. No credit cards. Daily 5am–10:30pm. AMERICAN/PUERTO RICAN.

The food service area of this place occupies one end of a store otherwise devoted to the sale of rum, baked goods, and hardware. But it's so friendly and the counter setting is so appropriate for the food (bacon and eggs, hamburgers, spaghetti with sausage, or such local fare as rice with seafood) that we wanted to add it to our listings. You'll find this Formica-clad heaven about 1 1/2 miles south of the center of Rincón. The staff when we last visited was charming, brightening the day with acts of cheerfulness that went beyond the call of duty.

Tamboo Tavern/Larry B's Restaurant. Sandy Beach. ☎ **787/823-8550.** Reservations not accepted. Main courses $7–$18. AE, V. Daily 11am–midnight. AMERICAN.

The allure of this place derives from the crowd of surfing enthusiasts who gather here for drinks and fuel before braving the sometimes treacherous waters at Sandy Beach. The spot sports a Rastafarian color scheme of green and yellow. Owned by investors from Vermont, it's a new-wave kind of place that prides itself on knowing the latest surfing conditions. Burgers and sandwiches are the most frequently ordered items, although rum and cokes ($2 each) and piña coladas ($4 each) are enduringly popular too.

2 Southwest Coast Beach Resorts

The true native of Puerto Rico heads not to the fancy resorts along the north coast near San Juan, but instead to the southwestern corner, a region with a distinctly island flavor. Here are some of Puerto Rico's great beaches, notably at Boquerón, and a lot of mom-and-pop operations offering nightly rentals and good seafood dinners.

For bird watchers, the Guánica State Forest is a sanctuary with the greatest number of birds on the island. For beachcombers, there are many hidden places, such as Gilligan's Island off the coast of the little village of Guánica. For snorkelers, there are miles of coral reefs awash with tropical fish and coral and marine life. The Cabo Rojo lighthouse, south of Bouquerón, offers views of the rocky coastline and a panoramic sweep of the Caribbean.

BOQUERÓN

Lying 85 miles southwest of San Juan and 33 miles west of Ponce is the little beach resort of Boquerón. The location is just south of Cabo Rojo, west of the historic city of San Germán, and near the western branch of the Boquerón Forest Preserve.

What puts sleepy Bouquerón on the tourist map is its lovely public beach, called **balnerio,** one of the island's finest for swimming. It is also known for the shellfish found offshore. The beach has facilities, including lockers and changing places, plus kiosks that rent water-sports equipment. Parking is $2. On weekends the resort tends to be crowded with families driving down from San Juan.

From Boquerón you can head directly south to **El Faro de Cabo Rojo** at the island's southernmost corner. The century-old Cabo Rojo Lighthouse lies on Route 301, along a spit of land between Bahia Sucia and Bahia Salinas. Looking down from the lighthouse you'll see a 2,000-foot drop along jagged limestone cliffs. The lighthouse dates from 1881 when it was constructed under Spanish rule. The famous pirate, Roberto Cofresi, used to terrorize the coast along here in the 19th century and was said to have hidden out in a cave nearby.

DIVING & SNORKELING

The **Bouquerón Dive Shop,** Muñoz Rivera St. 58 (☎ 787/851-2155), can direct you to one of the best dive spots on the island. This spot, near the village of La Parguera (see below), is known to divers throughout the Caribbean and includes the fabled Black Wall where black coral flourishes abundantly and 6-foot moray eels are regularly spotted. A two-tank dive costs $70 per person, with a one-tank night dive going for $40. This is a fully certified PADI dive center, and all equipment needed for diving can be rented here. Three-hour snorkeling trips can also be arranged, costing $35 per person, equipment included.

WHERE TO STAY

Cofresi Beach Club. Calle Muñoz Rivera 58, P.O. Box 910, Boquerón, PR 00622. ☎ 787/ 851-2155. 12 units. A/C TV TEL. $69 double; $99 quad. AE, MC, V.

Set across from one of the area's best dive shops, this is a choice for clients who want no maid service or resort-oriented amenities—there is no full-time reception or concierge staff. Accommodations have kitchens with cutlery, plates, and cooking equipment, durable furniture, and comfortable beds. There's a swimming pool on the premises. It's about as laissez-faire as they come.

Parador Boquemar. 101 Rte. 307 (P.O. Box 133), Boquerón, Cabo Rojo, PR 00622. ☎ 787/851-2158. Fax 787/851-7600. 75 units. A/C TV. $65–$74 double; $80 junior suite. AE, DC, MC, V.

The pink-walled Parador Boquemar was built in the late 1980s a block or so from Boquerón Beach. Rooms are at the end of long corridors that evoke a college dormitory, or worse, an anonymous office building. Despite small units, Puerto Rican families like this place a lot, causing readers to complain that children sometimes run up and down the corridors. Rooms are simple, stripped down to the bare essentials. Surprisingly, the hotel has one of the best restaurants in the area, Las Cascadas. Here, in a windowless dining room with a splashing wall fountain, you'll be offered regional fare. This usually includes lobster *asopao*, a form of seafood gumbo; filet mignon; and fillets of rolled fish stuffed with shrimp and chunks of lobster. Main courses cost from $8.75 to $29.75. Mealtimes are daily from noon to 3pm and 5 to 10pm. The place is a little too rustic and not maintained enough for our tastes, but the beach somehow compensates. Stay here only if you plan to spend most of your time outside of the hotel.

WHERE TO DINE

Parador Boquemar (see above) is also known for its cuisine. For some reason, Boquerón has more shellfish vendors than any other resort in western Puerto Rico. They display their bounty on wooden tabletops along the town's main street. Most of the shellfish is not refrigerated, and as such, we cannot vouch for its safety. But if you're adventurous, know in advance that a dozen clams are a bargain at between $4 and $6 a dozen depending on their size, whereas oysters sell for around $5 a dozen. Most vendors offer a selection of spicy sauces to accompany the shellfish.

Roberto's Fish Net. Calle José de Diego s/n (without number). ☎ 787/851-6009. Reservations not necessary. Main courses $9.95–$18.95. AE, MC, V. Wed–Sun 11am–10pm. PUERTO RICAN.

This is one of two restaurants, both named "Roberto," on the same sleepy street in the .center of Boquerón. Both belong to Roberto Aviles and offer roughly equivalent versions of the same food. We prefer this spot to Roberto's Restaurant Villa Playera (☎ 787/254-3163), just a few steps away. However, the Villa Playera is still a good choice, particularly on Monday and Tuesday when the Fish Net is closed. Within the Fish Net's simple environment, a cross between a luncheonette and a bar, you can order tender beefsteaks, well-flavored chicken breasts, or fresh fish, any of which comes with rice and beans. More unusual are the *pilones,* tall wooden cups filled with an old-fashioned mortar, which is actually a combination of mashed plantains flavored with your choice of shrimp, conch, or octopus, usually served with salsa.

BOQUERÓN AFTER DARK

Eduardo's Pub. Calle de Diego 13. ☎ **787/255-6221.**

Crowded, convivial, and pulsating with merengue and rock and roll, even at lunchtime during the week, this is one of the most popular bars in Boquerón. Expect a party at any time. A Melon's Mama, made with vodka, watermelon liqueur, cream of coconut, grenadine, and a combination of pineapple and orange juice, and priced at $3.50 each, will help get you into the rhythm of things. It's open daily from 10am to midnight (till 1am on Friday and Saturday). Eduardo Iglesias is the establishment's founder and namesake.

Schamar Bar & Hotel. Boquerón Beach, PR 00622. ☎ **787/851-0542.**

No other watering hole in Boquerón commands as wide a recognition, or as animated a crowd of locals, as the Schamar. Set within a cement-sided pavilion, which opens onto the rocky coastline, it's filled most afternoons and evenings with clients of all ages, most of whom seem to know each other, all of whom seem to put away enormous amounts of beer, priced from $1.25 to $1.75 a bottle, or rum. The bar is open daily from 7:30am to very late at night, at least 2am or even later whenever there is a crowd at the resort. On the premises are five simple but comfortable bedrooms, each suitable for up to four occupants. Rooms come with air-conditioning but no phone or TV. They rent for $80 a night (MasterCard and Visa accepted) with breakfast included.

LA PARGUERA

This charming fishing village lies 78 miles southwest of San Juan and 26 miles west of Ponce, just south of San Germán. From San Germán, take route 320 directly south following the signposts. However, this route, the same highway, changes its name several times along the way, becoming Route 101, 116, 315, 305, and then 304 before reaching La Parguera. This area is known for its scuba diving and Phosphorescent Bay.

The name of the village comes from *pargos,* meaning snapper. Its main attraction, other than its beaches and diving, is **La Bahia Fosforescente,** a phosphorescent bay containing millions of luminescent dinoflagellates, a microscopic plankton. A disturbance causes them to light up the dark waters. For dramatic effect, they are best seen on a moonless night. Boats leave nightly from 7:30pm to 12:30am from La Parguera pier, depending on demand. The round-trip between La Parguera and the bay costs $5 per person.

Offshore are some 12 to 15 reefs with a variety of depths. The Beril reef goes down to 60 feet, then drops to 2,000 feet. This wall is famous among divers, and visibility ranges from 100 to 120 feet. These reefs also provide some of the best snorkeling possibilities in Puerto Rico. Marine life is both abundant and diverse, including big morays, sea turtles, barracudas, nurse sharks, and manatees. **Paradise Scuba Center,** Hotel Casa Blanca Building, at La Parguera (☎ 787-899-7611), offers the best diving and snorkeling. A two-tank dive costs $70, a night dive $50; a 4-hour snorkeling jaunt goes for $35 per person. Full equipment can be rented.

WHERE TO STAY

La Jamaka. Collinas de la Parguera, P.O. Box 303, Lajas, La Parguera PR 00667. ☎ and fax **787/899-6162.** 8 units. A/C. $60–$71 double. MC, V.

Set on a low but breezy hillside, a 10-minute hike from the town's congested center, this is a tasteful vacation compound in a verdant setting with bougainvillea and flowering shrubs. Guests here are pulled into the gregarious life of the establishment simply by the warmth of the family who runs it. Elsie Cintron and Carlos Rosado are the creative force, providing a small swimming pool, a communal kitchen, and a garden-style setting for the relaxation of their guests. Bedrooms are small, if a bit claustrophobic, well maintained, and filled in midsummer with holidaymakers from other parts of Puerto Rico. The indoor/outdoor restaurant is open Thursday through Sunday from noon to 10:30pm, charging $14 to $23 for items that include mahimahi in Créole sauce, and fillets of both *capitán* and hake in tamarind-based Créole sauce.

Parador Posada Porlamar. Rte. 304 (P.O. Box 405), La Parguera, Lajas, PR 00667. ☎ **787/899-4015.** Fax 787/899-5558. E-mail: posadoporlamar@hotmail.com. 40 units. A/C TV TEL. $75–$100 double EP, or $145–$175 double MAP. AE, MC, V. Drive west along Rte. 2 until you reach the junction of Rte. 116; then head south along Rte. 116 and Rte. 304.

Developed by the Pancorbo family in 1967 as one of the first full-service hotels in town, this *parador* evokes life in a simple fishing village. A horseshoe-shaped compound that overlooks a narrow channel flanked by mangroves, it conducts an ongoing business with dive enthusiasts, thanks to an on-site scuba shop. Bedrooms are plain and neat but don't invite lingering. Some have balconies, minibars, and small sitting rooms. The social center revolves around a patio overlooking the channel. The restaurants and bars of La Parguera are within a short walk of this centrally located place. On the premises is a rather formal restaurant, La Pared, that's open nightly from 6 to 11pm. Main courses cost from $16 to $40 each. Specialties include seafood in Créole sauce, lamb chops in Dijon mustard, and sautéed shrimp in soursop-flavored butter sauce. The venue has air-conditioning.

Parador Villa Parguera. 304 Main St. (P.O. Box 273), La Parguera, Lajas, PR 00667. ☎ **787/899-7777.** Fax 787/899-6040. www.elshop.com. E-mail: elshop@elshop.com. 70 units. A/C TV TEL. Sun–Fri $80–$85 double; Sat $90–$93 double. Two children under 10 stay free in parents' room. AE, DC, DISC, MC, V. Drive west along Rte. 2 until you reach the junction with Rte. 116; then head south along Rte. 116 and Rte. 304.

Although the water in the nearby bay is too muddy for swimming, guests can enjoy a view of the harbor and take a dip in the swimming pool. Situated on the southwestern shore of Puerto Rico, this *parador* is favored by *sanjuaneros* for weekend escapes from the capital. It's also known for its seafood dinners (the fish are not caught in the bay), comfortable and uncomplicated bedrooms, and location next to the bay's famous phosphorescent waters. Bedrooms are standardized, each with either a balcony or terrace. This place is more gregarious and convivial, and usually more fun, than the Porlamar, a few steps away.

The spacious, air-conditioned restaurant, where the occasionally slow service might remind you of Spain in a bygone era, offers traditional favorites, such as fillet of fish stuffed with lobster and shrimp. It's open daily from 7am to 9:30pm. Nonresidents are welcome. There's a play area for children.

Because the inn is popular with Puerto Rican families, especially on weekends, there's a special weekend package for a 2-night minimum stay; $325 to $350 (depending on the exposure of your room) covers the price of a double room, welcome drinks, breakfasts, dinners, flowers, and dancing with a free show. We prefer to stay here during the week, when it's more tranquil.

Puerto Rico's Secret Beaches

Some of Puerto Rico's most beautiful and isolated beaches lie on the island's southwestern coast, facing south toward the Caribbean Sea, far from major highways. Stretching between Ponce, in the east, and Cabo Rojo, on Puerto Rico's extreme southwestern tip, these beaches flank some of the least densely populated parts of the island. And because the boundaries between them are relatively fluid, only a local resident (or perhaps a professional geographer) could say for sure where one ends and the other begins.

If you consider yourself an aficionado of isolated beaches, it's worth it to rent a car and strike out for these remote locales. Drive westward from Ponce along Highway 2, branching south along Route 116 to **Guánica,** the self-anointed gateway and capital of this string of "secret beaches." Don't expect a lot—you're likely to see only a handful of simple bars, tacky luncheonettes, and gas stations peppering a verdant and perpetually sun-baked landscape.

By far the most accessible and appealing beach is **Caña Gorda.** Set about a quarter-mile south of Guánica, at the edge of a legally protected marsh that's known for its rich bird life and thick reeds, Caña Gorda is a sprawling expanse of pale beige sand that's dotted with ramshackle-looking *bohíos* (huts) crafted from tree branches and palm fronds. Despite its rusticity, it's a site that's been improved and developed by the local authorities. The centerpiece here is a well-recommended hotel, the **Copamarina** (☎ **800/468-4553** in the U.S. or 787/821-0505). Here you can check in for a night or two of sun-flooded R&R, along with the occasional beachgoer and honeymooner. Even if you're staying at the hotel, consider dropping in for a cuba libre, a margarita, or a meal. The Copamarina is about a 45-minute drive from Ponce.

Stray even farther west from Ponce, along coastal highways like 324, 304, and 323, and you'll pass beaches with such names as **Tamarindo, Manglillos, Rosado,** and **Playa Santa.** Most westerly of all is **Bahia Sucia** (whose name rather unappetizingly translates as "Dirty Beach"), 45 minutes west of Ponce, at the end of rutted and badly potholed roads. All of these beaches may be hard to reach, but persevere and you'll be met with warm water and long, uncrowded stretches of white sand, where towering king palms and salt-tolerant sea grapes provide an idyllic tropical backdrop for sun and surf. Keep in mind that with the exception of Caña Gorda, the beaches mentioned above have virtually no services and public utilities. Pack what you'll need for the day—food, water, sunscreen, and so forth.

WHERE TO DINE

La Jamaka (see above) also serves excellent cuisine.

La Casita. Calle Principal 304. ☎ **787/899-1681.** Reservations not necessary. Main courses $12.95–$35. AE, DC, MC, V. Tues–Sun 11am–10:30pm. Closed 2 weeks in September. SEAFOOD.

The town's most consistently reliable and popular restaurant has flourished here since the 1960s within a simple, wooden building. Inside, lots of varnished pine acts as a decorative foil for platters of local and imported fish and shellfish. Fillets of fish can be served in any of seven different styles; lobster comes in five. Even the Puerto Rican starchy staple of *mofongo* comes in versions stuffed with crab, octopus, shrimp, lobster, or assorted shellfish. Begin with fish chowder, a dozen cheese balls, or fish croquettes. End with coconut-flavored flan. Don't expect grand service or decor, but rather a setting where food is the focus.

GUÁNICA

This little resort on the Caribbean Sea lies 73 miles southwest of San Juan and 21 miles west of the city of Ponce. Part of the area is a UNESCO-designated world biosphere reserve adjacent to the famed Guánica dry forest, home to more than 100 species of migratory and resident birds, the largest number in Puerto Rico.

The beach at Guánica is pristine and the water, crystal clear, ideal for swimming, snorkeling, and diving. Directly offshore is the famed Gilligan's Island, plus six of Puerto Rico's best sites for night or day dives.

Once the area was known for its leaping bullfrogs. The Spanish conquerors virtually wiped out this species. But the bullfrogs have come back and live in the rolling, scrub-covered hills that surround the 18-acre site of the Copamarina, the area's major hotel (see below.)

Guánica is adjacent to the unique "Dry Forest" and experiences very little rainfall. Nearby mountains get an annual rainfall of 15 feet, but Guánica receives only about 15 inches. This is the world's largest dry coastal forest region. The upper hills are ideal for hiking.

Guánica was once the haunt of the Taíno Indians, and was the place where Ponce de León first explored Puerto Rico in 1508. One of his descendants later founded the nearby city of Ponce in 1692.

SCUBA DIVING & SNORKELING

The best dive operation is **Dive Copamarina** (☎ **787/821-0505**), part of the Copamarina resort recommended below. Copamarina has a long pier where fishing is permitted and a 42-foot Pro Jet dive boat. Guánica is one of the Caribbean's best areas for day and night dives. A two-tank dive costs $85, and full diving equipment can be rented. You can also rent snorkeling gear. Whale-watching excursions January to March are arranged at the hotel's tour desk, which also offers eco tours, kayaking, deep-sea fishing, and sunset sails. Horseback riding and sunset biking are also available.

At one of the local beaches, **Playa Santa,** west of town, **Pino's Boat & Water Fun** (☎ 787/821-6864) will rent you a paddleboat or kayak for $15 an hour.

One of the most visited sites is **Gilligan's Island,** a series of mangrove and sand cays near the Caña Gorda peninsula. Part of the dry forest reserve, it is set aside for recreational use. A small ferry departs from in front of Restaurant San Jacinto, just past the Copamarina, every hour daily from 10am to 5pm, weather permitting; round-trips cost $4.

WHERE TO STAY

✪ **Copamarina Beach Resort.** Rte. 333, km 6.5, Caña Gorda (P.O. Box 805), Guánica, PR 00653. ☎ **800/468-4553** or 787/821-0505. Fax 787/821-0070. www.copamarina.com. 106 units. A/C TV TEL. $165–$230 double; $400 suite. AE, DC, DISC, MC, V. From Ponce, drive west along Rte. 2 to Rte. 116 and go south to Rte. 333, then head east.

Charming, low-key, and discreetly elegant, this resort was originally built in the 1950s as the private vacation retreat of the de Castro family, Puerto Rican cement barons. In 1991, it was enlarged and upgraded by talented entrepreneurs. Today, it stands head and shoulders above everything else along Puerto Rico's western coast, surpassing even the Horned Dorset Primavera (its strongest competitor). Situated beside a public beach, amid a landscaped palm grove, the resort is airy and relaxing. A favorite destination of *sanjuaneros,* it also draws a well-heeled crowd of clients from Europe and North America, who know good value when they see it.

The bedrooms are in one- and two-story wings that radiate from the resort's central core. Attractively decorated, units have tile floors, lots of exposed wood, and louvered doors with screens that open onto large verandas or terraces. Everything is airy and comfortable. Bathrooms are larger than you might expect and up-to-date.

Dining: The resort houses two restaurants, one of which reigns as the finest in western Puerto Rico. Established by culinary superstar Wilo Benet, Copamarina Coastal Cuisine is a destination for clients from as far away as San Juan. Less formal, and staffed with a hardworking crowd of young people, is Las Palmas, which is set in the open air beneath a canopy.

Amenities: Its dive facilities are the best and most varied in western Puerto Rico, attracting divers of all levels of expertise. Baby-sitting, laundry, two swimming pools for adults, wading pool for children, two tennis courts, program of water sports (including snorkeling and scuba diving).

Mary Lee's by the Sea. Rte. 333, km 6.7 (P.O. Box 394), Guánica, PR 00653. ☎ 787/ 821-3600. Fax 787/821-3600. 8 units. A/C. $110 double with kitchen; $130–$140 suite with kitchen for up to 4; $160–$225 suite with kitchen for up to 6. No credit cards.

Owned and operated by Michigan-born Mary Lee Alvarez, a former resident of Cuba and a self-described "compulsive decorator," this is an informal collection of cottages, seafront houses, and apartments located 4 miles east of Guánica. Five California-style houses are subdivided into eight living units, each suitable for one to three couples. Rooms are whimsically decorated in an airy, somewhat bohemian way, with a sense of 1960s comfort and a sometimes soothing sense of clutter. The entire compound, which grew in an artfully erratic way, is landscaped with flowering shrubs, trees, and vines. Overall, the ambience is kind and low-key.

There aren't any formally organized activities here, but the hotel sits next to sandy beaches and a handful of uninhabited offshore cays. The management maintains rental boats with motors, two waterside sundecks, and several kayaks for the benefit of active guests. Hikers and bird watchers can go north to the Guánica State Forest.

Don't come here looking for nighttime activities or enforced conviviality. The place is quiet, secluded, and appropriate for low-key vacationers looking for privacy. There isn't a bar or restaurant here, although each unit includes a modern kitchen and an outdoor barbecue pit. The rooms are serviced weekly, although guests can arrange daily maid service for an extra fee.

WHERE TO DINE

✪ **Copamarina Coastal Cuisine.** In the Copamarina Beach Resort, Rte. 333, km 6.5, Caña Gorda (P.O. Box 805), Guánica. ☎ 787/821-0505. Reservations recommended. Main courses $19–$34. AE, DC, DISC, MC, V. Sun–Thurs 6–10:30pm, Fri–Sat 6–11pm. INTERNATIONAL.

This is a genuinely excellent restaurant whose culinary inspiration originated with Puerto Rico's most celebrated chef, Wilo Benet. Despite his departure, a team of disciples continues with delectable dishes that include fried red snapper with Créole sauce; fillet of mahimahi with pigeon peas, garlic shrimp with local rice, and beef parmigiana with red wine sauce. The interior is air-conditioned but tropical in its feel, providing a welcome dose of relaxed glamour.

Guánica Seafood. Calle 16 de Marzo (at the junction of Rte. 333 and Rte. 116). ☎ 787/ 821-3000. Reservations recommended. Main courses $14.95–$35. AE, MC, V. Wed–Sun 11am–11pm. SEAFOOD.

The port of Guánica has a reputation for harboring the boats of some of Puerto Rico's most productive fishermen. This restaurant, located a few steps from the town's wharves, usually gets the first pick of the day's catch. As such, diners come from throughout the region for ultra-fresh versions of red snapper, yellowtail, grouper, shrimp, and lobster. Lobster can be prepared 15 different ways, some of which might surprise you—there's a lobster pie made with sweet plantain, which looks something like lasagna with a Hispanic twist. The modern, unremarkable setting is merely a foil for very fresh fish.

3 Paradores of Western Puerto Rico

Two programs that have helped the Puerto Rico Tourism Company successfully promote the commonwealth as "The Complete Island"—the *paradores puertorriqueños* and the *mesones gastronómicos*—will help make your travels even more enjoyable.

The *paradores puertorriqueños* (see chapter 2 for more details about these government-sponsored inns) are a chain of privately owned and operated country inns under the auspices and supervision of the Commonwealth Development Company. These hostelries are easily identified by the Taíno grass hut that appears in the signs and logos of each one. The Puerto Rico Tourism Company started the program in 1973, modeling it after Spain's *parador* system, although many of the *paradores* here are mere shanties when compared to some of the deluxe Spanish hostelries. Each *parador* is situated in a historic or particularly beautiful spot. They vary in size, but most share the virtues of affordability, hospitable staffs, and high standards of cleanliness. Most but not all of their rooms are air-conditioned; however, each contains a private bathroom.

For reservations or further information, contact the **Paradores Puertorriqueños Reservation Office,** P.O. Box 4435, Old San Juan Station, San Juan, PR 00905 (☎ **800/443-0266** in the U.S., 787/721-2884 within San Juan, or 800/981-7575 outside of San Juan but within Puerto Rico).

Except for those in major hotels, you'll find few well-known restaurants as you tour the island. However, there are plenty of roadside places and simple taverns. For authentic island cuisine, you can rely on the *mesones gastronómicos* (gastronomic inns). This established dining "network," sanctioned by the Puerto Rico Tourism Company, highlights restaurants recognized for excellence in preparing and serving Puerto Rican specialties at modest prices.

Mesón gastronómico status is limited to restaurants outside the San Juan area that are close to major island attractions. Membership in the program requires that restaurants have attractive surroundings and comply with strict standards of service. Members must specialize in native foods, but if you order fresh fish, chances are you'll be pleased.

Regrettably, there are no maps listing these myriad restaurants, but they are easy to spot as you drive around the island.

JAYUYA

This village 30 miles southwest of San Juan and 12 miles north of Ponce lies in the middle of the Cordillera Central, a mountain massif. To get here, motorists follow Route 140 south through some of the most dramatic scenery in Puerto Rico. Then take 141 south all the way to Jayuya. This is the best overnight base for exploring this mountainous section of the island.

Jayuya is a small town that still retains strong Taíno cultural influences, particularly in the language. At the Jayuya Indian Festival on September 3 of every year, you'll see craft markets, parades, and displays of Taíno dances. The festival honors the patron saint of the town, Nuestra Señora la Monserrate.

Here you'll also find the Paradora Hacienda Gripinas, a former coffee plantation (see below), where you can glimpse the good old days in Puerto Rico. In 1950, Jayuya received worldwide attention when *independentistas* proclaimed the "Republic of Puerto Rico," and held the town under siege until the National Guard was called in.

WHERE TO STAY & DINE

Parador Hacienda Gripiñas. Rte. 527, km 2.5 (P.O. Box 387), Jayuya, PR 00664. ☎ **787/ 828-1717.** Fax 787/828-1718. 20 units. A/C TV. $125 double. Rates include 2 meals a day. AE, MC, V. From Jayuya, head east via Rte. 144; at the junction with Rte. 527, go south 1 1/2 miles.

A former coffee plantation about 2¹/₂ hours from San Juan, Hacienda Gripiñas is reached by a long, narrow, and curvy road. This home-turned-inn is a delightful blend of old-world hacienda and modern conveniences. The plantation ambience is everywhere—created by ceiling fans, splendid gardens, porch hammocks, and more than 20 acres of coffee-bearing bushes. You'll taste the homegrown product when you order the inn's aromatic brew.

The modest rooms vary in size, but all are kept as neat as a pin. For meals, stick to the restaurant's Puerto Rican dishes rather than going for the international cuisine. You can swim in the two chilly mountain pools (away from the main building), soak up the sun, or enjoy the nearby sights, such as the Taíno Indian Ceremonial Ball Park at Utuado. Boating and plenty of fishing are just 30 minutes away at Lake Caonillas. The parador is also near the Río Camuy Cave Park.

UTUADO

Another good base in the Cordillera Central massif is this little mountain town, which lies northwest of Jayuya (see above). Its location is 33 miles southwest of San Juan and 18 miles north of Ponce.

Utuado is a stronghold of *jibaro* or "hillbilly" culture, reflecting the mountain life of the island as few other settlements do.

This is the heartland of karst, an irregular limestone terrain with sinkholes, underground streams, and caverns. This unique landscape was created over several millennia by heavy rainfall.

Petroglyphs left over from the Taíno civilization have been found in the area. One depicted an Indian woman with frog legs and elaborate headdress. From Utuado, you can continue west for 20 miles on Route 111 to kilometer 12.3 to reach the Taíno Indian Ceremonial Center (see box).

WHERE TO STAY & DINE

Parador La Casa Grande. P.O. Box 616, Caonillas, Utuado, PR 00641. ☎ **888/343-2272** or 787/894-3939. Fax 787/894-3939. 20 units. $93 double. AE, MC, V. From Arecibo, take Rte. 10 south to Utuado; then head east on Rte. 111 to Rte. 140; head north on Rte. 140 to Rte. 612 for a quarter-mile.

This parador, situated on 107 acres of a former coffee plantation in the Caonillas Barrios district, about 2¹/₂ hours from San Juan, has been vastly improved since its takeover by Steven Weingarten and his wife, Marlene, a gourmet cook. Steven is still a practicing attorney in New York City, commuting to Puerto Rico on a regular basis. All the comfortably but simply furnished bedrooms have ceiling fans in lieu of air-conditioning, hardly needed during the cool nights here. Each room has a balcony, hammock, and mountain view. There is a swimming pool and nature trails carved out of the jungle.

Life After Death

The Taíno Indians who lived in Puerto Rico before Europeans came here were ruled by *Caciques,* or chiefs, who controlled their own villages and several others nearby. The Taínos believed in life after death, which led them to take extreme care in burying their dead. Personal belongings of the deceased were placed in the tomb with the newly dead, and bodies were carefully arranged in a squatting position. Near Ponce, visitors can see the oldest Indian burial ground uncovered in the Antilles (see chapter 8).

Even at the time of the arrival of Columbus and the conquistadores who followed, the Taínos were threatened by the warlike and cannibalistic Carib Indians coming up from the south. But though they feared the Caribs, they learned to fear the conquistadores even more. Within 50 years of the Spanish colonization, the Taíno culture had virtually disappeared, the Indians annihilated through either massacres or European diseases.

But Taíno blood and remnants of their culture live on. The Indians married with Spaniards and Africans, and their physical characteristics—straight hair, copper-colored skin, and prominent cheekbones—can still be seen in some Puerto Ricans today. Many Taíno words became part of the Spanish language that's spoken on the island even today. Hammocks, the weaving of baskets, and the use of gourds as eating receptacles are part of the heritage left by these ill-fated tribes.

Still standing near Utuado, a small mountain town, **Taíno Indian Ceremonial Center,** Route 111, km 12.3 (☎ 787/894-7325), was built by them for recreation and worship some 800 years ago. Stone monoliths, some etched with petroglyphs, rim several of the 10 *bateyes* (playing fields) used for a ceremonial game that some historians believe was a forerunner to soccer. The monoliths and petroglyphs, as well as the *dujos* (ceremonial chairs), are existing examples of the Taínos' skill in carving wood and stone.

Archaeologists have dated this site to approximately 2 centuries before Europe's discovery of the New World. It is believed that the Taíno chief Guarionex gathered his subjects on this site to celebrate rituals and practice sports. Set on a 13-acre field surrounded by trees, some 14 vertical monoliths with colorful petroglyphs are arranged around a central sacrificial stone monument. The ball complex also includes a museum, open daily from 9am to 4:30pm; admission is free.

There is also a gallery, Herencia Indigena, where you can purchase Taíno relics at very reasonable prices, including the sought-after *Cemis* (Taíno idols) and figures of the famous little frog, the coquí. The Taínos have long gone, and much that was here is gone with them. The site is of special interest to those with academic pursuits, but of only passing interest to the lay visitor.

Marlene presides over Jungle Jane's Restaurant, which serves an array of delectably prepared international and Puerto Rican dishes. Even if you're not a guest, you can feast here daily from 7:30am to 9:30pm. It might make an ideal luncheon stopover if you're touring in the area.

QUEBRADILLAS

Quebradillas is one of the sleepy municipalities of northwest Puerto Rico. With its flamboyantly painted houses, narrow streets, and spiritualist herb shops, it is like a town of long ago. Quebradillas lies 70 miles west of San Juan, only about a 15-mile trip from the city of Arecibo along Route 2.

The Atlantic waters along the northwest coast of Puerto Rico tend to be rough, with the rugged coastline seemingly plunging right into the ocean. Both snorkelers and scuba divers are drawn to a protected beach area known as "Shacks," close to the town of Isabela, northwest of Quebradillas. The reefs and coral caverns here are some of the most dramatic in Puerto Rico. Surfers also flock to Isabela's Jobos Beach. Neither beach, however, is ideal for swimming.

Also northwest of Quebradillas lies beautiful **Guajataca Balneario,** with its white sands, raging surf, and turbulent, deep waters. This is a fine beach for sunning and collecting shells, but it's a *playa peligrosa* (dangerous beach) unless you're a skilled swimmer. You can also visit **Lago de Guajataca,** another beauty spot, by heading south for 7 miles on Route 113. This man-made lake is a lovely place for hiking and the site of two *paradores* (see below). The staff at these government-sponsored inns will give you advice about jaunts in the **Guajataca Forest Reserve** to the immediate west.

WHERE TO STAY & DINE

Parador El Guajataca. Rte. 2, km 103.8 (P.O. Box 1558), Quebradillas, PR 00678. ☎ **800/ 964-3065** or 787/895-3070. Fax 787/895-3589. 38 units. A/C TV TEL. $76–$113 double. AE, DISC, MC, V. From Quebradillas, continue northwest on Rte. 2 for 1 mile (the parador is signposted).

You'll find this place on a rolling hillside reaching down to a surf-beaten beach along the north coast. Stay here for the stunning natural setting and don't expect too much, because the hotel itself is somewhat seedy. Each room is rather standard and has its own entrance and private balcony opening onto the turbulent Atlantic. Bathrooms are slightly battered but functional.

Served in a glassed-in dining room where all the windows face the sea, the cuisine isn't much more memorable than the accommodations, with little care going into the preparation of the often-canned ingredients. A local musical group plays for dining and dancing on Friday and Saturday evenings. The bar is open daily from 4 to 10pm (until 1 or 2am on Friday and Saturday). Room service is available from 7 to 8:30am. There are two swimming pools (one for adults, another for children), plus a playground for children.

Parador Vistamar. 6205 Rte. 113N (P.O. Box T-38), Quebradillas, PR 00678. ☎ **787/ 895-2065.** Fax 787/895-2294. 55 units. A/C TV TEL. $73.85–$96.30 double. Up to 2 children under 12 stay free in parents' room. AE, DC, MC, V. At Quebradillas, head northwest on Rte. 2, then go left at the junction with Rte. 113 and continue for a half-mile.

In the Guajataca area, this parador, one of the largest on Puerto Rico, sits like a sentinel surveying the scene from high atop a mountain overlooking greenery and a seascape. There are gardens and intricate paths carved into the side of the mountain where you can stroll while enjoying the fragrance of the tropical flowers. Or you may choose to search for the calcified fossils that abound on the carved mountainside. For a unique experience, visitors can try their hand at freshwater fishing just down the hill from the hotel. Flocks of rare tropical birds are frequently seen in the nearby mangroves.

Bedrooms are comfortably furnished in a rather bland motel style. Bathrooms are functional, but without much decorative zest. There's a dining room with an ocean view, where you can have a typical Puerto Rican dinner or choose from the international menu.

A short drive from the hotel will bring you to the Punta Borinquén Golf Course. Tennis courts are just down the hill from the inn itself. Sightseeing trips to the nearby Arecibo Observatory—the largest radar/radio-telescope in the world—and to

Monte Calvario (a replica of Mount Calvary) are available. Another popular visit is to the plaza in the town of Quebradillas.

COAMO

Legend has it that the hot springs in this town, located inland on the south coast about a 2-hour drive from San Juan, were the Fountain of Youth sought by Ponce de León. It is believed that the Taíno peoples, during pre-Columbian times, held rituals and pilgrimages here as they sought health and well-being. For more than a century between 1847 and 1958, the site was a center for rest and relaxation for Puerto Ricans and others, some on their honeymoon, others in search of the curative powers of the geothermal springs, which lie about a 5-minute walk from **Parador Baños de Coamo.** Nonresidents can come here to use the baths, but the experience is hardly special today. The baths are in poor condition.

South of Coamo you can get on the expressway (no. 52) and head east for a 40-minute drive to **Guayama,** a green and beautiful small town with steepled churches and the Casa Cautiño Museum, on the main plaza of town (☎ 787/864-0600). It is open Tuesday through Sunday from 10am to 4pm. Admission is $1 for adults and 50¢ for seniors, students, and children 7 to 12 (free for 6 and under). This museum is in a turn-of-the-century mansion that once was occupied by the Cañuelo family. It contains all of their original belongings and is a showplace for fine turn-of-the-20th-century furnishings and pictures of the prize horses for which Guayama is famous. Just minutes from town is Arroyo Beach, a tranquil place to spend an afternoon, but lacking facilities.

WHERE TO STAY & DINE

Parador Baños de Coamo. P.O. Box 540, Coamo, PR 00769. ☎ **787/825-2186.** Fax 787/825-4739. 48 units. A/C TV TEL. $81 double. AE, DC, DISC, MC, V. From Rte. 1, turn onto Rte. 153 at Santa Isabel; then turn left onto Rte. 546 and drive west 1 mile.

The spa at Baños de Coamo features this parador offering hospitality in traditional Puerto Rican style. The Baños has welcomed many notable visitors over the years, including Franklin D. Roosevelt, Frank Lloyd Wright, Alexander Graham Bell, and Thomas Edison, who came here to swim in the on-site hot springs, said to be the most radioactive in the world. (Locals sometimes purchase a day pass and use the pool, which leads to noise, confusion, and overcrowding on weekends.)

The buildings range from a lattice-adorned two-story motel unit with wooden verandas to a Spanish colonial pink stucco building, which houses the restaurant. The bedrooms draw a mixed reaction from visitors, so ask to see your prospective room before deciding to stay here. Many of the often-dark rooms are not well maintained, and the bathrooms seem more appropriate for a campsite. Mildew is also evident. The cuisine here is both Créole and international, and the coffee Baños style is a special treat.

Swimming is limited to an angular pool, but you can easily drive to a nearby public beach. The staff can arrange for you to ride the island's unique breed of show horse called *paso fino*.

The northeast corner of the island, only 45 minutes or so from San Juan, contains the island's major attractions, El Yunque Rain Forest and Luqillo Beach (see chapter 7), as well as a variety of landscapes ranging from miles of forest to palm groves and beachside settlements. Here you will find two of the best resorts on the island, El Conquistador and Palmas del Mar. This is also the site of Fajardo, a preeminent sailor's haven, where you can catch ferries to the offshore islands of Vieques and Culebra (see chapter 11).

Driving Tour of Eastern Puerto Rico

If you are not staying at either Palmas del Mar or El Conquistador, consider a 2-hour driving tour of the region. Seasonal changes transform the landscape here. In November the sugarcane fields burst into bloom, and in January and February red and orange blossoms cover the flowering trees along the roads. Springtime brings delicate pink flowers to the Puerto Rican oak and deep red blossoms to the African tulip tree. Summer is a flamboyant time when the roadsides seem to be on fire with blooming flowers.

From San Juan, take Route 26 southeast for 7 miles to the junction with Route 3, which you follow east for another 25 miles to Fajardo. Make a left onto Route 194, heading toward the eastern shore. At the traffic light at the corner of the Monte Brisas Shopping Center, turn left; stay on this road until the next traffic light, turn right, and continue to the intersection with Route 987. Turn left onto Route 987 and continue north until you reach the entrance to **Cabezas de San Juan Nature Reserve,** better known as *El Faro,* or "The Lighthouse" (see box in this chapter)

After visiting the reserve, you can take the same road back, heading south to Route 3. Then follow the highway signs south to **Fajardo,** a fishing port that was hotly contested during the Spanish-American War. Puerto Ricans are fond of giving nicknames to people and places—for many years, the residents of Fajardo have been called *cariduros* ("the hard-faced ones"). Don't let the label mislead you; local residents are very friendly. Sailors and fishermen are attracted to the shores of Fajardo and nearby **Las Croabas,** which has several seafood restaurants. If you have time, you can take a very satisfying trip by

To the Lighthouse: Exploring Las Cabezas de San Juan Nature Reserve

Better known as *El Faro* or "The Lighthouse," this preserve in the northeastern corner of the island, north of Fajardo off Route 987, is one of the most beautiful and important areas on Puerto Rico. Here you'll find seven ecological systems and a restored 19th-century Spanish colonial lighthouse. From the lighthouse observation deck, majestic views extend to islands as far off as St. Thomas in the U.S. Virgin Islands.

Surrounded on three sides by the Atlantic Ocean, the 316-acre site encompasses forestland, mangroves, lagoons, beaches, cliffs, offshore cays, and coral reefs. Boardwalk trails wind through the fascinating topography. Ospreys, sea turtles, and an occasional manatee are seen from the windswept promontories and rocky beach. Under the tutelage of Las Cabezas' guides, every visitor becomes a naturalist for a few absorbing hours.

The nature reserve is open Wednesday through Sunday; reservations are required, so call before going. For reservations throughout the week, call ☎ 787/722-5882; for reservations on Saturday and Sunday, ☎ 787/860-2560 (reservations on weekends can be made only on the day of your intended visit). Admission is $5 for adults, $2 for children 11 and under, and $2.50 for seniors. Guided 2¹/₂-hour tours are conducted at 9:30am, 10am, 10:30am, and 2pm (in English at 2pm).

---

ferry from Fajardo to either Vieques or Culebra, small islands off the Puerto Rican coast that make urban troubles seem far, far away (see chapter 11).

Continue south on Route 3, following the Caribbean coastline. At Cayo Lobos, just off the Fajardo port, the Atlantic meets the Caribbean. Here, the vivid colors of the Caribbean seem subdued compared to those of the deep blue ocean.

Go through the town of Ceiba, near the Roosevelt Navy Base, until you reach **Naguabo Beach,** a 30-minute drive from Fajardo. Here you can have coffee and *pastelillos de chapin,* pastry turnovers that were actually used as tax payments during Spanish colonial days. At kilometer 70.9 of Route 3, take a brief detour to the town of Naguabo, but only if you wish to enjoy the town plaza's scented, shady laurel trees, imported from India. There isn't much else to see.

Continue south along Route 3, going through **Humacao** and its sugarcane fields. When the cane blooms during November and December, the tops of the fields change colors according to the time of day. Humacao itself isn't of much interest, but it has a *balneario*-equipped beach with changing facilities, lockers, and showers. From here you can detour to **Palmas del Mar,** the sprawling resort covered in this chapter. You can stop here or continue along Route 3 through Yabucoa, nestled amid some hills. The view along the road opens up at Cerro La Pandura, a mountain from which there's a panoramic outlook over giant boulders onto the Caribbean.

Directly to the west of Yabucoa, you can connect to Route 182, heading west through some of the most dramatic scenery in Puerto Rico along the mountain chain of Cuchilla de Pandura. This road changes its number unexpectedly to Route 181 (but it's still the same road). After a sharp bend, it becomes Route 7740 (again the same road), and before it reaches the mountain station of Cerro La Santa, it becomes Route 184. Stay on Route 184, heading northwest and following the signs to Route 52, the major highway cutting across the heart of Puerto Rico. If you continue southwest on

Eastern Puerto Rico

Key to map (image):
- Cabezas de San Juan Nature Reserve 7
- El Yunque 1
- Fajardo 5
- Humacao 2
- Las Croabas 6
- Luquillo Beach 8
- Naguabo 4
- Palmas del Mar 3

Route 52, you'll come to Ponce (see chapter 8). But if you want to return to San Juan, head northeast, following the signs back into the heart of Puerto Rico's capital.

1 Las Croabas

35 miles E of San Juan

Las Croabas, near Fajardo, is the site of the famous El Conquistador resort. Overlooking both the Caribbean Sea and the Atlantic Ocean from atop a 300-foot cliff at the northeastern tip of Puerto Rico, El Conquistador was the acknowledged leader in luxury resorts in the Caribbean from the 1960s through the late 1970s. Celebrities Elaine May, Jack Gilford, Celeste Holm (with her husband and two poodles), Elaine Stritch (and her dog), Amy Vanderbilt, Jack Palance, Burt Bacharach, Angie Dickinson, Omar Shariff, Marc Connelly, Maureen O'Sullivan, and Xavier Cugat attended its grand inaugural in 1968. Later, its circular casino, in black and stainless steel, appeared in the last scene of the James Bond movie *Goldfinger*. The original hotel closed in 1980, however, but was reborn in 1993 as the distinctive, $250 million El Conquistador we have today. Former President George Bush was among its first guests.

ESSENTIALS

GETTING THERE   El Conquistador staff members greet all guests personally at the San Juan airport and transport them to the resort. Guests at the resort can take a taxi or a hotel courtesy car, or drive their rental car to Luquillo Beach.

If you're driving from San Juan, head east on Route 3 toward Fajardo. At the intersection, cut northeast on Route 195 and continue to the intersection with Route 987, at which point you turn north.

OUTDOOR ACTIVITIES

In addition to the lovely beach and the many recreational facilities that are part of El Conquistador itself (see the review below), there are other notable places to play in the vicinity. Don't forget that not far from Las Croabas is ✪ **Luquillo Beach,** one of the island's best and most popular public stretches of sand (see Chapter 7).

BOATING, SAILING & SNORKELING

For a cruise, your best bet in Las Croabas is **Erin Go Bragh Charters** (☎ 787/ 860-4410), where they still fondly remember the visit of their famous guest, Ricky Martin. This is a 50-foot Gulstar ketch operated by Captain Bill Henry. He is licensed to carry six passengers. The boat is available for day charters, sunset and evening cruises, and has equipment for water sports, including a windsurfer and masks and fins. A full-day tour costs $75 per person, including a barbeque lunch.

For scuba divers, the best deal is offered by **Palomino Diver,** (☎ 787/863-1000, ext. 7917), at the Puerto del Rey marina, the lowest level of El Conquistador. This is a PADI outfit. You can go for ocean dives on the outfitter's boats, a one-tank dive costing $69 or a two-tank dive for $99, including tanks and weight belt. A PADI snorkel program at $45 per person is also available.

Nearby in Fajardo, the Caribbean's largest and most modern marina, **Puerto del Rey** (☎ 787/860-1000), has facilities for 70 boats, including docking and fueling for yachts up to 200 feet in length, and haul-out and repair for yachts up to 90 feet. The marina has boat rentals, yacht charters, and water sports, in addition to several shops and a French restaurant.

WHERE TO STAY

✪ **Wyndham El Conquistador Resort & Country Club.** 1000 Conquistador Ave., Las Croabas (P.O. Box 70001, Fajardo), PR 00738. ☎ **800/468-5228** in the U.S. or 787/ 863-1000. Fax 787/863-6500. www.wyndham.com. 915 units. A/C MINIBAR TV TEL. Winter $395–$595 double; $1,375–$1,925 suite for 1–4 people; $775–$1,575 casita, with kitchen, for 1–6 people. Off-season $245–$295 double; $1,125–$1,570 suite for 1–4 people; $575–$1,075 casita, with kitchen, for 1–6 people. Additional bed for 3rd or 4th occupant $40 extra. MAP (breakfast and dinner) $82 extra per adult per day, $42 extra per child 12 and under. Children 15 and under stay free in parents' room. AE, DC, DISC, MC, V. Parking $10 per day.

One of the most impressive resorts anywhere in the tropics, El Conquistador is a destination unto itself, with an incredible array of facilities. Rebuilt in 1993 at a cost of $250 million, it encompasses 500 acres of forested hills sloping down to the sea. Accommodations are divided into five separate sections, which all have Mediterranean architecture and lush landscaping. Most of them lie several hundred feet above the sea, within two sections (Las Brisas and La Vista) of the bulky main building. At the same altitude, a bit off to the side, is a replica of an Andalusian hamlet, Las Casitas Village, which seems straight out of the south of Spain; these plush, pricey units, each with full kitchen, are a self-contained enclave. If money is no object, join the likes of John Travolta and Janet Jackson, who have checked into the casitas to enjoy peace and pampering. A short walk downhill is a circular cluster of tastefully modern accommodations, Las Olas Village. And at sea level, adjacent to an armada of pleasure craft bobbing at anchor, is La Marina Village, whose balconies seem to hang directly over the water. All accommodations are outfitted with comfortable and stylish furniture, excellent mattresses, bathrobes, ironing boards, coffeemakers, hair dryers, and thick towels. All the far-flung elements of the resort are connected by serpentine, landscaped walkways, and by a railroad-style funicular that makes frequent trips up and down the hillside.

Dining/Diversions: The resort contains 16 different restaurants and lounges, one of which is a tropical deli; some of the others are highlighted in "Where to Dine," below. There's also a casino, a piano bar, and bars. Drake's Cigar Bar is outfitted with books, mahogany, and a billiards table. Amigos Bar and Lounge offers flamenco reviews twice a week in summer, and nightly in winter.

Amenities: One of the most upscale and comprehensive spas in the world, the Golden Door, maintains a branch—one of only three in the world—within this resort. The hotel is sole owner of a "fantasy island" (Palomino Island), with caverns, nature trails, horseback riding, and water sports such as scuba diving, windsurfing, and snorkeling. Located about half a mile offshore, the island is connected by free, private ferries that travel to the main hotel at frequent intervals. There's also a 25-slip marina, where some of the boats are for rent; six pools; many whirlpool tubs; a fitness center; and state-of-the-art conference facilities. Seven tennis courts are lit for night play, and there's an 18-hole championship golf course designed by Arthur Hills with unbelievable views; greens fees are $95 to $155 per person. Arcade of about 20 retail shops, room service (from 7am to 11:30pm), baby-sitting, men's and women's beauty salon, laundry/dry cleaning, massage, spa services, special activities area and games room for kids. Camp Coquí for children 3 to 12 ($38 per day; from 9am to 3:30pm) provides fishing, sailing, arts and crafts, nature walks, or treasure hunts.

WHERE TO DINE
VERY EXPENSIVE

✪ **Cassava.** In Wyndham El Conquistador Resort. ☎ **787/863-1000.** Reservations recommended. Main courses $28–$35. AE, DISC, MC, V. Daily 6–10pm. PUERTO RICAN/ CARIBBEAN.

This is the most experimental and unusual restaurant at the El Conquistador Resort. You'll find it within earshot of the casino, in a location adjacent to the resort's lobby. The interior sports a colorful setting in which pinks, greens, and yellows explode in your eyes, as do the flavors on your palate. Appetizers get off to a dazzling start with fried curried calamari in lemongrass vinaigrette or steamed garlic clams flavored with cilantro lemon sauce. The tuna carpaccio is served on seaweed salad with *tamarindo* sauce (a legume with a sweet-and-sour flavor). The main courses also have some culinary pyrotechnics, as exemplified by the seafood *mofongo,* a medley of lobster, shrimp, octopus, and scallops, one of the most Puerto Rican–inspired dishes on the menu. Live Maine lobsters are flown in, or you might opt for a seared sea bass with grilled vegetables. Desserts, which change frequently, all taste homemade and are most satisfying if you have any room left.

✪ **Isabela's Grill.** In Wyndham El Conquistador Resort. ☎ **787/863-1000.** Reservations recommended. Main courses $32–$45. AE, DISC, MC, V. Mon–Sat 6–10pm, Sun 11:30am–3pm and 6pm–midnight. SPANISH/INTERNATIONAL.

Of all the restaurants in El Conquistador Resort, this is the most inspired by stateside tastes. The severely dignified baroque room may have the air of a Spanish monastery, but if Jack Benny, Jackie Gleason, or even President Eisenhower were to miraculously return, they would feel right at home with this 1950s menu. The service is impeccable, and the steaks are tender, the seafood fresh.

Portal of Luxury

Perched atop a stunning 300-foot bluff overlooking both the Caribbean Sea and the Atlantic Ocean, the **Golden Door,** in Las Casitas Village complex at the El Conquistador Hotel (☎ 787/863-1000), was established in 1999. This is the most sophisticated, well-managed, and comprehensive spa in the Caribbean, and one of the finest in the world. One of only three branches of a spa founded in Escondido, California, and today administered by the Wyndham group, it's devoted to the relaxation and healing of body, soul, and mind. Spa rituals are taken seriously; New Age mysticism is gracefully dispensed within a postmodern setting that's a cross between a Swiss clinic, a state-of-the-art health club, and a Buddhist monastery.

Designed with an artful simplicity, which cost a huge amount of money to build, it concentrates beauty treatments (hair, manicures, etc.) and boutiques on the ground floor, weight-training and aerobics facilities on the second floor, and massage and relaxation therapies on the third. Fifty-minute treatments on the third floor begin at $99 each. These innovative therapies include massage for pregnant women, massage for feet, massage with warm oil rubbed onto the "third eye" in the middle of your forehead, and full-body massage that stimulates an all-inclusive glow that quickly grows addictive.

One especially appealing treatment involves massaging the body with smooth lava rocks, heated to above-body temperatures, as a means of dissipating both tension and pain. If you just want to come and exercise, for a fee of $15 per day, the equipment here is the most sophisticated in the world, and administered by a staff who knows every detail about how a client should use it. The spa is open daily from 6:30am to 8:30pm. American Express, Diners Club, MasterCard, and Visa are all accepted.

Appetizers range from black-bean soup to Cajun crab cakes. Special care is taken with the beef dishes, even though the meat has to be imported frozen. Treats range from an extra-thick cut of veal chop to a prime rack of lamb. Prime rib of beef is a feature, as are New York strip and porterhouse. You might opt for the seafood, everything from grilled fillet of salmon in pink peppercorn sauce to grilled tuna flavored with ginger and tomato salsa. (While here, make sure to check out the massive gates—the most spectacular pieces of wrought iron on Puerto Rico.)

EXPENSIVE

Blossoms. In Wyndham El Conquistador Resort. ☎ **787/863-1000.** Reservations recommended. Main courses $17.50–$39.50. AE, CB, DC, MC, V. Daily 6–11:30pm; CHINESE/JAPANESE.

This restaurant on the Mirador level features three culinary styles, including a sushi bar, and boasts some of the freshest seafood in eastern Puerto Rico. Sizzling delights are prepared on teppanyaki tables, and there's a zesty selection of Hunan and Szechuan specialties. On the teppanyaki menu, you can choose dishes ranging from chicken to shrimp, from filet mignon to lobster. Sushi bar selections range from eel to squid, from salmon roe to giant clams.

Otello's. In Wyndham El Conquistador Resort. ☎ **787/863-1000.** Reservations required in winter, recommended off-season. Main courses $19.95–$36.95. AE, DISC, MC, V. Daily 6pm–midnight. NORTHERN ITALIAN.

Here you can dine by candlelight in the old-world tradition, with a choice of both indoor and outdoor seating. The decor is neo-Palladian. You might begin with one of the soups, perhaps pasta fagioli, or select one of the zesty Italian appetizers, such as clams Posillipo. Pastas can be ordered as a half-portion appetizer or as a main dish, and they include the likes of homemade gnocchi or fettuccine with shrimp. The chef is known for veal dishes. A selection of poultry and vegetarian food is offered nightly, along with several shrimp and fish dishes. When we last dined here, the salmon fillet in champagne sauce had beautiful accents, as did the veal chop in an aromatic herb sauce.

2 Palmas del Mar

46 miles SE of San Juan

A 60-minute drive east of San Juan, this residential resort community lies on the island's southeastern shore near Humacao. Here you'll find one of the most action-packed sports programs in the Caribbean, offering golf, tennis, scuba diving, sailing, deep-sea fishing, and horseback riding.

Palmas del Mar's location is one of its greatest assets. The pleasing Caribbean trade winds steadily blow across this section of the island, stabilizing the weather and making Palmas del Mar ideal for many outdoor sports.

The resort is no longer what it was in its heyday in the early '90s. Today it is a real estate conglomerate, promoting vacation properties to investors, although outsiders can stay here. Many of the occupants are residents of San Juan who come here on weekends.

GETTING THERE

No airline has regularly scheduled flights to **Humacao Regional Airport,** 3 miles north of Palmas del Mar. The resort (☎ **787/852-6000**) will arrange minivan or bus transport from Luis Muñoz Marín International Airport in San Juan to Humacao. The fare is $25 each way.

If you're driving from downtown San Juan, take Highway 52 south to Caguas, then take Highway 30 east to Humacao (trip time: 1 hr.). Follow the signs from there to Palmas del Mar.

BEACHES & OUTDOOR ACTIVITIES

Doral Palmas del Mar Resort offers a variety of choices to keep active vacationers in shape (many are also open to the public with prior reservation). Following are details on some of the most popular, along with a few other offerings in the area that are not connected with the resort complex.

BEACHES

The resort has 3 exceptional miles of white-sand beaches (all open to the public). Nonguests will pay a $1 charge for parking and 25¢ for a changing room and a locker. The waters here are calm year-round, and there's a water-sports center and marina (see "Scuba Diving & Snorkeling," below).

FISHING

Some of the best year-round fishing in the Caribbean is found in the waters just off Palmas del Mar. **Capt. Bill Burleson,** based in Humacao (☎ **787/850-7442**), operates charters on his fully customized, 46-foot sport-fisherman, *Karolette,* which is electronically equipped for successful fishing. Burleson prefers to take fishing groups to Grappler Banks, 18 nautical miles away. The banks are two seamounts, rising to about 240 feet below the surface and surrounded by depths of 6,000 to 8,000 feet. They lie in the migratory paths of the wahoo, tuna, and marlin. A maximum of six people are taken out, costing $500 for 4 hours, $675 for 6 hours, and $900 for 9 hours. He also offers snorkeling expeditions to Vieques Island at $85 per person for up to 5 hours. Other snorkeling locations include half- and full-day trips.

GOLF

Few other real-estate developments in the Caribbean devote as much attention and publicity to their golf facilities as the ✪ **Palmas del Mar Golf Club** (☎ 787/ 285-2256. Today, both the older course, the Gary Player–designed Palm Course, and the newer course, the Reese Jones–designed Flamboyant, have pars of 72 and layouts of around 6,800 feet each. Crack golfers consider holes 11 to 15 of the older course among the toughest five successive holes in the Caribbean. The pro shop that services players on both courses is open daily from 7am to 5pm. The Flamboyant course costs $170 for 18 holes; the Palm Course, $155 for 18 holes.

HIKING

Hiking on the resort's grounds is another favorite activity here, for Palmas del Mar's land is an attraction in its own right. Here you'll find more than 6 miles of Caribbean ocean frontage—3$^1/_2$ miles of sandy beach amid rocky cliffs and promontories. Large tracts of the 2,700-acre property have harbored sugar and coconut plantations over the years, and a wet, tropical forest preserve with giant ferns, orchids, and hanging vines covers about 70 acres near the resort's geographic center.

SCUBA DIVING & SNORKELING

Coral Head Divers & Water Sports Center, P.O. Box 10246, Humacao, PR 00792 (☎ 800/635-4529 or 787/850-7208), operates out of a building on the harbor at the Doral Palmas del Mar Resort. The dive center owns two fully equipped boats, measuring 26 and 48 feet. The center offers daily two-tank open-water dives for certified divers, plus snorkeling trips to Monkey Island and Vieques. The two-tank dive includes tanks, weights, and computer for $80. A snorkeling trip to Monkey Island includes use of equipment and a beverage for $45 per person; a scuba resort lesson costs $45.

TENNIS

The ✪ **Tennis Center** at Palmas del Mar (☎ 787/852-6000, ext. 51), the largest on Puerto Rico, features 15 hard courts and 5 clay courts open to hotel residents and non-residents. Court fees are $18 per hour during the day and $22 at night. Special tennis packages, including accommodations, are available. Call for more information. The resort contains a **fitness center,** located within the resort's tennis compound, which has the best-equipped gym in the region, open daily from 7am to 9pm. The center is free for guests of the resort.

WHERE TO STAY

The Hotel. 170 Candalero Dr., Palmas del Mar, Humacao, PR 00791. ☎ **800/725-6273** in the U.S. or 787/852-6000. Fax 787/852-6320. www.palmasdelmar.com. 102 units. A/C TV TEL. Winter $230–$263 double. Off-season $166–$191 double. MAP (breakfast and dinner) $45 per person extra. AE, DC, MC, V.

Although the acreage within the Palmas del Mar development contains thousands of privately owned villas, many of which can be rented or purchased, this is the only conventional, full-service hotel. At least some of its business derives from newcomers who want to experience the resort firsthand before taking the plunge into total immersion—actually buying one of the villas. It was extensively renovated in 1997, and again in 1999 under the directives of the Wyndham group. None of the well-furnished bedrooms overlooks the sea, but many have private patios or verandas, and most are roomier than you might expect. Rooms have tile floors, tropical furnishings, large closets, fine linens, and either king- or queen-size beds with good mattresses. The beach, tennis center, and golf courses are close at hand, and the staff will help you enjoy the many diversions available within the Palmas del Mar compound. Here also is a highly visible cadre of salespeople showing off the charms of the development, which is moving more into the role of full-time residential community, with less emphasis on temporary hotel guests. The Toco Coco, one of the many dining options available at Palmas del Mar, is within the hotel.

The Villas at Palmas. 170 Candelero Dr., Palmas del Mar, Humacao, PR 00792. ☎ 800/725-6273 in the U.S. or 787/852-6000. Fax 787/852-6320. 135 town house–style suites. A/C TV TEL. Winter $331–$495 1-bedroom suite; $482–$650 2-bedroom suite; $620–$817 3-bedroom suite. Off-season $221–$297 1-bedroom suite; $321–$390 2-bedroom suite; $413–$490 3-bedroom suite. MAP $34.50 extra per person year-round. Minimum bookings ranging from 3 to 7 nights required during some peak seasons, depending on the accommodation.

Set almost adjacent to The Hotel, this complex of red-roofed, white-walled town houses is a good choice for a family vacation. Divided into five separate clusters and carefully landscaped with tropical plants, each unit is furnished and decorated according to the taste of its individual owner. Each contains a working kitchen, a sense of privacy, and views of either the ocean or the gardens. Rental fees depend on the unit's proximity to the beachfront or golf course; an additional handful of villas built against a steep hillside overlook the resort's 20 tennis courts.

WHERE TO DINE

Thanks to the kitchens that come built into virtually every unit here, many guests opt to prepare at least some of their meals "at home." This is made relatively feasible thanks to the on-site general store at the Palmanova Plaza, selling everything from fresh lettuce and sundries to liquor and cigarettes. In addition to the romantic (or at least cheap) meal you prepare yourself, you'll have several other dining options within the Palmas del Mar complex.

Blue Hawaiian. In the Palmanova Shopping Center, Palmas del Mar. ☎ 787/852-0897. Reservations recommended. Main courses $13.95–$29.95. AE, MC, V. Daily noon–11pm. CHINESE.

This is the best Chinese restaurant in the region, a venue that's often selected by groups of friends from the surrounding villas of Palmas del Mar. The venue combines Polynesian themes (similar to that of a toned-down Trader Vic's) with an Americanized version of Chinese food that's flavorful and well suited to Puerto Rico's hot, steamy climate. Menu items include lobster with garlic-flavored cheese sauce; blackened salmon or blacked steaks reminiscent of styles in New Orleans; and a superb house version of honey chicken. You'll find the place within the dignified courtyard of the resort's shopping center, with tables for alfresco dining. Your host is Tommy Lo, former chef aboard the now-defunct ocean liner, SS *United States*.

Chez Daniel/Le Grill. Marina de Palmas del Mar. ☎ 787/852-6000. Reservations required. Main courses $22–$35. AE, MC, V. Fri–Sun noon–3pm; daily 6:30–10pm. Closed June and Tues Apr–Dec. FRENCH.

It's French, it's nautical, it's fun, and it's the preferred venue for occupants of the yachts moored at the adjacent pier. Normandy-born Daniel Vasse and his French Catalonian wife, Lucette, maintain twin dining rooms that in their way are the most appealing at Palmas del Mar. Le Grill is a steak house with a Gallic twist and lots of savory flavor in the form of béarnaise, garlic, peppercorn sauce, or whatever else you specify. Chez Daniel shows a more faithful allegiance to the tenets of classical French cuisine, placing an emphasis on such dishes as bouillabaisse (both the Catalonian and Marseillaise versions), onion soup, and snails, as well as lobster and chicken dishes. For dessert, consider a soufflé au Cointreau.

Toco Cocos. In The Hotel. ☎ **787/852-6000,** ext 50. Reservations required for 6 or more. Main courses $16–$40. AE, DISC, MC, V. Daily 6:30–11am, noon–2:30pm, and 6–10:30pm. INTERNATIONAL.

Cooled by trade winds, this restaurant overlooking a courtyard and pool is an ideal choice for any casual meal. The lunch menu always includes sandwiches and burgers; if you want heartier fare, ask for the Puerto Rican specialty of the day, perhaps red snapper in garlic butter, preceded by black-bean soup. Dinner is more elaborate— begin with stuffed jalapeño or chicken tacos, followed by Caribbean lobster, New York sirloin, paella, or the catch of the day. The cooking, although of a high standard, is never quite gourmet—it's just good, hearty food. Every night in winter has a theme, ranging from Italian on Monday to Puerto Rican on Saturday.

PALMAS DEL MAR AFTER DARK

The **casino** in the Palmas del Mar complex (☎ **787/852-6000,** ext. 10142) is close to the reception area. It has 12 blackjack tables, 2 roulette wheels, a craps table, and dozens of slot   machines. The casino is open daily year-round, Sunday through Thursday from 6pm to 2am, Friday and Saturday from 6pm to 3am. Under Puerto Rican law, drinks cannot be served in a casino.

Vieques & Culebra 11

They still may be virtually unknown to many visitors, but the off-shore islands of Vieques and Culebra are where Puerto Ricans go for their own vacations. Sandy beaches and low prices are the powerful attractions of both islands. Culebra still slumbers in the early 1950s, but Vieques is fast becoming one of the hottest tropical destinations in the Caribbean. The unspoiled beaches and stylish inns have created quite a buzz. When you spot Sandra Bernhard on the beach, you know that the times are a changin'.

Vieques, with more tourist facilities than Culebra, lies 7 miles off the eastern coast of Puerto Rico. It is visited today mainly for its 40-odd white-sand beaches. The island had been occupied at various times by both the French and the British before Puerto Rico acquired it in 1854. The ruins of many sugar and pineapple plantations testify to its once-flourishing agricultural economy.

The U.S. military took control of two-thirds of the island's 26,000 acres in 1941 and still uses the area for military training with live-fire maneuvers. However, the fact that the island is a military base should not deter a visit. It is unlikely that you'll hear planes flying low over-head, and it's very rare to hear any test bombs exploding, as you might have a few years ago. You probably won't be aware of any military equipment and personnel when you visit.

Culebra, 18 miles east of the Puerto Rican "mainland" and 14 miles west of St. Thomas in the U.S. Virgin Islands, is surrounded by coral reefs and edged with nearly deserted, powdery white-sand beaches. Much of the island has been designated a wildlife refuge by the U.S. Fish and Wildlife Service.

1 Vieques

41 miles E of San Juan, 7 miles SE of Fajardo

About 7 miles east of the big island of Puerto Rico lies Vieques (Bee-ay-kase), an island about twice as large as New York's Manhattan with about 8,000 inhabitants and some 40 palm-lined white-sand beaches.

Although Vieques remains a bit primitive—you can still hear wild horses galloping in the middle of the night—change is on the way with the opening of some of the most sophisticated inns in the Caribbean. The kind of trendsetters who discovered St. Barts and Anguilla years ago are now showing up here. Can visits by Tom Cruise, Madonna, and Ricky Martin be far away?

Since World War II, about two-thirds of the 21-mile-long island has been controlled by the U.S. military forces. Much of the government-owned land is now leased for cattle grazing, and when there are no military maneuvers, the public can visit the beaches, although you might be asked to produce some form of photo ID. Freedom to use the land has not, however, totally defused local discontent at the presence of Navy and Marine Corps personnel. In fact, the military has come under increased attack by Vieques's residents and top-ranking members of the Puerto Rican government. Some claim that the Navy's presence is strangling economic development; others cite potential dangers such as accidental deaths. Navy officials are adamant about wanting to stay on Vieques, but the Navy's role here is under consideration by Washington. As of this writing, the Naval presence remains in doubt.

Unlike the military, the Spanish conquistadores didn't think much of Vieques. They came here in the 16th century but didn't stay long, reporting that the island and neighboring bits of land held no gold and were, therefore, *las islas inutiles* (the useless islands). The name Vieques comes from a native Amerindian word for "small island," *bieques.*

The Spaniards later changed their minds and founded the main town, **Isabel Segunda,** on the northern shore. Construction on the last Spanish fort built in the New World began here around 1843 during the reign of Queen Isabella II, for whom the town was named. The fort, never completed, is not of any special interest. Now the island's fishermen and farmers conduct much of their business here. The **Punta Mula lighthouse,** north of Isabel Segunda, provides panoramic views of the land and sea.

On the south coast, **Esperanza,** once a center for the island's sugarcane industry and now a pretty little fishing village, lies near **Sun Bay (Sombe) public beach.** Sun Bay, a government-run, panoramic crescent of sand, is the beach to visit if you have only 1 day to spend on the island. The fenced area has picnic tables, a bathhouse, and a parking lot. A recently built resort, marina, and other facilities add to the allure of the many scalloped stretches of sandy waterfront.

ESSENTIALS

GETTING THERE   Flights to Vieques leave from Isla Grand Airport near the heart of San Juan—not to be confused with the main Luis Muñoz Marín International Airport near Isla Verde. **Vieques Air Link (☎ 787/253-3644)** operates four daily flights from San Juan. **Isla Nena (☎ 787/741-1577)** also flies to Vieques from San Juan three times daily. Both charge $63 one-way.

The Puerto Rico Port Authority operates two **ferryboats** a day to Vieques from the eastern port of Fajardo; the trip takes about an hour. The round-trip fare is $4 for adults and $2 for children. Tickets for the morning ferry, leaving Saturday and Sunday, sell out quickly, so passengers should be in line at the ticket window in Fajardo before 8am to be certain of a seat on the 9:30am boat. Otherwise, they'll have to wait until the 3pm ferry. For more information about these sea links, call ☎ 787/723-2260. For reservations, call ☎ 787/863-0705 or 787/863-0852.

GETTING AROUND   Public cabs or vans called *públicos* transport people around the island. We recommend that you rent a car for at least some of the time, just for the purposes of seeing the layout. To do this, contact **Island Car Rental (☎ 787/741-1666),** in the hamlet of Florida, about a 12-minute ride southwest of Isabel Segunda, or 5 minutes from the airport. The office is next door to the Crow's Nest Guest House. The cost of the local vehicles begins at $55 per day, plus another $10 for collision damage-waiver insurance. American Express, MasterCard, and Visa cards are accepted.

Vieques & Culebra

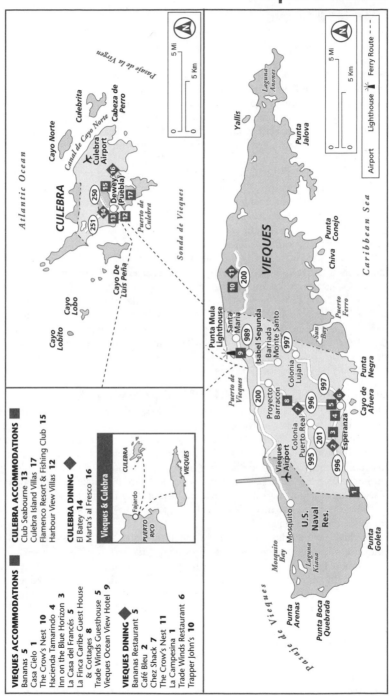

VIEQUES ACCOMMODATIONS ■
Bananas **5**
Casa Cielo **1**
The Crow's Nest **10**
Hacienda Tamarindo **4**
Inn on the Blue Horizon **3**
La Casa del Francés **5**
La Finca Caribe Guest House
  & Cottages **8**
Trade Winds Guesthouse **5**
Vieques Ocean View Hotel **9**

VIEQUES DINING ◆
Bananas Restaurant **5**
Café Bleu **2**
Chez Shack **7**
The Crow's Nest **11**
La Campesina **1**
Trade Winds Restaurant **6**
Trapper John's **10**

CULEBRA ACCOMMODATIONS ■
Club Seabourne **13**
Culebra Island Villas **17**
Flamenco Resort & Fishing Club **15**
Harbour View Villas **12**

CULEBRA DINING ◆
El Batey **14**
Marta's al Fresco **16**

Vieques & Culebra

BEACHES & DIVING

Few of Vieques's beaches have been named, but most have their loyal supporters—loyal, that is, until too many people learn about them, in which case the devotees can always find another good spot.

The U.S. Navy named some of the beaches, such as **Green Beach,** a beautiful, clean stretch at the island's west end. **Red and Blue Beaches** are great jumping-off points for snorkelers. ✪ **Sun Bay (Sombe)** is also a very beautiful white-sand beach, which offers picnic tables, a bathhouse, tent sites, and good snorkeling offshore. Other popular beaches are **Navia, Half Moon, Orchid,** and **Silver,** but if you continue along the water, you may find your own nameless secluded cove with a fine strip of sand.

If you'd like to go diving, the best outfitter is **Blue Caribe Dive Center,** Esperanza Beach (☎ **787/741-2522**). It offers full PADI instruction and certification. A morning one-tank dive goes for $70, and you can also take bioluminescent bay tours by kayak for $25 per person. Your instructor is Denny Johnson, a retired U.S. Navy SEAL.

Interesting tours are offered by **Get Snorked,** 376 Girasoles (☎ **787/741-1980**). Captain Richard Barone conducts a 3-hour reef tour for $30. You can see some of the most dramatic reefs in Puerto Rico offshore.

A well-rehearsed outfit that's good at leading newcomers into the island's most savage landscapes is **La Dolce Vita Mountain Bike and Adventure Company,** c/o La Finca Caribe Guest House & Cottages, Rte. 995, km 1.2 (P.O. Box 1332), Vieques, PR 00765 (☎ **787/741-0495;** www.bikevieques.com). Karl Husson or a member of his staff will lead mountain bikers on half-day ($25 per person) and full-day ($50 per person) tours of obscure trails that are noteworthy for their panoramas and technical difficulties. Use of a mountain bike, usually an aluminum-framed 28-speed state-of-the-art model, is included in the price. You can rent one of these bikes, without the services of a trail guide, for $20 a day.

THE LUMINOUS WATERS OF PHOSPHORESCENT BAY

One of the major attractions on the island is ✪ **Mosquito Bay,** also called Phosphorescent Bay, with its glowing waters produced by tiny bioluminescent organisms that live near the surface. These organisms dart away from boats, leaving eerie blue-white trails of phosphorescence. The *Vieques Times* wrote: "By any name the bay can be a magical, psychedelic experience and few places in the world can even come close to the intensity of concentration of the dinoflagellates called pyrodiniums (whirling fire). They are tiny ($1/500$-inch) swimming creatures that light up like fireflies when disturbed but nowhere are there so many fireflies. Here a gallon of bay water may contain almost three-quarters of a million."

The ideal time to tour is on a cloudy, moonless night. You should wear a bathing suit since it's possible to swim in these glowing waters.

Shannon Grasso (☎ 787/741-0720) operates trips aboard her *Luminosa* from La Casa del Francés (see "Where to Stay," below). These trips are not offered around the time of the full moon. The charge is $20, and most jaunts last about 90 minutes. A similar tour on a kayak and costing the same price is offered by **Blue Caribe Dive Center** (☎ 787/741-2522 for complete details).

SEEING THE SIGHTS

The **Fort Conde de Mirasol Museum** at Magnolia 471 (☎ 787/741-1717) is the major man-made attraction on the island.

In the 1840s, Count Mirasol convinced the Spanish government to build a defensive fortress here. Today the carefully restored fort houses a museum of art and history celebrating the story of Vieques. There are Indian relics, displays of the Spanish conquest, and old flags of the Danes, British, and French. The French sugarcane planters and their African slaves are depicted, and there's even a bust of Simón Bolivar based on a visit to Puerto Rico by the great liberator. A unique collection of maps shows how the world's cartographers envisioned Vieques. Since the U.S. Navy occupies more than two-thirds of the island, its presence and controversial role are chronicled. The museum and fort are open Wednesday through Sunday from 10am to 4pm, charging $1 for adults, 50¢ for children.

WHERE TO STAY

Many in-the-know guests, including repeat visitors who fall in love with the island, rent private villas by the week. Two-, three-, and four-bedroom houses are available at moderate rates, and some have swimming pools or are by the ocean. One of the most spectacular is **Glass House** at Puerto Real (☎ **310/452-9999**), costing $5,000 a week, but it's a stunning bit of modern architecture with two bedrooms and a pool. More modest in price is **Cane Garden,** also at Puerto Real (☎ **207/338-3618**), a pair of two-bedroom cottages costing $1,500 each weekly. Or else you can check out **Casa Dos Cuervos,** La Llave (☎ **314/533-9995**), for a small palazzo that sleeps four. It's a bit minimalist, and the cost is $1,500 a week.

EXPENSIVE

✪ **Casa Cielo.** Calle 995, km 1.1, Vieques, PR 00765. ☎ and fax **787/741-2403.** www. enchanted-isle.com/casacielo/. E-mail: casacielo@worldnet.att.net. 9 units. A/C. Winter $175–$225 double. Off-season $126–$165 double. MC, V. Closed Sept.

Former restaurateurs Ken Hartley and Russell Miller have chosen this hilltop guest-house, flanked by the Atlantic on the north and the Caribbean on the south, as the site of their inn of charm and sophistication. Fashion designer Narciso Rodríguez was one of the first guests, and since then Casa Cielo has captured the attention of the beautiful people. Reaching this hypermodern piece of New Age architecture is part of the fun. It lies within the hilly terrain in the island's center. Expect the most from your car's transmission as you bump and jog your way across impossibly rutted roads to reach it. Once here, the venue is pure *Architectural Digest,* thanks to big windows, large rectangular indoor-outdoor spaces, and a sense that the fashion world has checked in here before you.

On a 6-acre retreat, this is truly the island hideaway. You can lounge poolside or take a cool drink in the gazebo bar. All rooms are nonsmoking; have a light, breezy decor; either king or two full-size beds; and ceiling fans. Some have air-conditioning. All units come with private balconies to take in the ocean views. On site is a large swimming pool, around which a continental breakfast is served. The staff can arrange scuba diving, horseback riding, snorkeling, hiking, biking, kayaking, day sailing, and charter fishing.

✪ **Inn on the Blue Horizon.** Rte. 996 (P.O. Box 1556), Vieques, PR 00765. ☎ **787/ 741-3318.** Fax 787/741-0052. www.enchanted-isle.com/bluehorizon. 9 units. A/C. Winter $150–$200 double. Off-season $125–$175 double. AE, MC, V.

Set on the island's southern coastal road, less than a mile west of Esperanza, this is the most charming hotel on Vieques, and the one that has repeatedly earned the highest accolades from the international press. (In its January 2000 edition, *In Style* magazine defined any room at this inn as one of the 10 hottest items in the world.) In winter, it reigns as the most hip and stylish gathering place in the Caribbean for the low-key rendezvous of North America's fashion photographers and supermodels, who appreciate its offbeat glamour and urban sophistication. Its centerpiece is an airy seafront house, built in a Mediterranean style in 1975, whose soaring living area opens directly onto a view of the faraway blue horizon.

In the mid-1990s, the site was transformed into an inn by hotel and restaurant entrepreneurs William Knight and James Weis, refugees from the New York fashion world. Three of the bedrooms are in the main house; a half-dozen others are in a trio of bungalows, each of which contains two spacious and comfortable units, each with a private balcony and sea view. Airy and clean, they're outfitted with early 19th-century North American antiques, eclectic art from a variety of artists, and the kind of books you'd really like to read.

One of the most appealing spots in the hotel is the bar. Set beneath a red tin roof, it's a blue-and-yellow painted circular arrangement nestled within an octagonal room that's partially open to the ocean breezes. Loaded with beautiful people and their entourages during midwinter, it was recently defined by *Newsweek* magazine as one of the best bars in the world. (A plaque to that effect is proudly displayed inside.)

Nearby, symmetrically positioned arbors are covered with cascades of bougainvillea, centering a swimming pool and lawns that slope gracefully down to cliffs at the edge of the sea. Café Blu, the in-house restaurant, doesn't serve lunch (most clients are at the beach anyway), but dinners are island events (see "Where to Dine," below). The hotel maintains a strict policy of never accepting children under 14. The seafront adjacent to the hotel has a rocky coastline, but the staff will direct you to the dozens of fine local beaches.

MODERATE

Hacienda Tamarindo. Rte. 996 (P.O. Box 1569), Vieques, PR 00765. ☎ **787/741-8525.** Fax 787/741-3215. www.enchanted-isle.com/tamarindo. 16 units. A/C. $115–$140 double; $175 suite. Rates include breakfast. AE, MC, V.

Established in the late 1990s on the site of an expanded nightclub, less than a mile west of Esperanza, this inn has lots of flair, style, and pizzazz. Vermont-born owners Burr and Linda Vail transformed a thick-walled, rather unimaginative-looking concrete building into a replica of a Spanish colonial hacienda, thanks to Linda's skills as a decorator. The inn was built around a massive 200-year-old tamarind tree, whose branches rise majestically through the hotel's atrium. Its production of fruit (between February and March) is heralded with much excitement by the owners. Rooms are stylish, tile-covered, and spacious. Each contains an appealing mishmash of art and antiques, some of which were brought from Vermont. Bathrooms are modern, clean, and well designed. Although the inn is set about an eighth of a mile inland from the sea, there's access to a beach and swimming pool via a footpath. Breakfast is a generous continental one. There's no restaurant on the premises, but the Café Blu, at the Inn on the Blue Horizon, lies within a 5-minute walk.

La Casa del Francés. Barrio Esperanza (P.O. Box 458), Vieques, PR 00765. ☎ **787/ 741-3751.** Fax 787/741-2330. www.enchanted-isle.com/LaCasa/details.htm. 19 units. Winter $139 double. Off-season $119 double. AE, MC, V.

La Casa del Francés is about a 15-minute drive southeast of Isabel Segunda, just north of the center of Esperanza. Set in a field near the southern coastline, the hotel has an imposing column-fronted facade that rises from the lush surrounding landscape. It was built in 1905 by a retired French general as the headquarters for his working sugar plantation. The present owner has installed a swimming pool and transformed the high-ceilinged bedrooms into old-fashioned hotel accommodations, which are both quirky and cozy. Bathrooms are in good working order, although not particularly plush. Many units enjoy access to the sweeping two-story verandas ringing the white facade.

Scattered throughout the dozen acres surrounding the main house are century-old tropical trees. The estate's architectural highlight is the two-story interior courtyard, whose center is lush with bamboo, palms, philodendron, and well-chosen examples of Haitian art.

The fixed-price dinners attract many island residents who partake of Italian, barbecue, or Puerto Rican buffets, which the staff spreads out beneath a 200-year-old mahogany tree.

INEXPENSIVE

Bananas. Barrio Esperanza (P.O. Box 1300), Vieques, PR 00765. ☎ **787/741-8700.** Fax 787/741-0790. 8 units. $45–$65 double. AE, MC, V.

While filming *Heartbreak Ridge* here in 1986, the actors and crew transformed this establishment's windswept porch into their second home. Located on the island's south shore, on the main tourist "strip" of Esperanza, and best known for its bar and restaurant, this guesthouse also has eight simple rooms, some recently renovated. Each has a ceiling fan; three rooms are air-conditioned and have screened-in porches. We urge you to consider one of the air-conditioned rooms ($65) rather than those without ($45), simply as a means of cutting down on heat and noise from the outside. None of the rooms has a phone. Each is an unadorned cubicle with little architectural interest, providing shelter and calm and a basic level of comfort. There's a bar, sometimes rather animated, on the premises that serves mango coladas, pizzas, burgers, sandwiches, and platters priced from $4.75 to $14.50. Overall, the ambience is convivial, the staff friendly and accommodating.

Crow's Nest. Rte. 201, km 1.6, Barrio Florida, Box 1521, Vieques, PR 00765. ☎ **787/ 741-0033.** Fax 787/741-1294. 14 units. $65–$90 double. AE, MC, V.

Set high on 5 acres of forested hillside, about 1¹/₂ miles west of Isabela, this inn enjoys northward-facing views over the Atlantic and a cozy, responsive setting that's favored by many repeat guests. Each of the units contains some kind of cooking facilities, and all but two offer air-conditioning. Rooms are more upscale-looking than those at either Bananas (which is very basic) or Tradewinds, but less elegant and charming than those at Blue Horizon. There is a rectangular swimming pool on the premises, a bar with a sweeping view, and a restaurant that's favored by nonresidents as something of an island staple for dine-arounds. Like most of the other hotels on the island, this one requires a car ride of around 10 minutes for access to the nearest worthwhile beach.

La Finca Caribe Guest House & Cottages. Rte. 995, km 1.2 (P.O. Box 1332), Vieques, PR 00765. ☎ **787/741-0495.** . E-mail: lafinca@lafinca.com. 6 units (none with bathroom), 2 cottages. Winter $70–$85 double; off-season $60–$75 double. One-week cottage rental for 2–4 occupants, winter $675–$900; off-season $450–$675. MC, V. Closed Sept.

This bare-bones, eco-sensitive establishment caters to budget-conscious travelers and youthful adventurers. The present owners, the Merwin family, have renamed it *Finca,* which means a rustic estate in Spanish. The centerpiece of the property is a guesthouse with a spacious porch outfitted with hammocks and swinging chairs. An admirably maintained garden wraps itself around the scattered components of the compound. The rustic-looking outbuildings include a bathhouse, a communal kitchen, and two self-contained cottages suitable for up to three (the casita) or four (the cabana) occupants. Both have private decks and kitchens. There's a relatively new nonchlorinated pool on the premises (it stays clean through frequent recirculation of water from a mountain stream) and a crew of entrepreneurs who takes clients off on bike tours to obscure parts of Vieques. For more on this, see "Beaches & Diving," above. The property is situated on a forested hillside 3 miles from Sun Bay in the center of the island, north of Esperanza and southwest of Isabel Segunda.

Trade Winds Guesthouse. 107C Calle Flamboyan, Barrio Esperanza (P.O. Box 1012), Vieques, PR 00765. ☎ and fax **787/741-8666.** 14 units. Winter $60–$80 double. Off-season $50–65 double. AE, MC, V.

Along the shore on the south side of the island, in the fishing village of Esperanza, this oceanside guesthouse offers 9 units, four of them air-conditioned and with terraces. The others have ceiling fans, and some open onto terraces. Bedrooms are white-walled and durable, with absolutely no imagination in terms of decor; the units might remind you of a barracks. They're almost equivalent to the rooms at Bananas, a few buildings away, although just a bit better. Because of their low rates, they're usually booked solid, often with divers from the United States or residents of the Puerto Rican mainland who want low rates. This place is well known for hospitable ambience and its open-air restaurant overlooking the ocean (see "Where to Dine," below).

Vieques Ocean View Hotel. Isabel Segunda (P.O. Box 124), Vieques, PR 00765. ☎ **787/ 741-3696.** Fax 787/741-1793. 30 units. A/C TV. $75 double. AE, MC, V.

Situated in the heart of Isabel Segunda, directly on the coast and a block from the wharf where the ferryboat lands, this three-story building is one of the tallest on Vieques. Built in the early 1980s, it offers simple rooms with uncomplicated furniture and balconies overlooking either the sea or the town. Twenty-five of the 30 rooms are air-conditioned. The hotel has a restaurant serving Chinese food, open daily from 11am to 11pm, and there's a swimming pool here.

WHERE TO DINE
MODERATE

✪ **Café Blu.** In the Inn on the Blue Horizon, Rte. 996. ☎ **787/741-3318.** Main courses $19–$24. AE, MC, V. Winter Thurs–Mon 6–10pm. Off-season Thurs–Sun 6–10pm. Closed September. INTERNATIONAL.

In the premises of the Inn on the Blue Horizon (see "Where to Stay," above), this restaurant serves the best food on Vieques. Also on site is a bar that a team of journalists declared as one of their favorites in the world, so consider starting your evening with a drink or two in the octagonal Blue Bar. Meals are served within the inn's main building or beneath an awning on a seafront terrace lined with plants. Menu items include pan-blackened tuna; tenderloin of Black Angus beef; fillet of rainbow trout with saffron-flavored butter sauce; and tenderloin of pork, pan-seared, and served with dark rum and sweet spices, with a sauce of caramelized red onions. Expect a crowd of fashion industry folk, temporarily absent from New York and Los Angeles, and local residents, all mixing in ways that are gregarious, stylish, and usually a lot of fun.

La Campesina. La Hueca. ☎ **787/741-1239.** Reservations recommended. Main courses $12–$20. MC, V. Tues–Sun 6–10pm. Closed Oct. INTERNATIONAL.

Consciously designed to reflect indigenous dwellings, this unusual and excellent restaurant was built a few steps from one of the richest archeological deposits of Taíno artifacts in the Caribbean. It's located on the southwestern end of the island (follow the coast road from Esperanza) in the untrammeled fishing village of La Hueca.

In a room lined with baskets and weavings amid trailing vines of jasmine and flickering candles, you can enjoy a cuisine of distinctly tropical or uniquely Puerto Rican flair. Fresh herbs such as cilantro, tasty varieties of local vegetables, and fruits such as papaya, mango, and tamarind served in relishes and pastries complement the menu. Nightly specials might include avocado rémoulade, conch fritters, lobster ravioli, local fish, and great steak.

Trapper John's. In the Crow's Nest Hotel, Rte. 201, km 1.6. ☎ **787/741-0011.** Reservations recommended. Main courses $16–$35; Saturday night prime rib special $20. AE, MC, V. Restaurant open Fri–Wed 6–10pm. Bar open Fri–Wed 5pm–midnight. AMERICAN.

The setting is a cement-sided, indoor-outdoor terrace, within a building inspired by an hacienda. It's one of the genuinely respected restaurants on Vieques, offering consistent quality without any particular imagination or variation from one season to the next. But residents seem to appreciate the monotony, as it does a reliable business with both locals and visitors. Look for two-fisted portions of fish, ribs, steaks, and seafood, and stiff, party-colored drinks from the tropical bar. John and Barbara are your stateside-born hosts.

INEXPENSIVE

Bananas Restaurant. In Bananas hotel, Barrio Esperanza. ☎ **787/741-8700.** Main courses $14–16; sandwiches at lunch $4–$7.50. AE, MC, V (tab must exceed $15 to use a credit card). Daily 11am–10pm. INTERNATIONAL.

Bananas has some of the best food on the island, including familiar fare such as charbroiled New York sirloin, barbecued baby-back ribs, and marinated boneless breast of chicken. Slightly more exotic main dishes might include the grilled Jamaican-style jerk chicken or the lemon chicken sautéed in butter and wine. You might opt instead for the grilled fresh catch of the day served with lemon butter. The chef also makes pizzas with a wide choice of toppings. Baked potatoes in four different versions, including one with broccoli and chili, also appear on the menu. Sandwiches are available at lunch, including grilled chicken and fresh fish. You can also order a juicy half-pound burger with a number of toppings.

Chez Shack. Highway 995 (Airport Rd.). ☎ **787/741-2175.** Reservations recommended. Main courses $14–$18. No credit cards. Dec–May Wed–Mon 6–11pm; June–Nov Thurs–Sat 6:30–11pm. INTERNATIONAL.

It wins, almost without competition, as the most bohemian and counterculture restaurant on Vieques. The setting is exactly what the name implies—a battered wood-sided utility building that evolved from a virtual ruin after it was acquired by a grizzled and outspoken entrepreneur, Hugh Duffy, who was instrumental in the career of the Mamas and the Papas. This group, when still getting its act together, worked at Duffy's Love Shack in St. Thomas where Mama Cass was said to have been the world's worst waitress. Today, replete with naughty (and sometimes unprintable) anecdotes that are among the most valuable currency-in-trade on the island, the site is defined as a local monument. Chez Shack opens for business on off-season nights even when other restaurants are closed. Menu items include tried-and-true favorites, many of which attract repeat diners who memorized the menu long, long ago. Examples include baked crab, seafood cocktail, steaks, fish fillets, and barbecued ribs. You'll find the place near the edge of the highway, within the closest thing on Vieques to a tropical rain forest, in a remote location 6 miles northwest of Esperanza.

Trade Winds Restaurant. In Trade Winds Guesthouse, Calle Flamboyan, Barrio Esperanza. ☎ **787/741-8666.** Reservations recommended. Main courses $11.50–$35. AE, MC, V. Daily 7:30–10:30am and 6–9pm; bar, daily 4–11pm. STEAK/SEAFOOD.

This restaurant is often recommended by hotel owners across the island, and, as such, manages to feed the residents of a large cross-section of island hotels. It lies beside the oceanfront esplanade in the fishing village of Esperanza, on the south side of the island. A dining experience here often begins with a drink at the open-air Topside Bar. For dinner, the chef's specialties revolve around steak, fish, and lobster, which is often served with butter-flavored rum sauce. Among the steaks, the best is an 8-ounce filet,

Center Vieques: About to Lose Its Innocence

In the Spring of 2000, a historic event changed the hotel and restaurant land-scape of Vieques forever—the Dallas-based Rosewood chain opened a 156-unit luxury hotel. **Martineau Bay, A Rosewood Hotel & Resort,** Rte. 200, km 3.4, Vieques, PR 00765-9800 (☎ **888/ROSEWOOD** in the U.S. or 787/741-4100; www.rosewood-hotels.com), is set on a 40-acre tract adjacent to a horseshoe-shaped beach and flanked with a pair of rocky promontories. The first truly upscale hotel to open on the island, it's a cluster of neo-colonial buildings, each painted a contrasting shade of pastels and capped with a hip-shaped roof. Regrettably, it was scheduled to open after the deadline for this edition, so although we were able to tour the building site long before any of the 156 rooms were completed, a full review won't occur until the next edition of this guide.

Look for casually elegant tropical-weather living, lots of wrought iron and decorative tile work, and rooms with double sinks and sheathings of stone, tile, and marble. There will be at least two swimming pools, a center for children and teens, tennis courts, and a spa with spaces for massage indoors or in the open air. Bedrooms will have electronic hookups for fax and computer modems. Rooms will be the most expensive ever on the island, ranging from $450 for a double to $3,000 for a three-bedroom villa.

What is the reaction of this notoriously laid-back island to the construction of what will be Vieques's largest and splashiest hotel? A mixture of fear and respect, and uncertainty for what it will do for the island's already-crowded infrastructure. Important concerns involve the island's narrow roads (too small, they say, for the new traffic the hotel will bring); the island's lack of sophisticated medical facilities, including a bona fide emergency room; and the pressures it will place on the island's fragile ecosystems.

cooked just right over the char-broiler and served with a baked potato and a house or Caesar salad; also available is herb-marinated pork loin with mashed potatoes. The fresh fish special varies according to the luck of local fishermen, but is usually a good item to order, as is the jumbo shrimp sautéed with fresh garlic and lemon, or served with curry sauce. Black-bean soup is a good opener. Any main course can be served with *mofongo,* a mixture of mashed plantains with garlic, fried onions, and bacon.

Trapper John's at the Crow's Nest. Rte 201, km 1.6. ☎ **787/741-0033.** Reservations recommended. Main courses $14–$21 (lobster can go as high as $35). AE, MC, V. Daily 6–10:30pm. Closed Thursday in midsummer. INTERNATIONAL.

Perched on a second-floor deck with a view of El Yunque rain forest on the faraway Puerto Rican mainland, this is a soothing, laid-back, and popular dining venue. It's managed by an Italian-born couple, John and Barbara Orsillo, who also own a lobster boat in New England. As such, Maine coast lobster is invariably featured, prepared in any of at least five different ways. Many of the clients arrive Friday or Saturday night, when thick slabs of prime rib are the house specialty. Other dishes are uncomplicated but well prepared, including pork tenderloin, grilled chicken, Angus sirloin of beef, and honey-flavored chicken with sesame sauce resting on a bed of coconut-flavored rice. Fresh fish, either local or imported from New England, is also important here. Don't be afraid to get here early, as the bar opens every night at 5pm (closed Thursday in midsummer) and does a rollicking business.

SHOPPING

There aren't a lot of shopping possibilities in Vieques; however, you might want to visit **Siddhia Hutchinson Fine Art Studio & Gallery,** Calle 3, A15, Isabel Segunda (☎ 787/741-8780), located between the lighthouse and the ferry dock. Here you can purchase prints of local sea- and landscapes, along with native flowers, fish, and birds. There are also lovely bowls, mugs, and platters for sale.

2 Culebra

52 miles E of San Juan; 18 miles E of Fajardo

A tranquil, inviting little island, Culebra lies in a miniarchipelago of 24 chunks of land, rocks, and cays, 18 miles east of Puerto Rico's main island and halfway to St. Thomas, U.S. Virgin Islands. It's just 7 miles long and 3 miles wide and has only 2,000 residents. The landscape is dotted with everything from scrub and cacti to poincianas, frangipanis, and coconut palms.

Today vacationers and boaters can explore the island's beauties, both on land and under water. Culebra's white-sand beaches (especially Flamenco Beach), its clear waters, and its long coral reefs invite swimmers, snorkelers, and scuba divers.

This little-known year-round vacation spot in what was once called the Spanish Virgin Islands was settled as a Spanish colony in 1886, but like Puerto Rico and Vieques, it became part of the United States after the Spanish-American War in 1898. In fact, Culebra's only town, a fishing village called **Dewey,** was named for Admiral George Dewey, an American hero of that war, although the locals defiantly call it **Puebla.**

Both illustrious and notorious characters have visited Culebra in the past. It is believed that Columbus spotted the island on his second voyage to the New World in 1493. When the Spanish started colonizing Puerto Rico, many of the Taíno Indians fled to Culebra as a last refuge. It wasn't many decades later that the swashbuckling Sir Henry Morgan and other notorious pirates used Culebra as a hideout. The island supposedly still shelters their buried loot.

From 1909 to 1975, Culebra was used by the U.S. Navy as a gunnery range, even serving as a practice bomb site in World War II. Today the four tracts of the **Culebra Wildlife Refuge,** plus 23 other offshore islands, are managed by the U.S. Fish and Wildlife Service. The refuge is one of the most important turtle-nesting sites in the Caribbean, and it also houses large seabird colonies, notably terns and boobies.

Culebrita, a mile-long coral-isle satellite of Culebra, has a hilltop lighthouse and crescent beaches.

ESSENTIALS

GETTING THERE   Vieques Air-Link (☎ 787/723-9882) flies to Culebra five times daily from San Juan's Isla Grande Airport. One-way transit costs $50; round-trip is $95.

The Puerto Rico Port Authority operates one or two **ferryboats** a day (depending on the day of the week) from the mainland port of Fajardo to Culebra; the trip takes about an hour. The round-trip fare is $4.50 for adults, $2.25 for children 3 to 12 (free for 2 and under). For information and reservations, call ☎ 787/863-4560.

BEACHES & DIVING

The island's most popular beach is ✪ **Flamenco Beach,** a mile-long horseshoe-shaped cove on the island's northwestern edge. It's popular partly because of its nearness to Dewey, partly because of its soft sands.

From Leathernecks to Leatherbacks

In one of his last executive orders before leaving the White House in 1909, President Theodore Roosevelt established Culebra as a national wildlife refuge. Today this pint-sized archipelago, one of the last frontier outposts of the Caribbean, is one of only two nesting sites in the United States for the leatherback sea turtle, one of the world's largest marine reptiles. It and three other endangered species of turtles—the loggerhead, green, and hawksbill—are protected by the wildlife refuge.

Although Culebra was a national wildlife refuge, the U.S. Navy and Marine Corps began to use it as a practice bombing range during World War II. Culebrans massively protested the decision, especially when word leaked out that the Navy planned to relocate them to Vieques.

Arguments between Culebrans and the U.S. government didn't end with the war. Molotov cocktail–throwing violence erupted in 1971, with several islanders imprisoned for their hostile acts of defiance. President Richard Nixon finally brought peace to Culebra by ending all weapons training on the island. By 1975, the Navy swabbies and Marine Corps leathernecks had ceased shelling the island.

The leathernecks may be long gone, but the leatherbacks are still here. The **Culebra Leatherback Project,** P.O. Box 190, Culebra, PR 00775 (☎ **787/ 851-7297**), gathers statistics about the nesting sea turtles and takes applications on a first-come, first-served basis from eco-tourists who want to participate in its nightly patrols from April to July. Early reservations are advised, since many nature-minded travelers want to participate.

More isolated is **Zoni Beach,** a 1-mile strip of sand flanked by large boulders and scrub. Located on the island's northeastern edge, about 7 miles from Dewey (Puebla), it's one of the most beautiful beaches on the island. Snorkelers, but not scuba divers, find it particularly intriguing, despite the surf that makes underwater visibility a bit murky during rough weather.

Known for its beautiful corals, unspoiled underwater vistas, and absence of other divers, Culebra is what the Caribbean used to be before crowds of divers began exploring the sea. At least 50 dive sites, on all sides of the island, are considered worthwhile.

Culebra Dive Shop, 138 Escobar St. (☎ **787/742-0566;** fax 787/742-1953), offers a resort course for novice divers, including training in a sheltered cove and a tank dive in 15 to 20 feet of water ($70). Full PADI certification costs $450 and requires 5 days of participation in both classroom and ocean experience. Certified divers pay $85 for a two-tank open-water dive. The outfitter provides all the equipment you'll need for any of the above-mentioned dive experiences. It's rare that more than six divers go out in one of these boats on any day.

WHERE TO STAY

If you operate happily within a rented villa, preparing your own meals, consider making a call to **Pelican Enterprises Vacation Rentals** (☎ 787/742-0052). Jim Galasso, the rental agent, knows what's happening with most of the island's rental villas and can usually come up with something that's appropriate for your needs.

MODERATE

Club Seabourne. Fulladosa Rd. (P.O. Box 357), Culebra, PR 00775. ☎ **787/742-3169.** Fax 787/742-3176. 13 units. A/C. $95–$110 double in the clubhouse; $125 double in a villa or the Crow's Nest. Rates include continental breakfast. AE, MC, V. From Dewey (Puebla), follow Fulladosa Rd. along the south side of the bay for 1¹/₂ miles.

About an 8-minute drive from the center of town, this concrete-and-wood structure is set in a garden of crotons and palms, at the mouth of one of the island's best harbors, Enseñada Honda. It offers scattered villas and four rooms inside the clubhouse. All units are equipped with small refrigerators and air-conditioning. Dive packages and day sails can be arranged at the office.

Overlooking Fulladosa Bay, the club's dining room serves some of the best food on Culebra, with fresh lobster, shrimp, snapper, grouper, and conch, as well as steaks and other specialty dishes. The hotel also has a large patio bar with a nightly happy hour, plus the only freshwater swimming pool on the island.

Culebra Island Villas. Punta Aloe (P.O. Box 596), Culebra, PR 00775. ☎ **787/742-0333.** 10 units. Winter $695 per week studio or 1-bedroom suite; $175 per day; $995 per week 2-bedroom suite. Off-season $495 per week studio or 1-bedroom suite; $150 per day; $695 per week 2-bedroom suite. No credit cards.

Punta Aloe lies south of Enseñada Honda, half a mile south of Dewey, and separated from the Culebran mainland by a canal with a drawbridge. Here you'll find forested hillsides sheltering about 20 privately owned houses. Four of these houses, built by different owners between 1980 and around 1990, include rental units with views of the bay and simple kitchens. The studios and one-bedroom suites can accommodate one to three guests; the two-bedroom suites can hold two to six occupants. None of the units has air-conditioning, but the buildings have direct access to the trade winds. No meals are available, nor is there maid service.

Flamenco Resort & Fishing Club. 10 Pedro Marquez, Flamenco Beach (P.O. Box 183), Culebra, PR 00775. ☎ **787/742-3144.** Fax 787/742-3144. 32 units. A/C. $115 studio; $150 1-bedroom suite; $185 2-bedroom suite. MC, V.

This is the only guesthouse or hotel near the white sands of Flamenco Beach, one of the best in the region. Each unit has its own kitchen. This place would really be attractive to a group of friends or an extended family, since the accommodations are situated around spacious sitting rooms much like those in an informal beach house. The owner has studio apartments suitable for two, one-bedroom apartments suitable for four, two-bedroom bungalows suitable for six, and a three-bedroom unit that can house eight (it contains two bathrooms). All units are air-conditioned. Varied activities are available, including day trips on a sailboat to one of the nearby islands, snorkeling, and fishing expeditions. A small on-site restaurant, Coconut Beach Grill, serves food, usually seafood, Thursday through Sunday nights.

INEXPENSIVE

Harbour View Villas. Melones Beach, west of Dewey (P.O. Box 216), Culebra, PR 00775. ☎ **800/440-0070** or 787/742-3855. www.culebrahotel.com. 6 units. A/C. Winter $75–$125 double; $175 triple or quad. Off-season $75–$95 double; $145 triple or quad.

Set on a 5-acre estate and offering one of the best values on the island, these villas and suites are private but not isolated. They were designed for tropical living with 12-foot ceilings and big French doors, which open onto the main balcony with its 180-degree view of the ocean. The bedrooms also have private balconies. From the rooms, you'll have panoramic views of the ocean. The complex lies within walking distance of Melones Beach. Five of the units have a full kitchen, the other a smaller kitchenette.

Each unit has a master bedroom with a queen-size bed; two of the villas have a second bedroom for two more guests.

WHERE TO DINE

El Batey. 250 Carretera. ☎ **787/742-3828.** Sandwiches $2.75–$3.75. No credit cards. Sun–Thurs 9am–3pm; Fri 9am–midnight, Sat 9am–2am. DELI.

Across from the harbor, this large, clean establishment maintains a full bar and prepares an array of deli-style sandwiches. They'll hand you a cold beer when the afternoon sun is out, and the pool tables make the place lively, especially on weekends when many locals are there. Disco reigns on Saturday night. Weekdays, it's much calmer. The owners, Digna Feliciano and Tomás Ayala, have many fans on the island. Breezes from the harbor cool the place.

Marta's al Fresco. 10 Pedro Marquez. ☎ **787/742-3575.** Main courses $10–$25; sandwiches $3–$7. MC, V. Thurs–Sun 8am–10pm. AMERICAN/PUERTO RICAN.

In a simple building near the wharf where the ferryboats from Puerto Rico's mainland arrive and depart, this restaurant is named after its owner's wife, Marta Canovas. The setting has rattan furniture and big windows with a view of the sea. In addition to the deli-style sandwiches, the menu lists a wide range of fresh seafood, as well as steaks, *asopaos*, burgers, grilled chicken breasts, and pork chops with rice and beans. Although hardly memorable, the cooking is home-style and satisfying.

Appendix A:
Puerto Rico in Depth

"It's heaven and hell—all rolled into one tiny island," a Trenton, New Jersey, woman confided to us about Puerto Rico on a return flight from San Juan to Miami. "My husband loved it. I couldn't wait to get back home. But then he's a golfer and a fisherman, and while he was doing that, there were only so many crafts I could buy."

Ever since Castro in the early 1960s started chasing the gringos out of Havana, Puerto Rico has blossomed as a tourist destination, with its towering mountains, rain forests, long beaches, and vibrant Spanish culture.

The woman saw only the island's crime, unemployment, bad traffic, and what to her was "poor food." But in spite of its many critics, Puerto Rico must be doing something right. Of course, you can get bad food here, but in many places the island's cuisine, an adaptation of many cooking styles, is the finest in the Caribbean.

"If you want your Caribbean with a Latin beat, come here," one tour operator told us. "There's nobody who does it better than us." And he's basically right.

History buffs will get more ancient buildings and monuments here than anywhere else in the entire Caribbean, many of them dating back to the Spanish conquistadores some 500 years ago. Add some of the best golf and tennis in the West Indies, posh beach resorts, tranquil and offbeat (though not luxurious) government *paradores* (guest houses), and lots of Las Vegas–type gambling, glitter, and even extravagant shows, and you've got a formidable attraction.

There are problems here. As in many major cities, you could be mugged or have your car stolen or even hijacked. Service personnel are often gruff and unhelpful. Although there are country retreats where you can escape the masses, San Juan and most of the rest of the island is simply overcrowded.

There is also some anti-American sentiment here. Not all locals passionately embrace Uncle Sam. When we were seeking some real lowdown salsa joints away from the tourist hordes, a taxi driver told us, "I can take you to a club—maybe several clubs—but I'm not sure you'd get back in one piece."

Yet, for all its drawbacks, we still love Puerto Rico and rate it as one of the top destinations in the Caribbean, right up there with Aruba, St. Thomas, Jamaica, Barbados, and all the other front-running islands. Visit after visit over so very many years confirms our original impression: Puerto Rico brings life to the sleepy Caribbean.

1 The Natural Environment: Beaches, Mountains, the Rain Forest & More

Roughly half the size of New Jersey, this American commonwealth with 272 miles of Atlantic and Caribbean coastline sits strategically some 1,000 miles southeast of Florida at the hub of the Caribbean chain of islands. You'll probably fly in and out of San Juan at least once if you're doing much touring in the region. And with a 2-year, $2.8 million project that restored its waterfront, this oldest capital city under the U.S. flag is also the world's second-largest home port for cruise-ship passengers.

Puerto Rico has experienced many political changes since the days of its first Spanish governor, Juan Ponce de León, the conquistador who sailed with Columbus and who tried in vain to find a fountain of youth in Florida. With nearly 500 years reflected in its restored Spanish colonial architecture, Old San Juan is the Caribbean's greatest historic center.

Puerto Rico is the most easterly and the smallest of the four major islands that form the Greater Antilles. The other three are Cuba, Jamaica, and Hispaniola (which is home to two nations, Haiti and the Dominican Republic). Surrounded by the Atlantic Ocean to the north and the Caribbean Sea to the south, Puerto Rico is flanked by a trio of smaller islands—Vieques and Culebra to the east and Mona to the west—which are its political and geologic satellites.

The island's terrain ranges from palm-lined beaches on four coastlines to rugged mountain ranges, gently rolling hills, and dry desert-like areas. There are 20 designated forest reserves in Puerto Rico, and 6 more may be added.

BEACHES

The island has dozens of miles of sandy beaches, some long and straight, others broken into coves by headlands. On the northern coast, the Atlantic waters are often more turbulent than those along the more tranquil southern coast. Some stretches near San Juan and the major resorts are incredibly crowded, but it's still possible to find a quiet, remote beach. The big resorts have claimed the most ideal beaches, but even so, they are still open to the public. Public bathing beaches in Puerto Rico are called *balnearios.* These are government-run, with lifeguards, parking, and dressing rooms. For more information about Puerto Rico's beaches, refer to the **Department of Recreation and Sports** (☎ 787/722-1551).

In the northeast of the island are 6 miles of relatively unspoiled beaches, with waters ranging from calm to raging. Visits to El Yunque, the rain forest, are often combined with a stopover at the most popular (and the best) beach in the northeast, **Luquillo Beach,** a *balneario.* There's a huge stand of majestic coconut palms that shade more than a mile of sand. Dressing facilities, parking, and lockers are found here. It is the major beach used by residents of San Juan, and it tends to be overcrowded on weekends, especially at places where the most facilities are located.

Some of the best beaches of Puerto Rico are in the east—but offshore—on the two small islands of **Culebra** and **Vieques.** In Culebra, the white-sand beaches, particularly Flamenco Beach, have clear waters and scenic coral reefs, including a mile-long formation off Culebrita, where there is also a lighthouse.

The adjoining island, Vieques, contains numerous scalloped beaches along the north and northwest coasts, all of which lie on U.S. Navy land and are open to the public when no military maneuvers are going on.

On the south coast, the best beaches are centered near the fishing village of **La Parguera,** which becomes busy and bustling on weekends, when locals pour in for fun in the sun. Numerous mangrove cays and islets here form ornate channels in places, attracting boaters. Swimmers and picnickers prefer **Rosada Beach** or **Mata de la Gata Cay,** the best beaches in the area. Snorkelers and scuba divers explore the reefs and the outer shelf walls that lie 7 miles offshore.

On the west coast the best beach is along the bay at **Boquerón,** part of the municipality of Cabo Rojo. The area opens onto a mile of white sand bordered by clear water. Long a *balneario,* it is frequented mainly by locals. The beach is popular for swimming and picnicking under coconut palms. Nearby is the Boquerón Lagoon, a refuge for ducks and other birds.

In the northwest, rough Atlantic waters deter bathers but attract surfers. Scuba divers and snorkelers also gravitate to a beach here known as **The Shacks,** lying near Isabela. They swim among its coral caverns and reefs, whereas surfers head for **Jobos Beach.**

TOWERING MOUNTAINS

Other than these beaches, the island's most noteworthy geological feature is the **Cordillera**—the towering mountains that rise high above its central region. Geologists have identified the island's summits as the high parts of a chain of mountains whose mass is mostly submerged beneath the sea. These mountains, the oldest of the many land masses of the West Indies, form a dramatic relief in Puerto Rico.

What makes the mountain altitudes even more impressive is the existence, about 75 miles to the island's north, of one of the deepest depressions in the Atlantic, the Puerto Rico Trough. Running more or less parallel to the island's northern shoreline, it plunges to depths of up to 30,000 feet. Although not as obvious as this trench near the northern coastline, the sea floor a few miles from the island's southern coast also drops off, to nearly 17,000 feet below sea level. Geologists have calculated that if the base of this mountain chain were at sea level, it would be one of the highest landmasses in the world. Puerto Rico's highest summit—Cerro de Punta at 4,389 feet—would exceed in altitude even Mt. Everest, the world's tallest peak.

Most of Puerto Rico's geology, especially its mountain peaks, resulted from volcanic activity that deposited lava and igneous rock in consecutive layers. To a lesser degree, the island is also composed of quartz, diomites, and, along some of its edges, coral limestone.

EL YUNQUE & THE RAIN FORESTS

The mountains are home to the island's greatest natural attraction, ✪ **El Yunque** (☎ 787/887-2875 for information), a 45-minute drive east of San Juan. Given national park status by President Theodore Roosevelt, this 28,000-acre preserve is the only tropical rain forest on U.S. soil and is protected by the U.S. Forest Service. On these soaring peaks, the virgin forest remains much like it was in 1493 when Columbus first sighted Puerto Rico.

Today, El Yunque offers its visitors close encounters of the natural kind, from picnics amid rare flora and fauna to hikes along the scenic trails. Encompassing four distinct forest types, it is home to 240 species of tropical trees; flowers, including more than 20 kinds of orchids; and other wildlife, including millions of tiny tree frogs whose distinctive cry of *coquí* (pronounced *ko-kee*) has given them their name. Tropical birds include the lively, greenish blue– and red-fronted Puerto Rican parrot, once nearly extinct and now making a comeback. Other rare animals include the Puerto Rican boa, which grows to 7 feet, and 26 animal species found nowhere else in the world.

El Yunque also offers a number of walking and hiking trails, including the rugged El Toro, which passes through four different forest systems en route to the 3,523-foot Pico El Toro, the highest peak in the forest. El Yunque Trail leads to three of the recreation area's most spectacular lookouts, and Big Tree Trail is an easy walk to the panoramic La Mina Falls. Just off the main road is La Coca Falls, a sheet of water cascading down mossy cliffs.

Puerto Rico also has 19 other forest preserves. Directly east of San Juan lies **Piñones Forest,** which contains the island's largest mangrove forest. West of Ponce, **Guánica Forest** borders several white-sand beaches and the historic bay where U.S. troops first landed in 1898 during the Spanish-American War. **Cambalache Forest,** east of Arecibo, contains plantations of eucalyptus, teak, and mahoe trees. The driest vegetation is found in **Maricao Forest,** which also has a new visitor center and expansive views to the west coast. **Toro Negro Forest,** which straddles the peaks of the Cordillera in the center of the island, boasts the island's tallest peak with stunning drops to the Caribbean and the Atlantic. All these forests are open to visitors, and several have picnic areas and campsites.

THE KARST COUNTRY & CAVES

One of the most interesting areas of Puerto Rico to explore is the **Karst Country.** One of the world's strangest rock formations, karst is formed by the process of water sinking into limestone. As time goes by, larger and larger basins are eroded, forming sinkholes. Mogotes or karstic hillocks are peaks of earth where the land didn't sink into the erosion pits. The Karst Country lies along the island's north coast, directly northeast of Mayagüez in the foothills between Quebradillas and Manatí. The region is filled with an extensive network of caves. One sinkhole contains the 20-acre dish of the world's largest radio/radar telescope at the Arecibo Observatory.

Reached by Route 446, the **Guajataca Forest Reserve** is found here, offering some 25 miles of trails that take you through some of the most rugged parts of this country.

Eons ago, one of the world's largest underground rivers carved the **Río Camuy Caves** in northwest Puerto Rico, which experts today consider to be among the most spectacular on earth. Although relatively new to today's visitors, the Río Camuy Caves contain evidence of occupation long before the island was sighted by Columbus in 1493. The first professional explorers of the system were led to the site by local boys already familiar with some of the entrances.

Camuy Cave Park opens access to **Tres Pueblos Sinkhole,** measuring 65 feet in diameter with a depth of 400 feet—room enough to fit in all of El Morro Fortress in San Juan. Tres Pueblos, located on the boundaries of the Camuy, Hatillo, and Lares municipalities, is one of two sinkholes in the Río Camuy Cave system now adapted for visitors. The other, Cueva Clara de Empalme, opened in 1986 and has been the park's featured attraction for the past 7 years.

In Tres Pueblos, visitors can walk along two platforms—one on the Lares side facing the town of Camuy and the other on the Hatillo side overlooking Tres Pueblos Cave and the Río Camuy.

2 Puerto Rico Today

At the millennium, Puerto Rico continues to make headlines in mainland newspapers. Sometimes the news is good; at other times, troubling.

First the good. At the beginning of the 21st century, Puerto Rico's tourism figures are rising annually, as the island's aggressive hotel and marketing promotion seems to be paying off. Travelers from the United States are the major visitors and their numbers rose steadily throughout the late '90s. Canadian tourism is also on the rise, but the greatest increase is in visitors from other Latin American countries.

Indeed, the island's 3.56 million people—including a million in the San Juan metropolitan area—have forged ahead economically and made rapid strides. Their annual income is now the highest in Latin America, and their average life expectancy has risen to 73.8 years. And with the island's economy evolving from agriculture to manufacturing and tourism, a demand for an educated workforce has resulted in the ordinary worker having at least 12 years of schooling.

Tourism represents about 6% of the gross national product. Puerto Rico's present governor, Dr. Pedro Rosselló, has challenged both the private and public sectors of the tourism industry to double that contribution to the GNP within the next decade. At once both labor intensive and environmentally friendly, tourism is seen as the island's best alternative to continued heavy industrialization in pursuit of new jobs for its people.

Even in the now-prosperous tourism industry, storm clouds loom. The unspoken fear among developers of megaresorts is the possible impact of Cuba reopening to the American tourism market. Before Fidel Castro took over Cuba in 1959, Americans by the thousands flocked to Havana, and Puerto Rico was a mere dot on the tourist map. The island's growth was fueled enormously by the embargo imposed on Castro's communist government.

Now the bad. As part of legislation raising the nation's minimum wage in 1996, President Clinton vetoed a set of tax breaks for U.S. companies operating on the island. That ended 75 years of federal incentives that attracted stateside industries and helped make Puerto Rico the industrial powerhouse in the West Indies. For example, it produces about half the prescription drugs sold in the United States. What impact losing its special tax status will have in the long run remains to be seen.

Even with the tax breaks, Puerto Rico struggles with a 12.5% unemployment rate and a per capita income of $8,509, about half the level of America's poorest state, Mississippi.

Mirroring the U.S. mainland, rising crime, drugs, the AIDS crisis, chronic unemployment, overpopulation, and more troubles plague Puerto Rico. The island has America's third-highest AIDS rate and the dubious distinction of being a major gateway into the United States for drugs from Latin America. All the violence and social ills associated with drugs have beset the island. A newspaper headline said it best: "Puerto Rico Reeling Under Scourge of Drugs and Rising Gang Violence." Although the drug issue is still of epidemic proportions, you can visit Puerto Rico and be completely unaware that all this criminal activity is going on around you, especially if you're heading to one of the big, self-sufficient resorts. And efforts are being made to solve the drug problem. In the mid-1990s, the government increased the number of police officers, enacted harsher prison sentences for drug dealers, and conducted arms and drug raids—all part of a continuing battle to stop the flow of illegal drugs into the United States.

Making headlines at the end of the 20th century was the little offshore island of Vieques, which is experiencing a bit of a tourist boom in spite of the fact that the Navy has used it for years for target practice. In December 1999, President Clinton ordered a halt to live-fire military training on the island and an end to all exercises here within 5 years unless local residents agree to an extension. If islanders will agree to the continued use of Vieques as a military exercise target, the U.S. government might pour millions of dollars of developmental money into the offshore territory.

Governor Rosselló is the leading supporter of statehood for Puerto Rico, although a U.S. backlash has developed over the Navy's use of Vieques Island. This cause has tapped a tremendous reservoir of Puerto Rican nationalism, and may doom Rosselló's party in the 2000 elections.

Rosselló's New Progressive Party wants to make Puerto Rico the 51st state, but the opposition is strong, both on the island and in Congress. A nonbinding reference in 1998 resulted in a defeat of statehood. In addition, Puerto Rican militants pardoned in September 1999 were welcomed in San Juan as heroes even as President Clinton endured criticism for having set "terrorists" loose.

3 History 101

IN THE BEGINNING

Although the Spanish occupation was the decisive factor defining Puerto Rico's current culture, the island was settled many thousands of years ago by Amerindians. The oldest archeological remains yet discovered were unearthed in 1948. Found in a limestone cave a few miles east of San Juan, in Loíza Aldea, the artifacts consisted of conch shells, stone implements, and crude hatchets deposited here by tribal peoples during the first century of the Christian Era. These people belonged to an archaic, seminomadic, cave-dwelling culture that had not developed either agriculture or pottery. Some ethnologists suggest that these early inhabitants originated in Florida, immigrated to Cuba, and from there began a steady migration along the West Indian archipelago.

Around A.D. 300, a different group of Amerindians, the Arawaks, migrated to Puerto Rico from the Orinoco Basin in what is now Venezuela. Known by ethnologists as the Saladoids, they were the first of Puerto Rico's inhabitants to make and use pottery, which they decorated with exotic geometric designs in red and white. Subsisting on fish, crabs, and whatever else they could catch, they populated the big island as well as the offshore island of Vieques.

By about A.D. 600, this culture had disappeared, bringing to an end the island's historic era of pottery making. Ethnologists' opinions differ as to whether the tribes were eradicated by new invasions from South America, succumbed to starvation or plague, or simply evolved into the next culture that dominated Puerto Rico—the Ostionoids.

Much less skilled at making pottery than their predecessors but more accomplished at polishing and grinding stones for jewelry and tools, the Ostionoids were the ethnic predecessors of the tribe that became the Taínos. The Taínos inhabited Puerto Rico when it was explored and invaded by the Spanish beginning in 1493. The Taínos were spread throughout the West Indies but reached their greatest development in Puerto Rico and neighboring Hispaniola (the island shared by Haiti and the Dominican Republic).

Taíno culture has impressed both the colonial Spanish and modern sociologists. This people's achievements included construction of ceremonial ballparks whose boundaries were marked by upright stone dolmens, development of a universal language, and creation of a complicated religious cosmology. There was a hierarchy of deities who inhabited the sky. The god Yocahu was the supreme creator. Another, Jurancán, was perpetually angry and ruled the power of the hurricane. Myths and traditions were perpetuated through

Ponce de León: Man of Myth & Legend

For an explorer of such myth and legend, Juan Ponce de León still remains an enigma to many historians, his exploits subject to as much myth as fact.

It is known that he was born around 1460 in San Tervas de Campos, a province of Valladolid in Spain, to a noble Castilian family. The red-haired youth grew into an active, aggressive, and perhaps impulsive young man, similar in some respects to Sir Francis Drake in England. After taking part in Spain's Moorish wars, Ponce de León sailed to America with Columbus on his second voyage, in 1493.

In the New World, Ponce de León served as a soldier in the Spanish settlement of Hispaniola, now the island home of Haiti and the Dominican Republic. From 1502 to 1504, he led Spanish forces against Indians in the eastern part of the island, finally defeating them.

In 1508, he explored Puerto Rico, discovering gold on the island and conquering its native tribes within a year. A year later, he was named governor of Puerto Rico and soon rose to become one of the most powerful Europeans in the Americas. From most accounts Ponce de León was a good governor of Puerto Rico before his political rivals forced him from office in 1512.

At that time he received permission from King Ferdinand to colonize the island of Bimini in the Bahamas. In searching for Bimini, he came upon the northeast coast of Florida, which he at first thought was an island, in the spring of 1513. He named it La Florida because he discovered it at the time of Pascua Florida or "Flowery Easter." He was the first explorer to claim some of the North American mainland for Spain.

The following year, he sailed back to Spain, carrying with him 5,000 gold pesos. King Ferdinand ordered him back to Puerto Rico with instructions to colonize both Bimini and Florida. Back in Puerto Rico, he ordered the building of the city of San Juan. In 1521, he sailed to Florida with 200 men and supplies to start a colony. This was to be his downfall. Wounded by a poison arrow in his thigh, he was taken back to Cuba in June of 1521 and died there from his wound.

Legend says Ponce de León searched in vain for the so-called Fountain of Youth, first in Bimini and then later in Florida. He never once mentioned it in any of his private or official writings—at least those writings that still exist—and historians believe his goal was gold and other treasures, and perhaps to convert the natives to Catholicism.

His legacy lives on at the Casa Blanca in Old San Juan (see "Seeing the Sights" in chapter 6). Casa Blanca is the oldest continuously occupied residence in the western hemisphere and the oldest of about 800 Spanish colonial buildings in Old San Juan's National Historic Zone. In 1968, it became a historic national monument placed in the care of the Institute of Puerto Rican Culture. Today the building is the site of the Juan Ponce de León Museum. The carved conquistador's coat of arms greets visitors at the entrance.

ceremonial dances *(areytos),* drumbeats, oral traditions, and a ceremonial ball game played between opposing teams (of 10 to 30 players per team) with a rubber ball; winning this game was thought to bring a good harvest and strong, healthy children.

Skilled at agriculture and hunting, the Taínos were also good sailors, canoe makers, and navigators.

About 100 years before the Spanish invasion, the Taínos were challenged by an invading South American tribe—the Caribs. Fierce, warlike, sadistic, and adept at using poison-tipped arrows, the Caribs raided Taíno settlements for slaves (especially female) and bodies for the completion of their rites of cannibalism. Some ethnologists argue that the preeminence of the Taínos, shaken by the attacks of the Caribs, was already jeopardized by the time of the Spanish occupation. In fact, it was the Caribs who fought the most effectively against the Europeans; their behavior led the Europeans to unfairly attribute warlike tendencies to all of the island's tribes. A dynamic tension between the Taínos and the Caribs certainly existed when Christopher Columbus landed on Puerto Rico.

To understand Puerto Rico's prehistoric era, it is important to know that the Taínos, far more than the Caribs, contributed greatly to the everyday life and language that evolved during the Spanish occupation. Taíno place names are still used for such towns as Utuado, Mayagüez, Caguas, and Humacao. Many Taíno implements and techniques were copied directly by the Europeans, including the *bohío* (straw hut), the *hamaca* (hammock), the musical instrument known as the maracas, and the method of making bread from the starchy cassava root. Also, many Taíno superstitions and legends were adopted and adapted by the Spanish and still influence the Puerto Rican imagination.

SPAIN, SYPHILIS & SLAVERY

Christopher Columbus became the first European to land on the shores of Puerto Rico, on November 19, 1493, near what would become the town of Aguadilla, during his second voyage to the New World. Giving the island the name San Juan Bautista, he sailed on in search of shores with more obvious riches for the taking. A European foothold on the island was established in 1508 when Juan Ponce de León, the first governor of Puerto Rico, imported colonists from the nearby island of Hispaniola. They founded the town of Caparra, which lay close to the site of present-day San Juan. The town was almost immediately wracked with internal power struggles among the Spanish settlers, who pressed the native peoples into servitude, evangelized them, and frantically sought for gold, thus quickly changing the face of the island.

Meanwhile, the Amerindians began dying at an alarming rate, victims of imported diseases such as smallpox and whooping cough, against which they had no biologic immunity. The natives also paid the Spanish back, giving them diseases such as syphilis against which they had little immunity. Both communities reeled, disoriented, from their contact with one another. In 1511, the Amerindians rebelled against attempts by the Spanish to enslave them. The rebellion was brutally suppressed by the Spanish forces of Ponce de León, whose muskets and firearms were vastly superior to the hatchets and arrows of the native peoples. In desperation, the remnants of the Taínos joined forces with their traditional enemies, the Caribs, but even that belated union did little to check the inexorable growth of European power.

Because the Indians languished in slavery, sometimes preferring mass suicide to imprisonment, their work in the fields and mines of Puerto Rico was soon taken over by Africans who were imported by Spanish, Danish, Portuguese, British, and American slavers.

By 1521, the island had been renamed Puerto Rico (Rich Port) and was one of the most strategic islands in the Caribbean, which was increasingly viewed as a Spanish sea. Officials of the Spanish Crown dubbed the island "the strongest foothold of Spain in America" and hastened to strengthen the already impressive bulwarks surrounding the city of San Juan.

PIRATES & PILLAGING ENGLISHMEN

Within a century, Puerto Rico's position at the easternmost edge of what would become Spanish America helped it play a major part in the Spanish expansion toward Florida, the South American coast, and Mexico. It was usually the first port of call for Spanish ships arriving in the Americas; recognizing that the island was a strategic keystone, the Spanish decided to strengthen its defenses. By 1540, La Fortaleza, the first of three massive fortresses built in San Juan, was completed. By 1600, San Juan was completely enclosed by some of the most formidable ramparts in the Caribbean, whereas, ironically, the remainder of Puerto Rico was almost defenseless. In 1565, the king of Spain ordered the governor of Puerto Rico to provide men and material to strengthen the city of San Agustin (St. Augustine) in Florida.

By this time, the English (and to a lesser extent, the French) were seriously harassing Spanish shipping in the Caribbean and North Atlantic. At least part of the French and English aggression was in retaliation for the 1493 Papal Bull dividing the New World between Portugal and Spain—an arrangement that eliminated all other nations from the spoils and colonization of the New World.

Queen Elizabeth I's most effective weapon against Spanish expansion in the Caribbean wasn't the Royal Navy; rather, it was buccaneers such as John Hawkins and Sir Francis Drake. Their victories included the destruction of St. Augustine in Florida, Cartagena in Colombia, and Santo Domingo in what is now the Dominican Republic, and the general harassment and pillaging of many Spanish ships and treasure convoys sailing from the New World to Europe with gold and silver from the Aztec and Inca empires. The Royal Navy did play an important role, however, for its 1588 defeat of the Spanish Armada marked the rise of the English as a major maritime power. The Spanish then began to aggressively fortify such islands as Puerto Rico.

In 1595, Drake and Hawkins persuaded an uncertain Queen Elizabeth to embark on a bold and daring plan to invade and conquer Puerto Rico. An English general, the Earl of Cumberland, urged his men to bravery by "assuring your selves you have the maydenhead of Puerto Rico and so possesse the keyes of all the Indies." Confident that the island was "the very key of the West Indies which locketh and shutteth all the gold and silver in the continent of America and Brasilia," he brought into battle an English force of 4,500 soldiers and eventually captured La Fortaleza.

Although the occupation lasted a full 65 days, the English eventually abandoned Puerto Rico when their armies were decimated by tropical diseases and the local population, which began to engage in a kind of guerrilla warfare against the English. After pillaging and destroying much of the Puerto Rican countryside, the English left. Their short but abortive victory compelled the Spanish king, Philip III, to continue construction of the island's defenses. Despite these efforts, Puerto Rico retained a less-than-invincible aspect as Spanish soldiers in the forts often deserted or succumbed to tropical diseases.

A DUTCH TREAT

In 1625, Puerto Rico was covetously eyed by Holland, whose traders and merchants desperately wanted a foothold in the West Indies. Spearheaded by the Dutch West India Company, which had received trading concessions from the Dutch Crown covering most of the West Indies, the Dutch armies besieged

El Morro Fortress in San Juan in one of the bloodiest assaults the fortress ever sustained. When the commanding officer of El Morro refused to surrender, the Dutch burned San Juan to the ground, including all church and civil archives and the bishop's library, by then the most famous and complete collection of books in America. Fueled by rage and courage, the Spanish rallied their forces and soon threw out the Dutch.

In response to the widespread destruction of the strongest link in the chain of Spanish defenses, Spain threw itself wholeheartedly into improving and reinforcing the defenses around San Juan. King Philip IV justified his expenditures by declaring Puerto Rico the "front and vanguard of the Western Indies and, consequently, the most important of them and most coveted by the enemies of Spain."

Within 150 years, after extravagant expenditures of time and money, the city's walls were considered almost impregnable. Military sophistication was added during the 1760s, when two Irishmen, Tomas O'Daly and Alejandro O'Reilly, surrounded the city with some of Europe's most technically up-to-date defenses. Despite the thick walls, however, the island's defenses remained precarious because of the frequent tropical epidemics that devastated the ranks of the soldiers; the chronically late pay, which weakened the soldiers' morale; and the belated and often wrong-minded priorities of the Spanish monarchy, which were decided thousands of miles away.

A CATHOLIC CRUSADE

From the earliest days of Spanish colonization, an army of priests and missionaries embarked on a vigorous crusade to convert Puerto Rico's Taínos to Roman Catholicism. King Ferdinand himself paid for the construction of a Franciscan monastery and a series of chapels, and required specific support of the church from the aristocrats who had been awarded land grants in the new territories. They were required to build churches, provide Christian burials, and grant religious instruction to both Taíno and African slaves.

Among the church's most important activities were the Franciscan monks' efforts to teach the island's children how to read, write, and count. In 1688, Bishop Francisco Padilla, who is now included among the legends of Puerto Rico, established one of the island's most famous schools. When it became clear that local parents were too poor to provide their children with appropriate clothing, he succeeded in persuading the king of Spain to pay for their clothes.

Puerto Rico was declared by the pope as the first *see*—ecclesiastical headquarters—in the New World. In 1519, it became the general headquarters of the Inquisition in the New World. (About 70 years later, the Inquisition's headquarters was transferred to the important and well-defended city of Cartagena, in Colombia.)

FROM SMUGGLING TO SUGAR

The island's early development was shackled by Spain's insistence on a centrist economy. All goods exported from or imported to Puerto Rico had to pass through Spain itself, usually through Seville. In effect, this policy prohibited any trade (officially, at least) between Puerto Rico and its island neighbors.

In response, a flourishing black market developed. Cities such as Ponce became smuggling centers. This black market was especially prevalent after the Spanish colonization of Mexico and Peru, when many Spanish goods, which once would have been sent to Puerto Rico, ended up in those more immediately lucrative colonies instead. Although smugglers were punished if caught, nothing could curb this illegal (and untaxed) trade. Some historians estimate that almost everyone on the island—including priests, citizens, and military and civic authorities—was actively involved.

By the mid-1500s, the several hundred settlers who had immigrated to Puerto Rico from Spain heard (and sometimes believed) rumors of the fortunes to be made in the gold mines of Peru. When the island's population declined because of the ensuing mass exodus, the king enticed 500 families from the Canary Islands to settle on Puerto Rico between 1683 and 1691. Meanwhile, an active trade in slaves—imported as labor for fields that were increasingly used for sugarcane and tobacco production—swelled the island's ranks. This happened despite the Crown's imposition of strict controls on the number of slaves that could be brought in. Sugarcane earned profits for many islanders, but Spanish mismanagement, fraud within the government bureaucracy, and a lack of both labor and ships to transport the finished product to market discouraged the fledgling industry. Later, fortunes were made and lost in the production of ginger, an industry that died as soon as the Spanish government raised taxes on ginger imports to exorbitant levels. Despite the arrival of immigrants to Puerto Rico from many countries, diseases such as spotted fever, yellow fever, malaria, smallpox, and measles wiped out the population almost as fast as it grew.

MORE SMUGGLING

As the philosophical and political movement known as the Enlightenment swept both Europe and North America during the late 1700s and the 1800s, Spain moved to improve Puerto Rico's economy through its local government. The island's defenses were beefed up, roads and bridges were built, and a public education program was launched. The island remained a major Spanish naval stronghold in the New World. Immigration from Europe and other places more than tripled the population. It was during this era that Puerto Rico began to develop a unique identity of its own, a native pride, and a consciousness of its importance within the Caribbean.

The heavily fortified city of San Juan, the island's civic centerpiece, remained under Spain's rigid control. Although the victim of an occasional pirate raid, or an attack by English or French forces, the outlying countryside was generally left alone to develop its own local power centers. The city of Ponce, for example, flourished under the Spanish Crown's lax supervision and grew wealthy from the tons of contraband and the high-quality sugar that passed through its port. This trend was also encouraged by the unrealistic law that declared San Juan the island's only legal port. Contemporary sources, in fact, cite the fledgling United States as among the most active of Ponce's early contraband trading partners.

RISING POWER

During the 18th century, the number of towns on the island grew rapidly. There were five settlements in Puerto Rico in 1700; 100 years later, there were almost 40 settlements, and the island's population had grown to more than 150,000.

Meanwhile, the waters of the Caribbean increasingly reflected the diplomatic wars unfolding in Europe. In 1797, the British, after easily capturing Trinidad (which was poorly defended by the Spanish), failed in a spectacular effort to conquer Puerto Rico. The *criollos,* or native Puerto Ricans, played a major role in the island's defense and later retained a growing sense of their own cultural identity.

The islanders were becoming aware that Spain could not enforce the hundreds of laws it had previously imposed to support its centrist trade policies. Thousands of merchants, farmers, and civil authorities traded profitably with privateers from various nations, thereby deepening the tendency to evade or ignore the laws imposed by Spain and its colonial governors. The attacks by privateers on British shipping were especially severe, since pirates based in Puerto Rico ranged as far south as Trinidad, bringing dozens of captured British ships into Puerto Rican harbors. (Several decades earlier, British privateers operating out of Jamaica had endlessly harassed Spanish shipping; the tradition of government-sanctioned piracy was well established.)

It was during this period that coffee—which would later play an essential role in the island's economy—was introduced to the Puerto Rican highlands from the nearby Dominican Republic.

Despite the power of San Juan and its Spanish institutions, 18th-century Puerto Rico was predominantly rural. The report of a special emissary of the Spanish king, Marshal Alejandro O'Reilly, remains a remarkably complete analysis of 18th-century Puerto Rican society. It helped promote a more progressive series of fiscal and administrative policies that reflected the Enlightenment ideals found in many European countries.

Suddenly, Puerto Rico began to be viewed as a potential source of income for the Spanish Empire, rather than a drain on income. One of O'Reilly's most visible legacies was his recommendation that people live in towns rather than be scattered about the countryside. Shortly after this, seven new towns, some in the island's interior, were established.

Meanwhile, as the island prospered and its bourgeoisie became more numerous and affluent, daily life became more refined. New public buildings were erected; concerts were introduced; and the everyday aspects of life—such as furniture and social ritual—grew more ornate. Insights into Puerto Rico's changing life can be seen in the works of its most famous 18th-century painter, José Campeche, whose portraits, religious frescoes, and landscapes are among his era's most distinctive legacies.

THE LAST BASTION

Much of the politics of 19th-century Latin America cannot be understood without a review of Spain's problems at that time. Up until 1850, there was political and military turmoil in Spain, a combination that eventually led to the collapse of its empire. Since 1796, Spain had been a military satellite of post-revolutionary France, an alliance that brought it into conflict with England. In 1804, Admiral Horatio Lord Nelson's definitive victory for England over French and Spanish ships during the Battle of Trafalgar left England in supreme control of the international sea lanes and interrupted trade and communications between Spain and its colonies in the New World.

These events led to important changes for Spanish-speaking America. The revolutionary fervor of Simón Bolívar and his South American compatriots spilled over to the entire continent, embroiling Spain in a desperate attempt to hold onto the tattered remains of its empire at any cost. Recognizing that Puerto Rico and Cuba were probably the last bastions of Spanish Royalist sympathy in the Americas, Spain liberalized its trade policies, decreeing that goods no longer had to pass through Seville.

The sheer weight and volume of illegal Puerto Rican trade with such countries as Denmark, France, and—most important—the United States, forced Spain's hand in establishing a realistic set of trade reforms. A bloody revolution in Haiti, which had produced more sugarcane than almost any other West

Indies island, spurred sugarcane and coffee production in Puerto Rico. Also important was the introduction of a new and more prolific species of sugarcane, the Otahiti, which helped increase production even more.

By the 1820s, the United States was providing ample supplies of such staples as lumber, salt, butter, fish, grain, and foodstuffs, while huge amounts of Puerto Rican sugar, molasses, coffee, and rum were consumed in the United States. Meanwhile, the United States was increasingly viewed as the keeper of the peace in the Caribbean, suppressing the piracy that flourished while Spain's navy was preoccupied with its European wars.

During Venezuela's separation from Spain, Venezuelans loyal to the Spanish Crown fled en masse to the remaining Royalist bastions in the Americas—Puerto Rico and, to a lesser extent, Cuba. Although many arrived penniless, having forfeited their properties in South America in exchange for their lives, their excellent understanding of agriculture and commerce probably catalyzed much of the era's economic development in Puerto Rico. Simultaneously, many historians argue, their unflinching loyalty to the Spanish Crown contributed to one of the most conservative and reactionary social structures anywhere in the Spanish-speaking Caribbean. In any event, dozens of Spanish naval expeditions that were intended to suppress the revolutions in Venezuela were outfitted in Puerto Rican harbors during this period.

A REVOLT SUPPRESSED & SLAVERY ABOLISHED

During the latter half of the 19th century, political divisions were drawn in Puerto Rico reflecting both the political instability in Spain and the increasing demands of Puerto Ricans for some form of self-rule. As governments and regimes in Spain rose and fell, Spanish policies toward its colonies in the New World changed, too.

In 1865, representatives from Puerto Rico, Cuba, and the Philippines were invited to Madrid to air their grievances as part of a process of liberalizing Spanish colonial policy. Reforms, however, did not follow as promised, and a much-publicized and very visible minirevolt (during which the mountain city of Lares was occupied) was suppressed by the Spanish governors in 1868. Some of the funds and much of the publicity for this revolt came from expatriate Puerto Ricans living in Chile, St. Thomas, and New York.

Slavery was abolished in March 1873, about 40 years after it had been abolished throughout the British Empire. About 32,000 slaves were freed following years of liberal agitation. Abolition was viewed as a major victory for liberal forces throughout Puerto Rico, although cynics claim that slavery was much less entrenched in Puerto Rico than in neighboring Cuba, where the sugar economy was far more dependent on slave labor.

The 1895 revolution in Cuba increased the Puerto Rican demand for greater self-rule; during the ensuing intellectual ferment, many political parties emerged. The Cuban revolution provided part of the spark that led to the Spanish-American War, Cuban independence, and U.S. control of Puerto Rico, the Philippines, and the Pacific island of Guam.

THE YANKS ARE COMING, THE YANKS ARE COMING!

In 1897, faced with intense pressure from sources within Puerto Rico, a weakened Spain granted its colony a measure of autonomy, but it came too late. Other events were taking place between Spain and the United States that would forever change the future of Puerto Rico.

On February 15, 1898, the U.S. battleship *Maine* was blown up in the harbor of Havana, killing 266 men. The so-called yellow press in the United

States, especially the papers owned by the tycoon William Randolph Hearst, aroused Americans' emotions into a fever pitch for war, with the rallying cry "Remember the *Maine.*"

On April 20 of that year, President William McKinley signed a resolution demanding Spanish withdrawal from Cuba. The president ordered a blockade of Cuba's ports, and on April 24, Spain, in retaliation, declared a state of war with the United States. On April 25, the U.S. Congress declared war on Spain. In Cuba, the naval battle of Santiago was won by American forces, and in another part of the world, the Spanish colony of the Philippines was also captured by U.S. troops.

On July 25, after their victory at Santiago, American troops landed at Guánica, Puerto Rico, and several days later took over Ponce. U.S. Navy Capt. Alfred T. Mahan later wrote that the United States viewed Puerto Rico, Spain's remaining colonial outpost in the Caribbean, as vital to American interests in the area. Puerto Rico could be used as a military base to help the United States maintain control of the isthmus and to keep communications and traffic flowing between the Atlantic and the Pacific.

Spain offered to trade other territory for Puerto Rico, but the United States refused and demanded Spain's ouster from the island. Left with little choice against superior U.S. forces, Spain capitulated. The Spanish-American War ended on August 31, 1898, with the surrender of Spain and the virtual collapse of the once-powerful Spanish Empire. Puerto Rico, in the words of McKinley, was to "become a territory of the United States."

Although the entire war lasted just over 4 months, the invasion of Puerto Rico took only 2 weeks. "It wasn't much of a war," remarked Theodore Roosevelt, who had led the Rough Riders cavalry outfit in their charge up San Juan Hill, "but it was all the war there was." The United States had suffered only four casualties while acquiring Puerto Rico, the Philippines, and the island of Guam. The Treaty of Paris, signed on December 10, 1898, settled the terms of Spain's surrender.

A DUBIOUS PRIZE

Some Americans looked on Puerto Rico as a "dubious prize." One-third of the population consisted of mulattoes and blacks, descended from slaves, who had no money or land. Only about 12% of the population could read or write. About 8% were enrolled in school. It is estimated that a powerful landed gentry—only about 2% of the population—owned more than two-thirds of the land.

Washington set up a military government in Puerto Rico, headed by the War Department. A series of governors-general were appointed to rule the island, with almost the authority of a dictator. Although ruling over a rather unhappy populace, these governors-general brought about much-needed change, including tax and public health reforms. But most Puerto Ricans wanted autonomy, and many leaders, including Luís Muñoz Rivera, tried to persuade Washington to compromise. However, their protests generally fell on deaf ears.

Tensions mounted between Puerto Ricans and their new American governors. In 1900, U.S. Secretary of War Elihu Root decided that military rule of the island was inadequate; he advocated a program of autonomy that won the endorsement of President McKinley.

The island's beleaguered economy was further devastated by an 1899 hurricane that caused millions of dollars' worth of property damage, killed 3,000 people, and left one out of four people homeless. Belatedly, Congress allocated the sum of $200,000, but this did little to relieve the suffering.

Thus began a nearly 50-year colonial protectorate relationship as Puerto Rico was recognized as an unincorporated territory with its governor named by the president of the United States. Only the president had the right to override the veto of the island's governors. The legislative branch was composed of an 11-member executive committee appointed by the president, plus a 35-member chamber of delegates elected by popular vote. A resident commissioner, it was agreed, would represent Puerto Rico in Congress, "with voice but no vote."

As the United States prepared to enter World War I in 1917, Puerto Ricans were granted American citizenship and, thus, were subject to military service. The people of Puerto Rico were allowed to elect their legislature, which had been reorganized into a Senate and a House of Representatives. The president of the United States continued to appoint the governor of the island and retained the power to veto any of the governor's actions.

FROM HARVARD TO REVOLUTION

Many Puerto Ricans continued, at times rather violently, to agitate for independence. Requests for a plebiscite were constantly turned down. Meanwhile, economic conditions improved, as the island's population began to grow dramatically. Government revenues increased as large corporations from the U.S. mainland found Puerto Rico a profitable place in which to do business. There was much labor unrest, and by 1909, a labor movement demanding better working conditions and higher wages was gaining momentum.

The emerging labor movement showed its strength by organizing a cigar workers' strike in 1914 and a sugarcane workers' strike the following year. The 1930s proved to be disastrous for Puerto Rico, since it suffered greatly from the worldwide depression. To make matters worse, two devastating hurricanes—one in 1928 and another in 1932—destroyed millions of dollars' worth of crops and property. There was also an outbreak of disease that, along with starvation, demoralized the population. Some relief came in the form of food shipments authorized by Congress.

As tension between Puerto Rico and the United States intensified, there emerged Pedro Albizu Campos, a graduate of Harvard Law School and a former U.S. army officer. Leading a group of militant anti-American revolutionaries, he held that America's claim to Puerto Rico was illegal, since the island had already been granted autonomy by Spain. Terrorist acts by his followers, including assassinations, led to Albizu's imprisonment, but terrorist activities continued.

In 1935, President Franklin D. Roosevelt launched the Puerto Rican Reconstruction Administration, which provided for agricultural development, public works, and electrification of the island. The following year, Sen. Millard E. Tidings of Maryland introduced a measure to grant independence to the island. His efforts were cheered by a local leader, Luís Muñoz Marín, son of the statesman Luís Muñoz Rivera. The young Muñoz founded the Partida Popular Democratica (Popular Democratic Party) in 1938, which adopted the slogan "Bread, Land, and Liberty." By 1940, this new party had gained control of more than 50% of the seats of both the upper and the lower houses of government, and the young Muñoz was elected leader of the Senate.

Roosevelt appointed Rexford Guy Tugwell as governor of Puerto Rico; he spoke Spanish and seemed to have a genuine concern for the plight of the islanders. Muñoz met with Tugwell and convinced him that Puerto Rico was capable of electing its own governor. As a step in that direction, Roosevelt appointed Jesús Piñero as the first resident commissioner of the island.

Impressions

It is a kind of lost love-child, born to the Spanish Empire, and fostered by the United States.

—Nicholas Wollaston, *Red Rumba,* 1962

In 1944, the U.S. Congress approved a bill granting Puerto Rico the right to elect its own governor. This was the beginning of the famed Operation Bootstrap, a pump-priming fiscal and economic aid package designed to improve the island's standard of living.

SHOOTING AT HARRY

In 1946, President Harry S. Truman appointed native-born Piñero as governor of Puerto Rico, and the following year the U.S. Congress recognized the right of Puerto Ricans to elect their own governor. In 1948, Luís Muñoz Marín became the first elected governor and immediately recommended that Puerto Rico be transformed into an "associated free state." Endorsement of his plan was delayed by Washington, but President Truman approved the Puerto Rican Commonwealth Bill in 1950, providing for a plebiscite in which voters would decide whether they would remain a colony or become a U.S. commonwealth. In June 1951, Puerto Ricans voted three to one for commonwealth status, and on July 25, 1952, the Commonwealth of Puerto Rico was born.

This event was marred by a group of nationalists who marched on the Governor's Mansion in San Juan, resulting in 27 deaths and hundreds of casualties. A month later, two Puerto Rican nationalists made an unsuccessful attempt on Truman's life in Washington, killing a policeman in the process. And in March 1954, four Puerto Rican nationalists wounded five U.S. congressmen when they fired down into the House of Representatives from the visitors' gallery.

In spite of this violence, during the 1950s Puerto Rico began to take pride in its own culture and traditions. In 1955, the Institute of Puerto Rican Culture was established in San Juan, and 1957 saw the inauguration of the Pablo Casals Festival, which launched a renaissance of classical music and a celebration of the arts, a tradition that continues to this day. In 1959, a wealthy industrialist, Luís A. Ferré, donated his personal art collection toward the establishment of the Museum of Fine Arts in Ponce.

GIVE ME LIBERTY OR GIVE ME STATEHOOD

Luís Muñoz Marín resigned from office in 1964, but his party continued to win subsequent elections. The Independent Party, which demanded complete autonomy, gradually lost power. An election on July 23, 1967, reconfirmed the desire of most Puerto Ricans to maintain commonwealth status. In 1968, Luís A. Ferré won a close race for governor, spearheading a pro-statehood party, the Partida Progressiva Nueva (New Progressive Party). It staunchly advocated statehood as an alternative to the island's commonwealth status, but in 1972, the Partida Popular Democratica returned to power; by then, the island's economy was based largely on tourism, rum, and industry. Operation Bootstrap had been successful in creating thousands of new jobs, although more than 100,000 Puerto Ricans moved to the U.S. mainland during the 1950s, seeking a better life. The island's economy continued to improve, although perhaps not as quickly as anticipated by Operation Bootstrap.

Puerto Rico grabbed the world's attention in 1979 with the launching of the Pan-American Games. It is vigorously attempting to bring the Summer Olympics there in 2004. The island's culture received a boost in 1981 with the opening of the Center of the Performing Arts in San Juan, which attracted world-famous performers and virtuosos. The international spotlight again focused on Puerto Rico at the time of the first papal visit there in 1986. John Paul II (or Juan Pablo II, as he was called locally) kindled a renewed interest in religion, especially among the Catholic youth of the island.

In 1996, Puerto Rico lost its special tax-break status, which had originally lured American industry to the island. Down the road, some dire consequences to the island economy are predicted as a result of this loss.

A flare-up between the U.S. Navy and Puerto Ricans, especially the islanders of Vieques, burst into the headlines in 1999. President Clinton ordered an end to target practice by the Navy and to all military exercises within 5 years unless local residents agree to an extension. To entice residents, the U.S. is prepared to offer millions of dollars in developmental money. All military exercises were suspended in April 1999 when a civilian Puerto Rican guard, David Sanes Rodríguez, was killed after Marine jets dropped bombs that unintentionally hit an observation tower.

4 A Portrait of the Puerto Ricans

The people of Puerto Rico represent a mix of races, cultures, languages, and religions. They draw their unique heritage from the original native population, from Spanish royalists who sought refuge here, from African slaves imported to work the sugar plantations, and from other Caribbean islanders who have come here seeking jobs. The Spanish they speak is a mix, too, with many words borrowed from the pre-Columbian Amerindian tongue right up to modern-day English. Even the Catholicism they practice blends some Taíno and African traditions.

THE ISLANDERS

Some 3.56 million people inhabit the main island, making it one of the most densely populated in the world. It has an average of about 1,000 people per square mile, a ratio higher than that within any of the 50 states. It is estimated that if the 2 million Puerto Ricans who have migrated to the United States (more Puerto Ricans are said to live in New York City than in San Juan) were to return home, the island would be so crowded that there would be virtually no room for them to live.

When the United States acquired the island in 1898, most Puerto Ricans worked in agriculture, but today most jobs are industrial and are situated in the cities. One-third of the commonwealth's population is concentrated in the San Juan/Carolina/Bayamón metropolitan area.

The people of Puerto Rico represent a cultural and racial mix. When the Spanish forced the Taíno peoples into slavery, virtually the entire indigenous population was decimated, except for a few Amerindians who escaped into the remote mountains. Eventually they intermarried with the poor Spanish farmers and became known as *jíbaros*. Because of industrialization and migration to the cities, few *jíbaros* remain.

Besides the slaves imported from Africa to work on the plantations, other ethnic groups joined the island's racial mix. Fleeing Simón Bolívar's independence movements in South America, Spanish loyalists fled to Puerto Rico—a fiercely conservative Spanish colony during the early 1800s. French families

Sweet Songs of Love

The Spanish colonialists first recorded some of the Taíno tribespeople's legends, which they had passed down orally from generation to generation. Many of these were ghost tales about demons who roamed the island after dark, pursuing food or people or else protecting gold and loot that pirates long ago stashed away for safekeeping.

But one such tale, dated from about 1511, is the Puerto Rican version of *Romeo and Juliet* or the early Virginian legend of Capt. John Smith and his Native American bride, Pocahontas.

The story is called "Guanina" because it tells of Don Cristóbal de Sotomayor, a young man from Valladolid, Spain, who was enchanted by a graceful Amerindian girl, Guanina. At its end, the two are found dead, Guanina's head resting on his bloody chest.

It was said that a witch doctor buried their bodies under the roots of a towering ceiba tree, and that white lilies and red poppies grew from their graves. Locals claimed to hear sweet songs of love rustling through the leaves of the giant ceiba.

Some people on the island say the lovers still come out on moonlit nights to renew their vows of devotion.

also flocked here from both Louisiana and Haiti, as changing governments or violent revolutions turned their worlds upside down. Meanwhile, as word of the rich sugarcane economy reached economically depressed Scotland and Ireland, many farmers from those countries also journeyed to Puerto Rico in search of a better life.

During the mid-19th century, labor was needed to build roads. Initially, Chinese workers were imported for this task, followed by workers from such countries as Italy, France, Germany, and even Lebanon. American expatriates came to the island after 1898. Long after Spain had lost control of Puerto Rico, Spanish immigrants continued to arrive on the island. The most significant new immigrant population arrived in the 1960s, when thousands of Cubans fled from Fidel Castro's Communist state. The latest arrivals in Puerto Rico have come from the economically depressed Dominican Republic.

THEIR LANGUAGES

Spanish is the language of Puerto Rico, although English is widely spoken, especially in hotels, restaurants, shops, and nightclubs that attract tourists. In the hinterlands, however, Spanish prevails.

If you plan to travel extensively on Puerto Rico but don't speak Spanish, pick up a Spanish-language phrase book. The most popular is *Berlitz Spanish for Travelers,* published by Collier Macmillan. The University of Chicago's *Pocketbook Dictionary* is equally helpful. If you already have a basic knowledge of Spanish and want to improve both your word usage and your sentence structure while in Puerto Rico, consider purchasing a copy of *Spanish Now,* published by Barron's.

Many Amerindian words from pre-Columbian times have been retained in the language. For example, the Puerto Rican national anthem, titled "La Borinqueña," refers to the Arawak name for the island Borinquen, while Mayagüez, Yauco, Caguas, Guaynabo, and Arecibo are all pre-Columbian place names.

Many Amerindian words were borrowed to describe the phenomena of the New World. The natives slept in *hamacas,* and today Puerto Ricans still lounge in hammocks. The god Juracán was feared by the Arawaks just as much as contemporaries fear autumn hurricanes. African words were also added to the linguistic mix, and Castilian Spanish was significantly modified.

With the American takeover in 1898, English became the first Germanic language to be introduced into Puerto Rico. This linguistic marriage led to what some scholars call Spanglish, a colloquial dialect blending English and Spanish into forms not considered classically correct in either linguistic tradition.

The bilingual confusion was also greatly accelerated by the mass migration to the U.S. mainland of thousands of Puerto Ricans, who quickly altered their speech patterns to conform to the language used in the urban Puerto Rican communities of such cities as New York.

THEIR RELIGIONS

The majority of Puerto Ricans are Roman Catholic, but religious freedom for all faiths is guaranteed by the Commonwealth Constitution. Catholic services are conducted throughout the island in both English and Spanish. There is a Jewish Community Center in Miramar, plus a Jewish Reformed Congregation in Santurce. There are English-speaking Protestant services for Baptists, Episcopalians, Lutherans, and Presbyterians, and other interdenominational services.

Although predominantly Catholic, Puerto Rico does not follow Catholic dogma and rituals as assiduously as do the churches of Spain and Italy. Because the church supported slavery, there was a long-lasting resentment against the all-Spanish clergy of colonial days. Island-born men were excluded from the priesthood. When Puerto Ricans eventually took over the Catholic churches on the island, they followed some guidelines from Spain and Italy but modified or ignored others. For example, many Catholic couples in Puerto Rico practice birth control and are married outside the Catholic Church.

Following the U.S. acquisition of the island in 1898, Protestantism grew in influence and popularity. There were Protestants on the island before the invasion, but their numbers increased after Puerto Rico became an American colony. Many islanders liked the idea of separation of church and state, as provided for in the U.S. Constitution. In recent years, a Pentecostal fundamentalism has swept across the island. There are perhaps some 1,500 evangelical churches in Puerto Rico today.

As throughout Latin America, the practice of Catholicism in Puerto Rico blends certain native Taíno and African traditions with mainstream tenets of the faith. It has been said that the real religion of Puerto Rico is *espiritismo* (spiritualism), a quasi-magical belief in occult forces. Spanish colonial rulers outlawed spiritualism, but under the U.S. occupation it flourished in dozens of isolated pockets of the island.

Students of religion trace spiritualism to the Taínos, and to their belief that *jípia* (the spirits of the dead—somewhat like the legendary vampire) slumbered by day and prowled the island by night. Instead of looking for bodies, the *jípia* were seeking wild fruit to eat. Thus arose the Puerto Rican tradition of putting out fruit on the kitchen table. Even in modern homes today, you'll often find a bowl of plastic, flamboyantly colored fruit resting atop a refrigerator.

Many islanders still believe in the "evil eye," or *mal de ojo.* To look on a person or a person's possessions covetously, according to believers, can lead to that individual's sickness or perhaps death. Little children are given bead charm bracelets to guard against the evil eye. Spiritualism also extends into healing, folk medicine, and food. Some spiritualists, for example, believe that cold food should never be eaten with hot food. Various island plants, herbs, and oils are believed to have certain healing properties, and spiritualist literature is available throughout the island.

5 Puerto Rican Handicrafts

SANTOS

The most impressive of the island's crafts are the *santos,* carved religious figures that have been produced since the 1500s. Craftspeople who make these are called *santeros;* using clay, gold, stone, or cedar wood, they carve figurines representing saints, usually from 8 to 20 inches tall. Before the Spanish colonization, small statues called *zemi* stood in native tribal villages and camps as objects of veneration, and Puerto Rico's *santos* may derive from that pre-Columbian tradition. Every town has its patron saint, and every home has its *santos* to protect the family. For some families, worshipping the *santos* replaces a traditional mass.

Art historians view the carving of *santos* as Puerto Rico's greatest contribution to the plastic arts. The earliest figures were richly baroque, indicating a strong Spanish influence, but as the islanders began to assert their own identity, the carved figures often became simpler.

In carving *santos,* craftspeople often used handmade tools. Sometimes such natural materials as vegetable dyes and even human hair were used. The saints represented by most *santos* can be identified by their accompanying symbols; for example, Saint Anthony is usually depicted with the infant Jesus and a book. The most popular group of *santos* is the Three Kings. The Trinity and the Nativity also are depicted frequently.

Art experts claim that *santos* making approached its zenith at the turn of the 20th century, although hundreds of *santeros* still practice their craft throughout the island. Serious *santos* collectors view the former craftsmen of old as the true artists in the field. However, many skilled *santeros* still take this art most seriously. To pick up a list of these artisans, you can visit the **Popular Arts and Crafts Center,** Calle Cristo 253 (☎ 787/722-0621), run by the Institute of Puerto Rican Culture in Old San Juan. They will provide you with contacts of studios where visitors are welcome. See also "Shopping" in chapter 6 for outlets selling these *santos* figures.

Some of the best *santos* on the island can be seen at the Capilla del Cristo in Old San Juan. Perhaps at some future date, a museum devoted entirely to *santos* will open on Puerto Rico.

OLD LACE

Another Puerto Rican craft has undergone a big revival just as it seemed that it would disappear forever: lace. Originating in Spain, *mundillos* (tatted fabrics) are the product of a type of bobbin lace making. This craft, 5 centuries old, exists today only in Puerto Rico and Spain.

The first lace made in Puerto Rico was called *torchon* (beggar's lace). Early examples of beggar's lace were considered of inferior quality, but artisans today have transformed this fabric into a delicate art form, eagerly sought by collectors. Lace bands called *entrados* have two straight borders, whereas the other traditional style, *puntilla,* has both a straight and a scalloped border.

The best place to see the craft of the *mundillo* is the **Folk Arts Center** at the Dominican Convent at Calle Norzagaray 98 in Old San Juan (☎ 787/721-6866). This center has information on island shops that make and sell *mundillos.* You can also attend the Puerto Rican Weaving Festival, held annually at the end of April in the town of Isabela. For more information on how to purchase Puerto Rican lace, refer to "Shopping" in chapter 6.

GROTESQUE MASKS

The most popular of all Puerto Rican crafts are the frightening *caretas*—papier-mâché masks worn at island carnivals. Tangles of menacing horns, fang-toothed leering expressions, and bulging eyes of these half-demon, half-animal creations send children running and screaming to their parents. At carnival time, they are worn by costumed revelers called *vejigantes*. *Vejigantes* often wear bat-winged jumpsuits and roam the streets either individually or in groups.

The origins of these masks and carnivals may go back to medieval Spain and/or tribal Africa. A processional tradition in Spain, dating from the early 17th century, was intended to terrify sinners with marching devils in the hope that they would return to church. Cervantes described it briefly in *Don Quijote*. Puerto Rico blended this Spanish procession with the masked tradition brought by slaves from Africa. Some historians believe that the Taínos also were accomplished mask makers, which would make this a very ancient tradition indeed.

The predominant mask colors, at least traditionally, were black, red, and yellow, all symbols of hellfire and damnation. Today, pastels are more likely to be used. Each *vejigante* sports at least two or three horns, although some masks have hundreds of horns in all shapes and sizes. Mask making in Ponce, the major center for this craft, and in Loíza Aldea, a palm-fringed town on the island's northeastern coast, has since led to a renaissance of Puerto Rican folk art.

You can purchase these masks year-round at various places, even in the homes of the mask makers, providing that you have their addresses. Although many masks are extremely elaborate and expensive, they typically range in price from $15 to $100. The premier store selling these masks is **Puerto Rican Art and Crafts,** at Calle Fortaleza 204 in Old San Juan (☎ 787/725-5596). Masks can be seen in action at the three big masquerade carnivals on the island: the Ponce Festival in February, the Festival of Loíza Aldea in July, and the Día de las Mascaras at Hatillo in December.

WHERE TO SEE THE BEST ARTS & CRAFTS

Serious students of Puerto Rican art always go to the **Folk Arts Center** at the Dominican Convent at Calle Norzagaray 98 in Old San Juan (☎ 787/721-6866). It's the best source of information on the island about Puerto Rican arts and crafts. For actual purchases of Puerto Rican crafts, the best outlet is **Puerto Rican Arts and Crafts** at Calle Fortaleza 204 (☎ 787/725-5596), also in Old San Juan.

With its dozen or so museums and even more art galleries, Old San Juan is the greatest repository of Puerto Rican arts and crafts. Galleries sell everything from pre-Columbian artifacts to paintings by relatively contemporary artists such as Angel Botello, who died in 1986. The **Galleria Botello,** at Calle del

Impressions

A machete is the only instrument used in their work. With it, they cut the sticks, vines, and palm leaves to build their houses and also clear the ground and plant and cultivate their crops.

—Fray Inigo Abbad

Cristo 208 (☎ 787/723-2879), was his former home. He restored the colonial mansion himself; now his paintings and sculptures are on display here.

Another good place to see Puerto Rican art is the **Museum of History, Anthropology and Art,** Avenida Ponce de León, Río Piedras Campus (☎ 787/764-0000). Because of space limitations, the museum's galleries can exhibit only a fifth of their vast collection at one time, but the work is always of top-notch quality. The collection ranges from pre-Columbian artifacts to works by today's major painters.

The greatest art on the island is at the **Museo de Arte de Ponce,** Avenida de las Americas, #25 (☎ 787/848-0505), in Puerto Rico's second-largest city. The collection, donated by former governor Luís A. Ferré, ranges from Jan van Eyck's *Salvatore Mundi* to Rossetti's confrontational *Daughters of King Lear.* The museum building was designed by Edward Durell Stone, who also designed New York's Museum of Modern Art. Works are displayed here in a honeycomb of skylit hexagonal rooms. Puerto Rican artists who are represented include José Campéche (see above) and Francisco Oller. In addition to such European masters as Reubens, van Dyck, and Murillo, the museum features works by Latin American artists, including some by the Mexican Diego Rivera.

6 Puerto Rico's Exotic Bill of Fare

Although Puerto Rican cooking is somewhat similar to both Spanish and Mexican cuisine, it has a unique style, using such indigenous seasonings and ingredients as coriander, papaya, cacao, nispero, apio, plantains, and yampee.

Cocina Criolla (Créole cooking) can be traced back to the Arawaks and Taínos, the original inhabitants of the island, who thrived on a diet of corn, tropical fruit, and seafood. When Ponce de León arrived with Columbus in 1493, the Spanish added beef, pork, rice, wheat, and olive oil to the island's foodstuffs.

The Spanish soon began planting sugarcane and importing slaves from Africa, who brought with them okra and taro (known in Puerto Rico as *yautia*). The mingling of flavors and ingredients passed from generation to generation among the different ethnic groups that settled on the island, resulting in the exotic blend of today's Puerto Rican cuisine.

APPETIZERS & SOUPS

Lunch and dinner generally begin with sizzling-hot appetizers such as *bacalaítos,* crunchy cod fritters; *surullitos,* sweet and plump cornmeal fingers; and *empañadillas,* crescent-shaped turnovers filled with lobster, crab, conch, or beef.

Soups are also a popular beginning. There is a debate about whether one of the world's best-known soups, *frijoles negros,* is Cuban or Puerto Rican in origin. Wherever it started, black-bean soup makes a savory if filling opening to a meal. Another classic soup is *sopón de pollo con arroz*—chicken soup with rice—which manages to taste somewhat different in every restaurant. One traditional method of preparing this soup calls for large pieces of pumpkin and diced potatoes or *yautias* (the starchy root of a large-leaved tropical plant whose flesh is usually yellow or creamy white).

The third classic soup is *sopón de pescado* (fish soup), prepared with the head and tail intact. Again, this soup varies from restaurant to restaurant and may depend on the catch of the day. Traditionally, it is made with garlic and spices plus onions and tomatoes, the flavor enhanced by a tiny dash of vinegar and varying amount of sherry. *Caldo gallego* (Galician broth) is a dish imported from Spain's northwestern province of Galicia. It is prepared with salt pork,

Strange Fruit

Reading of Capt. James Cook's explorations of the South Pacific in the late 1700s, West Indian planters were intrigued by his accounts of the breadfruit tree, which grew in abundance on Tahiti. Seeing it as a source of cheap food for their slaves, they beseeched King George III to sponsor an expedition to bring the trees to the Caribbean.

In 1787, the king put Capt. William Bligh in command of H.M.S. *Bounty* and sent him to do just that. One of Bligh's lieutenants was a former shipmate named Fletcher Christian. They became the leading actors in one of the great sea yarns when Christian overpowered Bligh, took over the *Bounty,* threw the breadfruit trees into the South Pacific Ocean, and disappeared into oblivion.

Bligh survived by sailing the ship's open longboat 3,000 miles to the East Indies, where he hitched a ride back to England on a Dutch vessel. Later he was given command of another ship and sent to Tahiti to get more breadfruit. Although he succeeded on this second attempt, the whole operation went for naught when the West Indies slaves refused to eat the strange fruit of the new tree, preferring instead their old, familiar rice.

Descendants of those trees still grow in the Caribbean, and the islanders prepare the head-size fruit in a number of ways. A thick green rind covers its starchy, sweet flesh whose flavor is evocative of a sweet potato. *Tostones*—fried green breadfruit slices—accompany most meat, fish, or poultry dishes served today in Puerto Rico.

white beans, ham, and *berzas* (collard greens) or *grelos* (turnip greens), and the whole kettle is flavored with spicy *chorizos* (Spanish sausages).

Garbanzos (chickpeas) are often added to give flavor, body, and texture to Puerto Rican soups. One of the most authentic versions of this is *sopón de garbanzos con patas de cerdo* (chickpea soup with pig's feet). Into this kettle is added a variety of ingredients, including pumpkin, *chorizos,* salt pork, chile peppers, cabbage, potatoes, tomatoes, and fresh cilantro leaves.

Not really a soup, the most traditional Puerto Rican dish is *asopao,* a hearty gumbo made with either chicken or shellfish. One well-known version, consumed when the food budget runs low, is *asopao de gandules* (pigeon peas). Every Puerto Rican chef has his or her own recipe for *asopao. Asopao de pollo* (chicken *asopao*) takes a whole chicken, which is then flavored with spices such as oregano, garlic, and paprika, along with salt pork, cured ham, green peppers, chile peppers, onions, cilantro, olives, tomatoes, *chorizos,* and pimientos. For a final touch, green peas or asparagus might be added.

MAIN COURSES

The aroma that wafts from kitchens throughout Puerto Rico comes from *adobo* and *sofrito*—blends of herbs and spices that give many of the native foods their distinctive taste and color. *Adobo,* made by crushing together peppercorns, oregano, garlic, salt, olive oil, and lime juice or vinegar, is rubbed into meats before they are roasted. *Sofrito,* a potpourri of onions, garlic, and peppers browned in either olive oil or lard and colored with *achiote* (annatto seeds), imparts the bright yellow color to the island's rice, soups, and stews.

Stews loom large in the Puerto Rican diet. They are usually cooked in a *caldera* (heavy kettle). A popular one is *carne guisada puertorriqueña* (Puerto Rican beef stew). The ingredients that flavor the chunks of beef vary according to the cook's whims or whatever happens to be in the larder. These might include green peppers, sweet chile peppers, onions, garlic, cilantro, potatoes, olives stuffed with pimientos, or capers. Seeded raisins may be added on occasion.

Pastelon de carne, or **meat pies,** are the staple of many Puerto Rican dinners. Salt pork and ham are often used for the filling and are cooked in a *caldero* (small cauldron). This medley of meats and spices is covered with a pastry top and baked.

Other typical main dishes include fried beefsteak with onions *(carne frita con cebolla),* veal *(ternera)* à la parmesana, and roast leg of pork, fresh ham, lamb, or veal à la criolla. These roasted meats are cooked in the Créole style, flavored with adobo. *Chicharrónes* is very popular, especially around Christmastime— fried pork with the crunchy skin left on top for added flavor.

Puerto Ricans also like such dishes as *sesos empanados* (breaded calf's brains), *riñones guisados* (calf's kidney stew), and *lengua rellena* (stuffed beef tongue).

A festive island dish is *lechón asado,* or **barbecued pig,** which is usually cooked for a party of 12 to 15. It is traditional for picnics and alfresco parties; one can sometimes catch the aroma of this dish wafting through the palm trees, a smell that must have been familiar to the Taíno peoples. The pig is basted with *jugo de naranja agria* (sour orange juice) and achiote coloring. Green plantains are peeled and roasted over hot stones, then served with the barbecued pig as a side dish. The traditional dressing served with the pig is *aji-li-mojili,* a sour garlic sauce. The sauce combines garlic, whole black peppercorns, and sweet seeded chile peppers, flavored further with vinegar, lime juice, salt, and olive oil.

Puerto Ricans adore **chicken,** which they flavor with various spices and seasonings. *Arroz con pollo* (chicken with rice) is the most popular chicken dish on the island, and it was brought long ago to the U.S. mainland. Other favorite preparations include *pollo al Jerez* (chicken in sherry), *pollo en agridulce* (sweet-and-sour chicken), and *pollitos asados à la parrilla* (broiled chickens).

Most visitors to the island prefer the fresh **fish and shellfish.** A popular dish is *mojo isleno* (fried fish with Puerto Rican sauce). The sauce is made with olives and olive oil, onions, pimientos, capers, tomato sauce, vinegar, and a flavoring of garlic and bay leaves. Fresh fish is often grilled, and perhaps flavored with garlic and an overlay of freshly squeezed lime juice—a very tasty dinner indeed. Caribbean lobster is usually the most expensive item on any menu, followed by shrimp. Puerto Ricans often cook *camarones en cerveza* (shrimp in beer). Another delectable shellfish dish is *jueyes hervidos* (boiled crab).

Many tasty **egg dishes** are served, especially *tortilla española* (Spanish omelet), cooked with finely chopped onions, cubed potatoes, and olive oil.

The rich and fertile fields of Puerto Rico produce a wide variety of **vegetables.** A favorite is the **chayote,** a pear-shaped vegetable called *christophine* throughout most of the English-speaking Caribbean. Its delicately flavored flesh is often compared to that of summer squash.

Fried *tostones* are made with both **breadfruit** (see box) and **plantains.** In fact, the plantain is the single most popular side dish served on the island. Plantains are a variety of banana that cannot be eaten raw. They are much coarser in texture than ordinary bananas and are harvested while green, then baked, fried, or boiled. When made into *tostones,* they are usually served as an appetizer with before-dinner drinks. Fried to a deep golden yellow, plantains may accompany fish, meat, or poultry dishes.

THE AROMA OF COFFEE

It is customary for most Puerto Ricans to finish their meal with the strong, black aromatic coffee grown here. Originally imported from the nearby Dominican Republic, coffee beans have been produced in the island's high-altitude interior for more than 300 years and still rank among the island's leading exports.

Puerto Rican coffee, in the view of many connoisseurs, rivals that of the more highly touted product from Colombia. Coffee has several degrees of quality, of course, the lowest ranking one being *café de primera,* which is typically served at the ordinary family table. The top category is called *café super premium.* Only three coffees in the world belong to super-premium class: Blue Mountain coffee of Jamaica, kona coffee from Hawaii, and Puerto Rico's homegrown Alto Grande, platinum coffee beans sought by coffee connoisseurs around the world.

The best brand names for Puerto Rican coffee are Café Crema, Café Rico, Rioja, and Yaucono.

You can ask for your brew *puya* (unsweetened), *negrito con azúcar* (black and sweetened), *cortao* (black with a drop of milk), or *con leche* (with milk).

RUM: KILL-DEVIL OR WHISKEY-BELLY VENGEANCE

Rum is the national drink, and you can buy it in almost any shade. Since the island is the world's leading rum producer, it's little wonder that every Puerto Rican bartender worthy of the profession likes to concoct his or her own favorite rum libation.

Of course, you can call for Puerto Rican rum in many mixed drinks such as rum collins, rum sour, rum screwdriver, and rum and tonic. The classic sangría, which is prepared in Spain with dry red wine, sugar, orange juice, and other ingredients, may be given a thoroughly Puerto Rican twist with a hefty dose of the island's rum.

Today's version of rum bears little resemblance to the raw and grainy beverage consumed by the renegades and pirates of the Spanish Main. Christopher Columbus brought sugarcane, from which rum is distilled, to the Caribbean on his second voyage to the New World, and in virtually no time it became *the* regional drink.

It is believed that Ponce de León introduced rum to Puerto Rico during his governorship, which began in 1508. In time, there emerged large sugarcane plantations. From Puerto Rico and other West Indian islands, rum was shipped to colonial America, where it lent itself to such popular and hair-raising 18th-century drinks as Kill-Devil and Whiskey-Belly Vengeance. After America became a nation, rum was largely displaced as the drink of choice by whisky, distilled from grain grown on the American plains.

It took almost a century before Puerto Rico's rum industry regained its former vigor. This occurred during a severe whisky shortage in the United States at the end of World War II. By the 1950s, sales of rum had fallen off again, as more and different kinds of liquor became available on the American market.

The local brew had been a questionable drink because of inferior distillation methods and quality. Recognizing this problem, the Puerto Rican government drew up rigid standards for producing, blending, and aging rum. Rum factories were outfitted with the most modern and sanitary equipment, and sales figures (encouraged by aggressive marketing campaigns) began to climb.

No one will ever agree on what "the best" rum is in the Caribbean. There are just too many of them to sample. Some are so esoteric as to be unavailable in your local liquor store. But if popular tastes mean anything, then Puerto Rican rums, especially Bacardi, head the list. There are 24 different rums from Puerto Rico sold in the United States under 11 brand names—not only Bacardi, but Ron Bocoy, Ronrico, Don Q, and many others.

Puerto Rican rums are generally light, gold, or dark. Usually white or silver in color, the biggest seller is light in body and dry in taste. Its subtle flavor and delicate aroma make it ideal for many mixed drinks, including the daiquiri, rum collins, rum mary, and rum and tonic or soda. It also goes with almost any fruit juice, or on the rocks with a slice of lemon or lime. Gold or amber rum is aromatic and full-bodied in taste. Aging in charred oak casks adds color to the rum.

Gold rums are usually aged longer for a deeper and more mellow flavor than light rums. They are increasingly popular on the rocks, straight up, or in certain mixed drinks in which extra flavor is desired—certainly in the famous piña colada, rum and coke, or eggnog.

Finally, dark rum is full-bodied with a deep, velvety, smooth taste and a complex flavor. It can be aged for as long as 15 years. Enjoy it on the rocks, with tonic or soda, or in mixed drinks when you want the taste of rum to stand out.

All resorts offer the *piña colada,* made with cream of coconut, white Puerto Rican rum, and canned pineapple juice. The ingredients are thoroughly blended and served frappé style in a tall, cool glass, usually garnished with a maraschino cherry and a small paper parasol. But you may want to be more adventurous and sample some of the island's other cocktails, many of which are made with fresh fruit juices. Planter's punch, served over cracked ice, is the second-most-popular mixed rum drink for tourists. Often, it combines dark Puerto Rican rum, dark brown Jamaican rum, citrus juice, and Angostura bitters.

Your best introduction to Puerto Rican rum making is to visit the Bacardi distillery in Cataño, just a short ferryboat ride across the San Juan harbor.

7 Salsa & Bomba: Dancing to the Beat

One of Puerto Rico's notable exports is its music, which along with that of Jamaica is the predominant Caribbean music heard in the United States. Few if any American ears haven't been exposed to the vibrant Latin beats of the salsa, the bomba, and the plena.

Regrettably, you can often go to more Puerto Rican clubs in New York than you can in San Juan to hear this music. You would think that since Puerto Ricans like music so much, San Juan would be filled with dives offering a Latin beat. There are many dives in San Juan with music, but it's usually recorded. The best artists are hired to perform at the hotels, and even so, performances are irregular. Live music is heard more frequently in the winter than in the summer months, when there are fewer visitors.

Why so few clubs? Puerto Ricans often hear their music on radio or recorded instead of going to clubs. It's a way for them to listen to good music without paying high tabs. For a representative sampling of what's available—and admittedly it's limited—see "San Juan After Dark" in chapter 6.

At least some of the unique sounds of salsa, bomba, and the plena come from instruments that originated with the Taíno peoples. Most noteworthy is the *güícharo,* or *güiro,* a notched, hollowed-out gourd adapted from pre-Columbian days. The musical traditions of the Spanish and Africans can also be heard in Puerto Rico's music. At least four different instruments were adapted from the six-string Spanish classical guitar: the *requinto,* the *bordonua,* the *cuatro,* and the *tiple,* each of which produces a unique tone and pitch. The most popular of these, and the one for which the greatest number of adaptations and compositions have been written, is the cuatro, a guitar-like instrument with 10 strings (arranged in five pairs). Usually carved from solid blocks of laurel wood and known for resonances and pitches different from those produced by its Spanish counterpart, this instrument's graceful baroque body has been revered for decades as the national instrument of Puerto Rico.

Also prevalent on the island are such percussion instruments as *tambours* (hollowed tree trunks covered with stretched-out animal skin), *maracas* (gourds filled with pebbles or dried beans and mounted on handles), and a variety of drums whose original designs were brought from Africa by the island's slaves. All these instruments contribute to the rich variety of folk music with roots in the cultural melting pot of the island's Spanish, African, and Taíno traditions.

PUERTO RICAN FOLK MUSIC

During Puerto Rico's colonial years, a series of musical traditions evolved based on the folk songs and romantic ballads of 18th- and 19th-century Spain. Eventually, these became fused with music either imported or native to the Hispanic New World. Dealing with life, death, and everyday events of an agrarian society far removed from the royal courts of Europe, this music has been studiously collected and reorchestrated for modern audiences.

One collector of this music was Don Felo, whose 19th-century compositions were based on the melodic traditions of both Spain and the Spanish-speaking Caribbean. In the 20th century, Narciso Figueroa continued the tradition of collecting folk songs and reorchestrating them for chamber orchestras; his recordings have been sponsored by the Institute of Puerto Rican Culture.

Today, the most widely applauded—and, to many, most enjoyable—of the island's folk music are the hillbilly pieces created by the mountain-dwelling *jíbaros.* Using the full array of stringed and percussion instruments described above, they give lyrical performances whose live or recorded versions are popular at everything from island weddings to commencement exercises. Despite the appeal of other island musical forms, such as salsa, it could be argued that the *jíbaro* tradition of *cuatro* with drums is the island's most notable—and the one most likely to evoke homesickness in the hearts of any expatriate Puerto Rican.

Puerto Rico, unfortunately, doesn't have clubs featuring folk music on a regular basis. It's a "sometimes" thing. However, folk music is often incorporated into shows presented by music groups that seem to float from one hotel to another.

SALSA

The major type of music coming out of Puerto Rico is salsa, *the* rhythm of the islands. Its name literally translates as the "sauce" that makes parties happen. Originally developed within the Puerto Rican community of New York, it draws heavily from the musical roots of the Cuban and the African-Caribbean experience. Highly danceable, its rhythms are hot, urban, rhythmically sophisticated, and compelling. Today, the center of salsa has probably shifted from New York back to Puerto Rico, where local musicians compete fiercely with those from Cuba for the most infectious melodies.

Cuban salsa tends to be less avant-garde than the constantly mutating versions produced in Puerto Rico. Even within the salsa tradition, different groups adhere more or less fervently to the traditions of mainstream jazz, popular Latin song, and African inspirations.

Salsa is not an old form of music at all. Music critics claim that it originated in New York City nightclubs in the years following World War II, an evolution of the era's big-band tradition. The first great salsa musician was Tito Puente, who, after a stint with the U.S. Navy, studied percussion at New York's Juilliard School of Music. He went on to organize his own band, Puente's Latin Jazz Ensemble, which has been heard by audiences around the world. One critic said that the music is what results when the sounds of big-band jazz meet African-Caribbean rhythms. Other critics say that salsa is a combination of fast Latin music that embraces the rumba, mambo, cha-cha, guaguancho, and merengue.

Salsa has definitely made Puerto Rico famous in the world of international music. Salsa bands require access to a huge array of percussion instruments, including güiros, the gourds on which the Taíno peoples may have played music. Other instruments include maracas, bongos, timbales, conga drums, and claves—and to add the *jíbaro* touch, a clanging cowbell. Of course, it also takes a bass, a horn section, a chorus, and a lead vocalist to get the combination right.

No one quite agrees about who is the king of salsa today, but Willie Colón, El Gran Combo de Puerto Rico, and Hector Lovoe are on everyone's list as the grand masters of today's salsa beat. Chances are you won't get to see them on their home turf because they may be touring internationally. However, appearances on the island by one of these stars are widely heralded in the media and tickets are hard to come by. Hundreds of young *salseros* are waiting to take their thrones as the popularity (and income levels) of the emerging salsa stars continues to climb.

BOMBA & PLENA

Although usually grouped together, *bomba y plena* are actually two entirely different types of music that are coupled with dance. Pure African, **bomba** was brought over by black slaves who worked on the island's sugar plantations. It's a rhythmic music using barrel-shaped drums covered with tightly stretched animal skins and played by hand. This form of music is produced by one large drum plus a smaller drum called a *subidor*. The drums are accompanied by the rhythmical beating of sticks and maracas to create a swelling tide of drumbeats, in which aficionados can hear the drummers bang out a series of responses from one to another.

Bomba is described as a dialogue between dancer and drummer. It's as if the drummer were challenging the dancer to a rhythmic duel. The dance can go on just as long as the dancer can continue. Although critics are uncertain about the exact origins of bomba, it is divided into different rhythmic backgrounds and variations, such as the Euba, Cocobale, and Sica. As the dance and the drummer's beat continue, the music grows more spirited and more complex. Bomba is sometimes incorporated into folkloric shows presented infrequently in San Juan. Otherwise, it's nearly impossible to find a club presenting it with regularity. Count yourself fortunate if you get to see a performance.

Whereas bomba is purely African in origin, **plena** blends elements from Puerto Ricans' wide cultural backgrounds, including music that the Taíno tribes may have used during their ceremonies. This type of music first

La Vida Loca

Not since the mambo craze of the '50s has a Latin heartthrob wriggled his way onto the American pop music scene. Of course, it's Ricky Martin, the world's most famous Puerto Rican. He achieved megastardom in nearly every corner of the world, eventually becoming a household word in America. Today he's the frontrunner in a vanguard of Latin pop stars that includes Enrique Iglesias and Marc Anthony. Martin's first English-language album became the biggest-selling number 1 single in the history of Columbia Records.

Born in San Juan on December 24, 1971, Martin first became famous in 1984 when he was part of the Latin boy group Menudo. Dropping out of the group after 5 years, he then achieved success with bubblegum music on two Spanish-language albums. Later he worked as a bartender in Los Angeles (1994), appearing as a nightclub singer on weekends. His 1995 album, *A Medio Vivir,* marked a turning point in his career.

Today he's not bartending anymore, but is an international superstar who has sold more than 15 million records worldwide.

His "Livin' La Vida Loca" is a sensuous celebration of life driven by a loaded rock bass line, sexy smart lyrics, raw vocals, and pulsating rhythms. As for all the tabloids' speculation about his sexual orientation, Ricky's not saying.

appeared in Ponce, where performing the plena became a hallmark of Spanish tradition and coquetry.

Instruments used in plena include the *güiro,* a dried-out gourd whose surface is cut with parallel grooves, and, when rubbed with a stick, produces a raspy and rhythmical percussive noise. The Taínos may have invented this instrument. From the guitars brought to the New World by the Spanish conquistadores emerged the 10-stringed *cuatro.* To the *güiro* and *cuatro* is added the tambourine, known as *panderos,* originally derived from Africa. Dancing plena became a kind of living newspaper. Singers recited the events of the day and often satirized local politicians or scandals. Sometimes plenas were filled with biting satire; at other times, they commented on major news events of the day, such as a devastating hurricane.

Bomba y plena remain the most popular forms of folk music on the island, and many cultural events highlight this music for entertainment. In a somewhat commercialized form, *bomba y plena* shows are often presented at resort hotels along San Juan's Condado beachfront strip. It may not be "the real thing," but often it's just as good even if presented at a hotel instead of a local dive in some forgotten Puerto Rican village.

Appendix B: Useful Terms & Phrases

1 Basic Spanish Phrases & Vocabulary

ENGLISH-SPANISH PHRASES

English	Spanish	Pronunciation
Good day	**Buenos días**	*bway*-nohss-*dee*-ahss
How are you?	**¿Cómo está usted?**	*koh*-moh ess-*tah* oo-*sted*?
Very well	**Muy bien**	mwee byen
Thank you	**Gracias**	grah-see-ahss
You're welcome	**De nada**	day nah-dah
Good-bye	**Adiós**	ah-*dyohss*
Please	**Por favor**	pohr fah-*vohr*
Yes	**Sí**	see
No	**No**	noh
Excuse me	**Perdóneme**	pehr-*doh*-ney-may
Give me	**Déme**	*day*-may
Where is . . . ?	**¿Dónde está . . . ?**	*dohn*-day ess-*tah*?
the station	**la estación**	lah ess-tah-*seown*
a hotel	**un hotel**	oon oh-*tel*
a gas station	**una gasolinera**	oon-uh gah-so-*lee*-nay-rah
a restaurant	**un restaurante**	oon res-tow-*rahn*-tay
the toilet	**el baño**	el *bahn*-yoh
a good doctor	**un buen médico**	oon bwayn *may*-thee-co
the road to	**el camino a/hacia**	el cah-*mee*-noh ah/*ah-see*-ah
To the right	**A la derecha**	ah lah day-*reh*-chuh
To the left	**A la izquierda**	ah lah ees-ky-*ehr*-thah
Straight ahead	**Derecho**	day-*reh*-cho
I would like	**Quisiera**	key-see-*ehr*-ah
I want . . .	**Quiero . . .**	*kyehr*-oh
to eat	**comer**	ko-*mayr*
a room	**una habitación**	oon-nuh ha-bee tah-*seown*
Do you have . . .	**¿Tiene usted . . . ?**	tyah-nay oos-*ted*?
a book	**un libro**	oon *lee*-bro
a dictionary	**un diccionario**	oon deek-seown-*ar*-eo
How much is it?	**¿Cuánto cuesta?**	*kwahn*-to *kwess*-tah?

English	Spanish	Pronunciation
When?	¿Cuándo?	*kwahn*-doh?
What?	¿Qué?	kay?
There is (Is there . . . ?)	(¿)Hay (. . . ?)	eye?
What is there?	¿Qué hay?	kay eye?
Yesterday	Ayer	ah-*yer*
Today	Hoy	oy
Tomorrow	Mañana	mahn-*yawn*-ah
Good	Bueno	*bway*-no
Bad	Malo	*mah*-lo
Better (best)	(Lo) Mejor	(loh) meh-hor
More	Más	mahs
Less	Menos	*may*-noss
No smoking	Se prohíbe fumar	say pro-*hee*-bay foo-mahr
Postcard	Tarjeta postal	tar-hay-ta pohs-*tahl*
Insect repellent	Rapellante contra insectos	rah-pey-*yahn*-te *cohn*-trah een-*sehk*-tos

MORE USEFUL PHRASES

English	Spanish	Pronunciation
Do you speak English?	¿Habla usted inglés?	*ah*-blah oo-*sted* een-*glays*?
Is there anyone here who speaks English?	¿Hay alguien aquí qué hable inglés?	eye *ahl*-ghee-en kay *ah*-blay een-*glays*?
I speak a little Spanish.	Hablo un poco de español.	*ah*-blow oon *poh*-koh day ess-pah-*nyol*
I don't understand Spanish very well.	No (lo) entiendo muy bien el español.	noh (loh) ehn-tee-*ehn*-do moo-ee bee-ayn el ess-pah-*nyol*
The meal is good.	Me gusta la comida.	may *goo*-sta lah koh-*mee*-dah
What time is it?	¿Qué hora es?	kay *oar*-ah ess?
May I see your menu?	¿Puedo ver el menú (la carta)?	*puay*-tho veyr el may-*noo* (lah *car*-tah)?
The check please.	La cuenta por favor.	lah *quayn*-tah pohr fa-*vorh*
What do I owe you?	¿Cuánto lo debo?	*Kwahn*-toh loh *day*-boh?
What did you say?	¿Mande? (colloquial expression for American "Eh?")	*Mahn*-day?
More formal:	¿Cómo?	*Koh*-moh?
I want (to see)	Quiero (ver)	Key-*yehr*-oh vehr
a room	un cuarto or una habitación	oon *kwar*-toh, *oon*-nuh ha-bee-tah-*seown*
for two persons.	para dos personas	*pahr*-ah doss pehr-*sohn*-as
with (without) bath.	con (sin) baño.	kohn (seen) *bah*-nyoh
We are staying here only	Nos quedamos aquí solamente . . .	nohs kay-*dahm*-ohss ah-*key* sohl-ah-*mayn*-tay
one night.	una noche.	oon-ah *noh*-chay
one week.	una semana.	oon-ah say-*mahn*-ah
We are leaving	Partimos (Salimos)	Pahr-*tee*-mohss (sah-*lee*-mohss)
tomorrow.	mañana.	mahn-*nyan*-ah

English	Spanish	Pronunciation
Do you accept traveler's checks?	¿Acepta usted cheques de viajero?	Ah-*sayp*-tah oo-*sted chay*-kays day bee-ah-*hehr*-oh?
Is there a Laundromat near here?	¿Hay una lavandería cerca de aquí?	Eye *oon*-ah lah-*vahn*-day-*ree*-ah *sehr*-ka day ah-*key*?
Please send these clothes to the laundry.	Hágame el favor de mandar esta ropa a la lavandería.	*Ah*-ga-may el fah-*vhor* day mahn-*dahr* ays-tah *rho*-pah a lah lah-*vahn*-day-*ree*-ah

NUMBERS

1	**uno** (*ooh*-noh)	17	**diecisiete** (de-*ess*-ee-*syeh*-tay)
2	**dos** (dohs)	18	**dieciocho** (dee-*ess*-ee-*oh*-choh)
3	**tres** (trayss)	19	**diecinueve** (dee-*ess*-ee-*nway*-bay)
4	**cuatro** (*kwah*-troh)	20	**veinte** (*bayn*-tay)
5	**cinco** (*seen*-koh)	30	**treinta** (*trayn*-tah)
6	**seis** (sayss)	40	**cuarenta** (kwah-ren-tah)
7	**siete** (*syeh*-tay)	50	**cincuenta** (seen-*kwen*-tah)
8	**ocho** (*oh*-choh)	60	**sesenta** (say-*sen*-tah)
9	**nueve** (*nway*-bay)	70	**setenta** (say-*ten*-tah)
10	**diez** (dee-ess)	80	**ochenta** (oh-*chen*-tah)
11	**once** (*ohn*-say)	90	**noventa** (noh-*ben*-tah)
12	**doce** (*doh*-say)	100	**cien** (see-en)
13	**trece** (*tray*-say)	200	**doscientos** (*dos*-se-en-tos)
14	**catorce** (kah-*tor*-say)	500	**quinientos** (*keen*-ee-ehn-tos)
15	**quince** (*keen*-say)	1000	**mil** (meal)
16	**dieciseis** (de-*ess*-ee-sayss)		

2 Menu Terms

SOUPS

caldo gallego	Galician broth	**sopa de fideos**	noodle soup
caldo de gallina	chicken soup	**sopa de guisantes**	pea soup
sopa de ajo	garlic soup	**sopa de lentejas**	lentil soup
sopa de cebolla	onion soup	**sopa de pescado**	fish soup
sopa clara	consommé	**sopa de tomate**	tomato soup
sopa espesa	thick soup	**sopa de verdures**	vegetable soup

FISH

almejas	clams	**gambas**	shrimp
anchoas	anchovies	**langosta**	lobster
anguilas	eels	**langostinos**	prawns
arenque	herring	**lenguado**	sole
atún	tuna	**mejillones**	mussels
bacalao	cod	**merluza**	hake
calamares	squid	**necoras**	spider crabs
cangrejo	crab	**ostras**	oysters
caracoles	snails	**pescadilla**	whiting
centollo	sea urchin	**pijotas**	small whiting
chocos	large squid	**pulpo**	octopus
cigalas	small lobsters	**rodaballo**	turbot

Useful Terms & Phrases

salmonete   mullet
sardines   sardines

trucha   trout
vieiras   scallops

MEATS

albondigas   meatballs
bistec   beefsteak
callos   tripe
cerdo   pork
chuleta   cutlet
cocido   stew
conejo   rabbit
cordero   lamb
costillas   chops

gallina   fowl
ganso   goose
higado   liver
jamón   ham
lengua   tongue
paloma   pigeon
pato   duck
pavo   turkey
perdiz   partridge

VEGETABLES

aceitunas   olives
alcachofa   artichoke
arroz   rice
berenjena   eggplant
cebolla   onion
col   cabbage
colifior   cauliflower
ensalada   salad
esparragos   asparagus
espinacas   spinach

guisantes   peas
judías verdes   string beans
nabo   turnip
patata   potato
pepino   cucumber
remolachas   beets
setas   mushrooms
tomate   tomato
zanahorias   carrots

FRUITS

albaricoque   apricot
aquacate   avocado
cerezas   cherries
ciruela   plum
datil   date
frambuesa   raspberry
fresa   strawberry
Granada   pomegranate
higo   fig

limón   lemon
manzana   apple
melocoton   peach
naranja   orange
pera   pear
piña   pineapple
plátano   banana
toronja   grapefruit
uvas   grapes

DESSERTS

buñuelos   fritters
compota   stewed fruit
flan   caramel custard
fruta   fruit

galletas   tea cakes
helado   ice cream
pastels   pastries
torta   cake

BEVERAGES

agua   water
agua mineral   mineral water
café   coffee
cerveza   beer
ginebra   gin
jerez   sherry
jugo de naranjas   orange juice
jugo de tomate   tomato juice

leche   milk
sangría   red wine and fruits
sidra   cider
sifon   soda
té   tea
vino blancho   white wine
vino tinto   red wine

Useful Terms & Phrases

BASICS

Aceite oil
ajo garlic
azucar sugar
hielo ice
mantequilla butter
miel honey
frito fried

mostaza mustard
pan bread
pimienta pepper
queso cheese
sal salt
vinagre vinegar

Index

Index

FROMMER'S® COMPLETE TRAVEL GUIDES

Alaska
Amsterdam
Arizona
Atlanta
Australia
Austria
Bahamas
Barcelona, Madrid &
  Seville
Beijing
Belgium, Holland &
  Luxembourg
Bermuda
Boston
British Columbia & the
  Canadian Rockies
Budapest & the Best of
  Hungary
California
Canada
Cancún, Cozumel &
  the Yucatán
Cape Cod, Nantucket &
  Martha's Vineyard
Caribbean
Caribbean Cruises & Ports
  of Call
Caribbean Ports of Call
Carolinas & Georgia
Chicago
China
Colorado
Costa Rica
Denmark
Denver, Boulder & Colorado
  Springs
England
Europe

European Cruises & Ports
  of Call
Florida
France
Germany
Greece
Greek Islands
Hawaii
Hong Kong
Honolulu, Waikiki &
  Oahu
Ireland
Israel
Italy
Jamaica
Japan
Las Vegas
London
Los Angeles
Maryland & Delaware
Maui
Mexico
Miami & the Keys
Montana & Wyoming
Montréal & Québec City
Munich & the Bavarian
  Alps
Nashville & Memphis
Nepal
New England
New Mexico
New Orleans
New York City
New Zealand
Nova Scotia, New Brunswick
  & Prince Edward Island
Oregon
Paris

Philadelphia & the
  Amish Country
Portugal
Prague & the Best of the
  Czech Republic
Provence & the Riviera
Puerto Rico
Rome
San Antonio & Austin
San Diego
San Francisco
Santa Fe, Taos & Albuquerque
Scandinavia
Scotland
Seattle & Portland
Singapore & Malaysia
South Africa
Southeast Asia
South Pacific
Spain
Sweden
Switzerland
Thailand
Tokyo
Toronto
Tuscany & Umbria
USA
Utah
Vancouver & Victoria
Vermont, New Hampshire
  & Maine
Vienna & the Danube Valley
Virgin Islands
Virginia
Walt Disney World &
  Orlando
Washington, D.C.
Washington State

FROMMER'S® DOLLAR-A-DAY GUIDES

Australia from $50 a Day
California from $60 a Day
Caribbean from $70 a Day
England from $70 a Day
Europe from $60 a Day

Florida from $60 a Day
Hawaii from $70 a Day
Ireland from $60 a Day
Italy from $70 a Day
London from $85 a Day

New York from $80 a Day
Paris from $85 a Day
San Francisco from $60 a Day
Washington, D.C.,
  from $60 a Day

FROMMER'S® PORTABLE GUIDES

Acapulco, Ixtapa &
  Zihuatanejo
Alaska Cruises & Ports of Call
Bahamas
Baja & Los Cabos
Berlin
California Wine Country
Charleston & Savannah
Chicago

Dublin
Hawaii: The Big Island
Las Vegas
London
Maine Coast
Maui
New Orleans
New York City
Paris

Puerto Vallarta, Manzanillo
  & Guadalajara
San Diego
San Francisco
Sydney
Tampa & St. Petersburg
Venice
Washington, D.C.

Frommer's® National Park Guides

Family Vacations in the
    National Parks
Grand Canyon

National Parks of the
    American West
Rocky Mountain

Yellowstone & Grand Teton
Yosemite & Sequoia/
    Kings Canyon
Zion & Bryce Canyon

Frommer's® Memorable Walks

Chicago
London

New York
Paris

San Francisco
Washington D.C.

Frommer's® Great Outdoor Guides

New England
Northern California

Southern California & Baja
Southern New England

Washington & Oregon

Frommer's® Born to Shop Guides

Born to Shop: China
Born to Shop: France

Born to Shop: Italy
Born to Shop: London

Born to Shop: New York
Born to Shop: Paris

Frommer's® Irreverent Guides

Amsterdam
Boston
Chicago
Las Vegas

London
Los Angeles
Manhattan
New Orleans

Paris
San Francisco
Seattle & Portland
Vancouver

Walt Disney World
Washington, D.C.

Frommer's® Best-Loved Driving Tours

America
Britain
California

Florida
France
Germany

Ireland
Italy
New England

Scotland
Spain
Western Europe

The Unofficial Guides®

Bed & Breakfasts in
    California
Bed & Breakfasts in
    New England
Bed & Breakfasts in
    the Northwest
Beyond Disney
Branson, Missouri
California with Kids
Chicago

Cruises
Disneyland
Florida with Kids
Golf Vacations in the
    Eastern U.S.
The Great Smoky &
    Blue Ridge
    Mountains
Inside Disney

Hawaii
Las Vegas
London
Miami & the Keys
Mini Las Vegas
Mini-Mickey
New Orleans
New York City
Paris

Safaris
San Francisco
Skiing in the West
Walt Disney World
Walt Disney World
    for Grown-ups
Walt Disney World
    for Kids
Washington, D.C.

Special-Interest Titles

Frommer's Britain's Best Bed & Breakfasts and
    Country Inns
Frommer's Britain's Best Bike Rides
The Civil War Trust's Official Guide
    to the Civil War Discovery Trail
Frommer's Caribbean Hideaways
Frommer's Food Lover's Companion to France
Frommer's Food Lover's Companion to Italy
Frommer's Gay & Lesbian Europe
Frommer's Exploring America by RV
Hanging Out in Europe
Israel Past & Present

Mad Monks' Guide to California
Mad Monks' Guide to New York City
Frommer's The Moon
Frommer's New York City with Kids
The New York Times' Unforgettable
    Weekends
Places Rated Almanac
Retirement Places Rated
Frommer's Road Atlas Britain
Frommer's Road Atlas Europe
Frommer's Washington, D.C., with Kids
Frommer's What the Airlines Never Tell You